Looming Civil War

LOOMING CIVIL WAR

How Nineteenth-Century Americans Imagined the Future

JASON PHILLIPS

OXFORD
UNIVERSITY PRESS

OXFORD
UNIVERSITY PRESS

Oxford University Press is a department of the University of Oxford. It furthers the University's objective of excellence in research, scholarship, and education by publishing worldwide. Oxford is a registered trade mark of Oxford University Press in the UK and certain other countries.

Published in the United States of America by Oxford University Press
198 Madison Avenue, New York, NY 10016, United States of America.

Library of Congress Cataloging-in-Publication Data
Names: Phillips, Jason, 1973– author.
Title: Looming Civil War : how nineteenth-century Americans imagined the future / Jason Phillips.
Description: New York, NY : Oxford University Press, [2018] | Includes bibliographical references and index.
Identifiers: LCCN 2018000984 (print) | LCCN 2018025757 (ebook) | ISBN 9780190868178 (Updf) |
ISBN 9780190868185 (Epub) | ISBN 9780190868161 (hardcover)
Subjects: LCSH: United States—Civilization—19th century. |
United States—Social conditions—19th century. | United States—Social life and customs—19th century. |
Public opinion—United States—History—19th century.
Classification: LCC E169.1 (ebook) | LCC E169.1 .P5435 2018 (print) | DDC 973.9—dc23
LC record available at https://lccn.loc.gov/2018000984

For Trisha

Contents

Acknowledgments

I AM GRATEFUL TO so many people who contributed to this project. Thanks first to the financial supporters who made this book possible. An Andrew Mellon Research Fellowship from the Virginia Historical Society enabled me to make a critical research trip in the summer of 2012. Mississippi State University and West Virginia University funded other trips, granted me a sabbatical, and gave me manageable teaching assignments. I am deeply grateful to the Eberly family and other donors who have contributed to the Eberly Family Professorship in Civil War Studies. Their generosity sustained this work for the past five years.

This book would not have been possible without the curiosity, expertise, and good cheer of many librarians and archivists. At every archive listed in the notes, people cared about my research and went out of their way to find obscure sources. Like magic, these scholars would listen to my research problem, disappear into the bowels of a library, and return with manuscripts I had never considered. I thank them for their help and for permission to quote from materials in their collections.

So many colleagues at Mississippi State and West Virginia offered encouragement and advice throughout this project. In Starkville, I learned from Stephen Brain, Jim Giesen, Alison Greene, Alix Hui, Alan Marcus, Anne Marshall, Peter Messer, Chris Snyder, and many others. In Morgantown, I benefited from the help of Josh Arthurs, Tyler Boulware, Ken Fones-Wolf, Kate Staples, Michele Stephens, and many others. At both institutions I have been lucky to find a friend in the English Department. At Mississippi State, Farrell O'Gorman shared his insights on antebellum literature over barbecue. At West Virginia, it has been a pleasure talking with Tim Sweet about literary criticism over Indian food. Of all my colleagues, Brian Luskey deserves special thanks for his encouragement and help. Brian was the first to read a chapter of the manuscript. Together we organized and hosted a conference on Civil War material culture and edited a special issue of *Civil War History*. In all of our joint ventures, Brian's support and insights propelled my work to a higher level.

My students, undergraduate and graduate, aided this project for years. They were often the first people to hear new ideas and arguments as I routinely tested my research in the classroom. I am especially grateful for the graduate students who worked as research assistants on this book: Zac Cowsert, Jarrad Fuoss, Hannah McClearnen, Becky Oakes, Scott Thompson, and Chuck Welsko. To all of you, I hope the labor you devoted to this project was as rewarding for you as it was for this book. It was my genuine pleasure to work with such promising scholars.

Friends at other universities have cared about my research and contributed to it from the beginning. Peter Carmichael, more than anyone else, has championed this project. When a family illness prevented me from delivering the first paper from this research at the Organization of American Historians meeting in Seattle, Pete stepped up to give a "dramatic reading." He then organized and shared a panel with me at the Society of Civil War Historians meeting in Richmond. Pete even shared contacts to help me answer obscure questions about Henry Clay Pate and John Brown's pikes. At a symposium hosted by the German Historical Institute, Bruce Dorsey, Sebastian Jobs, Jen Manion, and Woody Register helped to hone the early phase of this project. Years later, when I crossed paths with Woody at the Library of Congress, a conversation with him over coffee helped me to weave the story of Pate's knife through the entire manuscript. At a symposium at Rice University, Ed Blum, Zach Dresser, Gaines Foster, Caleb McDaniel, Scott Nesbit, and Ben Wright helped me to wrestle with Edmund Ruffin's prophecy. Zach and Matt Gabriele later invited me to an interdisciplinary symposium hosted by the department of religion and culture at Virginia Tech, where Brian Britt and Nitzan Lebovic encouraged my theory about futures past.

So many other people have helped too. Michael Bernath, John Boles, Robert Bonner, John Brooke, Orville Vernon Burton, Joan Cashin, Catherine Clinton, Stephen Cushman, Greg Downs, Paul Escott, Lara Farina, James Goodman, Martha Hodes, Carrie Janney, Bob Kenzer, Melanie Kiechle, Derek Krissoff, Brian Craig Miller, Megan Kate Nelson, Kristen Oertel, Seth Rockman, Mary Ann Samyn, Aaron Sheehan-Dean, David Silkenat, Mark Simpson-Vos, Yael Sternhell, Frank Towers, Joan Waugh, Ashli White, Jonathan White, and many others have volunteered sources and asked important questions that never occurred to me.

Beyond the academy, two experts offered critical help to this project. My good friend, the Reverend Dr. Jeremy Rutledge, senior minister at Circular Congregational Church in Charleston, helped me to understand the bewildering universe of Judeo-Christian prophecy. Likewise, Peter R. Thomas Sr., an expert on bowie knives, helped me to understand the bewildering universe of American knife culture. The fact that Peter also happens to be a descendant of Edmund Ruffin sharpened his already penetrating correspondence.

Oxford University Press has provided an ideal home for this book thanks to Susan Ferber. From our first conversation, Susan sensed the broader ambition and appeal of this project. Her tireless work and careful attention to this book expedited its appearance and made it a better book than I could have imagined. I am so grateful for her help every step of the way. Oxford's unique faculty board offered sage advice that strengthened the manuscript. Jeremy Toynbee oversaw the production of the book with great care. I am forever indebted to the anonymous readers for Oxford. Their thorough critiques and brilliant recommendations caught my mistakes and focused my attention on the heart of this project when I was tempted to follow divergent interests. Any errors or digressions that remain are mine alone.

I gratefully acknowledge permission to reprint portions of this book that first appeared in other publications: Zachary Dresser and Benjamin Wright, eds., *Apocalypse and the Millennium: Providential Religion and the Era of the American Civil War* (Baton Rouge: Louisiana State University Press, 2013); Jimmy L. Bryan, Jr., ed., *The Martial Imagination: Cultural Aspects of American Warfare* (College Station: Texas A&M University Press, 2013); *Rethinking History* 18.1 (March 2014). The editors of these publications offered insightful critiques that improved this book.

Finally, my family supported this work the longest. I thank my parents, Fred and Nancy Phillips, for their interest and encouragement and for babysitting during a research trip. I thank my sons, Max and Charlie, for their love, happiness, and passion for learning. Most of all, I thank my wonderful wife, Trisha, whose partnership in life assures me that our future matters more than futures past. This book is for her.

Looming Civil War

Prologue

LOOMING

WHILE HIS COMRADES IN the Richmond Howitzers anticipated their first battle, Thompson Brown expected to die. Amid the excitement and whirl of preparations, Brown sat down to write his wife goodbye. He tried to articulate his "intensity of devotion" for her and asked her to take care of his mother. Looking to the future, he worried, "I hope I died a true Christian." Rumors spread that the enemy was planning a night assault, and the Howitzers had patrol duty from midnight to dawn. When Brown imagined the future, he saw his company ambushed by northern gunmen. The crack of rifle fire would wake comrades in camp who were ordered to sleep beside their arms. But friends would arrive too late for the Howitzers who would be far away, in the dark, where the enemy waited for them. Civil War archives preserve similar premonitions, letters penned by men who sensed this one would be their last, but none of them precede Brown's letter of November 27, 1859.[1]

Thompson Brown and the Howitzers guarded Harpers Ferry from a northern invasion to rescue John Brown from the gallows. As execution day loomed, Virginians tensed for another attack while John Brown faced eternity with peaceful resolve. An imminent Armageddon comforted Brown and terrified his jailors. The mounting suspense proved too much for some people. On November 17, the commanding officer of the local militia succumbed to the stress and sent a telegram across the Old Dominion screaming for reinforcements. In minutes, electric current transferred his anxiety to Alexandria, Fredericksburg, and Norfolk. The excitement pulsed through Richmond that night as the city's militia companies formed beneath glowing gas lamps. They were "anticipating orders for departure to the scene of action," as one of the men put it. Newspapers reprinted the colonel's call, sending his clamor to quiet hamlets still untouched by telegraph lines.[2]

Preparing for the worst, Governor Henry Wise flooded the area with militia. Thousands of soldiers walked the streets and scoured the countryside day and night for weeks. As Figure P.1 shows, the spectacle attracted untold numbers of gawkers who traveled to Harpers Ferry and Charlestown to witness history. Business stopped and people stood in their dooryards all day, swapping rumors and discussing the future. To control street traffic, soldiers instituted a pass system and curfew. They also expelled Yankee travelers from the area. Nervous citizens noted that so many visitors had swarmed the town that the enemy might already have a thousand secret agents walking the streets, waiting for the signal to attack.

Weeks of tense fears snapped on November 27 when people saw flares in the sky. Southerners who expected another raid imagined only one explanation for the heavenly signs: Yankee rescuers in the surrounding mountains must be coordinating their assault on the town. When mounted pickets stormed into the Howitzers' camp to report the blazing rockets, Thompson Brown picked up his pen and wrote his wife. The Civil War would begin with a midnight massacre in western Virginia and Thompson Brown expected to be its first casualty.

Edmund Ruffin wanted to believe those fires signaled the start of the Civil War. Ruffin had devoted decades to the cause of southern nationalism, but by 1859 he despaired of ever seeing his dream come true. On October 18, 1859,

Figure P.1 View of Charlestown, *Leslie's Illustrated Newspaper*, November 19, 1859. Periodical Collection, West Virginia State Archives.

he contemplated suicide. Expecting a future of dependence and death, he concluded, "I have lived long enough" and "have no object whatever to strive for." The next day John Brown saved Ruffin's life. Newspapers for October 19 reported a failed insurrection at Harpers Ferry, orchestrated entirely by northern men. The news rekindled his hope for the future, and Ruffin raced to the "seat of war" to watch it unfolding. "I wish that the abolitionists of the north may attempt a rescue," Ruffin confided in his diary on the night that Thompson Brown expected to die. "If an armed attempt to rescue is made, accompanied by blood-shed, whether successful or not, it will be a certain cause of separation of the southern from the northern states." While John Brown prophesied that bloodshed would free the slaves from their masters, Edmund Ruffin predicted that bloodshed would free the masters from abolitionists.[3]

Ruffin was there, standing in the street watching rockets rise in the sky, but he knew they were an illusion. His mind understood the flares were in fact sparks from nearby chimneys. Something small, insignificant, and low appeared large, portentous, and high because a dense layer of atmosphere bent rays of light from the sparks to create a superior mirage, an optical illusion that refracted light beams and lifted them above their true position. Because this effect happens close to the horizon, where air is most dense, it distorts stars in their courses and the setting sun.[4]

Nineteenth-century Americans called this phenomenon "looming," a term dubbed by sailors who often experienced the effect at sea, where refraction lifted land and ships into the sky. Superior mirages sparked seafaring legends like the Flying Dutchman and Fata Morgana. Ruffin first experienced looming years earlier when he thought he spied a large, dark island in Chesapeake Bay. "Had I not known that no such thing existed," Ruffin recalled, "I should have guessed it to be a castle." Truth did not diminish the power of the illusion. Ruffin noted, "The deception of the sight was not removed" when someone told him he was looking at a duck blind. At Harpers Ferry when atmospheric conditions were right, and people's imaginations were stirred, all that was needed to produce panic and dire visions of a looming civil war was a literal spark.[5]

Looming offers a metaphor for how nineteenth-century visions of the future formed, spread, and made history. First, some spark, an event or object, captured people's attention. Then, a unique atmosphere elevated and enlarged that spark, making it loom larger than reality. Finally, observers and visionaries focused on it and reported what appeared to be beyond the horizon. A series of sparks portended the Civil War. Bleeding Kansas, the Panic of 1857, Harpers Ferry, Abraham Lincoln's election, and secession sparked prophecies of different civil wars looming. Before the Civil War was fought or remembered, it was imagined by thousands of Americans who peered at the horizon through an apocalyptic atmosphere. Beliefs about approaching the end of history colored how Americans envisioned territorial disputes, immigration, economic depressions, slave revolts, divisive politics, and a host of other challenges.

Anxious visionaries watched for enemies throughout the sectional crisis. Reformers, secessionists, statesmen, economists, generals, and many other prominent people assumed prophetic voices before the war. But visions of the future were not merely handed down by leaders. Popular forecasts rose from women, slaves, immigrants, and common soldiers. Many people confined their expectations to private diaries and letters, but they also expressed their futures through actions and postures. Thousands of forecasts of the war—private dreams, fears, uncertainties, and hopes—repose in archives. Beyond appearing in manuscripts, forecasts of war spread through literature, political pamphlets, newspapers, sermons, songs, and cartoons. Widespread forecasting shaped politics, military planning, and the economy. Visions of the future influenced things big and small, from stock market values to the contents of men's haversacks as they marched to war. The Civil War may have been the most anticipated event of America's nineteenth century.

When individual imaginations of looming civil wars coalesced, they depicted different conflicts depending on visionaries' perspectives. Looking west, Americans envisioned the Civil War as a border war for the frontier that would decide the direction of national ambitions. Looking east, Americans speculated about the Civil War as a class war between competing labor systems that would shape the nation's economic prospects. Looking south, Americans spread rumors of a war that would spark racial extermination. Looking abroad, Americans prophesied about the Civil War as a revolution triggered by secession. When the Civil War began, all of these visions shaped how Americans perceived the looming conflict and waged it. Somehow the real war combined all of these antebellum prophecies without fulfilling any of them in detail.

How Americans understood time affected their visions of looming wars, and two prevailing temporalities coexisted in nineteenth-century America. Some people imagined themselves traveling through time, into a future ahead of them, and forging that future and their lives in the process. For these Americans, the future was open, opportunities abounded, and humanity made history. This modern temporality, defined as anticipation, believed in progress and free will. Other people imagined themselves stationary while time passed through them. The future remained ahead, but instead of moving toward it, these people watched as the future approached them. This temporality defined life and history as a series of reactions to events expected and unexpected. Instead of focusing on an open future that people fashioned with acts and ideas, these Americans imagined a closed future that other forces, impersonal and supernatural, had already determined. This older temporality, defined as expectation, privileged providence and fate.[6]

Nineteenth-century Americans appreciated these different temporalities, but many of them, like us, used "anticipation" and "expectation" as synonyms. Instead of defining their temporalities with precise language, people expressed them with metaphors, idioms, active or passive voice, and conduct. During the nineteenth century, the two words converged when anticipation, the more modern temporality, eclipsed expectations. The *Oxford English Dictionary* now defines expectation as anticipation—"the action or fact of anticipating or foreseeing something." It was not always so. The etymology of both words retains their earlier, distinct temporalities. Anticipation comes from *anticipare*, the Latin noun for action. Before it referred to acting on the future, anticipation meant using money before it was at hand or making a payment before it was due. Expectation is also Latin, from *exspectationem*, meaning "state of waiting in suspense." While anticipation approached modernity from the world of finance, expectation came from religion. An expectation was a right of succession to a church position granted by a pope or king. Traces of these definitions survived in the Civil War era when prospectors and speculators favored "go-ahead" anticipations while prophets and believers spread apocalyptic expectations.[7]

American anticipations and expectations of the Civil War remained fluid before, during, and even after the conflict. In some respects, how individuals oriented themselves toward the future was a personality trait, but external factors affected temporalities too. Age, race, gender, environment, class, and a host of other things influenced how people imagined tomorrow. Religion stressed the future in ways that other factors did not and explained how events unfolded. The Second Great Awakening convinced millions of antebellum Americans that Christ's second coming would occur during their lifetime. Some Americans anticipated how human progress would fashion the future and prepare the world for Christ's return at the end of the millennium. These postmillennialists championed reform movements to accelerate history and fulfill their prophecy. Other Americans expected God to initiate Christ's return at the beginning of the millennium. These premillennialists prepared their souls and looked for signs that divine intervention was coming. Though the anticipations of postmillennialists resonated more with antebellum society and culture, the expectations of premillennialists captured the imaginations of millions who sensed the end of history.[8]

Some groups seemed to favor certain temporalities. For example, white men who avoided church and belonged to middle- or upper-class families usually anticipated the future. They expressed control over their destiny and imagined traveling toward it with power and will. Conversely, enslaved women who prayed for Jubilee typically expected the future. They sensed how forces beyond their control shaped life and reacted to future circumstances that approached them. Patterns in historical records support these generalizations, but we cannot assume that individuals conformed to them. The most powerful white man of the era who avoided church and belonged to a prosperous family, Abraham Lincoln, expected the future throughout his life. The most famous enslaved woman of the century, Harriet Tubman, anticipated the future and moved toward it with initiative and determination her whole life. People also switched temporalities during the war. Thousands of white men who anticipated glory when they volunteered found themselves ensnared by a war that forced them to await the future with dreadful expectations. Thousands of enslaved women who expected freedom instead approached it with energetic anticipations and forged new futures for themselves. In other words, the Civil War changed more than America's future; it changed *how* Americans imagined the future, changes that resound through American temporalities today.[9]

Researching antebellum visions of looming conflicts has exposed a deeply rooted myth about the Civil War: an unquestioned belief that Americans predicted a short, glorious war when it began. This short war myth has a consensus of followers who agree on little else. Historians who debate what caused the war, who emancipated the slaves, why the Confederacy lost, and how the war changed America agree that most Americans imagined a swift, painless conclusion to decades of sectional discord. Giants of Civil War history Bell Wiley, Shelby Foote, and James McPherson have spread the short war myth to millions of readers. According to Wiley, "almost everyone seemed to think that the war would be decided by a battle or two in Virginia or Kentucky; it was necessary, therefore, to get to the fight with dispatch or run the risk of not making it at all." Foote struck the same note, claiming, "All shared a belief that the war would be short, and some joined in haste, out of fear that it would be over before they got there." As McPherson put it, "Many people on both sides believed that the war would be short—one or two battles and the cowardly Yankees or slovenly rebels would give up." Similar statements pepper Civil War scholarship, National Park waysides, and American history textbooks. Anyone who has learned about the Civil War has probably encountered the short war myth.[10]

Forecasts of a holiday frolic and ninety-day war were widespread among certain segments of American society. Republicans and secessionists had political motives for downplaying warnings of looming civil war during the crisis. New recruits questioned the likelihood of a long, destructive war to reassure loved ones and perhaps themselves. Emotions surged during the secession crisis, the siege of Fort Sumter, and the call for volunteers. As a result, short war predictions were louder than warnings of a dire, destructive conflict, but not more prevalent. Anecdotal evidence from secessionists, Republicans, and volunteers overshadows how other Americans envisioned the looming war differently. A popular source is South Carolina senator James Chesnut's promise to drink all the blood spilled by secession. Dire warnings that questioned Chesnut's boast were less vocal, because they ran counter to the patriotism of the hour. Thus we find forebodings of a long, ruinous war more frequently in private papers than in public statements. Nonetheless, terrifying prophecies appeared in contemporary newspapers, sermons, and speeches.[11]

The short war myth has also romanticized, whitewashed, and masculinized Civil War history. The myth privileges the rosy anticipations of politicians and soldiers over the dark expectations of women, African Americans, and civilians who felt dragged into a terrifying future by extremists from both regions. This problem not only erases how millions of Americans imagined the war but also homogenizes their temporalities. Though unintended, Civil War history normalizes modern, anticipatory time at the expense of an older, expectant time, thus elevating the futures of some groups over others. When scholars employ a modern temporality in their work, they perform a political act that lifts their vantage point and objectifies their subjects. Lost in this process are the ghosts of heterogeneous time, "unheard voices, unacknowledged bodies, foreclosed potentials," as literary scholar Carolyn Dinshaw puts it. Civil War historians have recovered the lives of women, African Americans, and others obscured by the short war myth but have yet to acknowledge the diverse temporalities that gave presence to their tomorrows. The future is unfamiliar territory for historians. Readers interested in the interdisciplinary work that informs this book will find more of it in the notes than the text, because Civil War Americans, not contemporary theorists, best explain how the future framed their present. The breadth of material about the future beckons historians. In a double sense, it is about time.[12]

Insights, however profound, cannot replace myths unless they tell a better story. A long war myth would be as false as a short war myth. Instead, Civil War narratives need a story that encompasses the rich diversity of American forecasts when the war came. Decades after he lived through the conflict, philosopher William James argued, "A large acquaintance with particulars often makes us wiser than the possession of abstract formulas, however deep." Generations of America's greatest storytellers have contributed to the short war myth, so this book merely proposes an alternative plot, an untold story that may be adopted and improved by other storytellers. Instead of silencing American Cassandras and black prophets, this story showcases their prescience. Instead of opening the Civil War with a sweeping generalization about white men, this story begins with a possession cherished by a generation of white men. Before he left for Bleeding Kansas, Virginian Henry Clay Pate received a gift from his friends, a handsome bowie knife. Shortly after he arrived in Kansas, Pate lost his knife to John Brown. As the nation approached the Civil War, Pate's knife traveled the country, attracted enemies, and projected different wars under different circumstances. In Kansas it threatened a frontier war in 1856. In Connecticut it transformed and multiplied into a thousand pikes for class warfare in 1857. In Virginia the pikes prophesied a race war in 1859. In South Carolina they triggered a revolution in 1860. In New York they promised a war for liberation in 1861. In Massachusetts, Pate's original knife reappeared and harbingered a destructive war in 1862. These weapons divided Americans without shedding blood.[13]

Telling this story requires taking material things seriously. Which objects captivated Americans when they imagined the Civil War mattered. During the antebellum era, weapons attracted increased attention, steeled resolves, and goaded men into confrontations. Significantly, people seldom focused on modern arms like rifles, revolvers, and cannons when they amassed relics of the future war. Brown could have kept Pate's pistol and his lieutenant's rifle but preferred their knife and sword. Southerners could have collected Brown's handguns and rifles but favored his knife and spears. The grim sharpness of edged weapons appealed to men and spoke volumes about the kind of war they projected. These totems foretold a brutal war of close combat and personal killings. Such things were more than symbols of imagined outcomes—these weapons realized the future. As Lorraine Daston explains, without things people would literally have nothing "to describe, or to explain, remark on, interpret, or complain about." Worrying about and contending for real things grounded Americans who fixated on the future.[14]

The material cultures of Civil War Americans can help us understand how things contributed to the looming war. Across the nation, people grasped things to forge futures. Just as postwar Americans would erect Civil War monuments and enshrine battlefield relics to substantiate their memory of a vanished past, antebellum Americans made and gathered things to realize their forecasts of an emerging future. The most compelling example of this ominous process is the story of Pate's knife and its progeny. Twice during their journey, versions of Pate's knife crossed borders to spark conflicts for freedom. Both invasions failed, the enemy captured things as trophies,and circulated them to promote radical politics—first abolition and then secession. This national circulation of things accomplished more than a series of thefts and gifts. The men who invaded Kansas and Virginia found courage, resolve, and identity in the things they carried. They could not have pressed forward without such things. The men who took those things to Connecticut and South Carolina gained a false sense of security by disarming their enemies. They too could not have pressed forward without such things. More than ideas distinguished the visions of border ruffians, abolitionists, slaves, and secessionists. They understood things differently and associated with things in diverse ways. People like Henry Clay Pate, John Brown, and Edmund Ruffin believed that they possessed the future. More than mute props, their weapons caused alarms, triggered controversies, and deepened hatred. The mere presence of their things harmed the body politic without piercing a single soul. Antebellum Americans owned relics of a visceral future.[15]

I

Horizons

IN SPRING 1856, HENRY CLAY PATE headed west on the Santa Fe Trail in search of glory and John Brown. He had always dreamed of being a soldier. As a child in Bedford County, Virginia, he listened to his grandfather tell war stories from the Revolution and envied the old man for accomplishing "that greatest of military achievements," spilling blood to win independence. Instead of fighting for freedom, Pate wasted time trying his hand at journalism and law. When a war for Kansas promised him a battle for sovereignty, Pate gathered his things and left for the territories. His friends in Virginia gave him a beautiful bowie knife as a parting gift. The weapon projected future conquests that Pate yearned to realize. Through bloody aggression and manly adventure, he would help to claim Kansas for slavery and the South. He would literally take matters into his own hands.[1]

Serving as a deputy US marshal, Pate chased John Brown and other free-state men who assembled militia and terrorized settlers. That spring, Missourians and US soldiers rounded up several free-state men, including two of Brown's sons, John Jr. and Jason. The captors beat John Jr. with fists and rifle butts. Jason narrowly avoided being lynched. Troops chained the brothers together like slaves and drove them across the plains at a blistering rate of twenty-five miles per day. Their father still evaded authorities and Pate hoped to burnish his reputation by bringing the free-state captain to justice. Pate's only description of Brown came from one of his victims, Mahala Doyle. "With an eye like a snake, he looks like a demon," she said. As a warning, Doyle relayed to Pate what Brown told her: "If a man stood between him and what he considered right, he would take his life as coolly as he would eat his breakfast."[2]

Before dawn on June 2, two squads of armed men approached Pate's camp. A guard fired his rifle at the looming figures and fled. Murderous crossfire raked through the Missourians. Seeking cover in the wagon ruts of the Santa Fe Trail, Pate's men shot wildly over the oncoming force. Pate rallied his troop and repulsed the assault. For three hours the battle raged. Then terrified screams from wounded horses announced its turning point. The enemy was gunning down Pate's exposed mounts, eliminating any chance of escape. At that moment shadows filled the sky above Pate's position. Vultures had caught wind of the bloodshed and swooped down on his wounded men and animals. Penned in a gully and separated from supplies, Pate pondered dark omens. [3]

While Pate despaired, a solitary horseman charged between the lines. Men paused amid wild gunplay to watch this mysterious figure dash between them. A massive, bearded man, threadbare as a scarecrow, waved a cutlass over his head while riding a red horse across the prairie. Pate's southerners shot at him to no effect. The scarecrow hollered in ecstasy, "Father, we have them surrounded and have cut off their communications," before vanishing in a stand of black timber. Others thought they heard him quoting scripture. He sounded like an angel reporting victory to God. Both sides puzzled over the messenger and his meaning. Only a lunatic would cross that field alone, reasoned Pate. The scarecrow must be leading reinforcements. He needed time. Time to gather men, time to think. He dispatched one man to find reinforcements and sent a prisoner toward the enemy under a white flag. Looking west, Pate thought he saw enemies looming on the horizon. [4]

John Brown asked the approaching figure if he led those men, and when he identified himself as a free-state ally, Brown sent him back with instructions to fetch Pate. The Virginian crossed the field and declared himself a deputy US marshal charged with enforcing the Lecompton Constitution, proslavery law in Kansas. Brown identified himself and told Pate the only proposal he would accept was Pate's "unconditional surrender." Pate was furious; "I was *taken prisoner under the flag of truce, a barbarity unlooked for in the country, and unheard of in the annals of honorable warfare*." Brown had concealed men nearby, and when signaled, they appeared with rifles pointed at Pate. His bowie knife was pointless in this situation. The southern commander had two choices, "submit, or run and be shot." With Pate as a hostage and shield, Brown and eight men walked toward the southern line. [5]

A long row of shoulders and rifles peeked above a bluff as Pate, Brown, and his men approached the proslavery camp. "Tell your men to lay down their arms," Brown hollered to Lieutenant W. B. "Fort Scott" Brockett, Pate's second in command. "If our captain says to do so we'll do it, but I do not think he is such a damned coward as to do it," replied Brockett. Brown turned to Pate, pressed a revolver to his chest, and told him to give the order. Stuck in an impossible situation, Pate said, "Boys, lay down your arms till we can talk it over." Twenty-eight men, all but Brockett, followed the command. "Captain is a damn coward," Brockett announced. Salmon Brown pointed a pistol at

Brockett's head and screamed, "Let go, let go." Brockett dropped a nickel-plated Sharps rifle and someone scooped it up as a battle trophy. The free-state men gathered much needed spoils of war—food, rifles, ammunition, and a handful of unharmed horses. In the end, thirty southerners surrendered to John Brown and eight other men. To signify their surrender, Brown took Brockett's sword and Pate's bowie knife. [6]

Thus ended the Battle of Black Jack, the first battle between northerners and southerners over slavery. Previous violence in Kansas and elsewhere had been retaliatory and destructive but unorganized. Black Jack was open combat, a pitched firefight that lasted for hours and involved about a hundred men at its peak. After surrendering, Pate spied the mysterious rider. He was John Brown's son, Frederick, who had been told to guard horses during the attack. No one, including Frederick, could explain what possessed him to ride between the lines and lie about the enemy being surrounded. Worse than being tricked by Yankees, Pate was deceived by his own imagination. He was wrong about enemy reinforcements arriving. Additional free-state militia led by James Abbott did not gallop to the scene until after Pate surrendered. When he looked west, Pate (Figure 1.1) saw enemies who were not there. [7]

Saddle Time

PATE'S FALSE VISION OF the western horizon reflected an old American penchant for looking west for a glimpse of the future and spying a looming conflict. Many people, events, and things forecasted violence on the frontier. Fears of a sectional war for the West rose as diminishing threats of Indian war on the frontier no longer united Americans against a common enemy. When conditions like sensational news coverage and filibustering mixed with fears of an approaching apocalypse and thoughts of an open, contentious future, any event or thing could spark vivid visions of looming bloodshed. As western settlement unfolded, events and their narratives shaped that arc of the western horizon by fostering certain visions about the future. But more than stories fashioned how people projected tomorrow. Every frontier settlement needed things to exist and expand. The spoils and trophies collected at Black Jack belonged to a material world of accumulation, theft, and ruin that made and remade the frontier. Western expansion spawned competing material cultures among northern and southern settlers who made and circulated different things that portended different futures, threatened different wars, assembled opposing sides, and goaded men to fight.[8]

Figure 1.1 Henry Clay Pate, Colonel (5th Virginia Cavalry), Confederate States of America, in suit. Boyd B. Stutler Collection, West Virginia State Archives.

As old as the nation itself, fears of civil war looming in the west first appeared in the eighteenth century when Americans shifted their gaze from east to west. At that time, the western landscape changed from being known as the "back-country," a term that illustrated how colonists oriented themselves toward the east and Europe, to being called the "frontier," an open territory in front of Americans in both space and time. This new perspective turned the West into the future of American history. Imagining civilization as a westward march through time put America in the vanguard and Europe in the past. Stepping out of his house for a walk, Henry David Thoreau invariably headed west or southwest. Some instinct or natural magnetism settled his needle in that direction, because "the future lies that way to me, and the earth seems more unexhausted and richer on that side." Historian Donald Worster notes that the East represented "the old closed world of diminished opportunity" while the West symbolized a "field of action . . . still open to fresh heroic deeds" in the nineteenth century. Reflecting on his travels, Thoreau concluded, "Eastward I go only by force; but westward I go free."

He believed his impulse reflected an American tendency. "We go westward as into the future."[9]

What Thoreau considered an American tendency was shared by European intellectuals who looked west to the United States as a harbinger of future reforms in politics and society. America was "the land of the future" for German philosopher G. W. F. Hegel who prophesied, "In the time to come, the center of world-historical importance will be revealed there." A host of prominent Europeans, including Marquis de Lafayette, Alexis de Tocqueville, Harriet Martineau, and Frances Wright, traveled to the early American republic to witness the future unfolding and report back to European readers. Irish philosopher George Berkeley expressed the same sentiment in his poem "On the Prospect of Planting Arts and Learning in America" with his forecast: "Westward the course of empire takes its way; The first four Acts already past, A fifth shall close the Drama of the day; Time's noblest offspring is the last." [10]

When Americans equated the western horizon with an open, national destiny, they articulated anticipation, a modern temporality born by the Enlightenment. Revolutions in politics, technology, and economics raised the prospect of human improvement and the possibility of realizing utopia on earth. Even the word "revolution" marked this shift. Instead of referring to predictable, repetitive patterns of nature like the earth's revolution of the sun, the word referred more frequently to unpredictable, unprecedented events caused by people. "Creativity" as a concept did not appear until the nineteenth century, perhaps, as philosopher Anders Schinkel explains, because "only in modern times did humans dare apply the label 'creative' to themselves." These ideas shared a new, open, and activist view of the future that challenged expectation—an older, closed, and passive temporality based on cyclical nature and biblical eschatology. Experiencing these profound changes fostered a sense that society and time were accelerating forward, an idea encapsulated by another modern word, "progress." [11]

Anticipations of the future and westward expansion developed during a watershed era that historian Reinhart Koselleck called the *Sattelzeit*, or saddle time. During this period, old and new ways of imagining the future competed for supremacy in Western civilization. Expectations imagined cyclical time in which the future returned to the present and past. Generations would experience the stages of life that their ancestors knew, until Christ returned. Anticipations envisioned linear time in which the future departed from the present and past. Generations would experience things their ancestors never knew by progressing toward a new world of experience. This new approach to the future changed how people understood history and their place within it. As Koselleck explains, "History could be regarded as a long-term process of growing fulfillment which, despite setbacks and deviations, was ultimately planned and carried out by men themselves." The adoption of standard time zones and the mass production of clocks and watches reinforced notions that man made time and owned it. But society did not shift temporalities over night. Modern anticipations of abstract, manmade history and pre-modern expectations of natural, divine time coexisted during the nineteenth century. Progress competed with providence, while prognosis challenged prophecy.[12]

These tensions raised hopes and fears. The confidence that Americans felt about shaping the future concealed uncertainties about tomorrow. Horizon lines may have seemed farther from the present and more clearly defined, but the world beyond remained unknowable. If time were linear not cyclical, history became a less reliable guide to what loomed ahead. This anxiety sparked apocalyptic and millennial prophecies. If the horizon could not be penetrated by history or science, perhaps older ways of knowing the future could reveal America's destiny. Maybe the future was already revealed in scripture. People who felt displaced and disoriented by the changes of modernity looked to religion to gain perspective and find an anchor amid the stormy present. This anxiety about a manmade future also created friction between people who sought competing projects. If man, not God, controlled the future, then tomorrow was a contested domain. The West was America's tomorrow land. A sense of moving into the future instead of awaiting the future's approach reflected this modern, anticipatory temporality that praised enterprise, exploration, and adventure. Viewing the future with anticipation encouraged people to be aggressive about fashioning the future to match their ambitions. Utopian visions justified drastic efforts, including wars, to fulfill them. As long as the future seemed open and pliable, clashing anticipations threatened perpetual conflicts.[13]

Fire-Bell in the Night

DURING THE NATION'S FOUNDING, Alexander Hamilton imagined western origins for civil war. Far from the reach of government authority, scheming men in the territories could conspire to tear the nation asunder. Territorial disputes in the West between competing states or sections could also cause a civil war in which the nation would be "deluged in blood." Hamilton predicted that sectional contests over the territories might delude rival regions into advocating disunion as a peaceful alternative to continued conflict out west. "A man must be far gone in utopian speculations who can seriously doubt that, if these States should either be wholly disunited or only united in partial confederacies, the subdivisions into which they might be thrown would have frequent and violent contests with each other." The kind of war that would follow disunion terrified Hamilton. Civil war "would be desultory and predatory. Plunder and devastation ever march in the train of irregulars." The crisis would encourage the belligerent sections to consolidate power in a central government, raise massive armies, and strengthen the executive branch, thereby ensuring citizens' safety at the expense of their liberties. [14]

When the Whiskey Rebellion threatened to realize Hamilton's dire predictions, he volunteered to command an army against it. The uprising rose on the frontier, spread from western Pennsylvania, crossed the Appalachian Mountains, and reached four western states and the Northwest Territory. President George Washington called out 13,000 troops to quell the largest rebellion against the federal government before the Civil War. Washington, Hamilton, and other nationalists worried that foreign agents conspired to rob the United States of western territories. Perhaps dissension on the frontier, financed by British or Spanish filibusters, would spread beyond the reach of federal authority and end America's experiment in self-government with civil war. As one Federalist put it, the "seeds of dissension" sown in New England and Pennsylvania "will not end without a civil war." Prophecies of frontier wars resurfaced wherever the nation expanded westward.[15]

Competing visions of the frontier divided the North and South during the Missouri crisis of 1819. Northern congressmen supported New York representative James Tallmadge's amendment that Missouri could enter the Union as a slave state provided it follow a plan for gradual emancipation similar to policies implemented by northern states. Sensing an ominous precedent, southerners opposed any federal legislation that affected slavery in a state. The Missouri controversy sparked apocalyptic visions of disunion and war among southerners, because the possibility of restricting slavery on the frontier combined so many southern fears about the future. Economic concerns about vanishing markets for slavery during the age of emancipation, political anxieties about becoming a minority section, and racist alarms about living amid an overgrowing black population convinced southerners that they needed to "diffuse" slavery across the western horizon. The intensity of southern resistance to gradual emancipation on the frontier surprised northern politicians who assumed that southerners still sought a way to end slavery and welcomed northern cooperation toward that end. [16]

Bloody imagery of a destructive civil war soaked southern prophecies about restricting slavery in Missouri. Senator Freeman Walker of Georgia imagined civil war, "a brother's sword crimsoned with a brother's blood," and homes wrapped in flames. Congressman John Scott of Missouri predicted that his constituents "might one day bleed in contending for and against this restriction." Francis Jones of Tennessee agreed that Missouri's name "will be written in characters of blood." Thomas W. Cobb of Georgia accused James Tallmadge of kindling a blaze that "seas of blood can only extinguish." The rhetoric blazed so hot that Virginian Edward Colston accused northern congressmen of "speaking to the galleries" to incite a race war, just as British filibusters had aroused Indian attacks on the Florida frontier. Andrew Jackson court-martialed and executed the foreign agents, and Colston thought his fellow congressmen deserved "no better fate." Such statements stunned Speaker of the House Henry Clay from Kentucky. The crisis had sparked candid conversations about disunion that would have been deemed criminal a few years earlier. He feared that southern anticipations were more than political rhetoric, because men discussed the prospect in private without emotion, as if they were considering common legislation. [17]

Northern congressmen preferred to imagine the frontier as an undeveloped wilderness than to entertain the possibility of western expansion spreading slavery and civil war. Harrison Gray Otis of Massachusetts wished the Mississippi River were "an eternal torrent of burning lava," as impassable as the lake of fire that divides evil from good. Better to leave Missouri a jungle haunt for wolves and panthers than to transform it into slave labor camps. Likewise Rufus King of New York would rather surrender Missouri to the moon or to wild beasts than give it to southern masters. Senator Prentiss Mellen from Massachusetts complained, "We have been again and again cautioned, in the language of terrifying prophecy, to pause and consider before it may be too late." Mellen refused to accept that "commotion and civil war may next present their horrors, and a dissolution of the Union may be the fatal result." Tallmadge, whose amendment ignited the crisis, marveled at southern congressmen who threatened "the dissolution of the Union; of civil war, and of seas of blood" while insisting that the spread of slavery benefited humanity. If civil war must come, Tallmadge could only say, "Let it come!" [18]

Northern politicians were rumored to be meeting in secret to form a sectional party. Clay credited the gossip and feared its consequences. If the problem of slavery on the frontier could not be settled, "it will lead to the construction of the worst of all parties," one based on regional interests alone. Clay would not be surprised when it happened. Within five years of a sectional party's birth, Clay predicted, the nation would be split into three confederacies.[19]

Seventy-seven-year-old Thomas Jefferson agreed that the question of slavery on the frontier would kill the Union. "A geographical line, coinciding with a marked principle, moral and political, once conceived and held up to the angry passions of men, will never be obliterated; and every new irritation will mark it deeper and deeper." He doubted that the nation could solve the issue peacefully because "justice is in one scale, and self-preservation in the other." Historian Peter Onuf writes, "Jefferson, the prophet of intractable sectional divisions, thus looked forward to the American Civil War." According to Onuf, "Jefferson could plumb the depth of such feelings because he shared them; he knew that the union he cherished was in jeopardy because he could not stop himself from imagining its destruction." [20]

Jefferson's reaction to the Missouri crisis reflected his concerns as a Virginian who lived to see the end of the Old Dominion's dominance in national politics. In 1820, the Virginia dynasty in the White House ended with James Monroe's second term. The allure of western prosperity contributed to the state's decline. Farmers abandoned Virginia's depleted soil for richer, western lands in Kentucky, Tennessee, and the Old Northwest. Fears about the state's future fostered a host of reactions from John Randolph's states' rights doctrines to shore up political power to John Taylor and Edmund Ruffin's plantation manuals to restore economic vitality. Nothing worked. By the end of the antebellum period, Henry Clay Pate joined a million Virginians who left their homes for western horizons, an exodus far exceeding that of any other state during the period. [21]

Jefferson's forecast is the most famous prediction sparked by the Missouri crisis. Writing to a northern congressman who sided with the South during the debate, Jefferson admitted that he had stopped paying attention to national affairs "confident they were in good hands" until the question of slavery in the territories arose. Then "this momentous question, like a fire-bell in the night, awakened and filled me with terror," he said. "I considered it at once as the knell of the Union. It is hushed, indeed, for the moment. But this is a reprieve only, not a final sentence." Jefferson despaired that he would die knowing that the revolutionary generation had bled for sovereignty and self-government that passionate sons would throw away. In his opinion, emancipation could be implemented through union, not secession. A luminary of the Enlightenment, he anticipated a future shaped, for better or worse, by humanity. When his self-governed nation died, it committed suicide instead of being destroyed by God. He raged against Yankee reformers whose shortsighted strategies would destroy the world's best hope for democracy in order to free slaves. [22]

John Quincy Adams saw things differently. On November 29, 1820, he imagined a civil war to end slavery on the frontier. While Jefferson approached the looming contest with active anticipation, Adams awaited the approaching conflict with passive expectation. "If the dissolution of the Union must come, let it come from no other cause but this," he said. Instead of mankind causing disunion, Adams imagined the calamity would "come" on its own as a consequence of impersonal forces and divine intervention. "If slavery be the destined sword in the hand of the destroying angel which is to sever the ties of this Union, the same sword will cut in sunder the bonds of slavery itself," Adams prophesied. Disunion over slavery would trigger "a servile war in the slave-holding States, combined with a war between the two severed portions of the Union." The only result he could foresee from such a looming civil war "must be the extirpation of slavery from this whole continent; and, calamitous and desolating as this course of events in its progress must be, so glorious would be its final issue, that, as God shall judge men, I dare not say that it is not to be desired." While Jefferson deemed disunion over slavery a tragic suicide, Adams considered it a just reckoning. [23]

Congress resolved the crisis by balancing Missouri's admission as a slave state with Maine's statehood as a free state, but legislators knew that the problem would recur whenever western populations sought statehood. Henry Clay forged the Missouri Compromise to anticipate these future conflicts and avoid them. The agreement banned slavery from all US territory north and west of Missouri. The remaining land of the Louisiana Purchase south of Missouri could extend slavery, but the bulk of the West, including what would become Kansas, was reserved for freedom.

The Great Nation of Futurity

THE COMPROMISE DID NOT stop antebellum scholars and clergy from framing the West as a final battleground for civilization and salvation. While the Missouri crisis consumed Congress in February 1820, Edward Everett, a Unitarian minister from Massachusetts, delivered a sermon in the US Capitol entitled "Brethren, the time is short." Written with the New Year in mind, Everett hoped to inspire his listeners to account for past transgressions and resolve to do better in the future. His sermon used recent scientific discoveries of the Earth's true age to reinforce an expectant temporality. According to Everett, history signified nothing within "that mighty unbeginning and unending infinity." All of time is short compared to God's existence. We fool ourselves into thinking that we move through time and mark its passage. In reality time moves through us and marks our passage. This year shrivels our skin, that one loosens our teeth, and another one dulls our senses. "Time is the great epidemic," Everett warned, "always mortal, always fatal, alike to individuals and nations, to men and things, art and nature."[24]

The Missouri crisis exposed the truth that the United States was as mortal as every other nation. "Go out in the morning of a nation," Everett told the congressmen. "How thriving, strong, and fresh—what forests of masts along the shore, what a living tide of population toward the west—how they spring up like an exhalation of the soil." Within a few years, luxury and poverty appear. Corruption ensues, the nation wars with itself, and a grave decline begins. In a few centuries the forests reclaim the capital. Everett assured his listeners, "Our country indeed will continue, God grant for long and happy ages," but "our generation is going off." What mark would these men of Congress leave? Soon, Everett warned, "it will be too late to strike off the fetters of the slave; death has already done it, he is free as you; and ready, when the trumpet shall sound, to start up in judgment against you." Everett asked America's leaders to "measure what progress we have made on that journey of eternity which all must travel; toward that vale of shadows, which all must pass." Everett sensed that the Missouri Crisis marked a crossroads. The direction the nation chose to follow in 1820 would decide its future and mark its history by blazing a trail for time to pass through the nation and judge it.[25]

Looking toward western horizons, many Americans hoped that expanding the space of the nation would extend the life of the republic by providing fresh soil and air for future generations. In his Second Inaugural Address, Thomas Jefferson dismissed predictions that "the enlargement of our territory would endanger its union." Instead he imagined how dispersing people across the plains would distribute power evenly through a republican empire. Such visions of the future responded to Thomas Malthus's "Essay on Population" that predicted an inevitable decline for all societies, because population growth would eventually surpass food production. When John O'Sullivan coined the phrase "manifest destiny," he addressed this looming fear by advocating America's "manifest destiny to overspread the continent allotted by Providence for the free development of our yearly multiplying millions." Time's inevitable passage and its ruin of the republic through generational growth was the principal concern of O'Sullivan, Jefferson, and other fervent expansionists. When southern congressmen objected to the Tallmadge amendment, they advocated diffusing the slave population in the West for the same Malthusian reasons. Proslavery advocates in old southern states like Virginia and South Carolina obsessed over Malthus's calculations.[26]

Northerners saw the western horizon from a different perspective—they insisted that how America acquired and settled the frontier had serious consequences for the future. Yankee congressmen made this point when they preferred to leave Missouri as a wilderness or surrender it to foreign powers rather than see it become additional slave states. During the Missouri crisis, New England educator and textbook author Emma Willard argued, "There is no physical cause" to prevent the nation from growing "in a peaceful manner, under a good government, till the end of time." She shared Everett's view that republics declined because of corruption and internal strife, not overpopulation. Conquest and war threatened the nation's future more surely than generational increase ever could. When her textbook described the acquisition of Florida from Spain, Willard admitted that "the addition of this peninsula . . . completes the ocean boundary of the United States," but she disapproved of the expansion because it ignited "a bloody war." Willard, Everett, and others challenged American exceptionalism by insisting that the United States risked the same fate and judgment as other nations. Willard closed her 1855 world history textbook with an ominous question for her students: "Has the Ruler of Nations given assurance, that he will set aside the order of his providence in our behalf? Has he given us a license to commit, with impunity, offences for which he has filled other nations with blood?" Willard argued, "Conquest by war is but an antiquated vulgarity." "As with ancient Rome," spilling blood to expand sovereignty would lead the United States "to decay and dissolution."[27]

Boosters of American exceptionalism countered these visions. Joseph Smith believed God designed a special fate for the United States as the place where Jesus Christ would return to Earth. In western New York, a frontier region known for religious revivalism and deemed the "burned-over-district," Smith experienced a series of visions in which an angel prophesied the Second Coming and revealed lost scripture buried beneath a hill. The documents revealed to Smith an ancient history of warring civilizations on the American frontier. According to Smith, a survivor of the virtuous, defeated nation buried the scripture at the site of the climactic battle. The Book of Mormon began as a battlefield relic.[28]

Smith warned that the United States' millennial role would not save the nation from God's wrath administered through the scourge of war. To prepare for looming bloodshed, Smith sent Mormon missionaries to convert Native Americans on the Great Plains. He hoped to establish a second

Jerusalem in the center of the continent, a haven in Missouri that he called Zion, to shield believers during Armageddon. On Christmas day, 1832, Smith received a vision that prophesied how apocalyptic wars would come to America. "VERILY, thus saith the Lord concerning the wars that will shortly come to pass, beginning at the rebellion of South Carolina, which will eventually terminate in the death and misery of many souls," Smith announced. "For behold, the Southern States shall be divided against the Northern States, and the Southern States will call on other nations, even the nation of Great Britain, as it is called, and they shall also call upon other nations, in order to defend themselves against other nations; and then war shall be poured out upon all nations." "And it shall come to pass," Smith prophesied, "slaves shall rise against their masters, who shall be marshaled and disciplined for war." Armageddon would begin in America with a civil war over slavery. Armies of slaves and masters would ally with powers across the globe until they consumed the Earth in fire. Though there was no escape from this future, Smith told his followers to "stand ye in holy places, and be not moved, until the day of the Lord come." Recurring phrases like "it shall come to pass" reveal how Smith and his followers understood time. Mormons opposed the modern notion that humanity made the future and shaped its destiny. For them God orchestrated time and made history. The future would come to pass regardless of human efforts. At best, believers could only prepare for tomorrow.[29]

Other prophets agreed that God destined the United States to be the final republic before the end times. George Berkeley expressed a millennial vision that America would build the last empire on the western horizon, complete the "fifth act" of history, and inaugurate Christ's return. Westward expansion would allow the American republic to transform European monarchies. As Jefferson put it in 1816, "That same light from our west seems to have spread and illuminated the very engines employed to extinguish it." Ardent expansionist John O'Sullivan agreed. In "The Great Nation of Futurity," he argued that the United States had "little connection with the past history of any of them, and still less with all antiquity." Instead "our national birth was the beginning of a new history . . . which separates us from the past and connects us with the future only." Here O'Sullivan illustrated a key concept of modernity: people anticipated a future that seemed liberated from historical precedents and limits. Jefferson shared this temporality. He confessed to John Adams, "I like the dreams of the future better than the history of the past."[30]

Bright anticipations of a western march that broke with the past conflicted with dreadful expectations that America's future merely reiterated historical cycles. If Indian wars and removal did not challenge American exceptionalism for many Americans, the Mexican War did. John Taylor Hughes, a private in Company C of the First Missouri Mounted Volunteers, envisioned a western horizon stained by bloody conquest. He recalled the image of his regiment marching on the same trail that Pate's men would take into Kansas, "the great Santa Fe Road which led to the enemy's country." The morning sun warmed their backs and glinted off their sabers and guns as they marched for miles over undulating prairie. Hughes described the sight: "The American eagle seemed to spread his broad pinions and westward bear the principles of republican government." This positive anticipation of human progress clashed with a heavenly sign that dreadful expectations loomed ahead. In early 1846, "before it was known, or even conjectured, that a state of war would be declared," a party of traders saw a sign in the heavens when they traveled toward Missouri. A storm blew past as the sun set on the horizon, leaving the image of "the American eagle, on the disc of the sun." The witnesses cried out in unison at the sight and all agreed "that in less than 12 months the eagle of liberty would spread his broad pinions over the plains of the West, and that the flag of our country would wave over the cities of New Mexico and Chihuahua." After the war, Hughes wrote, "The prediction has been literally and strikingly verified," but he could not shake the feeling that heavenly signs portended dark omens. He thought the omen deserved "quite as much credit" as the chariots of fire that Romans saw in the heavens before Caesar's assassination.[31]

Abraham Lincoln served in Congress during the Mexican War, and though his constituents supported the conquest of the neighboring republic, he opposed it. In December 1847 he challenged President James Polk to prove that the Mexican assault that justified the war took place on American soil. How the nation expanded its territory mattered to Lincoln. In a series of resolutions, he argued that American troops occupied a contested boundary, expelled Mexicans from a local settlement, built a fort there, and goaded the Mexican army to attack. Lincoln suspected that Polk was "deeply conscious of being in the wrong." "The blood of this war, like the blood of Abel, is crying to Heaven against him." To avoid scrutiny, Polk tried to woo the public with "military glory—that attractive rainbow that arises in showers of blood." God would punish such arrogant duplicity. The war escaped Polk's control, exceeded his anticipations, and left the president "he knows not where." Looking back on the start of the conflict, Lincoln recalled how Polk disgraced General Winfield Scott for "intimating that peace could not be conquered in less than three or four months." After twenty months of bloodshed, the war left the president "a bewildered, confounded, and miserably perplexed man." For Lincoln and many others, no amount of Mexican territory could pay for the costs of the war. No subsequent glory could excuse the war's corrupt origins.[32]

In 1854, the year Congress opened Kansas to slavery, southern evangelist Samuel Baldwin published *Armageddon*. Baldwin expected the last war on earth would soon begin in the American West. By translating biblical days into solar years and calculating the amount of time between the fall of the holy temple in 68 AD and its promised restoration, Baldwin calculated that Armageddon would occur "between this [time] and 1878, or about 1861–5." He based his prophecy on the books of Daniel and Revelation, and recent filibustering. Baldwin predicted that frontier warfare would ignite America's dominion over the world, burn up the earth's sins, and cauterize the land into God's paradise. American filibustering would usher in the millennium because it manifested "a national itching to extend the area of freedom on the ruins of thrones." Democracy's dominion on earth would mark a world historical event and "be attended in its march with the total extinction of some inferior races, as for instance, the Mexicans." People that Baldwin judged unfit for self-government would simply die out, leaving room for more advanced civilizations to enjoy the looming millennium. Baldwin's bloody vision of the western horizon excused all violence on the frontier because it ushered in the Second Coming of Christ.[33]

When framed by antebellum conflicts for western territory, these widespread prophecies of a looming apocalypse on the frontier shaped America's horizon of expectation in ominous directions. Edward Everett, Joseph Smith, and Samuel Baldwin spanned the spectrum of Protestant faiths, from Unitarianism to Mormonism to Southern Methodism, respectively. Nonetheless, all three looked west and saw the fate of civilization hanging in the balance. On their frontiers, good and evil would meet to determine the fate of the world. No event evoked this vision better than Bleeding Kansas.

The Theft

ANTEBELLUM HORIZONS OF EXPECTATION framed how Henry Clay Pate and John Brown viewed their clash at Black Jack, Kansas. Both men understood the event as a historic "first" that foreshadowed a looming civil war. Pate called it "the first time American citizens, of different States, professing different politics, had met in battle array." Brown described it as the "first regular battle fought between Free State & pro Slavery men in Kansas. May God still gird our loins & hold our right hands, & to him may we give the glory."

Their descriptions anticipated a postwar debate over Civil War memory years before the war itself occurred. The southerner stressed how a political dispute caused a war between men from "different States." All the belligerents were Americans, but Pate stressed, each side represented different sovereign powers, "different States." His explanation ignored slavery. The northerner did not see an abstract political debate but rather a war between freedom and slavery. Brown defined the battle as a contest within a common territory. While the southerner preferred chivalric imagery of "battle array," the northerner chose biblical allusions of girded loins. Pate imagined himself an agent of American empire sent to secure sovereignty just as his grandfather had done during the Revolution. Brown considered himself God's agent to clean the frontier of the sin of slavery. Their firefight on the prairie may have seemed inconsequential to them if generations of politicians, scholars, and clergy had not invested the American frontier with such ominous responsibility for the fate of civilization.[34]

To prove that Black Jack meant war, Brown and Pate drafted an article of surrender and prisoner exchange that afternoon. According to the agreement, John Jr. and Jason Brown would be exchanged for Pate and Brockett. The document specified, "The arms particularly the side arms of each one exchanged are to be returned with the prisoners." The exchange never occurred, because fifty US dragoons led by Colonel Edwin Sumner and Lieutenant J. E. B. Stuart arrived three days later. Sumner, a cousin of Massachusetts senator Charles Sumner, announced that he had orders from the president to disperse armed bands throughout the territory. He freed Pate and his men and forced Brown to return their things. Brown produced the signed article of prisoner exchange and insisted that Pate and Brockett were his prisoners until the proslavery forces released John Jr. and Jason Brown. Sumner told Brown that he would not parley "with lawless and armed men" and demanded that Brown release his prisoners and return their things.[35]

Staring at a column of US cavalrymen, Brown had no choice but to let Pate and Brockett go, but he protested in a striking way. The southerners would not honor the terms of their surrender, but Brown would. He could not keep the men, so he kept Pate's bowie knife and Brockett's sword instead. "Now, Colonel Sumner," John Brown complained, "I can't undertake to return every man his jack-knife." "Never mind, Captain," said Sumner, "in good faith—in good faith, sir—find all you can, and return these men their property." Soldiers often collect relics after their first battle, and Brown no doubt valued these artifacts as mementos of an important event in his life and the nation's history. He suffered no shortage of swords and knives. He stole those things for a reason. The things people carried and valued reveal how southerners and northerners hoped to realize competing visions of the future out west. [36]

When the Kansas-Nebraska Act gave settlers the power to make a sovereign state, it opened the territory to Americans, who rushed to gather enough people, arms, and votes to ensure their future republic in Kansas. These gatherings did not produce representative assemblies but arsenals. Bleeding Kansas was a political failure within the territory and in Washington, a breakdown that exposed how rising sectionalism undermined compromise and brought violence. But what happened in Kansas and the prophecies of blood that Kansas foretold were deeper than a generation's flaws or an era's propensity for violence. Kansas replayed a violent process of republic-making that Americans had inflicted on the British, Native Americans, Mexicans, and others. Ignoring treaties, laws, and boundaries, Americans threatened and inflicted bloodshed to impose their sovereignty. The principal difference in Kansas was that white Americans deployed these bloody methods against each other. Rival sections assembled things to realize their horizon of expectation. [37]

A chain of events that culminated at Black Jack illustrates how the material goods that settlers accumulated to realize their vision of Kansas defined what was possible on the frontier and shaped their western horizons. The political race to transform Kansas into a free or slave state relied on things as much as people, ideas, and actions. This was a time when popular sovereignty meant gathering arms, not votes, when a cane spoke louder than a senator. [38]

Both northerners and southerners gathered and circulated objects that threatened bloodshed, consolidated opposing sides, and goaded them into violent clashes over sovereignty. But *how* each region assembled, spread, and employed things reflected and affected its vision of the future. Southerners carried arms in defiance of social norms, against laws, and across borders to assert personal sovereignty against all comers. They expected their enemies would cower in submission instead of risking death to oppose men hell-bent on aggressive conquest. This behavior reflected "martial manhood," a popular form of nineteenth-century American masculinity that idealized physical strength, wildness, violence, honor, and adventure. Northerners, by contrast, concealed weapons and flaunted capital, labor, and goods as key ingredients to settle the West. They anticipated overwhelming southern squatters and Native Americans by transplanting a superior civilization en masse to the prairie. Their design related to "restrained manhood," a rival form of American masculinity during the period that stressed morality, control, domesticity, and temperance. The story behind this portentous process reveals how things, especially weapons, were harbingers of civil war.[39]

Bowie-Knife Gentry

THE BOWIE KNIFE EMBODIED a martial manhood and southern threats to conquer the West. Bowie knives first appeared in the early republic after civilians stopped wearing swords. A sign of aristocracy, swords went out of fashion after the American and French Revolutions, and even British gentlemen stopped wearing them. Social pressures encouraged men to replace swords with concealed weapons, and changes in clothing accommodated this shift by introducing more pockets in men's coats and pants. Sword canes and percussion pistols offered more discreet forms of self-defense, but sword canes took time to unsheathe and were brittle, while pistols were inaccurate and unreliable. After the sword became socially taboo, none of the period's other weapons replaced its usefulness in a melee.[40]

Such fracases flourished on the southwestern frontier. Slavery was predicated on violence, and white men resorted to physical brutality to assert their authority over blacks, women, children, and each other. A code of honor encouraged men to duel and feud over misunderstandings and insults. Unsettled territories like the Old Southwest fostered fighting because they lacked local law enforcement and efficient courts. If lawmen existed, they often belonged to feuding clans. No wonder people literally took matters into their own hands.[41]

In 1827, brothers James and Rezin Bowie entered this world in Rapides, Louisiana, and made a knife to combat it. Rezin sharpened one side of an old iron file, called it a "hunting knife," and presented it to his brother as a gift. Europeans wore similar knives when hunting but never in public. James was recovering from a gunshot wound he had received from Norris Wright and was preparing for an inevitable second encounter. When James recovered, he stuck the knife in his belt and carried it with him everywhere. Their second fight erupted after a duel on a Mississippi River sandbar. Wright and Bowie belonged to rival groups who watched their principals exchange harmless shots on September 19, 1827. Satisfied that their honor had been vindicated, the men prepared to return to town for a drink. But their parties consisted of armed men with scores to settle. As the gangs dispersed, gunfire erupted between them. Bowie discharged his pistols and unsheathed his knife. Wright shot Bowie through the lung and drew a sword cane, but the flimsy blade stuck in Bowie's sternum. When Wright tried to extricate it, Bowie thrust his knife into Wright's heart, killing him instantly. Bowie cut another assailant in the side before the scuffle ended. Things spun out of control because of the extreme potential for violence that each man carried in his pockets and belt. [42]

The sandbar fight made the bowie knife more famous than its owner because it fulfilled a material need in southern society. Masters of their worlds, southern white men kept or broke the peace at will. Duelists and filibusters disregarded law and order. Personal sovereignty trumped all other authorities, whether they emanated from social customs, courtroom justice, state power, or even international borders. When a southern man pulled out his bowie knife, it meant war. By 1859, John Bartlett's dictionary of Americanisms insisted "they are worn as weapons by persons in the South and South-western States only." Southern men raced to purchase their own bowie knives without knowing what one looked like. Bowies of all shapes and sizes appeared. Two elements made a knife a bowie: the garish thing stuck out of a belt against all social proprieties, and it was made for murder. Its coffin-shaped hilt proved prophetic. After James Bowie died defending the Alamo, his knife embodied southern politics. [43]

In Kansas, southern men like Henry Clay Pate asserted popular sovereignty at the point of their bowie knives. People called them the "bowie-knife-and-pistol gentry." As the *Atchison Squatter Sovereign*, a proslavery Kansas newspaper, expressed it, settling Kansas required "war to the knife, and knife to the hilt." With "Blood for Blood!" emblazoned across its front page, the newspaper urged, "Let us purge ourselves of all abolition emissaries . . . and give distinct notice that all who do not leave immediately for the East, will leave for eternity!" In 1854, South Carolinian William Henry Trescot explained, "The history of the world is the history of encroachment, of invasion, of wrong, if you so will." God designed the future so that "you cannot bring into contact an earnest, living will, and a feeble, effete nature, without the absorption of the one into the other." Weeks before the battle of Black Jack, George Frederick Holmes, chancellor of the University of Mississippi, echoed this sentiment. "Conquest, extension, appropriation, assimilation, and even extermination of inferior races has been and must be the course pursued in the development of civilization," he explained. "Such is unquestionably the plan prescribed for the progressive amelioration of the world." Like Samuel Baldwin, Holmes and Trescot believed that exterminating undesirable people improved the world. They predicted that violent conquest and destruction would elevate humanity. The point of the bowie knife was the vanguard of progress. [44]

Henry Clay Pate and other members of the bowie-knife gentry served as the shock troops for southern conquest and extermination. One of the reasons Pate left Old Virginia was a sense of frustration that it was too focused on the past. "My native State seems to be doomed to the rule of enemies of progress, who say daily—let us rest at our ease, and live upon the glory of departed ancestors." His Virginia friends presented him with the bowie knife as a parting gift. Pate left Virginia and the past behind, named his Missouri newspaper "Star of the Empire," and crossed the border in search of fame and adventure. Thomas Gladstone, a correspondent for the *London Times*, reported many "incidents of bowie-knife voting" in Kansas while staying in Kansas City. Gladstone quoted border ruffians who applied the same logic as George Frederick Holmes and Pate but with more colorful language. One southern adventurer who called himself "General" Stringfellow told Gladstone that southern men were to "mark every scoundrel that was the least tainted with free-soilism or abolitionism, and to exterminate him." Stringfellow had no "qualms of conscience as to violating laws, state or national, the time had come when such impositions must be disregarded." According to the border ruffian, it was time to "enter every election district in Kansas, in defiance of the Governor and his vile myrmidons, and vote at the point of the bowie-knife."[45]

Southern settlers conveyed their future with possessions as much as words and actions. A Presbyterian clergyman, Frederic Starr, passed wagonloads of Missouri border ruffians returning from "bowie-knife voting" in Kansas elections. A flagpole in the front of their wagon waved a homemade skull and crossbones flag. The men lashed a revolver, powder horn, and bowie knife to the pole and plugged an inverted, empty whiskey bottle on the tip. Such were "the piratical symbols of Missouri ruffians," men hell-bent on claiming the future through intimidation and bloodshed. When their captain saluted Starr, he was stunned to recognize a prominent lawyer who had canvassed with him months earlier to promote local liquor laws. Even southern gentlemen condoned and participated in bowie-knife politics.[46]

Bowie knives so epitomized southern politics that southern legislators used them to settle debates. Theodore Dwight Weld noted that southern congressmen were "*in the habit* of wearing bowie knives" to work. Weld recounted the murder of Joseph Anthony, a member of the Arkansas House of Representatives, by John Wilson, Speaker of the House. On December 14, 1837, Wilson took offense at something Anthony said during a debate, left the Speaker's chair, drew a bowie knife with a ten-inch blade, and approached Anthony, who pulled out his own bowie. They exchanged thrusts until Wilson plunged his blade into Anthony's heart. The Speaker of the House paused to wipe the blood off his blade with his thumb and finger before returning to his chair. Though the attack occurred in the statehouse before dozens of witnesses, authorities did nothing for several days. Only fervent demands from Anthony's family led to Wilson's arrest and eventual trial for murder. After the jury found him innocent, Wilson bought them drinks at a local grog shop. Weld recounted similar murders with bowie knives in Arkansas and noted that the white population was similar in size to that of Litchfield County, Connecticut. "And we venture the assertion, that a public affray, with deadly weapons, has not taken place in that county for fifty years, if indeed ever since its settlement, a century and a half ago." When John Brown, a native of Litchfield County, stole Pate's bowie knife, he disarmed the southerner of his characteristic weapon.[47]

Crate Politics

NORTHERN EXPANSIONISTS DISPLAYED MORE ambivalence about their own arms. Massachusetts entrepreneur Eli Thayer thought he understood how things generated republics. Anticipating the need to finance the antislavery settlement of Kansas, he founded the Massachusetts Emigrant Aid Company a month before the Kansas-Nebraska bill became law. His organization mushroomed into a joint-stock company known as the New England Emigrant Aid Company that equipped thousands of settlers devoted to a free Kansas. Amos Lawrence, a wealthy textile manufacturer, bankrolled the operation. Southerners exaggerated the size and reach of the company, but it did provision more than a thousand emigrants. Some things, like passage on steamboats, helped people travel to Kansas. Others, like a printing press and type for a newspaper, precipitated the establishment of town politics. Emigrants named their largest town in Kansas after Lawrence.[48]

When a company agent in the territory, Charles Robinson, requested Sharps Rifles, the company quietly complied. Lawrence prophesied that "a revolution must take place in Kansas," and "when farmers turn soldiers they must have *arms*." Like Henry Clay Pate, Amos Lawrence understood the looming conflict by framing it within the historical memory of the American Revolution, which hinged on a violent contest over sovereignty. Other New Englanders agreed. Above his mantel, Theodore Parker proudly displayed the musket his father fired at the battle of Lexington, a clash precipitated by stockpiles of arms. The company reimbursed settlers who purchased guns, ordered rifles at a bulk rate and shipped them west, and presented arms to settlers when they embarked for the territory. In this atmosphere, abolitionists traded nonviolence for bloodshed that promised to accelerate emancipation.

In Kansas, conductors of the Underground Railroad gave guns to runaways. In 1856, James Birney confessed to Thomas Wentworth Higginson, "I regret that a civil war should rage but if slavery cannot be exterminated without one—& I don't see how it can be—I say let it come." Thayer told New Yorkers, "It might be well for the Emigrant to be furnished with his Bible and his rifle; and if he were not protected in his rights according to the principles of the first, let him rely upon the execution of the latter." Reverend Henry Ward Beecher conflated Bibles and rifles more directly. His congregation bought and shipped Sharps rifles to Kansas in crates labeled as Bibles. Before violence erupted on the prairie, northern settlement of Kansas contained key ingredients of a filibuster: financing men and arms to cross the border and claim territory for their form of government. One Illinois emigrant who headed to Kansas in an armed squad recalled, "It was a military company that could be changed to a colony or a colony ready for military service." His description was the definition of a filibuster campaign.[49]

If bowie-knife politics forwarded southern horizons of expectation, crate politics promoted northern visions of the future. Northerners' concealment of arms in crates labeled dry goods and Bibles reveals a desire to maintain, if in appearances only, restrained manhood on the frontier. Like restrained manhood, crate politics was self-contained. Northern filibustering cared about outward appearances, morality, and structural integrity. Supplying the frontier with boxes of Bibles and goods would convey civilization to the wilderness. Northern visions of the horizon evinced an unquestioned faith that their region's superior capital, manufacturing, and benevolence would trump southern swashbuckling on the prairie. While northerners criticized bowie-knife politics as barbaric, southerners accused crate politics of dishonesty.[50]

In October 1856, a New York City rally to supply Kansas illustrated how northern filibustering concealed its weaponry behind religious and idyllic visions. Poet William Cullen Bryant and writer Charles Dana organized the meeting and asked the Reverend Joseph P. Thompson to speak. While introducing Thompson, Bryant framed northern emigration within the story of Exodus. While Moses lifted his rod, the Israelites slew the Amalekites, but when his arms tired and lowered, the Amalekites prevailed. Only by supporting Moses's tired arms and keeping them aloft did Aaron and the Israelites triumph. Like the Hebrews' battle against the oppressive powers of the Egyptians and the Amalekites, northerners were fighting "the battle for the rights of the many against the rights of the few," a battle of the chosen people against oligarchies. Victory in that war required the material support of true religion. That was as close as Bryant would come to asking for money to buy arms for Kansans. "My friends," Bryant concluded, "let us accept this omen."[51]

When Thompson took the stage he contrasted northern and southern horizons of expectation. He prophesied that when Bryant went west he heard a prosperous and free future in the industrious hum of a bumblebee.

> I listen long
> to his domestic hum; and think I hear
> The sound of that advancing multitude
> Which soon shall fill these deserts. From the ground
> Comes up the laugh of children, the soft voice
> Of maidens, and the sweet and solemn hymn
> Of Sabbath worshippers. The low of herds
> Blends with the rustling of the heavy grain
> Over the dark-brown furrows.

"That picture," Thompson said, "is a picture of freedom; the home of free men, the homes of Christian families; the dignity of labor; the freedom of knowledge; the inviolable sanctity of worship; the peace and smile of God." Border ruffians threatened to "*blot out* that picture" by imposing a southern horizon of expectation, where "the clank of chains, the curse of the oppressor . . . the sigh of the needy" drown out the industrious hum of honest work. When that happened, when slavery contaminated Kansas, Oregon, Utah, "and Nicaragua to boot," slaveholders would become the majority, New York harbor would become "a mart of slavers," and leaders in Washington would become border ruffians who "bristle all over with bowie-knives and revolvers." Thompson urged New Yorkers to avoid this future. "That vision of yours was not the mere dream of the prophet; it was a prophecy inspired of God, and my children shall yet read your prophecy fulfilled upon these teeming prairies."[52]

The material culture of both sections triggered events that neither side prophesied. The gathering of armed Yankee settlers and their early clashes with proslavery citizens alarmed southerners who responded with rival assemblies. The Kansas Emigration Society of Missouri rallied the slave states to action. "It requires no foresight to perceive that if the 'higher law' men succeed in this crusade, it will be but the beginning of a war upon the institutions of the South, which will continue until slavery shall cease to exist in any of the states, or the Union is dissolved." Henry Titus was one of the first to answer the Missourians' appeals for help. A proslavery northerner, Titus participated in two failed filibusters to Cuba before he arrived in Kansas and built Fort Titus, a fortified log cabin, nine miles west of Lawrence. Titus allied with Major Jefferson Buford, a veteran of the Creek Indian War from Alabama, who financed a southern filibuster to Kansas. A wealthy slaveowner, Buford sold forty slaves to equip an army of four hundred settlers. He promised "forty acres of first rate land, a free passage to Kansas and the means of support for one year" to "men capable of bearing arms." Buford forecasted that a "great day of darkness" loomed before Kansas, and the rights of slave owners required men "crazy enough to peril even life in the deadly breach." He organized his emigrants into military units and told them that the fate of the South was in their hands. They marched to Kansas under a silk banner that read "The Supremacy of the White Race." When they arrived, Henry Clay Pate presented Buford with a horse, saddle, and bridle on behalf of "the cause of slavery for Kansas."[53]

That spring, Buford's army patrolled the area surrounding Lawrence to prevent wagonloads of guns and sabers sent by northern aid companies from reaching the town. A squad of Buford's men captured George Brown, antislavery editor of the newspaper *Herald of Freedom*, and imprisoned him at Lecompton, the proslavery capital. When these tactics failed to quell the antislavery threat, border ruffians from Missouri consolidated Buford's men into a proslavery posse and raided the town. Buford openly objected to the Missourians' plan to destroy Lawrence, but the filibuster he financed was running its course. Things were beyond his control. David Atchison, former senator from Missouri, urged the southern army to violence. "Draw your revolvers & bowie knives, & cool them in the heart's blood of all those damned dogs, that dare defend that damned breathing hole of hell." The group surrounded Lawrence and demanded that citizens give up their weapons. After the town surrendered some arms, the Missourians destroyed things that signified free-state principles. Northern propaganda dubbed the event the "Sack of Lawrence," but no citizens were physically assaulted. Instead, looters and arsonists descended upon the homes and personal effects of free-state leaders. They targeted the Free State Hotel, which served as an antislavery headquarters and fortress, bombarded it with four cannons, exploded kegs of gunpowder inside the building, and set it on fire.[54]

Thomas Gladstone witnessed the Missourians' triumphant return to a Kansas City hotel. Caked in dust and reeking of smoke, men overran the bar, "displaying with loud boasts the 'plunder' they had taken from the inhabitants." Gladstone noticed that the posse wore a uniform of sorts: red flannel shirts, "immense boots worn outside their trousers," and big beards. They were armed "to the teeth with rifles and revolvers, cutlasses and bowie-knives." The British writer had found "the seat of Western war," where "the strife of politics" affected personal character and "transmuted" Americans "into new forms." The posse decorated their outfits with battle trophies taken from Lawrence. Some wore a Yankee's satin vest or fine dress coat over their flannel shirts. Others "girded themselves with the cords and tassels which the day before had ornamented the curtains of the Free-State Hotel." Gladstone expressed revulsion at this "grotesque intermixture of dress," but the ruffians followed an old ritual of wearing their victims' clothing as battle trophies. Wearing someone's clothing violated that person's privacy and parodied the individual's values. It harmed opponents without laying a hand on them.[55]

Border ruffians who wore their victims' clothes also articulated a key feature of crate politics in Kansas: outward appearances were deceiving. Hotels were forts. Crates labeled dry goods, books, and Bibles contained weapons. Charitable societies like the New England Emigrant Aid Company secretly fronted filibusters. To expose the genteel façade of Lawrence settlers, the posse burned books in the street and destroyed the printing press of the *Herald of Freedom*. Smashing and scattering its type in the streets sent a clear message to free-state settlers: violence, not words, would decide the future of Kansas. Antislavery settlers got the message. In the aftermath of the raid, women gathered the type and gave it to free-state militia, who melted it into cannon balls. When they assaulted Fort Titus, the decisive turn in the battle occurred when militiamen fired the reconstituted type through the fortress walls. "'This is the second edition of the 'Herald of Freedom,'" the free-state militia jeered as they fired. "How do you like it?" Titus answered with a white flag.[56]

The "second edition" of the *Herald of Freedom* illustrates how weapons assembled political movements that goaded men to commit violence. The material culture of Washington, DC, also revolved around arms and produced similar results. Washington social life exuded hypermasculinity and violence, and as sectional tensions mounted over Bleeding Kansas, congressmen, senators, and spectators brought pistols, dirks, and sword canes into the Capitol. The presence of concealed weapons increased confrontational language and behavior inside the chamber. The heightened potential for violence raised politicians' aggression as men goaded each other to draw first. The day after border ruffians practiced bowie-knife politics in Lawrence, Congressman Preston Brooks broke the tension in Washington by using a cane to make his point against Senator Charles Sumner of Massachusetts.[57]

Caning Charles Sumner

A MODEL OF RESTRAINED manhood, Sumner never carried weapons. For him, armed statesmen signified civilization's decline toward barbarity and he blamed slavery. For months, Sumner crafted and memorized a long speech entitled "The Crime against Kansas" that contrasted the material cultures of slavery and freedom. The point of Sumner's two-day speech was lost because he opened with prefatory remarks that insulted Stephen Douglas, James Mason, and Andrew Butler, three senators who had supported slavery in Kansas. His barbs at Butler were particularly vile. An elderly senator from South Carolina, Butler was absent recovering from a stroke that affected his speech. Sumner mocked Butler's speech impediment. Worse, he implied that Butler had sex with his slaves. Sumner knew that he was insulting armed men. He provoked their response, because he expected victory from either outcome. If southern firebrands assaulted him, he would expose their barbarity. If they did not, he would reveal their vacant threats and cowardice. Stephen Douglas did not fully grasp Sumner's strategy. While listening to the speech, Douglas asked, "Does he want somebody to kick him?" Whether somebody kicked him or not, Sumner thought he had already won the political debate. When John Bingham overheard Douglas's remark, he thought it was "designed to produce or encourage an assault" against Sumner and relayed his concern to friends who pleaded with Sumner to let them escort him safely home. When they could not convince Sumner to accept their help, they spread rumors that Sumner was armed, hoping to discourage an attack.[58]

Their plan backfired. When Henry Edmundson heard the rumor from Sumner's friends, he shared the news with Preston Brooks, a distant cousin of Andrew Butler, who was already considering how best to confront the physically imposing Sumner. He considered whipping Sumner with a cowhide, a weapon used against slaves that would demean the Yankee, but he feared that Sumner would wrestle the whip from him. Instead Brooks selected a cane, which signified class and was less likely to end up in Sumner's hands. The rumors that Sumner was armed convinced Brooks to give the man no chance to defend himself.[59]

In his speech, Sumner explained how things in Kansas foreshadowed civil war. "Even now, while I speak," Sumner warned, "portents hang on all the arches of the horizon, threatening to darken the broad land, which already yawns with the mutterings of civil war." The crossing of Missouri's army into Kansas meant "the strife is no longer local, but national." People who tried to dismiss the organized violence as a frontier feud missed the point;

"the muster has begun," civil war armies were already gathering. Sumner prophesied "war—fratricidal, parricidal war—with an accumulated wickedness beyond the wickedness of any war in human annals." Americans were "justly provoking the avenging judgment of Providence and the avenging pen of history."[60]

The heart of Sumner's address contrasted northern and southern horizons of expectation. Sumner imagined civilized, northern expansion, a process through which territorial governments provided security and guarded freedoms, so that pioneers could pursue "the sweet employment of undisturbed industry." In Sumner's northern ideal, the settler "is not aggressive"; he is "accustomed to produce, and not to destroy, he is essentially peaceful" and "contented in the returns of bounteous nature." Governments based upon free labor progress toward civilization; governments founded on slavery regress into barbarism. Figure 1.2 depicts how antislavery northerners understood the blight of slavery on the South. Human bondage was transforming the region into an immoral world stained by knife fighting, dueling, lynching, gambling, and drinking. The "sack of Lawrence" testified that America was sliding backward into an age of iron savagery. "The border incursions, which, in barbarous ages or barbarous lands, have fretted and 'harried' an exposed people, have been here renewed." The agents of free governments rule by voice and consent; their citizens upheld the government with their votes. The agents of slave governments rule by weapons and violence; their citizens feared the government and consented to being subjugated like slaves.[61]

Sumner's clear distinction between free and slave governments blurred within his own speech. To understand the scale of border ruffian violence,

Figure 1.2 "Our Peculiar Domestic Institutions." Library of Congress, Rare Book and Special Collections Division.

Sumner compared the size, supplies, and organization of Missouri columns to historic American military forces. Sumner recognized that the "armed multitude of Missouri" invaded Kansas "in larger numbers than General Taylor commanded at Buena Vista, or that General Jackson had within his lines at New Orleans—larger far than our fathers rallied on Bunker Hill." Though all those forces gathered men and arms to assert sovereignty, Sumner tried to separate the border ruffians from the rest. "On they came as an 'army with banners,' organized in companies, with officers, munitions, tents, and provisions, as though marching upon a foreign foe, and breathing loud-mouthed threats that they would carry their purpose, if need be, by the bowie-knife and revolver." The Massachusetts senator conveniently forgot that patriots of the Revolution asserted their sovereignty with bloodshed first and declarations second. General Taylor's army mirrored the Missourians' habit of crossing borders to pick a fight over sovereignty. Taylor's men shared another characteristic with Missouri's border army: both forces fought to return slavery to land where it had been banned.[62]

Sumner's fading distinctions between free settlement and slave settlement vanished when he defended the Emigrant Aid Company as a benevolent society. Railing against the "false testimony" that southern senators made against the society, Sumner swore that it was "an association of sincere benevolence, faithful to the Constitution and laws, whose only fortifications are hotels, school-houses, and churches; whose only weapons are saw-mills, tools, and books; whose mission is peace and good will." Southerners accurately accused the company of trafficking in "cannon and rifles, in powder and lead, and implements of war," which Sumner said was "absolutely false. The officers of the company authorize me to give to this whole pretension a point blank denial," he proclaimed. He directly replied to Senator Butler's assertion that the association supplied Yankee settlers "with one uniform gun, Sharpe's rifles," by lying that "the company has supplied no arms of any kind to anybody." Instead, the company is planting "*capital in advance of population*" to accelerate emigration and "soften the hardships of pioneer life." Nonetheless, in Kansas, both sides gathered men and arms to assert sovereignty. Both sides filibustered for the future.[63]

Two days after the speech, Sumner sat at his desk attending to mail while the Senate adjourned. Absorbed by his work, Sumner did not notice a man standing beside him until he spoke, "I have read your speech twice over carefully. It is a libel on South Carolina, and Mr. Butler, who is a relative of mine." Sumner looked up to see a tall stranger. While he listened to the man's words, trying to catch his meaning and identity, a heavy cane struck him over the head. Stunned blind, Sumner raised his arms to protect himself, but the cane kept finding its mark. Uncounted blows cracked against Sumner's skull. He lost consciousness. When he awoke he found himself ten feet in front of his desk, his pounding head resting on someone's knee. Voices and faces of northern friends hovered over him. Stephen Douglas stood at a distance with southerners and Sumner thought he spied his assailant among them. Some gentlemen carried him to a sofa in the lobby. Blood covered Sumner's collar, waistcoat, and trousers. Blood soaked through the padded shoulders of his broadcloth coat. Blood splattered his back and sides.[64]

After the assault, the cane represented the event more than Brooks did. It underlined with blood the relationship between things, people, and social order in antebellum America. During the episode Brooks lost self-control but the cane continued its work and seemed to have a life of its own. When the cane shattered during the attack, the remnant in Brooks's hand continued to beat Sumner until someone intervened. No one could say how many times the cane "licked" Sumner. Some guessed ten times; others thought thirty. The testimony of witnesses is clear about the location of the cane after the event but unsure about the whereabouts of Brooks. People scrambled to collect fragments of the cane, relics soaked with a senator's blood. Henry Edmundson saw "three pieces broken off the small end of the cane" and people racing to grab them. One lucky winner was a "Senate boy" who pocketed "a piece about four inches in length." Brooks absently surrendered the prized piece, the golden head of his walking stick, to John Crittenden, a Kentucky compromiser who aspired to Henry Clay's legacy. Crittenden deplored "such violence in the Senate chamber" and spied the remaining piece of the stick in Brooks's hand. "I took hold of it," Crittenden explained, "and he very gently yielded and allowed me to take it out of his hand." Crittenden wanted no memento from an event that savagely divided North and South. He gave the head away without a second thought.[65]

When Brooks recovered his senses, he realized that he no longer owned a piece of the thing that now defined him and his future. Seeing his friend Edmundson nearby, Brooks implored him to recover the golden head, explaining that it was a cherished gift from a friend. When he found it, he did not give it to Brooks. Edmundson was one of the few people who knew that Brooks planned to assault Sumner. The last thing Edmundson wanted was to look like an accomplice, so he delivered the weapon to the Senate sergeant-at-arms, Adam J. Glassbrenner, who was in his office and unaware of the attack.

When Edmundson told him that "an assault had been committed by Mr. Brooks upon Mr. Sumner," Glassbrenner received the stick as evidence and put it in his safe. Then, instead of finding Brooks, Glassbrenner investigated the cane. "I have measured the stick carefully," he told the Senate Investigating Committee. "The fragment I have is the head of the stick, the smaller end having been broken off. It is twenty-one and three quarter inches in length, one inch thick at the large end, and three-quarters of an inch thick at the small end. The cane is hollow, and the hollow being three-eights of an inch in diameter at the small end, and seeming to increase proportionally to the head."[66]

Glassbrenner's focus on the cane proved prescient, because the Senate committee asked as many questions about the cane as they did about Brooks. The senators asked witnesses, "Do you know anything of the relative specific gravity of a gutta percha cane or of a hickory cane?" "How thick was the cane used by Mr. Brooks?" Witnesses who owned pieces of the cane brought them to the Senate investigation in their pockets. They asked the doctor who attended to Sumner if repeated blows to the head with "a stick from one-half to five-eights of an inch in diameter" could kill a man. "It would depend upon the character of the stick," the doctor replied, not the character of the assailant.[67]

When John Brown learned about the caning, he vowed revenge. His military company arrived too late to defend Lawrence, and Brown flew into a rage when he discovered that its inhabitants did not fight against Buford's filibusters and the Missourian hordes. Before he came to Kansas, Brown had collected money from New York abolitionist Gerrit Smith to arm his sons and other free-state militiamen. During his journey to the frontier, Brown stopped in Ohio and gathered swords from a filibuster who had planned to use them against Canada. The weapons were military surplus, artillerymen's short swords that imitated arms from the Roman republic. After the news from Lawrence and Washington, Brown decided it was time to deploy these weapons to punish the wicked and liberate the territory. On May 24, under cover of darkness, Brown and his band dragged five southern men from their beds and hacked them to death. Using their new broadswords, the men split open their victims' skulls, slashed their chests and sides, and severed their fingers, hands, and arms. None of their victims owned slaves. Their principal "crime" was associating with proslavery settlers including Buford's filibusters. Brown left his enemies' bodies where they fell and stole their horses. His actions ignited civil war in Kansas and compelled Henry Clay Pate to cross the state line in search of him.[68]

Annihilating Time

WHEN BRITISH CORRESPONDENT WILLIAM RUSSELL visited Montgomery, Alabama, during the spring of 1861, he marveled at the prevalence of bowie-knife politics during the creation of the Confederacy. Russell disliked the seedy, violent culture of Washington, where politicians gambled, drank, whored, and fought, but life in the new Confederate capital was worse. Russell stayed in a house "full of Confederate Congress men, colonels, and place-men with or without places, and a vast number of speculators, contractors, and the like, attracted by the embryo government." He met four filibusters who raved about the Knights of the Golden Circle, a shadowy society committed to spreading a slave empire from the Gulf South through the Caribbean and Latin America. One of Russell's friends complained to the hotel clerk "that he could scarce get down to the hall on account of the crowd, and that all the people who passed him had very hard, sharp bones." The clerk explained that those "bones" were "implements of defence or offense, as the case may be." "I suppose you and your friends are the only people in the house who haven't a bowie-knife, or six-shooter, or Derringer about them."[69]

Russell tried to understand why southerners carried so many sidearms and how those weapons affected their government policies. A conversation with a Mississippi gentleman answered his questions. The Mississippian explained that his state capital averaged "a murder a month," but "he used a milder name for the crime." Arguments between Mississippi politicians often ended at the point of a bowie knife when opponents settled their dispute outside a bar, hotel, or gambling house. Sitting in the shade with the man on a hot spring day, Russell listened to "tale after tale of blood." The Mississippian explained to Russell why southern gentlemen anticipated assaults on their property, person, and character by acting first to avoid danger. "If a gentleman with whom you are engaged in altercation moves his hand towards his breeches pocket, or behind his back, you must smash him or shoot him at once, for he is either going to draw his six-shooter, to pull out a bowie knife, or to shoot you through the lining of his pocket." The gentleman warned Russell not to rely on pocket pistols "because suppose you hit your man mortally he may still run in upon you and rip you up with a bowie knife." Either carry a knife or a revolver that can "drive a good heavy bullet into him." Russell heard secessionists applying the same logic when they founded the Confederacy. Waiting for Abraham Lincoln and Black Republicans to strike against slavery exposed the South to a lethal blow. Bowie-knife politics baited southerners to anticipate a blow, fight first, and ask questions later.[70]

When Russell boarded a train for Memphis, volunteers headed to a military camp at Corinth crowded the cars. Their whiskey and tobacco consumption led to hideous war cries as the train lurched through the night. Suffocating from the stifling heat and smell from these men, Russell felt trapped "in the land of Lynch law and bowie knives, where the passions of men have not yet been subordinated." A recent victory at Big Bethel cheered his fellow passengers, who anticipated whipping effete Yankees and walking all over the North. Russell marveled at their fancy names and colorful uniforms. His favorite was a group "with rifled pistols and enormous bowie knives, who called themselves 'The Toothpick Company.' They carried along with them a coffin, with a plate inscribed, 'Abe Lincoln, died ____,' and declared they were 'bound' to bring his body back in it, and that they did not intend to use muskets or rifles, but just go in with knife and six-shooter, and whip the Yankees straight away." Having been in the Crimean War, Russell knew modern warfare firsthand. "How astonished they will be when the first round shot flies into them, or a cap full of grape rattles about their bowie knives." [71]

Up river from Russell, Samuel Clemens echoed the British correspondent's prophecy. While his contemporaries rushed to war, Clemens sensed the war was rushing toward him and he wanted no part of it. Before Russell reached Memphis by train, Clemens left the city on one of the last riverboats that churned North before the Union blockade ended such traffic in the spring of 1861. For years Americans expected steamships would conquer the West and unite the North and South. From the deck of a Mississippi riverboat in 1842, J. S. Buckingham was captivated by "the signs of promise for the future, as contrasted with the wild and savage nature from which it has just emerged into a giant infancy, advancing on to manhood with colossal strides." By accelerating trade and settlement, "steam navigation colonized the West!" James Lanman argued. Steamboats "advanced the career of national colonization and national production at least a century!" Others predicted that steamboats' voluminous traffic and trade along a North/South axis would stitch together regional sentiments and economies like never before. Citizens of each section met on Mississippi riverboats and could more easily travel from the heart of Dixie to the upper Midwest.[72]

With their power to surge against the current, steamships encouraged anticipations that technology advanced against the river of time and controlled the future. Time no longer consumed civilizations as Edward Everett had preached, because man created machines that obliterated it. For Edmund Flagg, steam power "has in a few years anticipated results through the New World which centuries, in the ordinary course and consequence of cause and event would have failed to produced." Robert Baird used a more popular and suggestive phrase when he praised the steamboat's "annihilation of time." Built for speed, steamboats competed for the fastest time from New Orleans to Natchez, Cairo, and Louisville. Ships with evocative names like *Comet, Eclipse, Enterprise*, and *Telegraph* broke records. People sensed that time itself was accelerating because of human technology.[73]

Critics and prophets challenged this secular faith in technological progress. In 1852, Presbyterian minister Alfred Bryant warned his congregation, "There is no religion in railroads, steamships, magnetic telegraphs, or in the progress of the arts and sciences." Instead of accelerating time and ushering in the millennium, technology was a "stimulus to avarice, to worldliness, to selfishness in every form, and pleasure." What struck Bryant about steamboats was their sinfulness. The amount of drinking, gambling, and whoring onboard would send passengers to Hell faster than they could reach St. Louis. Herman Melville explored these themes in *The Confidence-Man: His Masquerade*, a satirical novel set on a Mississippi riverboat. The main character fleeces passengers by donning disguises that flatter their visions of the future. One of his victims expresses his deepest faith in technology and looks forward to an era when a "thousand new inventions" will replace labor and end slavery. From his pulpit at Dartmouth College, millennialist clergyman Nathan Lord did not share his contemporaries' faith in steamboats. "They are rather confusing the world," he warned. Instead of annihilating time and distance, new technology was "annihilating the necessary distinctions of life" and "precipitating the stew of human wickedness, whose end is death." Lord also stressed that a variety of accidents claimed the lives of passengers and crew. People were burned, drowned, snagged, or "sawyered" by passing obstacles, and blown to bits. The 1856 bestseller *Lloyd's Steamboat Directory, and Disasters on the Western Waters* quoted newspaper lists of the killed and wounded that eerily foreshadowed Civil War casualty reports. Graphic descriptions of steamboat accidents anticipated language that witnesses would use to convey the horror of battlefield carnage. The victims were "crushed, torn, mangled, and scattered in every direction." "Legs, arms, and the dismembered trunks of human bodies" covered the scene, while the wounded shrieked in agony.[74]

As a pilot, Samuel Clemens knew the ways of riverboats firsthand. Pilots embodied the era's ambiguous relationship with time. They never bothered to carry maps of the Mississippi River because its channels and hazards changed more quickly than any mapmaker could document. Instead, pilots scanned the horizon for trouble and tried to anticipate what was coming. When the war erupted, many people still assumed that they were the pilots of their destiny and their nation's future. They looked to history and thought that it offered a map to the future. They rushed forward with anticipation. Other Americans felt a different sensation. Instead of moving toward the future, they sensed that the future was rushing toward them, the same feeling that a pilot has when a snag looms toward the bow. He knows that the danger is stationary and he is moving toward it, but at the moment of peril, it feels like the danger is rushing toward him and he doesn't have the time or the power to stop it. When the river has no hazards, the pilot enjoys a sense of control, but an experienced man like Clemens knew that this too was an illusion.[75]

Despite his experience on the river, Clemens was disoriented in the spring of 1861. While onboard a steamer in April 1861, he wrote his brother, Orion, "I am on the wing for Louisiana," then crossed out the word when he remembered he was heading upriver to Missouri. Clemens promised to return to St. Louis tomorrow and asked his brother to do him a favor. "Orion bring down 'Armageddon' with you if have it. If not, *buy* it." Two weeks after the Civil War began, Sam Clemens was not eager to enlist and march to the center of the war with groups like "The Toothpick Company." Instead he wanted to read Samuel Baldwin's prophecy of a titanic war in the Mississippi Valley to get a clearer sense of what loomed on the horizon. In July he escaped the Valley before war consumed it. He and Orion traveled to Nevada territory for the remainder of the war. Like Henry Clay Pate, Clemens looked west, but instead of seeing approaching enemies, he spied peace.[76]

2

Speculations

MONTHS AFTER BLACK JACK, John Brown fled from Kansas arrest warrants to embark on a fundraising tour. Prone, sick in a wagon, he rumbled across the plains dreaming of future battles. In lucid moments, Brown feverishly scribbled the names of prospective recruits and sponsors in a notebook. In Ohio, Governor Salmon P. Chase met Brown and drafted him a letter of introduction to New England radicals. With a governor's endorsement, the fugitive boarded a train for New York and Boston, where he found sanctuary in the home of Massachusetts superior court judge Thomas Russell. Brown knew how to impress eastern voyeurs of western violence. Every night before retiring to his room in the judge's home, Brown made a show of inspecting his weapons. Russell recalled, "He used to take out his two revolvers and repeater . . . to make sure of their loads, saying 'Here are eighteen lives.'" Brown apologized to the judge's wife for the blood he would spill on her carpets if enemies came.[1]

His message for New England radicals was clear: abolition required more than sentiments for success. Brown told eastern bankers, merchants, and doctors how his small army had endured squalor, sickness, hunger, wounds, imprisonment, torture, and death to defend American liberty. All he asked from them was "the money that is *smoked away* during a single day in Boston." More than ideas, materials were needed to kill slavery. He asked them for "horses, baggage-wagons, tents, harness, saddles, bridles, holsters, spurs, and belts; camp equipage, such as cooking and eating utensils, blankets, knapsacks, intrenching-tools, axes, shovels, spades, mattocks, crowbars," plus ammunition, money to pay for freight expenses, and support for his family. With those things, Brown promised to end slavery by striking a blow against its foundation. Without them, human bondage would continue, and God would hold Americans accountable. Mary Stearns, the wife of prominent manufacturer George Stearns, was so impressed by Brown's speech that she asked for "a copy to preserve among my relics." In return, she convinced her husband to write Brown a check for $7,000.[2]

Brown understood the powers of possessions. On his trip east, he stopped in Chicago and exchanged his ragged Kansas clothing for a suit of brown broadcloth tailored an old-fashioned way, a gray military overcoat with a cape, and a fur cap, which gave him the appearance of a pious and militant pioneer torn from the past. He testified against southern violence with gory detail. "I saw three mangled bodies two of which were dead + one alive with twenty Buck shot + Bullet holes in him; after the two murdered men had lain on the ground to be worked at by flies for some 18 hours. One of those young men was my own Son." As proof of southern brutality, he showed people the shackles that Henry Clay Pate's posse had clamped on John Brown Jr. But his prized relic was Pate's knife. After listening to Brown's graphic, earnest lectures about Bleeding Kansas, audiences thrilled to see him pull the bowie knife out of his boot. People came to expect this dramatic flourish. When Emerson and Thoreau met Brown, they asked to see the knife and spent an afternoon by Thoreau's fireside hearing Brown's account of the battle of Black Jack and passing the knife around the room. Thoreau noticed that Brown (Figure 2.1) "referred to what his family had suffered in Kansas, without ever giving the

Figure 2.1 John Brown. Library of Congress, Prints and Photographs Division.

least vent to his pent-up fire." Brown's temperament "was a volcano with an ordinary chimney-flue," an arrangement bound to explode at any moment.[3]

When Brown took Pate's knife, he acquired a battle trophy. Soldiers often collected mementos after their first combat. These mute, fellow survivors expressed war's ineffable nature. When troops stripped a defeated enemy, they asserted supremacy. The enemy's private possessions, flags, and body parts had no practical value. John Brown did not need another piece of cutlery. By stealing Pate's knife, he disarmed the southerner of his characteristic weapon. When the prisoner exchange in Kansas unraveled, Brown retaliated by sticking a piece of the vainglorious Virginian in his boot and walking off with it. But battle trophies seldom remained with their collectors. Soldiers gave them to family and friends, gambled them away, or exchanged them for luxuries. In the process, trophies circulated from war front to home front and turned into gifts that forged friendships and strengthened family ties. What began with a theft that deepened hatreds between enemies transformed into tokens of respect and love. Such was the fate of Pate's knife.[4]

On December 10, 1856, the Canton Frémont Club held a fundraiser for Brown in Collinsville, Connecticut. After their Republican candidate for president, John C. Frémont, lost the election a month earlier, the Club sought new ways to attack slavery. Horatio Rust, a local druggist and radical abolitionist, organized the event. For one dollar, citizens could hear rousing music by the Middletown band and stirring speeches by John Brown and other gentlemen from the frontier. Dinner was included in the price of admission. All proceeds from the event would go to "the needy in Kansas," meaning Brown's family of freedom fighters. As darkness descended, crowds filed into the lecture hall. Brown mesmerized them with a graphic description of his war on the frontier. After covering expenses, Rust gave Brown $75.00.[5]

Following the fundraiser, Rust arranged a meeting between Brown and local blacksmith, Charles Blair. Standing in Rust's pharmacy, the men passed Pate's knife back and forth. The blacksmith admired the weapon. "It was a two-edged dirk, with a blade about eight inches long," Blair remembered. The blade had "a ridge in the middle and was beveled each way." It had a short guard and "a neat handle." Blair could tell "it was an expensive weapon." An expert in knives, Blair manufactured the finest machetes for southern sugar plantations. Now slavery's most determined enemy asked what it would cost to copy Pate's blade and attach its replicas to a thousand six-foot poles. According to Brown, Kansans needed such weapons to defend their homes from "border ruffians or wild beasts." Blair paused, then quoted Brown a stiff price, "a dollar a piece." Brown said he wanted them made. To express his gratitude to Rust for orchestrating the fundraiser and the pikes' production, Brown gave him the saber he had stolen from W. B. "Fort Scott" Brockett at Black Jack. "I would of no account have you buy it of me," Brown said, but he recognized that Rust had paid for the weapon by raising money for Brown and helping him negotiate a deal with Blair.[6]

Why pikes? Brown had already used edged weapons in Kansas when his men hacked to death five southerners with broadswords. Spreading a thousand blades across Kansas would intensify the scare Brown had started. Like the era's most wondrous invention, the telegraph, Brown's terrorism would range like lightning, sending his message to remote communities with predictable effects. His choice of weapon mattered. It would have been easier to ask Blair to make a thousand bowie knives, but those arms had a southern accent that did not send the message of terror Brown intended. He envisioned weapons defending free homesteads from slavery's myrmidons. Turning a bowie into a pike also illustrated the protean ways of Yankee radicals. Rifles arrived in Kansas labeled as Bibles or dry goods. Northern militia called their Lawrence fort the Free State Hotel. As Figure 2.2 shows, Brown continued this shape-shifting behavior by transforming a ruffian's knife into free-state pikes. He instructed Blair to use common hoe handles and to ship the blades separately in small bundles to avoid suspicion. His son Oliver referred to them as "Kansas butter knives."[7]

In Kansas, people concealed base motives behind benign façades. Northern settlement agencies were more than antislavery ventures. The first emigrant company was unconcerned about slavery in the territory. Eli Thayer

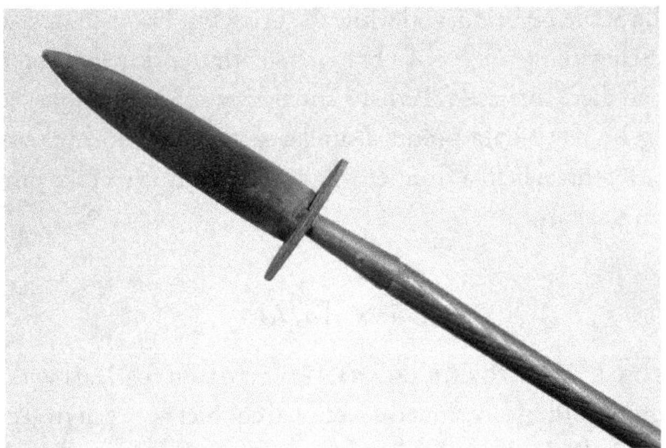

Figure 2.2 John Brown's Pike. Virginia Historical Society.

started the Massachusetts Emigrant Aid Society to steer settlers onto western land owned by a railroad directed by his cousin, Nathaniel Thayer. Their plan for the Hannibal & St. Joseph railroad was simple. The people whom Eli sent to Kansas would grow wheat on the railroad's land and ship it east along the finished line. Eli would make money by selling the settlers provisions and running the emigrant agency as a joint-stock company. Nathan would make his fortune by selling the settlers' mortgages to European investors and charging farmers for moving their grain. Missouri border ruffians threatened the Boston capitalists' scheme by scaring free settlers out of the territory and starting a slave republic that did not appeal to English investors. What started as a railroad venture transformed into an antislavery crusade to protect the investments of powerful Boston capitalists. Things were not what they seemed in Kansas.[8]

When Brown ordered a thousand pikes, he imagined a weapon ideal for the defense of northern free labor. An avid reader of European military history, Brown knew that European peasants used pikes to defend their homelands from invaders and overthrow tyrants. In medieval times, a knightly class of heavy horsemen assumed social and military dominance because a cavalry charge seemed physically unstoppable by lowly infantrymen. However, the supremacy of cavalry relied more on intimidation than power, and it succeeded until Swiss peasants skewered charging knights with pikes. A simple weapon in the hands of a determined underclass ended the reign of knights in Europe. Likewise, antebellum histories of the French Revolution praised Vendean peasants who grabbed pikes and defended their borders against tyrannical invaders. Brown would have approved of Archibald Alison's description of their valor. "Thus armed and organized, they offered up their vows to the Supreme Being, and while the priests and women were assembled in prayer, fell with the might of a brave and enthusiastic people on their foes, and crushed them to pieces." Perhaps circulating a thousand pikes to stalwart yeomen in Kansas would produce similar results against southern knights. If Pate's knife threatened a frontier war out West, Brown's pike prophesied a class war in the East.[9]

Class Warfare

WHILE SOME AMERICANS IMAGINED a civil war sparked by competition for the frontier, others envisioned a sectional conflict between rival classes and economies. Radicals in both regions imagined an unavoidable battle between free labor and slavery. Southern prophets forecasted unrest and revolution in northern cities teeming with discontented workers. Scanning the northern horizon, Dixie economists warned the North to adopt domestic slavery before a class war engulfed them. Northern visionaries countered that the entire nation must choose between freedom and slavery. Citing the 1850 census and the disparate tempos of life in each section, northern prophets insisted that their section was hurtling toward the future while the South was mired in the past. These prophets of economic clashes contended that bloodshed was only a matter of time.[10]

Visions of an economic showdown served competing political ideologies, but beneath this transparent service, such prophecies spread speculations—financial forecasts imbued with the confidence of prognosticators who saw the future and knew how to capitalize on it. Antebellum Americans distrusted speculators and branded them as confidence men who preyed on innocent hopes and accumulated wealth by fashioning prospects instead of goods. Not all speculators were land pirates, mining magnates, and bank executives. Others stood behind church pulpits and laboratory tables, wrote editorials and poetry, and served in Congress and reform societies. Despite its outspoken criticism of speculation, antebellum America was its epicenter, a world pregnant with prospects of fortune and misfortune as trivial as riverboat gambling and as momentous as the second coming of Christ.[11]

New material cultures quickened the pace of society in both sections and contributed to rampant speculations. Changes in technology and the economy shaped how people approached the future. Some new inventions and practices, telegraphy and an expanding postal service, fostered passive expectations by forcing people to wait for the future to reach them. But the wider reach of antebellum communications fostered more hopes of empowerment than feelings of passivity. Other changes, notably the railroad and steamboat, encouraged active anticipations by giving people a sense of traveling through time. All of these changes marked modernity and strengthened faith that a single person or small group could improve society. Despite the optimism such changes generated, they also raised fears and anxieties. Things happened too fast for some people, and not all of society benefited. The same speed that generated overnight fortunes brought thunderous panics in banking and commerce. Hidden forces seemed to shape the future, and many people feared them. If small groups could shape the future, secret cabals could undermine American principles and institutions.[12]

The same developments stirred utopian visions of human perfection and apocalyptic fears of impending doom, depending on the visionary's perspective, circumstances, and temperament. Living amid so much change uprooted people from cause and effect, past and future, and they addressed this disorientation by searching for an ending and telling stories about it. When antebellum Americans sensed the end times approaching, they responded with panic and joy, millennial faiths and social movements, political ideologies and economic speculations. As historian James H. Moorhead notes, "If postmillennialists had one foot in the world of steamships and the telegraph, the other was still firmly planted in the cosmos of John's Revelation—a universe where angels poured out vials of wrath, the dead would rise again, and the wicked would be cast into a lake of fire burning forever."[13]

The Universal Telegraph

BEFORE THE CIVIL WAR, revolutions in communications and transportation changed how Americans approached and thought about the future. Rising literacy rates and an expanding postal service fostered a golden age of American letter writing. Laws in 1845 and 1851 slashed the cost of mailing letters. From 1840 to 1860, letters delivered by the US post office jumped from 27 million to 161 million every year, representing a tripling in individual usage of the post. Due to western expansion and transportation changes, more people had distant loved ones to write. By mid-century, historian David Henkin explains that "a critical mass of Americans began reorganizing their perceptions of time, space, and community around the existence of the post." While millions of Americans experienced these postal changes directly, they also felt indirect effects of the telegraph. Wherever telegraph lines appeared, increased volatility of banking, commerce, and news coverage followed.[14]

The post and telegraph encouraged waiting for other people and things to fashion the future. Instead of seizing the future with anticipation, people at post offices and telegraph stations passively, if not patiently, expected the future to come to them. People expressed these expectations in spiritual terms. The first telegram read, "What hath God wrought," an outcry from the prophet Balaam in the book of Numbers. Often separated from home, John Brown understood the post as a spiritual link between him and his distant family. In March 1844, he wrote to his wife, "It is once more Sabbath evening, and nothing so much accords with my feelings as to spend a portion of it in conversing with the partner of my choice." Though "absent in body," thanks to the post Brown was "very much of the time present in spirit." This sense of being present in two places at once suggests how empowering the post and telegraphy could be. Both expanded an individual's reach across space and time, fostering faith that individuals could transform the world.[15]

The communication revolution reinforced notions that humanity centered the universe and affected space and time. In 1850, Edward Hitchcock, a Christian geologist and president of Amherst College, argued that all human activity is transmitted to the future via a "universal telegraph." According to Hitchcock, "material creation receives an impression from all our words and actions that can never be effaced." Hitchcock endorsed Charles Babbage's theory that human movement forever stirred atoms in earth, water, and air. Like billiard balls, unseen matter collided and caromed across creation, eternally disturbed by all human actions, even speech. As Babbage put it, "The air itself is one vast library, on whose pages are for ever written all that man has ever said or woman whispered." But Hitchcock's theory surpassed Babbage's in scope, by claiming that every thought moved the cosmos and lasted forever. He argued that the mind, like the telegraph, relies on electricity to convey thoughts. Morse's telegraph "seems to us a marvelous discovery" because it can transmit "thoughts at the distance of thousands of miles." Yet Hitchcock was convinced that "by means of the same power, all our thoughts are transmitted to every part of the universe, and can be read there by the acuter perceptions of other beings as easily as we can read the types of hieroglyphics of the electric telegraph." When future mathematicians discovered the equation for tracking the invisible reactions caused by human deeds, historians could know anything about the past as easily as reading Morse code.[16]

Babbage, Hitchcock, and others imagined humanity as central to the morality of the universe. The assumption that people exist at the heart of the cosmos is illustrated by Babbage's analogy of a stone thrown into a pool. Every human action is a stone that disturbs a serene environment, and the disturbance encircles the stone with ever expanding rings of reaction. Because the material world contains impressions of all human effort, the universe is a witness of human good and evil. As Hitchcock explains, "Nature, through all time, is ever ready to bear testimony of what we have said and done." Once people learned how to detect and read these traces in the material world, humanity would see how it forms the fabric of the universe.[17]

By this thinking, the evils of slavery could never be erased; they pulsated through creation forever, recording each slave's suffering and damning every enslaver. Babbage conveyed this idea by recounting the fate of slaves drowned during the middle passage. In 1837, a British naval vessel, *Thalia,* captured the slave ship *Adalia*. During the pursuit, *Adalia*'s crew threw more than 150 slaves overboard to lighten the ship. Waters that washed over the mouths of doomed souls would bear witness to the murders on Judgment Day. "When man and all his race shall have disappeared from the face of our planet, ask every particle of air still floating over the unpeopled earth, and it will record the cruel mandate of the tyrant," Babbage said. Men like the *Adalia*'s crew may escape humanity's justice, but God would summon the material record of creation and "confront the murderer with every corporeal atom of his immolated slave, and in its quivering movements he will read the prophet's denunciation" that Nathan said to David: "Thou art the man."[18]

If sins could not be effaced in a material sense, neither could kindness and courage. The actions, words, and even thoughts of reformers radiated across the universe forever, affecting its texture and trajectory. In 1850, Theodore Parker told his congregation how he imagined reformers' effects on the future. "I do not pretend to understand the moral universe; the arc is a long one, my eye reaches but little ways," he said. Nonetheless, Parker assured them "it bends towards justice." Parker's friend, Julia Ward Howe, shared his faith in the future and believed in Hitchcock's "universal telegraph." Howe wrote that Parker, "the Great Man of the party[,] refrains from his large theories, which, like circles made by the stone thrown into the water, begin somewhere and end nowhere." Howe believed that people who were attuned to the telegraphic effects of the moral universe could sense the future approaching them. "Mine eyes have seen the glory of the coming of the Lord," she attested in her greatest work. "I have seen Him in the watch-fires of a hundred circling camps." Like circling ripples in the water, the circling camps of war marked God's visitation upon a sinful nation.[19]

The telegraph shaped people's views of history, personal conduct, and salvation. John Brown believed that "Providence will lead us all more properly to appreciate the amazeing [*sic*], unforseen [*sic*], untold, consequences; that hang upon the right or wrong doing of things seemingly of trifling account." When he thought about contingency and the eternity of every human action, Brown mused, "Who can tell or comprehend the vast results for good, or for evil; that are to follow the saying of one little word. Evrything [*sic*] worthy of being done at *all*; is worthy of being done in *good earnest*, & in the best possible manner." Edgar Allan Poe agreed. "As no thought can perish, so no act is without infinite result," he wrote. In his story, "The Power of Words," Poe explained the same phenomenon:

> We moved our hands . . . and, in so doing, we gave vibration to the atmosphere which engirdled it. This vibration was indefinitely extended, till it gave impulse to every particle of the earth's air, which thenceforth, *and for ever*, was actuated by the one movement of the hand.

Charlotte Cushman, the great Shakespearean actress, imagined possibilities for eternal disturbance. "We cannot break a law of eternal justice, however ignorantly, but throughout the entire universe there be a jar of discord," she said. Cushman gave Fanny Seward, the daughter of William Seward, a copy of *The Poetical Works of James R. Lowell* and marked the poem "The Present Crisis," which begins, "When a deed is done for Freedom, through the/broad earth's aching breast/Runs a thrill of joy prophetic, trembling on from/east to west." The universal telegraph empowered individuals by convincing them that they could be the force that stirs creation forever.[20]

Their thoughts about such powers differed from a "butterfly effect," a popular term among chaos theorists for the claim that the smallest air disturbance, a butterfly flight in China, for instance, can determine whether an Atlantic hurricane ravages coastal Carolina or dissipates in the center of the sea. The butterfly effect lacks morality, admits randomness, and gives "lower" animals the power to affect human affairs. Hitchcock, Howe, Cushman, and Brown shared with chaos theorists a faith that something minuscule and insignificant can culminate in unexpected, gigantic consequences. Antebellum Americans, like chaos theorists, saw those minor signs, but everywhere. They insisted that every action has an equal, predictable reaction. The telegram, traveling at the speed of lightning, arrives with the same message that its sender conveyed. Humanity alone lays the cables and stirs the world.[21]

People caught within a swirling present imagined how someone threw the stone that set everything in motion. According to the telegraph effect, the dynamic process of antebellum immigration was really a concerted, covert invasion orchestrated by the pope and his monarchists. Diffuse political events and crises were not random or unpredictable outcomes caused by impersonal forces but instead were the intended effects of cabals of men. Financial panics were not caused by a random mixture of unfortunate events but rather by unscrupulous bankers. Religious revivals were not caused by social movements of the day but by God. Even scientists attuned to the complexity of the universe assumed that God orchestrated everything. For Hitchcock, the infinite reactions to human actions offered scientific proof of eternity. When Peter prophesied that fire would consume the world, Hitchcock theorized that the chemistry of apocalypse would not annihilate matter, because "fire only changes the form of substances." God's flames would leave behind a scorched platform for erecting a millennium of peace.[22]

Telegraphy raised expectations that technology would erase sectionalism and end war forever. In 1858, New Yorkers celebrated the transatlantic cable laid between England and the United States with a parade. Along the route, citizens displayed muskets with candles plugging their barrels. A sign read, "The Cable with its peaceful tricks/ Makes of muskets candlesticks." People hoped that the telegraph would end war by obliterating the distance between nations and clarifying communications. In a book that celebrated the engineering feat, Charles Briggs and Augustus Maverick predicted, "It is impossible that old prejudices and hostilities should longer exist, while such an instrument has been created for an exchange of thought between the nations of the earth." Within the United States, the telegraph would shrink the expanding nation by annihilating the distance between fellow citizens. The telegraph eased arcane fears that expansive republics were doomed to repeat the fall of Rome. With lightning speed, the telegraph transmitted intelligence across the nation. People expected this central nervous system to unite American thinking and action. By 1850, 10,000 miles of electric wire criss-crossed the nation, forming a web where instantaneous news, actions, and reactions spread. In 1859, the Reverend Henry Bellows of New York celebrated the era's "progress in true Humanity." Two inventions propelled civilization forward: "the discovery of vaccination and the union of the hemispheres by the Atlantic Cable." Both inventions spread goodness across creation through unseen paths.[23]

The promises and perils of telegraphy were embodied in its inventor, Samuel F. B. Morse. Unable to project his future, Morse darted through life with no apparent direction. At Yale he tried history, mathematics, chemistry, and a host of other disciplines while painting portraits to buy cigars and ice cream. After he married Lucretia Pickering Walker in Concord, New Hampshire, in 1819, the newlyweds traveled to Charleston, South Carolina, where the twenty-eight-year-old sought a fashionable life painting the portraits of wealthy slave owners. A slender couple with jet-black curls, the Morses drew attention from art patrons and gossips of the social season. In six years Morse would establish himself as one of America's premier artists. He was painting a portrait of Lafayette, the revolutionary hero, in Washington in 1825 when word reached him that his beloved Lucretia had died in New Haven. The mail was so slow that he did not return in time to attend her funeral.[24]

Grief made Morse wary of looming threats and committed to annihilating space and time that hindered communication. When he devised a code for his invention, he wanted to keep it a secret for the government to use against its enemies domestic and abroad. As a widower in the 1830s, he was obsessed with conspiracy theories. Living in New York City, Morse observed the influx of European immigrants. He was convinced that evil designs lurked behind the wave of immigration. Instead of accepting migration as a consequence of impersonal forces that pushed and pulled millions to American shores, he and thousands of other Americans explained it as a plot orchestrated by Catholic monarchs to infiltrate the young republic with subversive subjects who would dilute American patriotism and compromise self-government. Under the pen name "Brutus," Morse published his conspiracy theory in the *New York Observer* and later as a pamphlet titled *Foreign Conspiracy against the Liberties of the United States*. "Our institutions have already withstood many assaults from within and from without, but the war has now assumed a new shape," he warned. While Americans ignored the signs of a looming peril, the world watched powerless to stop the approaching danger. "Yes, it is the world that has its anxious eyes upon us; it is the world that cries to us in the agony of its struggles against despotism, THE WORLD EXPECTS AMERICA, REPUBLICAN AMERICA, TO DO HER DUTY." In 1836 he ran for mayor as an anti-immigration candidate.[25]

Morse's conspiracy theory expressed an expectant posture toward the future. Powerless to stop what was coming, he told a story that personalized the nebulous threat and narrated the future. The conspiracy simplified complex realities by replacing them with a secret cabal. He conjured a sinister network of menacing agents instead of accepting the idea that no one was in charge. Believing the pope ruled behind the scenes seemed more plausible than surrendering to the suspicion that no one was in control. Nineteenth-century conspiracy theorists, like Morse, believed they could make out the outlines of the network of people and events encircling American freedoms but were powerless to stop them. Only by raising an alarm and rallying the masses on the ground could theorists hope to avoid the looming threat.[26]

Foreign Conspiracy echoed earlier theories and anticipated how Americans would characterize sectional cabals in the 1850s. Morse accused the Leopold Foundation, a Jesuit missionary group, of orchestrating a papal network that ensnared American democracy. Quoting the missionaries' published correspondence, he described how the Jesuits financed Catholic settlement in America, helped Catholics pay travel expenses, built Catholic schools, and supported Catholic newspapers. For Morse, these actions by an emigrant aid company concealed their true designs. In the 1790s, his father, Jedediah Morse, had accused the Bavarian Illuminati of scheming to end the American republic. While Morse pointed a finger at the Leopold Foundation, thousands of Americans accused Freemasons of designing and financing a political overthrow. By the 1850s, when southerners focused on the New England

Emigrant Aid Company and northerners decried the Slave Power, thoughts about conspiracies against American freedoms traveled along grooved paths.[27]

Go-ahead Men

IF TELEGRAPHY FOSTERED EXPECTATIONS, another invention of the era, the railroad, encouraged anticipations. The railroad gave Americans a sense of traveling into the future and making history along the way. As Walt Whitman explained, the railroad was an "emblem of motion and power—pulse of the continent." Like steamboats, they "annihilated" time. This speed increased urban growth by carrying more food to cities and lowered prices by reducing shipping costs. Grain farmers in the North and West called for more tracks and greater speed because, unlike southern cotton, their crops fell prey to pests and fungi the longer they waited to be sold and consumed. Railroads worked in concert with the telegraph to spread news faster and farther. Both inventions demanded standardized time and more accurate timepieces. They put cheaper clocks and watches to use and raised social expectations for punctuality. These changes transformed the South. Masters adopted clock time to manage plantations and forbade slaves from owning watches. As historian Will Thomas explains, "Their effect was so profound, so pervasive, that those places without railroads and telegraphs in the nineteenth century measured time and distance by how close they were to the growing network."[28]

Traveling by rail changed how people approached the future and disoriented even ardent supporters of the development. Asa Whitney, a champion of the transcontinental railroad, recorded his first experience onboard a train in 1844. He was eager to see new places but could not, because "time & space are annihilated by steam, we pass through a City a town, yea a country, like an arrow from Jupiter's Bow." The train had passed Schenectady before Whitney thought to look for it. Dizzy when the cars stopped so that passengers could dine, Whitney had only a few minutes to consume food and had to take people's word that he was in Utica because he had lost all sense of time and direction. His diary exudes motion sickness: "Oh, this constant locomotion, my body & everything in motion, Steam Boats, Cars, & hotels all cramed [*sic*] & full the whole population seems in motion & in fact as I pass along with Lightning speed & cast my eye on the distant objects, they all seem in a whirl nothing appearing permanent even the trees are waltzing."[29]

Like the telegraph, the railroad encouraged speculation. "The mind too goes with all this, it speculates, theorizes, & measures all things by locomotive speed." Wondering about the end result of these changes, Whitney asked,

"Can it be happy?" and answered, "I fear not." Perhaps the new pace of life at mid-century would accelerate the end of time. His day on the train gave Whitney new respect for religious sects that predicted humanity was rapidly approaching the apocalypse. If the telegraph changed how people expected cause and effect to work in the universe, the railroad quickened the tempo of life and bent thoughts toward anticipations and prospects.[30]

As with steamboats, the progress of railroads was measured in speed, and breakneck competition superseded safety. Both machines relied on volatile, high-pressure boilers. Races to complete rail lines encouraged slapdash construction. John Quincy Adams experienced the harrowing consequences in 1833 on a trip from his home outside Boston to Philadelphia. The first phase of his journey conveyed him to Providence by stagecoach. The tempo of this travel, the bump and roll of the stage, affected his thinking and "verses were accordingly running in my head." "Winding round the Blue Hills, through Dedham and Walpole, always opens my poetical vein," he said. He composed "four stanzas upon Truth" that were "shaken out by the motion of the stage."[31]

When he switched to steamboat travel in Providence and then boarded a train at Amboy, New York, his poetical muse vanished. The ship was choked with passengers "of every land and language," and the train had "upwards of two hundred passengers." These modes of travel encouraged time keeping instead of poetry. A fellow train passenger marked their speed with his watch: two miles in four minutes, then "one mile in one minute and thirty-six seconds." While the train was accelerating, a wheel caught fire, burned for several minutes, and slipped off the rails. The car ahead of Adams lurched and tossed people across the tracks, while the engine refused to stop for two hundred feet. Escaping unharmed, Adams surveyed the scene: "Men, women, and a child scattered along the road, bleeding, mangled, groaning, writhing in torture, and dying." The car was "almost demolished." Stunned, Adams thanked God that "this torture, a thousand-fold worse than death, has been spared me." In his diary, Adams tried to slow down the event and reduce its chaos into a series of logical steps. In his mind, actions and equal reactions kept his car on the track. The "same pressure" on the right side of his car affected the left side of the car behind him, which "saved from injury all the passengers in it."[32]

The experiences of Whitney and Adams suggest that railroads and steamboats crowded American mental landscapes as fast as they spanned physical spaces. These changes affected people across society, not just its upper crust. Adams noted, with irritation, that "a whole tribe of wild Irish" traveled with him. Thousands of enslaved southerners rode the rails every month. The experience could foster anticipations, new ways of thinking about traveling through time. In 1839, French engineer Michel Chevalier remarked how a "passion for locomotion" infused American habits, attitudes, and thinking. Chevalier thought that competition, an unsettled landscape, and "an exaggerated estimate of the value of time" left the nation's "nervous system in a state of perpetual agitation." The quickening tempo of American life could exhilarate or terrify.[33]

People attached gender norms to emerging temporalities: stasis connoted femininity while movement signified masculinity. Women in particular wrote letters and awaited replies. The process and material culture of epistolary habits, being stationary with stationery, fostered an expectant posture that the future, in the form of a reply, would arrive on the spot. Paper bought at the stationer's store did the traveling, and a network of others conveyed it. The relationship between correspondence and feminine expectation was illustrated in *The Post-office*, written in 1844. When a boy asks his mother why she believes that her letter will reach its destination, she replies that there are "affairs of the greatest consequence to carry on, about which I must send far beyond this world" in the form of a prayer. She offers the boy four reasons why her confidence in the post matches her faith in prayer. She sends both "in the regular, appointed way," she has everything she needs to send them, she knows that thousands of others safely rely on the same system every day, and she has received answers "in the same way." Thus, she was encouraged "to hope and expect that I shall receive the blessing I need in answer to prayer." Whether seated at a writing desk or kneeling at a pew, she expected the future to arrive at her stationary spot.[34]

While the communication revolution raised expectations and made them feminine, the transportation revolution heightened anticipations and made them masculine. Historian Scott Sandage writes, "To the first generation reared on steamboat levies, canal embankments, stage platforms, and railroad beds, boyhood fascination with perpetual motion grew into an ideal of manhood." Masculinity meant winning at the "race of life," and the primary quality needed for success was a "go-ahead" attitude. Chevalier noted the "Go ahead!" spirit of the times: "If movement and the quick succession of sensations and ideas constitute life, here one lives a hundred fold more than elsewhere; all is here circulation, motion, and boiling agitation." Western expansion and the rise of capitalism rewarded men who anticipated where migration would develop new cities and which investments would yield the highest returns. The line between being visionary and reckless about the future blurred. As Philip Hone observed in his diary in 1837, "We have become the most careless, reckless, headlong people on the face of the earth. 'Go ahead' is our maxim and password; and we do go ahead with a vengeance." The economic results could be as disastrous as Adams's train ride to Philadelphia.[35]

A forgotten phrase today, "go-ahead" was a nineteenth-century American mantra. In 1859, Bartlett's *Dictionary of Americanisms* defined "go ahead" as "rapidly advancing, progressive." Bartlett quoted the *Philadelphia Press* for an example: "America is a dashing, go-ahead, and highly progressive country, giving by her institutions and enormous growth the solution of the greatest political problem in the world." Harnessing the ambition and speed to move forward was what Americans sought and how they distinguished themselves from other nations. When Samuel Morse tried to sell his invention to foreign governments, he decided that "there is more of the 'Go-ahead' character" in America than he could find anywhere in Europe. Only a go-ahead nation was "suited to the character of an electro-magnetic Telegraph." Morse could not bear "*standing still*." "I have been dealing too much in lightening [sic] lately to feel easy travelling on a snail's back."[36]

"Go-ahead" connoted many things that illustrate how a modern pace and temporality infused antebellum America. It meant blazing into the future in front of the competition. This anticipatory notion assumed that the future was an open country that ambitious men reached first. Land speculators and prospectors were "go-ahead men." So were inventors and businessmen whose foresight defined the future. In 1840, Chicago lawyer Joseph Balestier saw the go-ahead men in action. "Sagacious men, looking far into the future, now perceived that cities and villages, covering only a few acres of land, were soon destined to extend over an illimitable domain." Wherever they went, go-ahead men spread "visions of the glorious future [that] filled the imaginations of the multitude." P. T. Barnum embodied America's go-ahead habits when he toured England in search of things for his museum. His British friend, Albert Smith, confessed "that never before in his life had he accomplished a day's journey on the Yankee go-ahead principle." When Smith wrote an article about his day with Barnum, "he found the whole thing so confused in his brain."[37]

The go-ahead creed reflected democratization at work. The disestablishment of churches, dismantling of the national bank, opening of western lands, proliferation of mass travel and communication, rise of popular politics, explosion of reform movements, all these changes encouraged people to go ahead and do something or become someone. Go ahead and follow your own faith; go ahead and take a loan to invest in a new enterprise; go ahead to the territories; go ahead by steamboat or rail; go ahead and vote your interests;

go ahead and marry for love or join a commune. Whatever you yearn for, go ahead and do it.[38]

Henry Clay Pate considered himself a go-ahead man. He took his maxim from David Crockett, "First be sure you're right, and then go ahead." Once he knew he was in the right, Pate would "go ahead, regardless of consequences." For Pate, ambition was not inherent in men but acquired from culture. "Correct rules must be laid down to go by," or else go-ahead men would travel in the wrong direction. After all, the same ambition for glory animated George Washington and Benedict Arnold. Pate believed something in their education marked their divergent paths of patriotism and treason, fame and ignominy. "Let the youth of our land be ambitious," Pate pronounced. "A gun and its ball are useless without powder; and to the same extent are a man and his mind useless without ambition." But without proper guidance, the ball may miss its mark or prove fatal to the marksman. Society must give ambition its proper channels or else a generation of go-ahead men might destroy the nation.[39]

Go-ahead speculations raised anxieties as well as hopes. As society opened opportunities, the race of life became choked with runners, and getting ahead became more difficult. Anxieties of being left behind lurked beneath go-ahead cockiness. Missing the second coming of Christ; falling behind prosperous peers; failing to stake a claim for the best available lands; settling in a bust rather than a boom town; watching other factions control party politics. These and other fears gave a frantic edge to America's craze for velocity and getting ahead. Beneath concerns of missing opportunities festered a deeper fear that none of these speculations was anchored in reality. When prophets readjusted the date of the apocalypse, they not only defended false forecasts from the past as honest miscalculations but also buttressed themselves against rising doubts about any apocalypse. In 1838, James Fenimore Cooper depicted land speculators as delusional gamblers. Men who risked fortunes on paper surveys of fictional lots "are gambling as recklessly as he who places his substance on the cast of the die." "I anticipate a terrible blow," he prophesied; "the day is not remote" when Americans would wake from their illusions and learn that "nothing can be sustained without a foundation."[40]

The Irrepressible Conflict

ANXIOUS FINANCIAL OBSERVERS FORECASTED a clash between northern and southern labor systems. Senator William Seward prophesied an "irrepressible conflict between opposing and enduring forces" that meant "the United States must and will, sooner or later, become either entirely a slaveholding nation, or entirely a free-labor nation." Abraham Lincoln made the same prediction in his "House Divided Speech" when he intoned, "A house divided against itself cannot stand." The nation "will become *all* one thing, or *all* the other." Either slavery will become extinct or "its *advocates* will push it forward till it shall become alike lawful in *all* the States, *old* as well as *new*—*North* as well as *South*." Historian George Bancroft forecasted that America faced the same fall as Rome. "Slavery, by the gradual extermination of free labor and an industrious self-relying people, had poisoned the Roman State to the marrow." When slave labor overwhelmed freedom and industry, the Roman spirit of invention turned from engineering technological marvels to satisfying sensual pleasures. Slavery left Roman society vulnerable to revolt and invasion. The all-or-nothing logic and doomsday rhetoric of Seward, Lincoln, and Bancroft preyed on northern anxieties about the future.[41]

Rapid changes in economics, technology, and demographics destabilized American society, particularly in the antebellum Northeast. Any citizen of New York or New England could sympathize with Rip Van Winkle's disorientation. They too awoke in a world radically different from the one they knew from their youth. Beyond experiencing time travel, people sensed changes in time. The proliferation of clocks, railroads, and telegraphs changed temporality by accelerating life's tempos and expanding the present toward an ever present. In his definitive study of how different cultures keep time, psychologist Robert Levine concludes, "People are prone to move faster in places with vital economies, a high degree of industrialization, larger populations, cooler climates, and a cultural orientation toward individualism." His description fits antebellum New England perfectly.[42]

Many observers insisted that progress and pace separated the North from the South. Travelers commented that northern society was faster, which in the era of steam and telegraphy meant better, more progressive. Alexis de Tocqueville summarized the differences by comparing the banks of the Ohio while traveling on a steamboat toward the Mississippi River. "Upon the left bank of the stream the population is rare; from time to time one descries a troop of slaves loitering in the half-desert fields; the primaeval forest recurs at every turn; society seems to be asleep, man to be idle, and nature alone offers a scene of activity and of life. From the right bank, on the contrary, a confused hum is heard which proclaims the presence of industry; the fields are covered with abundant harvests, the elegance of the dwellings announces the taste and activity of the laborer, and man appears to be in the enjoyment of that wealth and contentment which is the reward of labor." Tocqueville attributed the different tempos to traveling "between liberty and servitude." On the left bank, in Kentucky, Cassius Clay agreed. "I cannot as a statesman, shut my eyes to the industry, ingenuity, numbers and wealth which are displaying themselves in adjoining states." Blaming slavery for stunting southern growth, Clay became a rare antislavery southerner.[43]

Northerners assumed their technology and enterprise elevated them above southerners. When Seward visited the South before the Civil War, he blamed slavery for sapping the region of enterprise, improvement, and industry. He passed exhausted fields and dilapidated towns while traveling over wretched roads. Slavery threatened to kill the nation's go-ahead spirit. Fellow New Yorker Frederick Olmsted published a trilogy of southern travel accounts that blamed slavery for the region's social and economic ills. Yet he doubted that "a mere setting free of the blacks, if it could be accomplished, would surely remedy these evils. An extraction of the bullet does not at once remedy the injury of a gun-shot wound; it sometimes aggravates it." Eric Foner summarizes this northern judgment of Dixie: "Instead of progress, the South represented decadence, instead of enterprise, laziness. . . . To those with visions of a steadily growing nation, slavery was an intolerable hindrance to national achievement." Some northern visionaries assumed that their region would have to colonize the South to fix its backwardness. After Eli Thayer populated Kansas with free settlers through his emigrant aid company, he started a similar enterprise to send northern settlers to western Virginia in 1857.[44]

Abolitionists expressed the same faith in posterity by touting the tempo and technology of the North as heralds of progress. Harriet Beecher Stowe equated railroads with modernity and assumed that "unsophisticated" places, "where there are no railroads," retained social norms "that prevailed in New England a century ago." Even William Lloyd Garrison lauded the railroad as progress. According to Ronald Walters, "Instead of imagining that it would compromise America's moral fiber and further the heartless exploitation of the country, Garrison believed it would foster human unity by bringing men closer to each other in time." Reformers' faith in railroads as engines of positive social change is illustrated by the song "Get off the Track," sung by abolitionists at an 1844 rally. Nathaniel Rogers attended the performance and described its energy and appeal:

> It represented the moral Rail Road in characters of living light and song, with all its terrible enginery and speed and danger. And when they came to that chorus-cry, that gives name to the song,—when

> they cried to the heedless pro-slavery multitude that were stupidly lingering on the track, and the Engine "Liberator" coming hard upon them, under full steam and all speed,—the Liberty Bell loud ringing, and they standing like deaf men right in its whirlwind path,—the way they cried 'Get off the track,' in defiance of all time and rule, was magnificent and sublime. They forgot their harmony, and shouted one after another, or all in confused outcry, alike an alarmed multitude of spectators, about to witness a terrible rail road catastrophe.

When the Hutchinson Family Singers wrote, "Get off the Track," they changed the lyrics to "Ole Dan Tucker," a song made popular by the blackface group Virginia Minstrels a year earlier. Like John Brown's plan to transform a pro-slavery bowie knife into free-state pikes, the Hutchinsons' efforts illustrated the strategy of northern reformers: change things to change society. Their music inspired Rogers to prophesy, "The world is out of tune now," but humanity would restore harmony by abolishing slavery. "The hills shall then break forth into singing, and all the trees of the field clap their hands." In 1856, the Republican Party transformed "Ole Dan Tucker" into John Frémont's campaign song.[45]

Northern prophets of a class war between free labor and slavery spread a conspiracy theory to support their speculations. They insisted that a cabal of masters schemed to seize the federal government and force slavery on northern citizens and western settlers. They called this shadowy force the Slave Power and used the telegraph effect to articulate its reach and influence. Theodore Parker, a devout believer in the telegraph effect and the Slave Power, claimed, "The slave power controls the President, and fills all the offices." Joseph Quincy, president of Harvard University, told an audience that his warnings were backed by "more than fifty years' attentive observation of the operations of the slave power." Aristocrats at the heart of the conspiracy devoted their lives and fortunes to a plot for governing free men as they controlled their slaves. "Though widely separate, the chiefs sit as spiders in the centre of their respective webs, throwing out filaments to every State in the Union, in every one of which the threads of some of them find points of attachment and reciprocation, in custom-houses, post-offices, those of contracting printers, and many others, from each of which ready sympathetic responses are returned, as sure and as quick as by the wires of the telegraph." Quincy expected the Slave Power's telegraphy to cause a class war. Looking to the future, he told his audience that "unborn millions" pleaded to them, "'On your faithfulness it depends, whether we shall become the depraved subjects or ministers of a slave despotism; whether fraud, violence, and an infamous traffic, shall be our destiny, or the enjoyment of the pure light of liberty, morality, and religion.'" When Republicans spread the Slave Power conspiracy they tarnished northern Democrats who compromised with southern statesmen. The conspiracy theory attracted white northerners to antislavery without stirring sympathy for the plight of black southerners. For this reason, radical abolitionists hoped the Slave Power succeeded until wage laborers were willing to attack the conspirators in their den by ending slavery in the South. John Brown told his wife, "I have no desire to have the Slave power cease from its acts of aggression. 'Their foot shall slide in due time.'" His prophecy drew from Deuteronomy: "To me belongeth vengeance and recompense; their foot shall slide in due time; for the day of their calamity is at hand."[46]

Die by Suicide

ALL THESE SPECULATORS FOSTERED a false dichotomy between a modern North and a pre-modern South. They assigned progressive traits to the North, including technology, industry, immigration, and democracy while they saddled the South with stagnant agriculture, declining population, arcane aristocracy, and chronic lassitude. As their "go-ahead" mantra and "get off the track" anthem implied, champions of the free labor North imagined one fixed track to modernity and the future. The South was as modern as the North but imagined a different course to the future. As Edward Ayers suggests, "The role of modernity in the Civil War might better be understood as a catalyst for both the North and the South rather than as a simple difference between them." Railroad growth in the South during the 1850s matched northern construction of lines, capitalism thrived in slave markets and land speculations, high literacy rates and a national print culture flourished, and popular politics fed modern nationalisms. Beneath these obvious elements was a modern temporality that encouraged anticipations. Across society in the South as in the North, people imagined living in the future.[47]

In 1838, Abraham Lincoln, a southerner by birth who had recently moved to Springfield, Illinois, understood that modernity shaped both regions. Speaking to new neighbors at the Young Men's Lyceum, Lincoln obsessed about the future. He approached his subject, "The Perpetuation of Our Political Institutions," from an expectant posture. Time was hurtling the future toward the nation faster than Americans could mature to face its looming dangers. Instead of embracing an anticipatory temporality in which people move into the future and forged it, Lincoln expected the future to approach him. Unlike Samuel Morse and other nativists, Lincoln did not expect danger to arrive from foreign shores. "All the armies of Europe, Asia, and Africa combined, with all the treasure of the earth . . . could not by force, take a drink from the Ohio, or make a track on the Blue Ridge, in a trial of a thousand years." The danger "cannot come from abroad," because republics either "live through all time, or die by suicide."[48]

What terrified Lincoln in 1838 was not immigration, sectionalism, or even slavery; he feared anarchy, mob rule, and tyranny spawned by the people's disregard for law. His speech tried to locate the nation's present spot along its timeline. At first glance, the times looked promising and the nation seemed blessed with peace. "We find ourselves in the peaceful possession, of the fairest portion of the earth, as regards extent of territory, fertility of soil, and salubrity of climate." But violence threatened the nation every day. "Accounts of outrages committed by mobs, form the every-day news of the times." The go-ahead spirit that encouraged all sorts of activities also bred lawlessness. In Mississippi, land speculation and gambling overlapped too much for society's comfort, so Vicksburg citizens "first commenced by hanging the regular gamblers." Then the mob lynched blacks suspected of conspiracy, "then, white men, supposed to be leagued with the negroes; and finally, strangers, from neighboring States, going thither on business." In the end "dead men were seen literally dangling from the boughs of trees upon every road side." Shortly before Lincoln's speech, abolitionist editor Elijah Lovejoy died defending his printing press from a mob in Alton, Illinois. Patriotic cohesion kept the nation together when the Revolution was still living history. But by 1838, the Revolutionary generation had disappeared, modernity atomized society, and reckless speculations were tearing the nation apart.[49]

A lawless nation would lose the allegiance of its best citizens and become vulnerable to tyrants. Lincoln warned his audience that ambitious men will "spring up amongst us." The go-ahead man "disdains a beaten path" and "seeks regions hitherto unexplored." Genius "*scorns* to tread in the footsteps of *any* predecessor." Lincoln prophesied that an American Caesar would not be satisfied maintaining a government crafted by others. He would seek distinction "whether at the expense of emancipating slaves, or enslaving freemen." Seeking God's help was not enough. Only after the sacredness of law was "preached from the pulpit, proclaimed in legislative halls, and enforced in courts of justice" would the nation be safe. He expected America to fail.[50]

Three years earlier, Lincoln failed when his New Salem store closed for good. He and co-owner, John Berry, lacked the business acumen needed to get ahead. According to Lincoln scholar Michael Burlingame, "they extended too much credit, bought and sold goods unwisely, failed to keep items properly stocked, and invested so much money in slow-selling merchandise that their stock became an unappealing hodge-podge." Historian Joshua Rothman explains why doing business in the 1830s challenged newcomers like Lincoln. "Engagement in an expanding market economy entailed trusting faceless forces that few thoroughly understood, and the temptations of easy money created epidemics of speculation that leery commentators feared would ruin the minds and finances of those they touched." When their store closed, Lincoln owed more than $1,000. Given his ambition, the setback must have hurt his pride. He confessed to a friend, "That debt was the greatest obstacle I have ever met in life." Struggling with the go-ahead culture of speculation, he declared bankruptcy and promised his creditors that if they "would let me alone, I would give them all I could earn over my living, as fast as I could earn it." The debt still hounded Lincoln when he ran for president in 1860.[51]

The expectancy in his Lyceum speech may have stemmed from this personal failure. Lincoln believed in the "race of life," the idea that every man deserved an "unfettered start," a chance to go as far as his intelligence and will would take him. But competitors and problems "spring up amongst us," as he said in Springfield. Lincoln understood that most aspects of the race were beyond control. "At what point shall we expect the approach of danger?" he wondered. The race of life approached men while they passed through it. He did not share the go-ahead man's faith in endless prosperity and forward progress. His was a melancholy future shaped by impersonal forces and shadowy dangers. Lincoln never went into business again.[52]

Cassandra—Warnings

WHEN THE ANTEBELLUM RACE of life intensified between labor and capital, many Americans feared an apocalypse. Few prophets imagined this imminent class war as vividly as Virginia planter Edmund Ruffin. Like Karl Marx, Ruffin understood that capitalists increased profits by depressing wages "to the lowest rate at which a bare subsistence can be purchased." But the proletariat would be pushed only so far before "the last evils of a vicious and unbridled and starving populace" revolted and made history. He sensed a looming class war each time the economy suffered a panic. When banks suspended payments and called in loans, when markets for commodities dried up, capitalists tried to recover their losses by firing workers or reducing their pay. If calls for work and bread went unanswered, the laboring class would pillage New York City and other urban centers swelled by immigrant hirelings. Echoing Ruffin's prophecy, David Hundley, a southern attorney living in Chicago, expected a "rebellion of the stomach" in his pamphlet *Work and Bread: or the Coming Winter & the Poor*. Hundley described capitalism as "warfare . . . between labor and capital, until the latter, being strongest, overrides the former, and drives the mechanic to the wall." For George Bagby, editor of the *Southern Literary Messenger*, this economic distinction between the regions justified secession and guaranteed southern success. In the North, "the deadly conflict between capital and labour is coming." Capitalists see it on the horizon and try to avoid the "irrepressible conflict" by reserving the territories for their teeming millions. "Here in the South, capital and labour are not at war," because "capital owns the labour. They are at peace. They work together in harmony, and are cordial friends." For Ruffin, Hundley, and Bagby, northern cities were tinderboxes ready to explode.[53]

Southern speculators of class warfare imagined global power for their system of labor. In 1859, Bagby predicted that the Republic of Virginia would claim dominion over the Americas, West Indies, Pacific Islands, Australia, and all of Europe except for Russia. "The first step will be to reduce the Yankee to slavery," he explained, and this will occur "after the terrible revolution and anarchy now impending at the North, have spent their force." Once southerners enslaved the other populations under their rule, the Republic of Virginia would thrive by harnessing the unique skills of each ethnicity. French cooks, British butlers, and German soldiers would join Yankee machinists and sailors. African laborers would farm every climate and soil, leaving the "untameable races," like Indians, Mexicans, Polynesians, and Aborigines, to go extinct. "The reconciliation of labour and capital being complete," poverty would vanish "and with it all chance of civil danger resulting from the state of smothered volcanic disaffection" that plagued industrialized Europe and the North. Bagby's vision was not exceptional. Other speculators dreamed of a slave republic from the South to Brazil that used the Gulf of Mexico and Caribbean Sea as a massive harbor for exporting cotton, tobacco, sugar, and coffee to the world.[54]

Southerners insisted that every society had a permanent laboring class. John C. Calhoun said, "There never has yet existed a wealthy and civilized society in which one portion of the community did not, in point of fact, live on the labor of the other." Looking to the future, Calhoun accused northern abolitionists of plotting a class war in the South. Emancipation would not bring social equality because class equilibrium is a social fiction. Instead, "we would soon find the present condition of the races reversed." Southern blacks "and their northern allies would be the masters, and we the slaves."

Calhoun's successor, James Henry Hammond, expressed this point in his "mudsill" speech. Like Calhoun, Hammond insisted, "In all social systems there must be a class to do the menial duties, to perform the drudgery of life." This "mud-sill of society" enables "that other class which leads progress, civilization, and refinement." He noted that his colleague in the Senate, William Seward, "said yesterday that the whole world had abolished slavery. Aye, the *name*, but not the *thing*." Virginia planter George Fitzhugh agreed. Northern laborers were wage slaves who suffered worse than southern slaves. "Whilst labor-saving processes have probably lessened by one half, in the last century, the amount of work needed for comfortable support, the free laborer is compelled by capital and competition to work more than he ever did before, and is less comfortable."

While Marx thought workers should unite to combat capitalism, southerners proposed that they accept the southern form of slavery instead. As Ruffin explained, even in dire economic crises, masters provided their workers with the basic necessities of life. Neither northern capitalism nor European socialism could deliver to the mudsills what southern blacks already had—food, shelter, and health care for life. Finally, southern prophets of a class war argued that slaves were safer than free laborers because African Americans, unlike immigrants and white Americans, were naturally docile and obedient. Virginia planter Beverley Tucker insisted that the slave's manners "are exactly suited to his situation. Their characteristic is proud humility," whereas northern laborers display "servile sulkiness." "If the tempers of our negroes were as ferocious, and their feelings as hostile, we should have to cut their throats in self-defense in six months."[55]

As a founder of scientific agriculture, Ruffin refuted the notion that modernity stemmed from technology, industry, and commerce that radiated from the North. When he discovered how marl, fossilized shells, prepared the soil for fertilizer, Ruffin realized the consequences of his experiment. "Agriculture had become profitable—a prospect was presented of comfort and wealth to the farmers of the country; energy and enterprise succeeded to indolence and idleness, and now it was no longer necessary to look for homes in the western forests for themselves and their descendants." His neighbors were wrong to declare this a barren land. The soil could be renewed by science and diligent work. He had changed more than the acidity of Virginia soil; he had replaced the fatalism of farming with a progressive, scientific view of agricultural management. The telegraph effect reigned supreme: humanity controlled nature, the material world was dynamic not static. Ruffin understood that his "high gratification" at the success of his experiments "can only be appreciated by a schemer and projector." Only a modern man, someone focused on the future, could grasp the magnitude of Ruffin's discovery. "It forms an essential part of the character of an enthusiastic and successful projector, and especially an agricultural projector, to be anxious to inform others as to profit himself." For Ruffin, farming was business, not a gentleman's avocation. "I was entirely opposed to following the universal practice in Virginia, of every gentleman's son, who cannot inherit a sufficient patrimonial estate (& many who do,) studying for either the profession of law or medicine." Instead Ruffin taught his oldest son geometry. Edmund Jr. became a civil engineer and worked on railroads.[56]

In 1859, Ruffin traveled through the South and witnessed signs of modernity everywhere. In July he stayed at the lavish, new Atlantic Hotel in Beaufort, North Carolina, owned by Josiah Pender, a dapper man with long black mustaches. Gossips reported that Pender spent $4,000 on his new investment with dreams of it becoming the premier resort in the state. Looking to the future, Pender anticipated how beach vacations would replace trips to sulfur springs and medicinal baths as a tourist destination. Pender's "house," as Ruffin called it, contained one hundred rooms and three stories. Its design captured all the pleasures of the shore. Triple-decker porches and rows of windows welcomed the fresh, salty air. Perched on pilings at the water's edge, the hotel afforded the best ocean views. The dining room offered the bounties of the sea: fish, oysters, and soft-shell crab. In the evening, fine music mixed with sounds of surf.[57]

The area's future seemed as enchanting and clear as the ocean view from Ruffin's window. The Atlantic and North Carolina Railroad recently linked Beaufort to Goldsboro and New Bern. Beyond bringing tourists, the new line would attract commerce to the sleepy shore. Local boosters were quick to point out the deep, navigable water here—seventeen feet deep, they said, with plenty of room to accommodate the world's trading vessels. Within a year of completing the railroad, two aspiring towns sprouted near Beaufort. Moorhead claimed real estate at the end of the line, while the more ambitiously named Carolina City established itself two miles above the terminus. Each community expected it would replace Wilmington as the state's largest port city. Perhaps they were constructing the next Charleston, Richmond, or even New Orleans. Who knew what the future might bring?[58]

Ruffin saw a different future. Styling himself a rational forecaster who relied on "the facts," he concluded that "prospects seem to show, as I had predicted, that mere deep water to the ocean, & a railroad to reach it, will not divert trade from its old channels & marts, to a new seaport where there is neither existing business, capital, nor merchants." Wilmington had a century head start against Moorhead and Carolina City. Sea captains, cotton factors, and bankers already had everything they needed in Wilmington. Why would they move their businesses here? While waiting for the Atlantic and North Carolina train to depart for the coast, Ruffin met three directors of the railroad company. They offered him a free roundtrip ticket to Beaufort as a token of their appreciation for the agricultural services Ruffin had rendered to the South.[59]

On his fourth day in Beaufort, Ruffin boarded a flat-bottomed sailboat with sixteen people and crossed Cane Sound to witness the catching, penning, and selling of wild ponies on an island. When locals promised him a memorable experience, they were right for the wrong reasons. Members of his party purchased nine ponies, which delayed the return to Beaufort and crowded the boat with animals. The added weight tested the black captain's ability to steer the ship and grounded them on several sand bars. While perched on one of them, the party watched helplessly as a looming storm darkened the horizon and headed toward them. Soon torrents of rain and strong winds pummeled the huddled group. Their boat offered no shelter. Thunder and lightning terrified the ponies. After the storm and several more groundings, the captain became disoriented. He did not know where they were, nor which direction they should travel. None of the tourists knew the Sound. When a rainy sunset found the party stranded on yet another bar, the captain announced they would have to spend the night there. With no fire or light on board, complete darkness enveloped the party. Wet with wind chilling his bones, Ruffin could not fall asleep. In the morning, the rising tide offered a chance to free the vessel from the ground. Some passengers stood in the water and pushed the sailboat off the bar. Once the captain regained his bearings, the ship made slow progress for Beaufort, though it ran aground repeatedly on the second day. This short, day tour that promised to be a wonderful experience turned into one of the most wretched incidents Ruffin could recall.[60]

Back safely at the Atlantic Hotel, Ruffin resumed his favorite pastime, writing. With a view of the sea and the salty air rustling his papers, Ruffin found a perfect place to mull over the South's modernity and ponder its future. His view of the South's horizon seemed clear, but he envisioned storm clouds instead of bright skies. He warned that a Republican president would free the slaves within two years of taking office. If that president had a Republican majority in Congress, he could "abolish slavery by general emancipation—without even a pretense of compensation to the owners of slaves." Ruffin's greatest fear was that "the people of the South may (as, unfortunately, many do) shut their eyes to these threatened and approaching calamities." If they waited too long, or headed in the wrong direction, southerners would find themselves as helpless as Ruffin and his party to Cane Sound. If they ignored the portentous signs on the horizon, they must be "content to yield everything valuable to freemen, and to submit to utter ruin of their country and degradation and misery." Black men played a critical, though unspoken, role in Ruffin's warning. If white southerners delayed taking action, they might find themselves under the direction of black men as lost as the boat's captain. Then the South would endure a dark, miserable, interminable night before the tide would shift and whites could lift the region past a degrading stagnation.[61]

The most arresting thing about the piece was its title, "Cassandra—Warnings." Ruffin alluded to the Trojan princess who was so intelligent and lovely that Apollo offered her the power of prophecy if she would surrender her virginity to him. Overwhelmed by the offer, she accepted his gift. Then, when she changed her mind, Cassandra found herself in an impossible position. Prophecy was not a gift she could return and she had incurred the wrath of a terrible god. Instead of taking his gift from her, the jilted Apollo cursed her prophecies with incoherence. No matter how Cassandra expressed her knowledge of the future, no one would ever believe her. Apollo's curse drove Cassandra insane. She raved, howled, and shrieked the future in vain. She anticipated the gruesome death her brother Hector would suffer at the hands of Achilles but she was powerless to stop it. She understood how the Trojan horse would lead to the ruin of her people but she could not convince her father, King Priam, to beware of Greeks bearing gifts. When Troy fell, she sought sanctuary in the temple of Athena where a Greek warrior found and raped her. Then King Agamemnon abducted her as a concubine and carried her back to Greece. Cassandra tried to convince him that they would both be killed by his jealous wife. Knowing her impending death, Cassandra threw all the language she could muster at Agamemnon. Baffled by her frantic, opaque warning, Agamemnon did nothing. Once in Greece, he and his war prize were murdered, as she had predicted.[62]

Ruffin empathized with Cassandra and feared that he shared her cursed fate. He emulated Greek tragedians' ability to present horrifying anticipations of the future through a succession of unfolding events, so that the storm looms closer and closer until it crashes upon us at the end. A future that casual observers think materializes slowly appears fixed and certain to the prescient writer. Ruffin recited events that led to the South's impending doom, a fate he does not reveal until the final sentence of his essay.[63]

Ruffin also chose Cassandra for his title because she embodied foreign conquest. Like Cassandra, Ruffin foresaw the fall of his civilization at the hands of a hostile, alien culture. The Trojans lost their freedom and became slaves of their enemies because they disregarded Cassandra's foreknowledge. Ruffin expected the same fate when he prophesied. Personal failure and a conquered South loomed. No matter how he expressed the imminent tragedy he envisioned for his civilization, society scoffed at his warnings. For years he had warned southerners of the danger posed to their world by the menace of northern abolitionists, but he could not convince them of the validity of his prophecies. Like Cassandra, he yearned for a fair hearing. He ached to be understood, because he knew in the broadest sense we are all Cassandra. We know death is coming, and we are powerless to stop it.

Another southern Cassandra, John Beauchamp Jones, edited a proslavery newspaper in Philadelphia and raged against northern readers who never took his warnings seriously. In 1859 he prophesied an imminent war in 502 detailed pages. From his vantage within a city teeming with new immigrants and underpaid laborers, Jones speculated that the collapse of the second party system would unleash more than a sectional conflict; it would spark a vicious class struggle that would rend the fabric of America to shreds. In Jones's speculations, self-government failed not only at the national level but also within regions, states, communities, and even individuals. Anarchy ensued. In the North, Republicans demanded the subjugation of the South and the enfranchisement of slaves. In the South, Democrats called for an invasion of the North to raze symbols of free labor capitalism, its factories, railroads, mines, cities, and wharves. The press incited revolts on its front pages and spread terror across the nation via telegraph lines. Northern prisons were blown open and ruthless mobs terrorized cities day and night. Predatory bands crossed the sectional border to rob banks, raid mansions, and murder outspoken men. "The gutters ran with blood, and the waysides were strewn with the dead."[64]

Southern prophets of a class war like Ruffin and Jones insisted that free labor could not match the steady order of a slave society during times of crisis. John C. Calhoun reassured his fellow masters that slavery "exempts us from the disorders and dangers" that stem from the conflict between labor and capital in the North. This sectional advantage "explains why it is that the political condition of the slaveholding States has been so much more stable and quiet than that of the North." Calhoun was confident that slavery would immunize the South from class warfare unless masters succumbed to the go-ahead craze, "the eager pursuit of gain which overspread the land." If infected by Yankee avarice, the southern economy might lose its natural advantages during times of panic and unrest. Hammond agreed that the South was immune from northern economic crises because "our slaves do not vote. . . . Yours do vote, and, being the majority, they are the depositories of all your political power." If southern critics of free labor published their disdain in the North as vehemently as abolitionists agitated for emancipation in the South, "your society would be reconstructed, your government overthrown, your property divided." Both Ruffin and Jones speculated that southern harmony would eventually overcome northern anarchy and win the looming civil war. Jones argued that the "great landed proprietors" of the South could stabilize or ruin northern capitalists by either purchasing their goods or boycotting them. He warned Philadelphians, "It is not in human nature to confer benefits on an enemy." George Fitzhugh offered northerners a solution to avoid this imminent fate. "We slaveholders say you must recur to domestic slavery, the oldest, the best, the most common form of Socialism," and "the natural and normal condition of the laboring men, white and black."[65]

Panic

IN AUGUST 1857, WEEKS after Fitzhugh published his recommendation, a financial panic crippled the North. In Europe, the Crimean War (1854–1856) had raised the value of American grain exports, one reason why the Thayer cousins dreamed of linking western grain to eastern markets. Too many Yankee capitalists shared their dream. Speculation in western lands, and bank loans to finance such schemes, mushroomed. As historian Elliott West explains, "The orgy of railroad construction far surpassed the needs of the day, and people invested merely on an imagined future." With the Crimean War over, the go-ahead market had gone too far. Critics sensed the crash before it happened. "That a storm is brewing on the commercial horizon there can be no doubt," said the financial writer for the *New York Herald*. He warned, "The same premonitory symptoms that prevailed in 1835–36 prevail in 1857 in a tenfold degree . . . paper bubbles of all descriptions, a general scramble for western lands and town and city sites, millions of dollars, made or borrowed, expended in fine houses and gaudy furniture." In the summer of 1857, financial forecasts resembled self-fulfilling prophecies.[66]

One of the first dominoes to fall was the Thayers's Hannibal & St. Joseph railroad. The line had been the brainchild of Missourian John Marshall Clemens, father of Samuel Clemens. Missouri senator David Atchison bribed congressmen and senators to pass legislation for the railroad because he dreamed of a direct line from Missouri to California goldfields. When

Boston investors took over the company, Atchison had political and economic reasons to squash the Yankee settlement agency that subverted his scheme. Politically, his career was over if he sponsored a bill that greased the pockets of Yankee capitalists. Economically, his investment vanished if the railroad he planned to link Missouri to California gold instead connected New England to midwestern grain. The Thayer cousins had outfoxed him in business, but Atchison had a political maneuver to trump them.[67]

Southern politicians passed a law on the last day of Congress, March 5, 1857, that undermined northern investments in western railroads, including the Hannibal & St. Joseph. The new law authorized state agents to identify swamplands in the public domain, drain them, and sell them at a profit. The agents claimed thousands of acres they did not bother to inspect, including property promised to railroad companies. According to the law, all the land claimed, swampy or not, would belong to the states at the end of 1857. Missouri was one of the most aggressive states to claim public lands as swamps, thus jeopardizing northern investments in speculative railroads like the Hannibal & St. Joseph.[68]

When northern investors got wind of the threat, railroad stocks and bonds crashed. Across the nation, telegraph wires connected banks, increasing their volatility. Rumors of trouble in the Midwest stirred panic in the Northeast. The Ohio Life Insurance & Trust Company, a major lender for speculative railroads, went under first. To make matters worse, the manager of the bank's New York office, Edwin C. Ludlow, embezzled funds. Public confidence in banks dropped and the New York Stock Exchange crashed on August 24, 1857. Philadelphia businessman Sidney George Fisher thought more than money linked banks and railroads. "A bank is a machine to facilitate trade, just as a railroad is." "Our people require a machine to make money fast although now & then it produces bankruptcy & confusion, and they require a machine by which they can travel fast & cheaply, altho now & then a collision occurs, by which fifty or a hundred people are maimed at a blow." The *Cincinnati Gazette* blamed the tempo of northern society: "We have been living too fast." Northerners understood the panic in apocalyptic terms. In 1848, financial stress had triggered a series of European revolutions that had spun into class warfare. When hundreds of thousands of Americans lost their jobs in 1857, people feared bloodshed. Angry workers marched in several northern cities. Mobs attacked merchant shops and threatened the US customs house in New York. Only an influx of specie could bolster the flagging financial system. In September, a ship carrying $1,500,000 in California gold to New York banks sank off the coast of South America.[69]

Instead of accepting how impersonal forces including legislation, credit, markets, and a shipwreck combined to cause the crisis, people looked for scapegoats and a telegraph effect. The country blamed "speculators" who worked at the center of the economy and tampered with it to get ahead. John Jacob Niles pinpointed "speculating madmen and visionary schemers," categories that did not eliminate many nineteenth-century Americans from blame. Frederick Jackson, a veteran of Wall Street, described the panic in telegraphic terms: "something which can be felt, but can neither be traced nor followed. It has the power of motion and flight . . . for it can pass from city to city." Like Hitchcock's eternal reaction, a panic "has the power of making itself invisible, and can stalk through the streets in the day time unseen, frightening every body by its presence." Like Babbage's eternal waves, a panic was "a kind of moral element, and like the fire, a single spark may kindle into a conflagration, which the whole nation cannot extinguish." Jackson understood that panic could be caused and explained by conspiracy theories. "The panic makers immediately conjure up the ghost of an earthquake, that is about to take place." Panics happened when anxieties heightened and "every man suspects his neighbor to be in possession of some secret, which he is not."[70]

Even the term "panic" implied that someone lurked behind the crisis. Some understood the event as God punishing the nation for its greed and luxury. A massive religious revival swept through the Northeast and centered in Boston and New York. People called it the "Businessmen's Revival" to stress that its converts, unlike people affected by previous awakenings, were predominantly male, solemn, and class conscious. People hoped that the panic would bring capitalists closer to heaven instead of bringing workers closer to revolution. George Barrell Cheever thought God was preparing the nation for the destruction of slavery. "I sometimes think I see, with the clearness of a death-bed vision, that the spirit of gain, and of a commercial expediency, and of an indolent love of ease and prosperity, even in spiritual things, has taken fast hold of the people." He blamed slavery for America's immoral economy and expected a divine reckoning on the horizon.[71]

But the panic and revival hardly touched the South. Cotton and tobacco prices recovered quickly. The South's export economy seemed immune from the boom and bust cycles that plagued the North. Southerners relished a chance to mock northern claims of economic superiority. The 1850 census had reported regional disparities in manufacturing, railroad mileage, population, wealth, and other statistics that favored the North. None of those statistics saved the region in 1857. "You may go to your trashy census books, full of falsehood and nonsense," Hammond told his northern colleagues in

Congress. The true measurement of economic strength for Hammond was surplus production. He estimated that southern exports in 1857 were worth $220 million, compared to $60 million for the North. When the panic hit, "when the abuse of credit had destroyed credit and annihilated confidence; when thousands of the strongest commercial houses in the world were coming down, and hundreds of millions of dollars of supposed property evaporating in thin air: when you came to a dead lock, and revolutions were threatened," southern exports saved the North from ruin. "We have poured in upon you one million six hundred thousand bales of cotton just at the crisis to save you from destruction."[72]

Hammond's take on the situation fostered fantasies of southern nationhood. After secession, the South would need no army or navy because cotton was too valuable to the world for any nation to make war against it. If necessary, a southern nation could muster a million men to arms, "a larger army than any Power of the earth can send against her," because southern slaves would maintain the economy while white knights marched to war. After the panic, Edmund Ruffin and William Yancey founded the League of United Southerners, a secret organization devoted to southern secession and empire. They conspired with William Walker, the southern filibuster who repeatedly tried to conquer Nicaragua and reintroduce domestic slavery there. Even if the South did not expand after secession, Hammond pointed out that it would be "as large as Great Britain, France, Austria, Prussia, and Spain. Is not that territory enough to make an empire that shall rule the world?"[73]

Blow Ye the Trumpet, Blow

THE PANIC RUINED JOHN BROWN'S fundraising tour. When he failed to pay for the pikes, Blair left them unfinished. This was the second time a financial disaster destroyed Brown's schemes. He lost almost everything after the Panic of 1837. Rumors of riot and revolt filled the papers. "The Nation has been drawing on the Future, and the Future dishonors the draft," one of them reported. In 1842, bankruptcy erased Brown's financial prospects and took everything he owned except the barest essentials: a few pieces of furniture, some tools, farm animals, and eleven Bibles and Testaments. When Lincoln failed in business, he turned to law and politics. Brown turned to family and religion.[74]

The Bibles that Brown saved from his bankruptcy taught him to depend on God for his future. He told his children to emulate the prophet Ezra, an Israelite who obeyed God's laws during trying times and punished those who strayed. According to religious scholar Abraham Joshua Heschel, prophets like Ezra insisted, "*the human situation can be understood only in conjunction with the divine situation.* The absurdity of isolating the human situation and treating it in disregard of the divine involvement is exemplified by the self-defeating course of man-made history." Go-ahead men and modern forecasters like Edmund Ruffin placed men at the center of the universe, believing that humanity reigns supreme over nature. In this universe, Heschel notes, "God is either nonexistent or unconcerned. It is human initiative that makes history." Crises, like the panics that Brown experienced, awaken the prophet to "forces he cannot completely control [that] emerge imperceptibly to stifle him and to defy his intentions, his plans, and his visions." For Brown, this admission of larger forces pointed to God standing above and beyond history. God unfolded the future by handling invisible forces and using people to fulfill His mysterious will. Brown convinced himself that he was God's weapon to punish America for the sin of slavery. For fifteen years he focused on family and tried various schemes to escape poverty. Farming, speculating in land, tanning hides, selling wool—each new plan was more ambitious than the last. They all failed. By 1857, Brown was determined to finish his pike project, but the financial and social support for such schemes had vanished along with so many people's fortunes.[75]

If the Panic of 1837 started Brown's turn away from society, the Panic of 1857 sealed it. He gave up public fundraising and turned to secret donors. Theodore Parker, Thomas Wentworth Higginson, Samuel Gridley Howe, and Franklin Sanborn backed him. All four were Transcendentalists who accepted Edward Hitchcock's theory that creation was a "universal telegraph" that "receives an impression from all our words and actions that can never be effaced." The deeper pockets to fund Brown's schemes came from Gerrit Smith, a rich millennialist, and George Stearns, a wealthy merchant who had financed the New England Emigrant Aid Company. This "Secret Six" embodied the creed articulated by George Light in his poem, "Go Ahead."

Do not ask too broad a test:
    Go ahead;
Lagging never clears the sight:
    When you do your duty best,
You will best know what is right.
    Go ahead.
Never doubt a righteous cause:
    Go ahead;

Throw yourself completely in:
    Conscience shaping all your laws,
Manfully, through thick and thin,
    Go ahead.
Do not ask who'll go with you;
    Go ahead:
Numbers! spurn the coward's plea!
    If there be but one or two,
Single handed, though it be,
    Go ahead.
. . .
Better days are drawing nigh;
    Go ahead:
Making Duty all your pride,
    You must prosper, live or die,
For all Heaven's on your side.
    Go ahead.

When Brown's conspirators wrote about his plans, they used the language of business to conceal his intentions. Instead of conceiving his plans as missionary work in a foreign field, they talked of him "arranging his wool business" and "raising the mill." A bankrupt many times over, Brown turned his speculations to a new field and finally found success in failure.[76]

Revolutions in communications and transportation, conspiracy theories, the go-ahead creed, panics, and revivals, all these forces shaped John Brown's worldview and convinced him to attack the Slave Power. The wonders of modern technology and God's omnipotence convinced Brown that a small band of devoted followers could change the world in a controlled way by transmitting a moral shockwave through violent action. He founded an African American self-defense group called the United States League of Gileadites. The name referred to Gideon's army of 300 that defeated 42,000 Midianites. Before battle, God told Gideon, "Whosoever is fearful or afraid, let him return and depart early from Mount Gilead." In the end, only 300 of Gideon's 32,000 men remained to fight. With God's help and Gideon's trickery his 300 won the battle. Gideon stationed his men around the Midianite camp and gave each of them a trumpet to blow. Gideon ordered his men: "When I blow with a trumpet, I and all that *are* with me, then blow ye the trumpets also on every side of all the camp, and say, *The sword* of the LORD, and of Gideon." This surprised and terrified the Midianites who panicked and fled. In the ensuing disorder, Gideon's men slaughtered the rest. "Blow Ye the Trumpet, Blow" was Brown's favorite hymn:

> Blow ye the trumpet, blow!
> The gladly solemn sound
> let all the nations know,
> to earth's remotest bound:
> The year of jubilee is come!
> The year of jubilee is come!
> Return, ye ransomed sinners, home.

With God's help, Brown would craft a new telegraph effect more potent than the Slave Power's conspiracy: terrorism.[77]

3

Rumors

IN OCTOBER 1859, SEVENTEEN men followed the pikes across Virginia's border toward Harpers Ferry. John Brown finally paid for the weapons three years after Black Jack when he returned to Charles Blair's shop unannounced. Blair wondered why Brown wanted them now that Kansas was settled. Brown said, "They might be useful if finished." While Blair found someone to complete the arms, Horatio Rust repaired rifles for his friend and shipped supplies from his pharmacy to Brown's lieutenant, John Kagi, in Chambersburg, Pennsylvania. Kagi quietly received Rust's supplies, collected the unassembled pikes, and shuttled them to Brown's secret headquarters in Maryland.[1]

An agnostic, Kagi lacked his leader's faith that God controlled history. Kagi knew Brown's plans before any of the other raiders, but foreknowledge did not comfort or empower him. Though he hoped to make history as a freedom fighter, he yielded power and will to a future he considered already sealed. Kagi's letters home revealed little about the imminent raid but much about his temporality. Instead of seeing an open future ahead, he imagined fate approaching him. In June 1859, Kagi encouraged his sister not to succumb to a feeling that haunted him, a premonition that "you were singled out by Fate from living chessmen in his game of horror and of death." Weeks before the raid, he told his father that the future "is bright and good," but instead of imagining how he and Brown would march into the future and forge it, Kagi insisted that the future "treads on to meet the hopeful with rapid strides." Events seemed to be accelerating, the future closing in.[2]

Other raiders surrendered their will to justice, duty, God, or John Brown. Like Kagi, they made a series of choices over time that anchored their future to John Brown's plans. They were instruments of forces beyond their control. Perhaps granting power to other people and things helped to ease anxiety about the impending violence they would commit. Osborne Anderson, a free black man from Canada, recalled that he and the rest of Brown's army marched toward the arsenal that night like "a funeral procession." Considering himself a weapon in God's hands, even Brown denied responsibility for the future.

When unexpected supplies and money arrived, he considered it a heavenly sign to launch the attack. "Men, get on your arms," he said. "We will proceed to the Ferry." [3]

Instead of prophesying a border war out West or a class war in the East, the pikes would threaten a race war down South. This future portended ironic justice. Hoe handles, a common implement in slaves' hands, would work for freedom instead of oppression. The sidearm of a white Virginian from the master class would become a thousand weapons for black Virginians. Pikes already meant something to slaveholders. Across the slaveholding Americas, masters used them to display the severed heads of captured rebels as a warning. The gruesome tradition parodied Macbeth, who suffered the same fate. When Macduff carries Macbeth's head on stage, aloft on a pike, he proclaims, "Behold, where stands/Th' usurper's cursed head: the time is free." In the nineteenth century, theaters cut the scene, because critics considered it a barbaric spectacle. However, blacks' heads still appeared on poles to warn others against resistance. Sarah Grimké saw a human head stuck up on a high pole while traveling through South Carolina. "On inquiry, I found that a runaway slave, who was outlawed, had been shot there, his head severed from his body, and put upon the public highway, as a terror to deter slaves from running away." After its metamorphosis, Pate's blade made a new point about conquest and progress. Instead of warning slaves against rebellion, pikes would enable revolt, seize masters, and kill them.[4]

For Osborne Anderson, the pikes harbingered a new era of slave insurrections. Older revolts sprang from midnight meetings in dark forests, "but John Brown reasoned of liberty and equality in broad daylight, in a modernized building." Insiders betrayed previous conspiracies, but none of Brown's men divulged a word. Most important, Brown relied on modern technology: "the telegraph, the post-office, the railway, all were made to aid the new outbreak." Though an ancient weapon, Brown's pikes were financed by leading capitalists, forged by one of the nation's leading blade smiths, transported by rail to the band's headquarters, and assembled for swift distribution on-site. This insurrection would not rely on farm implements and random weapons at hand. The pike became a modern weapon that promised freedom.[5]

During the raid, Anderson was responsible for giving pikes to slaves. Because he was in charge of things, slaves assumed he was captain of the band. This rumor was reinforced by the fact that Lewis Washington, a great-grandnephew of George Washington, surrendered his ancestor's sword to Anderson, not to Brown. Racial politics abounded in the gesture, a Washington surrendering his sword to a black man, but material culture was at the heart of the event. Brown's order 11 of the plan of attack explained his intentions for the exchange: "Anderson being a colored man, and colored men being only *things* in the South, it is proper that the South be taught a lesson upon this point." Brown exposed the legal fiction that blacks were property by having Washington surrender his prized possession to Anderson. [6]

Exchanging arms was Brown's way of proving black masculinity. "Give a slave a pike," he said, "and you make him a man." Making gifts of pikes would shed any submissiveness that slavery imposed on male slaves. Those pikes would transform black people as profoundly as Brown transformed Pate's knife. Brown imagined that white Americans would welcome a more aggressive, assertive manhood among blacks. After all, weapons conveyed virtues that Americans respected. "Nothing so charms the American people as personal bravery," Brown told African Americans. He sought to inspire them by recalling "the Greeks struggling against the oppressive Turks, the Poles against the Russians," and other heroic wars for sovereignty. Foreshadowing his own fate, Brown told them that the capital trial of one, determined race warrior would precipitate abolition faster than the dutiful, submission of millions of slaves. While other abolitionists wanted to give slaves freedom, Brown wanted to give them weapons. Too many reformers saw slaves as docile, inferior beings in need of charity. Brown sought to show the world that they were men. "Hold on to your weapons, and never be persuaded to leave them," he said.[7]

Martin Delany shared Brown's conviction. An African American doctor and radical abolitionist, Delany criticized the passive, expectant portrait of slaves spread by Harriet Beecher Stowe in *Uncle Tom's Cabin*. Delany answered her work by publishing *Blake*, a novel about a slave insurrectionist that encouraged blacks to fight instead of pray. According to Delany, Christianity overdeveloped a sense of hope among the slaves. "Consequently," Delany wrote, "they usually stand still—hope in God, and really expect Him to do that for them, which it is necessary they should do for themselves." Prayer might yield spiritual rewards but if slaves wanted physical freedom, they had to "go to work with muscles, hands, limbs, might and strength, and this, and nothing else will attain it." Delany tired of abolitionist strategies to end slavery by spreading morality and preferred Brown's politics that circulated weapons.[8]

In 1858, Delany hosted Brown, Kagi, and their fellow conspirators at a Constitutional Convention for the reformed United States they envisioned. The body adopted a "Provisional Constitution of the United States" that would redesign American government after Brown's raid succeeded. Three articles of the new constitution addressed weapons. The body proclaimed that all citizens, "whether male or female, shall be encouraged to carry arms openly." The time for crate politics and restrained manhood had ended. Anyone concealing weapons "shall be deemed a suspicious person," arrested, searched, and investigated. People identified themselves as true, loyal citizens by displaying their arms for all to see. According to this new Constitution, when Brown's pikes crossed into Virginia, they would accomplish more than assembling an army of slaves; they would grant citizenship to black Americans within a new national government.[9]

The result was electric. Throughout the raid, slaves handled and exchanged weapons to express allegiance, wield power, and spread fear. After Brown's men secured the town, Anderson and others fanned out to assemble a slave army by circulating pikes. They first shared their plan with black men on the road who said "they had been long waiting for an opportunity of this kind." Rumors of the raid quickly spread through slave quarters. Several slaves heard about the raid through "underground wires," traveled to Harpers Ferry, and asked Anderson for pikes. Black men materialized through the night. Armed free blacks stopped a mail express train in Maryland from reaching the Harpers Ferry bridge. Between twenty-five and fifty slaves joined the raiders. An elderly slave used Lewis Washington's shotgun to kill a white citizen as retaliation for the death of one of the raiders. Some slaves shuttled weapons from Brown's stockpiles in Maryland to the raiders at Harpers Ferry. Others used pikes to guard hostages, including their masters. The prisoners cried and begged for a chance to see their families one last time. "I saw what, indeed, looked like war," said John Dangerfield, the United States paymaster at Harpers Ferry, "negroes armed with pikes, and sentinels with muskets all around." Rumors spread that hundreds of blacks had joined the insurrection. Anderson enjoyed the torment he saw in captives' eyes. "Judgment-day could not have presented more terrors, in its awful and certain prospective punishment to the justly condemned." [10]

After a successful start, things got out of hand. Raiders stopped a train and then, inexplicably, let it continue to Baltimore to raise the alarm. Because Brown launched the assault unexpectedly and not at the appointed time, his support network was unprepared to join the attack. Martin Delany and other black leaders in the region planned to rise up on another date. Taking hostages consumed the raiders' time and immobilized them in town when they could have struck the arsenal, gathered arms, and headed for the mountains. Few scholars have considered how the raiders' obsession for weapons also derailed the invasion. Though he carried a thousand pikes and hundreds of firearms to Harpers Ferry, Brown targeted a town stockpiled with weapons. Thousands of slaves lived in the surrounding countryside, but when Brown's men fanned out that night they gathered more weapons than recruits. As Figure 3.1 suggests, arms seemed to attract the raiders more than the bodies they needed to fight a war.[11]

When the raid failed, African Americans immediately changed their relationship to weapons. Shields Green, one of five black men in Brown's party, dropped his rifle and stood beside six slaves, hoping to pass as one of them. When citizens gunned down Kagi, a nearby slave named Ben threw down his pike and begged for mercy. A minister saved him from being lynched. One of Washington's slaves expressed his loyalty by returning his master's shotgun days after the event. Others hid weapons as battle trophies. Washington lost his Belgian bird gun for good. Terence Byrne, a Maryland slaveholder who was a hostage during the raid, testified that he saw a black man carrying the fowling piece. Osborne Anderson hoped that a network of blacks would spread a race war. Instead it helped him escape to Canada along the Underground Railroad.[12]

Figure 3.1 **"Harper's Ferry Insurrection—Interior of the Engine-House,"** ***Leslie's Illustrated Newspaper*****, November 5, 1859. Library of Congress, Prints and Photographs Division.**

Darkness

THOUGH JOHN BROWN'S PIKES spilled no blood, they cast a long shadow on American politics and society. Grim and ancient like Old Testament justice, pikes in the hands of black men touched a nerve in antebellum America. Visions of disunion and a war for the West did not rend society like a race war could. Likewise, forecasts of economic clashes between competing labor systems were tame by comparison. Class warfare, with its threats of disorder, imagined a conflict that could not be resolved by redrawing a map. If class war barricaded streets and looted storefronts, race war murdered families in their beds.[13]

Themes of darkness and bloodshed seemed obvious given the facts of John Brown's attack, but they also resonated with apocalyptic visions of the future that gripped Americans of every section, race, and gender. While Brown awaited execution, rumors of abolitionist activity terrified local whites. For weeks, postmen delivered threats and warnings to the jailor, clerk of court, and sheriff. This correspondence contained dark designs to liberate Brown by firing the town or arming slaves. An anonymous note from New York menaced, "you will see every City—Town and Village South of Mason & Dixon's line in

> **Flames**
> We are determined to put down Slavery at any odds.
> Forcibly if it must. Peaceably if it can.
> Believe me when I tell you the end is not yet by a long odds.
> All of us at the North sympathize with the
> Martyrs of Harper's Ferry.

Local blacks who voiced such sympathy landed in jail. But more than talk kindled whites' fears. When night patrollers returned to their beds, arsonists burned wheat stacks and stockyards in the surrounding countryside. Some suspected abolitionist agents while others blamed local blacks and poor whites who associated with them. Farmers stood in their yards watching helplessly as flames consumed their harvest. In 1859, Thomas Jefferson's old prophecy that disunion would sound "like a fire-bell in the night" rang true in the Virginia county that carried his name.[14]

Meanwhile Governor Henry Wise received a warning sent by "an Onlooker" in Connecticut. The correspondent pointed out that only a US court could try cases of treason and urged Wise to suspend Brown's sentence until the Supreme Court could review the case. "If the South do not heed this counsel," Onlooker warned, "they will risk an attempt at rescue and farther bloodshed." The prophet from Connecticut could not resist the urge to play with the governor's name: " 'a word to the wise is sufficient.' 'Be wise in time, 'Tis madness to defer.' " Wise's anonymous tormentor was quoting a famous poem by Edward Young titled "The Complaint: or Night Thoughts on Life, Death, and Immortality." Young asked, "In human hearts what bolder thought can rise,/ Than man's presumption on tomorrow's dawn?/ Where is tomorrow? In another world." We live by projecting ourselves forward in time, presuming countless sunrises, building a mountain of hopes "And, big with life's futurities, expire." The South imagined slavery eternal and postponed schemes to change its institutions indefinitely. In 1859, Brown's nocturnal raid sparked night thoughts of death and the future in many southern minds. "Procrastination is the thief of time," Young warned. "Year after year it steals, till all are fled,/ And to the mercies of a moment leaves/ The vast concerns of an eternal scene." Perhaps it was already too late for the South.[15]

As they spread across the nation, Harpers Ferry stories generated terrifying expectations about the future. On one level, these rumors were acts of resistance. Whether true or false, word of imminent revolts empowered slaves by instilling fear in oppressors and destabilizing society. But the power of rumors derived from the possibility that they might be true. Beyond being an act of resistance, talk of race warfare was a socially constructed future, a vision that shaped how people approached tomorrow. Instead of diminishing rumors as falsehoods, this second perspective on them maintains their status as uncertain knowledge that formed reality. Masters went to bed differently after such talk. Communities reassessed their priorities, armed their militia, and thus changed the future whether rumors were true or false. Some rumors became reality; some prophecies proved self-fulfilling.[16]

Harpers Ferry rumors meant different things to different people. Henry Ward Beecher identified what bothered people most about the news from Virginia: it was not "connected with a cause or an effect!" A host of elements, including religion, race, region, class, gender, and politics, shaped how people interpreted Harpers Ferry as an omen, how they gave the story a beginning and end, a cause and effect. John Brown's actions sparked accusations and investigations that sought a motive and origin for his crimes. Instead of studying narrators who looked backward in search of a beginning, this chapter focuses on those storytellers who gazed forward to find the definitive conclusion to Harpers Ferry. They pointed in every direction in search of a plot that finished the story that John Brown started but would not live to conclude. These diverse anticipations nonetheless shared certain themes and messages that gave individual projections broader currency and credibility throughout the crisis.[17]

After Brown's raid, rumors gained a wider audience in the South if they were set in the dark. When white southerners gazed into the future after Harpers Ferry, they focused on the night. Uncertainty about what might happen to them while they slept unnerved people. The fact that John Brown commenced his raid at midnight encouraged predictions that rescue attempts, slave revolts, and other aftershocks of the affair would occur after dark. On the evening after Brown's raid failed, rumors of another night raid interrupted Lieutenant Colonel Robert E. Lee while he was composing his official report. A Mr. Moore, from Pleasant Valley, Maryland, claimed that "a body of men had, about sunset, descended from the mountains, [and] attacked the house of Mr. Gennett." Moore believed the "the residents of the valley were being massacred" because he heard "cries of murder and screams of the women and children." Lee considered the report "so improbable that I could give no credence to it," but the surrounding population did not share his cool reserve and their reaction compelled Lee to do something. When residents of Sandy Hook heard the rumor, they fled to Harpers Ferry and the protection of its assembled militia and Lee's marines. Sandy Hook's panic alarmed Harpers Ferry citizens who were still recovering from the previous days' events. Amid the hysteria, Lee admitted, "I thought it possible that some atrocity might have been committed." He started for Pleasant Valley, four and a half miles away, with two lieutenants and twenty-five marines. They found the town "quiet and unharmed" and Mr. Gennett and his family asleep.[18]

Southern panic about the dark designs of abolitionists and midnight assaults was not limited to the vicinity of Harpers Ferry. Tennessean James Williams was as safe from Brown and his imagined allies as possible. He was serving as United States minister to Turkey and living in Constantinople when he learned about John Brown's raid. Nonetheless, Williams shared the dread of darkness that seized southerners. Writing to British abolitionist Henry Peter Brougham, Williams explained that Brown was "a villain of no ordinary stamp" because "he did not slay in the flare of the noonday sun, as a common robber at the head of his band of retainers, but he killed in the quiet hours of the night, and the slumbers of innocence were startled by the death-shrieks of his unsuspecting victims." Williams identified a pattern of dark violence in Brown's career. At Pottawatomie Creek, "dreadful, indeed, were the scenes through which that poor woman passed during the brief space of one short night. She was sleeping in fancied security when the spoilers came to her humble log cabin, and passed through the unbarred door to the bedsides of her sleeping husband and children. . . . They were four when they lay down to rest, that dreadful night. The morning dawned upon the living woman, surrounded by the lifeless and mutilated bodies of her husband and children." At Harpers Ferry, "again was the hour of midnight made terrible by the death-struggles of his unwatching victims." Williams pinpointed what terrified southerners about Brown's violence: his victims never saw him coming. A grizzly end awaited them at night and they never knew it. After Harpers Ferry, white southerners feared that they and their cherished society were "sleeping in fancied security." A bloody night loomed ahead.[19]

Instead of dissipating after the false alarm at Pleasant Valley, rumors of night attacks increased. Nighttime arsonists stoked such rumors as did messages addressed to Brown that his jailors intercepted. On November 29, "WIL" wrote to Brown, "Don't give up all hopes of liberation for I have collected 2,500 men all in arms and they have been quietly entering the town for some time past and on the 1st at 12 o'clock at M[idnight] we will make an attact [*sic*]." Southerners as a result became afraid of the dark. As Amanda Edmonds confessed in her diary on November 11, "Reluctantly did we retire" for the night, because "as the sun lowered his clouded dise [*sic*] a dark foreboding crept over me. I could not find peace and that feeling clung to me through the night ever and anon." Edmonds lived with "a feeling of utter dread" about the future. "O! what is to become of us. Will the kind hand of Providence protect us? Or is this a judgement [*sic*] to befall this wicked people? Sometimes I think it is." Brown's raid and the rumors surrounding it darkened Edmonds's view of life. "We move in this bright beautiful world unsuspicious of the enemies prowling around just waiting for our lives."[20]

Some southerners suspected that their likeliest murderers lived among them: the slaves. Amanda Edmonds and her sister lived "in such suspense, concerning the darkeys" that it made them sick with fear. Afraid that local slaves set fires across Jefferson County, Edmonds imagined a gruesome retaliation for black arsonists. "I could see the fire kindled and those who did it singed and burnt while the last drop of blood was dried within them + every bone molders to ashes." Edmonds marveled that some masters, "those who own the most, the vilest ones, seem to be perfectly easy!" Slave owners reassured themselves that slaves were loyal by pointing to reports that Brown had failed to incite slaves to revolt. In Florida, Richard Call considered such news to be proof that slaves accepted their inferior position and loved their masters. "This is the reason why I sleep soundly with my doors unlocked, unbarred, unbolted, when my person is accessible to the midnight approach of more than two hundred African slaves." Call thought, "There should be no better evidence required of the fidelity and attachment of the slaves to their masters than the results developed in the mission of John Brown." He spread a rumor about Colonel John Washington's slave John. When Brown woke John "at midnight" and "told him he must fight, putting *a murderous pike into his hands to butcher* his master," John replied, "*On which side will Mass John fight? I want to be with him.*" Ruffin drew the same lesson from Brown's raid. "This entire failure, after months of preparation, of obtaining even one slave to join in the attempt at insurrection, must astonish the northerners, & remove much of their general & erroneous impression of the discontent of the slaves, & their readiness for revolt." Ruffin, like Call, announced his willingness to sleep behind unlocked doors and windows. "Not even the outer door is locked," Ruffin bragged. "We all know, that if our slaves so choose, they could kill every white person on any farm, or even through a neighborhood, in any night." And yet, "there is but little more of security, or of care to guard against either violence or thieving, in any country house in this slave-holding region." Ruffin implied that Yankees who barred every window and door in New York City had more to fear than he.[21]

Imaginary enemies lurked everywhere in nineteenth-century America. Southerners were not alone for fearing dark agents who imperiled their lives. The Republican Party ascended to power by stoking northern anxieties that a slave power conspiracy ruled the government behind closed doors and planned to return human bondage to every state. The Republicans' shadowy cabal of planters supplanted the American Party's imaginary enemies, papist spies who were infiltrating America to dismantle democracy. Both theories fueled American fears that republican governments were fragile, fleeting, and vulnerable to powerful, wealthy interests. The Republicans predicted how a southern aristocracy would undermine the majority and enslave it. Likewise, nativists warned that European monarchs and the pope had financed a silent coup that was already set in motion and would end with an Austrian emperor of the United States. Samuel F. B. Morse prophesied this danger in his pamphlet, *Foreign Conspiracy against the Liberties of the United States*. Morse expressed a paranoid sensibility shared by secessionists, Republicans, Anti-Masons, Anti-Mormons, and other nineteenth-century visionaries. "A conspiracy exists," Morse announced, and "its plans are already in operation. . . . [W]e are attacked in a vulnerable quarter which cannot be defended by our ships, our forts, or our armies." "The serpent has already commenced his coil about our limbs, and the lethargy of his poison is creeping over us," Morse warned. "Is not the enemy already organized in the land? Can we not perceive all around us the evidence of his presence?" he asked. "*We* may sleep, but the *enemy* is awake; he is straining every nerve to possess himself of our fair land. We must awake, or we are lost." Like southerners after John Brown's raid, Morse expressed terror of being asleep when the terrible end is imminent.[22]

The Secret Six, John Brown's unveiled financiers, proved that shadowy figures and dark designs were more than imaginary in antebellum America. As the Secret Six illustrate, conspiracy culture made the news by inspiring actions as well as reactions to events. As much as economics or politics, culture caused things to happen. New England intellectuals supported Brown because he promised to realize their hopes. These Transcendentalists imagined Brown's heroism inspiring Americans to trade their materialism for spirituality and their mob mentality for individualism. In John Brown they saw a man of action who could make their vision come true. Henry David Thoreau, champion of civil resistance, lionized Brown after Harpers Ferry. Ralph Waldo Emerson praised Brown because he "believed in two articles—two instruments, shall I say?—the Golden Rule and the Declaration of Independence; and used this expression in a conversation here concerning them: 'Better that a whole generation of men, women, children should pass away by violent death, than that one word of either should be violated in this country.'" Emerson embraced Brown's apocalyptic ending to American slavery.[23]

Southerners supported conspiracies too. While the Secret Six planned to invade Virginia, the Knights of the Golden Circle schemed to invade Latin America to filibuster for slavery. After the Secret Six became known, Congress, led by Virginia senator James Mason and Mississippi senator Jefferson Davis, launched an investigation to shed light on things. For months Mason and his committee interrogated people they suspected were accomplices to John Brown. The committee's findings illuminated nothing but paranoia. Southerners also crafted their own conspiracies. Edmund Ruffin conspired as much as anyone in antebellum America. He created the League of United Southerners to conspire for secession and joined the Association of 1860, a South Carolina group determined to foment secession.[24]

Ghost Stories

DURING THE AFTERSHOCK OF Harpers Ferry, Harriet Prescott Spofford published "Six by Seven," a ghost story about a dead prisoner who proves his innocence by mailing letters to the living from beyond the grave. The man, a humble New York artisan, was falsely accused by an aristocrat and convicted. His ghost haunted the spot where evidence of his innocence remained. In particular, he terrorized a young woman nearby. At night she felt "some phantom, some creature, or power" communicate with her in a "horrifying" unspoken voice. Though she was a common resident of a country town, fate singled her out to be a heroine who confronted a mystery that frightened her for the rest of her days. While awaiting execution, Brown too was a dead man who trusted posterity would vindicate him and wrote letters to women to express his innocence. He captivated the country by writing letters to Lydia Maria Child that Horace Greeley printed in the *New York Tribune*, the country's most widely circulated newspaper.[25]

Execution day, like the weeks that led to it, was charged with expectations and foreboding. By nine o'clock on December 2, fifteen hundred men formed two squares facing the scaffold. Ruffin had evaded a strict ban on civilian spectators by becoming the oldest cadet of the Virginia Military Institute, for a day. Too excited to sleep the night before, he had walked the streets of Charlestown with soldiers making the rounds, searching for abolitionist rescuers. He dined with David Hunter Strother, who showed Ruffin his unpublished drawings of Brown. In the morning he waited for a glimpse of the man himself. Two hours later a wagon arrived with Brown seated on his casket. Still displaying "complete fearlessness of & insensibility to danger and death," the old man scaled the steps and shook hands with his executioners. Ruffin was close enough to the gallows to notice that Brown wore red slippers.[26]

Ready to die, Brown requested, "Do not detain me any longer than is absolutely necessary." For fifteen minutes Brown stood on the trap door, hooded and noosed, waiting for death. Meanwhile the troops who escorted him found their places in line, but some observers suspected that the wait was a cruel, final test of Brown's courage. He stood motionless and silent. As Figure 3.2 depicts, the stillness afforded Strother time to draw a detailed picture of the scene. Major Thomas Jackson of the Virginia Military Institute marveled at Brown's "unflinching firmness." "I was much impressed with the thought that before me stood a man in the full vigor of health, who must in a few moments enter eternity." Jackson believed that souls journeyed for a few minutes before they found the afterlife. He prayed that Brown's soul would be saved from fire. When the trapdoor finally fell, Brown's noose was too short to break his neck. He endured five more minutes of spasms waiting for death. Then a warm breeze swayed his body like the pendulum of a clock. For thirty minutes soldiers watched in silence before doctors listened for a heartbeat and declared him gone. "So perish all such enemies of Virginia! all such enemies of the Union! all such foes of the human race!" announced Colonel John Preston. "Yet the mystery was awful," he confessed to his wife,

Figure 3.2 The Execution of John Brown. David Hunter Strother, West Virginia Historical Art Collection, West Virginia and Regional History Center.

"to see life suddenly stopped in its current, and to ask one's self the question without answer, 'And what then?' "[27]

On his final morning, Brown answered Preston's question. One of his guards asked Brown for his autograph, a relic to remember what would become a historic event. Instead Brown wrote, "I John Brown am now quite certain that the crimes of this guilty, land: will never be purged away; but with Blood. I had as I now think: vainly flattered myself that without very much bloodshed; it might be done." In hindsight, Brown's prophecy seems an accurate forecast of the Civil War, but the context in which it was written suggests that Brown envisioned an apocalyptic race war. Brown made this forecast hours before his execution, when self-sacrifice for freedom would have been foremost on his mind. He had hoped that his death and the deaths of his sons and comrades would be enough to purge the nation of the sin of slavery. His favorite scripture was Hebrews 9:22: "And almost all things are by the law purged with blood; and without shedding of blood is no remission." One thread of thought in Brown's plans from Kansas through Harpers Ferry was his persistent faith that a small band of resolute souls could dismantle the entire system. When Brown confessed in prison that he intended to free

Virginia's slaves with "eighteen men only," a militiaman in the room scoffed, "What in the world did you suppose you could do here in Virginia with that amount of men?" "Well," Brown answered, "perhaps your ideas and mine on military subjects would differ materially." Facing the scaffold made Brown realize that his death could not free the slaves, but he hoped it would provide a model for countless other self-sacrifices for freedom. Brown's soul was prepared for eternity; he used his final weeks on earth to prepare America for its bloody purge. With the nation watching his every move, John Brown showed people how to die for freedom.[28]

After the execution, people tried to assure themselves that normal life had resumed. When Ruffin returned home, he met with his most trusted slave, Jem Sykes, and "had a long conversation with him on the attempt & fate of Brown & his companions." In 1846, Ruffin made Sykes his plantation overseer, replacing a white hired manager. Ruffin shocked the neighborhood by leaving his plantation in Sykes's hands for months while vacationing at the springs of western Virginia. Ruffin had no doubts about slavery and his slaves. Nonetheless, he knew that slaves were spreading rumors about Brown's raid and execution. He wanted to give to Sykes, "& through him to his fellows, correct information" about Brown's "expectations, & the causes of his complete failure, & of which such must always operate." Ruffin stressed to Sykes how and why Brown failed to rally nearby slaves. What began as a news report about Brown's raid evolved into a history lesson about the origins of American slavery. Ruffin went on and on about abolitionists in general and slavery as an institution. No doubt this "conversation" was a one-sided affair, with Sykes gesturing agreement and Ruffin warming to his subject. This wasn't the time and place for an enslaved overseer to express his expectations. That opportunity would arrive with the Union army in the spring of 1864, when Jem Sykes disappeared.[29]

Brown still lurked in southern landscapes after his execution. On December 2, 1859 William Gwathmey noted in his diary with apparent satisfaction that "old ossawatomie brown," was hanged for "murder and insurrection" without trouble. The death of the "wicked beast" was confirmed by telegraph. Gwathmey took comfort in Psalm 31, particularly line 15, "My times are in thy hand: deliver me from the hand of mine enemies, and from them that persecute me." Gwathmey associated with David, who committed his future to God's hands, confident that the day was looming when the Lord would execute terrible justice against the wicked. Two days later, Gwathmey went to a meeting at Beulah Baptist Church and listened to a sermon based on John 15:25, "He hated me without a cause." A sixty-five-year-old physician and planter, Gwathmey was patriarch of a family of slaveholders that had led politics, society, and religion in King William County, Virginia, for two centuries. His world seemed to be returning to its old order, when, after the service, a rumor unsettled the contentment that Gwathmey felt about Brown's death. People swore that Brown had been in the neighborhood two years ago, calling himself McLane and selling trusses. Worst of all, the rumor asserted that he acted "very sanctified" and partook of the sacrament at Beulah. This news disturbed Gwathmey, who served as a trustee of Beulah. How many other hypocrites infested his world, scheming to unleash bedlam when he least expected it? It was difficult to maintain a calm assurance that the future was in God's hands when men like Brown passed through King William County.[30]

Similar rumors sprouted across the South. The same year Brown was purported to have scouted King William County, he was said to have been in Oxford, Mississippi. There, rumormongers said, Brown disguised himself as a clock repairer and was accepted by the neighborhood. When authorities found maps among Brown's possessions with black crosses dotting communities across the South, the rumors and terror spread like telegraphs. Osborne Anderson stoked southern fears in *A Voice from Harper's Ferry*. He refused to share specific information, but he promised that "preliminary arrangements were made in a number of places,—plans proposed, discussed and decided upon, numbers invited to participate in the movement, and the list of adherents increased." Imminent attacks could be anywhere.[31]

On December 7, someone left a note at the door of Mrs. Johnson's boarding house in Richmond, threatening that "an attack would be made upon the house between 10 and 12 o'clock." "Blood for Blood" was scribbled across the message, which was signed by "an accomplice." Colonel Western rushed the note to the mayor, who dispatched four policemen to guard the boarding house. When Robert Granniss and a friend returned from drilling with their militia company at half past nine, they found everyone in the boarding house assembled in the parlor. The ladies were very excited and frightened; the men were well armed and "prepared to resist all invasion." At half past ten the women retired upstairs to their bedrooms. Eight men, fortified with coffee, cold ham, excellent whiskey, and fine cigars, sat around the parlor fire, "spinning yarns, telling stories." When boredom crept in, they explored the house for signs of trouble. On one occasion, they roused Dick, a colored boy sleeping beside the basement fire, to check his pockets. Their inspection found nothing suspicious. The doctor turned in early and slept until half past two. Granniss "followed his example at a much later hour."[32]

Two nights later, three ladies of the house confessed that they had composed the letter as a prank. The poor women had miscalculated. It was too soon to joke about Harpers Ferry and southerners took anonymous threats seriously. Nothing linked this ordinary Richmond boarding house to John Brown and his associates, but authorities preferred to overreact to every threat. Southern men would go to extreme lengths to protect their women. When they discovered how much trouble their innocent prank stirred, the women were too frightened to tell the truth. It was easier for them to go along with the charade and accept their role as vulnerable ladies of the house than to admit they had penned the threat. Granniss noted, "The result was that 8 of us gentlemen and 4 policemen were kept out of bed watching for imaginary enemies."[33]

Blood

WHEN AMERICANS PROPHESIED AFTER John Brown's raid, blood loomed larger than darkness and ghosts. The phrase "Blood for Blood" summarized what Americans expected after Harpers Ferry. John Brown encouraged prophecies of blood with his actions and words. By striking white southerners, his attack emulated Old Testament justice, a violent reckoning that promised blood for blood, white southern blood for black southern blood spilled during centuries of bondage. The South responded with vigilante justice, its variety of blood for blood. Manhunts for Brown's accomplices fanned across the nation, but so did arbitrary violence against innocent people who raised suspicion. The South punished outsiders, expelling some and lynching others as far away as Texas. Northern peddlers, tutors, and piano tuners who stayed in the South in 1860 risked their lives. After Brown's death, northerners vowed to avenge his martyrdom by finishing his life's work, blood for blood.

In Brown's last address to the court on November 2, he predicted, "if it is deemed necessary that I should forfeit my life for the furtherance of the ends of justice, and mingle my blood further with the blood of my children and with the blood of millions in this slave country whose rights are disregarded by wicked, cruel, and unjust enactments, —I submit; so let it be done!" The statement is remarkable on a number of levels. First, Brown alluded to an interracial mingling of blood in a Virginia court that prohibited interracial sex. Second, he argued that God, not the court, would decide his fate. Through his last day in court, Brown expressed obedience to a higher law than Virginia's.[34]

A sampling of prophecies suggests the looming dimensions of America's bloody visions in 1860. Sarah Frances Williams was an antislavery northerner until she married a North Carolina planter. After she read about John Brown's attack in the newspaper, she mailed the account to her parents in New York. "I sent you a paper giving an account of the insane project in Virginia," she explained. She described the attack as "one of the diabolical schemes of a set of fanatics who, if they had their way, would deluge the land in blood." What frustrated Williams about John Brown and, perhaps, her northern relatives was their inability to separate lies from the truth about slavery. For Williams, uncertainties caused by the distance between northern perceptions and southern realities of slavery gave fanatics room to scheme and breed violence. "How I wish they could see this thing as it is," she complained, "but, there are none so blind as those who won't see." Moncure Conway's story mirrored Sarah Frances Williams's transition and prophecy. A native Virginian from a slaveholding family, Conway became an abolitionist while attending Harvard Divinity School. On the Sunday after John Brown's execution, Conway told his congregation in Cincinnati, Ohio, "This is a time when nothing should be disguised, and men must confront unwelcome but stubborn facts." Conway thought it was "an error to say we are on the verge of civil war; we are in the midst of civil war, whether much blood be shed or not." Like Brown, Conway had hoped that slavery would end without much bloodshed, but now he expected blood would deluge his native land and loved ones. "Last Friday the wind was sown: soon or late the whirlwind must be reaped." Williams and Conway forecasted as prophets who knew both sides of the looming conflict. Both urged their audiences to focus on the facts and see hard truths. When they looked to the future, they relied on scripture to provide contours and meanings to their horizon of expectation. Williams selected the Old Testament prophet Jeremiah to find a source for fanatics' unwillingness to see her world. Conway chose Hosea 8:7 to portend the coming storm.[35]

People in both regions prophesied that bloodshed would baptize the nation. Six days after John Brown's execution, Mississippi congressman Reuben Davis spoke before the House of Representatives. Davis warned, "The storm cloud of anarchy and blood and carnage and desolation has gathered darkly over our country." He noted that "its thunders and lightnings come together, telling us of its close proximity." Each crisis of the 1850s brought the flash of lightning and the clap of thunder closer in time and space. Now the tempest was nearly synchronous above America. Davis predicted, "A thousand other John Browns, may invade us and the Government will remain neutral—there will be no Army, no Navy, sent to resist any invasion." Like Samuel Morse, Davis imagined an enemy immune from military defenses. Facing his colleagues in Congress, Davis asked, "Ought we not, then, in frankness to tell our northern compatriots that if we are not to be protected in the Union, we will protect ourselves out of it, even at the hazard of deluging this vast country in a sea of blood?" Revolutions were written in blood and Davis saw one on the horizon. While Davis stormed, Theodore Parker kept abreast of American news as he convalesced in Rome. Anticipating Brown's final prophecy, Parker wrote, "A few years ago it did not seem difficult first to check Slavery, and then to end it without much bloodshed. I think this cannot be done now, nor ever in the future." This realization did not trouble Parker much because "all the great charters of HUMANITY have been writ in blood. I once hoped that of American Democracy would be engrossed in less costly ink; but it is plain, now, that our pilgrimage must lead through a Red Sea, wherein many a Pharaoh will go under and perish." Davis and Parker were sectional opposites in 1859, yet both anticipated apocalyptic bloodshed as the path to national greatness.[36]

Prophecies of blood after Harpers Ferry echoed persistent warnings from abolitionists that slavery would soon end in violence if the nation did not embrace emancipation. The coincidence that Nat Turner's insurrection occurred mere months after William Lloyd Garrison founded the *Liberator* created the impression that a bloody reckoning loomed if America did not accept the moral arguments for abolition. After Turner's revolt, Angelina Grimké, a southern abolitionist raised within a slaveholding household, prophesied,

> At one time I thought this system would be overthrown in blood, with the confused noise of the warrior; but a hope gleams across my mind, that *our* blood will be spilt, instead of the slaveholders, our *lives* will be taken and theirs spared. . . . I say a *hope*, for of all the things I desire to be spared the anguish of seeing our beloved country desolated with the horrors of a servile war.

William Jay voiced the same concern long before John Brown's raid. If the Union dissolved, "a civil war ensues—the moral means heretofore used by abolitionists give place to the confused noise of the warrior, and to garments rolled in blood; servile insurrection necessarily follows in the train of civil war, and if slavery perish it will perish only in a deluge of BLOOD." Both prophecies refer to Isaiah 9:5, "For every battle of the warrior *is* with confused noise, and garments rolled in blood; but *this* shall be with burning *and* fuel of fire." Isaiah promised that God reigned over warfare; all its chaos and gore would be consumed by fire to usher in eternal peace. But this promise offered little comfort to those who heard the tramping footsteps and feared the flames of retribution.[37]

As Osborne Anderson understood, visions of race war that intensified after Harpers Ferry began generations earlier with the Stono Rebellion, Haitian Revolution, Gabriel's Rebellion, Denmark Vessey, and Nat Turner's Revolt. In 1829, free black David Walker warned southerners that slaves had more cause to revolt than American colonists did in 1776. Using the book of Revelation, he prophesied Armageddon, "Americans!! I warn you in the name of the Lord . . . to repent and reform, or you are ruined!!!" As Revelation foretold, God would "tear up the very face of the earth" over slavery. Referring to Pharaoh's army in the Red Sea, the fall of the Roman Empire, and the Haitian Revolution, Walker assured Americans that all civilizations that think "the whole of mankind were made to be slaves to them; just as many of the Americans think now" have suffered violent deaths at the hands of slaves and an angry God. Walker relied on material culture, commerce, and the sea to spread his prophecy in the South. As owner of a secondhand apparel shop, Walker sewed his pamphlet inside clothing that black sailors bought, wore, and bartered in southern ports. When authorities in Savannah found sixty copies, the legislature held a secret session and banned black sailors from the state and put a price on Walker's head. They also made it a capital offense to spread the prophecy and other "pamphlets of evil tendency among our domestics." Walker died of mysterious causes a year later.[38]

Apocalyptic Politics

THE BLOOD OF HARPERS FERRY stained the 1860 presidential election. Democrats seized the chance to incriminate Republicans as Harpers Ferry conspirators. Weeks after the raid, Benjamin F. Dill, editor of the *Memphis Appeal*, urged Stephen Douglas to "seek the earliest occasion in the Senate to trace the Harpers Ferry Treason as a legitimate consequence of (as it is) of the doctrines taught by Seward & Lincoln, against which your public life has been one continual warfare." Douglas did just that. "The great principle that underlies the organization of the Republican party is violent, irreconcilable, eternal warfare upon the institution of American slavery," he said. Weeks after Brown's execution, Douglas introduced a bill to protect southerners from future invaders inspired by Republican doctrine. He urged Congress to seize the initiative, anticipate the looming danger, and avoid further bloodshed. "The causes that produced the Harper's Ferry invasion are now in active operation," he warned. "Can you expect people to be patient, when they dare not lie down to sleep at night without first stationing sentinels around their houses to see if a band of marauders and murderers are not approaching with torch and pistol?" Southern Democrats who supported John Breckinridge for president agreed: "The Republican party cannot wash its hands of this bloody transaction." "Look at their deifying a man, who, without provocation, at the dead of night, stole down upon the peaceful and unsuspecting inhabitants of a town, who had done him no wrong, inciting their slaves to cut their throats, and he and his followers imbruing their hands in their blood." The most graphic denunciation appeared in John Cooper's *Pennsylvania Statesman*, a Democratic newspaper published in Harrisburg. For the anniversary issue of Brown's attack, circulated weeks before the election, Cooper printed a pike on its front page, calling it "a graphic sketch of the Black Republican argument" that was "designed to *pierce the heart* rather than *convince the mind* of the southern people." "This *argument*, as delivered by old Brown, consisted of an Iron Pike precisely the size and shape of the drawing on our first page, fixed on a wooded staff six or seven feet long." Cooper said the Republican argument required no skill and was "just the thing to suit an ignorant and enraged negro." Brown's pikes "would go through and through the body of a man or a woman," and "a child could be impaled on them and carried aloft as a trophy." If the Republican Party won, the *Charleston Mercury* prophesied, "a war of races—a war of extermination—must arise, like that which took place in St. Domingo."[39]

This barrage of accusations affected the Republican race for president. Fears of a looming race war compromised William Seward's candidacy. Northern and southern critics argued that his "irrepressible conflict" prophecy inspired Brown's raid. It did not help his cause that Seward met Brown once and happened to be overseas when the attack occurred. " 'The irrepressible conflict has begun,' is heard accompanied with fierce denunciations, bad whiskey, profanity, and vulgarity," complained one Republican to another, but the charges stuck. The Tennessee legislature resolved that Brown's attack was the "natural fruit of this treasonable 'irrepressible conflict' doctrine put forth by this great head of the Black Republican party." If the Harpers Ferry raid could happen when the South was united behind a trustworthy president like James Buchanan, "what will be the measures of insurrection and incendiarism which must follow our notorious and abject prostration to Abolition rule at Washington?" asked the *Charleston Mercury*. The *New York Herald* answered that question in an article titled "The Irrepressible Conflict What Is It?" Seward's presidency would cause the worst slave revolt in history and a "bloody civil war." One week after Brown's execution, a Whig from Lynchburg, Virginia, who identified himself as "A Slaveholder" warned Republican congressman John Sherman of Ohio that "the Southern states will take up arms against a President elected by a sectional party, and that fact alone ought to induce all true patriots, and all men who have any regard for their own interest, to labor with none but a national party."[40]

Republicans searched for a candidate not affiliated with Brown, someone who could convince voters that he opposed slave revolts and enforced the law. In February 1860, Abraham Lincoln persuaded many voters that he was that candidate when he lectured to over a thousand people at the Cooper Institute in New York City. Lincoln denounced apocalyptic narratives that prevailed after Harpers Ferry. "When you speak of us Republicans, you do so only to denounce us as reptiles, or, at the best, as no better than outlaws. You will grant a hearing to pirates or murderers, but nothing like it to 'Black Republicans.'" He vehemently denied accusations that his party conspired with John Brown. "You charge that we stir up insurrections among your slaves. We deny it; and what is your proof? Harper's Ferry! John Brown!! John Brown was no Republican; and you have failed to implicate a single Republican in his Harper's Ferry enterprise." Lincoln also denied that Republican ideology fostered slave insurrections. Southerners simplified the party's doctrine to mean "insurrection, blood and thunder among the slaves," without admitting that Republicans opposed all interference with slavery where it exists. If the slaves knew about Republicans and saw them as allies, it was because southerners misrepresented them, not because of anything Republicans said or did. Lincoln portrayed Republicans as a conservative party that upheld the founders' vision for America, especially their plan for gradual emancipation. He quoted Thomas Jefferson: "It is still in our power to direct the process of emancipation, and deportation, peaceably, and in such slow degrees, as that the evil will wear off insensibly." He agreed with Jefferson's prophecy that the nation could replace slaves with "free white laborers" or leave the future to "force" and "shudder at the prospect." Emancipation could happen through "the peaceful channel of the ballot-box" or through a race war.[41]

Weeks after Brown's execution bloodshed seemed imminent on the floor of Congress because the Republican Party had subsidized an abridged edition of Hinton Helper's *The Impending Crisis*. Helper was a go-ahead man from North Carolina who went to California for gold but failed to make a fortune. Failure shifted Helper's temporality from anticipations to expectations. When he returned home, he blamed his misfortunes on the Slave Power. The master class kept honest yeomen like him down by not providing decent public education. Drawing from the 1850 census, Helper concluded that the free labor

North surpassed the slave South in every economic category, even agriculture. He prophesied a looming disaster and instructed his class "how to meet it." He rallied his fellow yeomen, who accounted for three-fourths of southern voters, to expel the planter class from power. According to Helper, the bowie knife sustained the Slave Power. He called slave owners "mere tyrants, whose manual exercises are wholly comprised in the use they make of instruments of torture, such as whips, clubs, bowie-knives and pistols." In other words, black slaves and white yeomen of the South wielded tools—hoes, hammers, and saws—that brought the region prosperity. Tyrannical masters did not know how to handle productive instruments; they only gripped destructive, oppressive things.[42]

Though Helper was no friend to the slave, his threat to the master class seemed more ominous after Harpers Ferry. Sixty-eight Republican congressmen endorsed the new edition of *Impending Crisis* that added the caption "Revolution—Peacefully if we can, Violently if we must." When one of those Republicans, John Sherman, was nominated for Speaker of the House, lawmakers from both sections brought weapons to work expecting a shoot-out. According to a southerner, slave-state congressmen "are willing to fight the question out, and to settle it right here. . . . I can't help wishing the Union were dissolved and we had a Southern confederacy." When disunion failed to arrive after Harpers Ferry, Ruffin traveled from Brown's execution to the halls of Congress and sat in the gallery awaiting civil war. The governor of South Carolina also anticipated civil war. If fighting broke out in the capitol building, William Gist wrote William Porcher Miles, "telegraph me, and I will have a regiment in or near Washington in the shortest possible time." As Allan Nevins explained in the 1950s, "Fear—honest fear of the future—was really at the root of much of the bluster. The Southerners had a general fear of losing their rights, a deadly fear of servile rebellion, and a growing fear of Northern onslaughts." People smelled gunpowder in the wind. "Now is the time," Helper told southern yeomen, to "strike for Freedom in the South."[43]

Porte Crayon

IT WAS NOT INEVITABLE that people would anticipate Armageddon after Harpers Ferry. Brown's bungling failure encouraged some storytellers to frame the experience as a comedy or fiasco, but their tales failed to acquire widespread appeal. The deaths of Brown's sons and other young people innocently caught in the maelstrom at Harpers Ferry could have fostered tragedies and romances about the attack, but such stories did not spread. No, when

Americans looked to the future after Harpers Ferry they saw an apocalypse. Some feared it and others prayed for it. Whether a story acquired popularity and credibility depended on its plot as much as its teller.

One of the nation's most popular storytellers, David Hunter Strother, lived near Harpers Ferry in the fall of 1859. Before he took the pen name Porte Crayon and published travel accounts, Strother studied oil painting under Samuel Morse and traveled to Europe for inspiration in 1839. "What adventures were to be mine?" he asked his journal. With wry humor, Strother imagined "a new revolution would break out" upon his arrival in Europe and he "would lead the fiery populace to victory." As his ship approached France, the entire horizon blazed with fire to mark the reburial of Napoleon. "The stupendous cliffs of flame, which towered above the deep green sea and relieved the leaden sky, almost black toward the horizon, seemed more like enchantment than reality." Watching Napoleon's funeral procession, Strother was disgusted by the crass commercialism of the event. Hawkers sold figurines of the emperor with cologne in his belly. People came to gawk at pageantry, not to honor history. Moving to Rome, where he met fellow American artist Thomas Cole, did not improve Strother's feelings about Europe but instead dampened his go-ahead enthusiasm. Instead of leading dramatic changes, Strother absorbed impressions that changed his temporality from anticipation to expectation. "We plan, we resolve, we imagine that we are shaping our own course but after all we have little to do with it. Chance, destiny, or providence like the wind with unresisting cloud, drives us whither it liketh and we know it not."[44]

Twenty years later, Strother was writing in his Martinsburg, Virginia, office when rumors of an insurrection at Harpers Ferry reached him. Not trusting the report, he waited to see how the Baltimore and Ohio train that passed through Martinsburg fared when it arrived in Harpers Ferry. The train passed by on schedule, but an hour later Strother saw it backing up from Harpers Ferry to the Martinsburg Depot. He raced to the station to hear the news. "I found a large and excited crowd there and all sorts of rumours afloat." One of the railroad men told Strother, "The arsenal and Rail Road Bridge at Harpers ferry had been seized by a band of Abolitionists whose object was to kill all the whites and free the slaves." Strother "rejected it as absurd and sought some other solution of the difficulty." A model Virginian, Strother assumed northern free labor was the root of the conflict. The trouble at the Ferry must be "a rebellion among the workmen at the Armory; a riot among the labourers . . . who had been defrauded of their pay by an absconding contractor; [or perhaps] an organized band of robbers from the cities." "Any idea that suggested itself was accepted rather than" the thought that abolitionists had incited a race war. Citizens called a town meeting, learned that Colonel Lewis Washington and other prominent people were hostages of the insurgents, and organized a company to rescue them. Strother did not go. He watched two carloads of men leave for the Ferry "armed with squirrel guns, fowling pieces, pistols, swords, and whatever was at hand."[45]

In the morning, Strother heard that the Martinsburg "boys had had a fight and that seven or eight of them had been wounded, two supposed mortally." Still convinced that the insurgents were robbers, Strother caught a train for Harpers Ferry. Sitting beside him was Jacob Kunkel, a Democratic candidate for Congress from Washington County, Maryland. Strother noticed Kunkel's "ill suppressed satisfaction" that the tragedy could elevate his political fortunes. "This thing will be worth three hundred votes to me in the coming election," Kunkel said. When he reached the Ferry, Strother saw streets choked with military men, "from the quiet effective looking United States Marines to the half armed, half drunk and noisy militiamen." An armed mob shot at three bodies lying in the Potomac. He passed the bloody corpse of a black man with glassy eyes and a gaping jaw. A dog smelled a bloody mess around the head while pigs rooted in the body. Three dead men, "ghastly and stiff," lay near the engine house where a fourth man writhed in spasms. A marine tried to suppress a crowd of gawkers that pressed forward to see the gore. Above the mayhem, Strother heard a voice "speaking in tones of rebuke to the rude men." He spotted "a mountain Beau with a girl on each arm, who seemed disgusted and astonished at the want of manners among the vulgar. 'Gentlemen,' said he, 'just give room here.' 'Cant you stand back and let the ladies see the corpses?' "[46]

The sights and sounds of Harpers Ferry turned Strother's thoughts to the future. In his journal he jotted down a line he recalled from Tocqueville: "to judge of the future, on the part of a being who is hourly deceived by the most palpable realities of life and who is constantly taken by surprise by circumstance with which he is most familiar." Brown's actions lit a powder keg of prophecies that exploded across the nation, but who could see with any confidence what loomed beyond the horizon? Tocqueville censured "the imprudence of attempting to limit the possible." The passage belonged to a section that considered the mortality of republics. "The history of the world affords no instance of a great nation retaining the form of a republican government for a long series of years." How frail was the Union, Strother wondered. Tocqueville expected "the existence of a great republic will always be exposed to far greater perils than that of a small one." Perhaps race wars were the "greater perils" that America faced.[47]

Strother used the event to shed light on despicable and embarrassing elements of society. Like Napoleon's reburial, John Brown's raid illuminated the ignorance and low character of the throng. He sketched John Brown as a frail old man, not the formidable fighter who sparked widespread panic and admiration. Strother mocked how Brown's "plan of government recognized complete equality between whites and blacks." The raiders' Provisional Constitution seized all the wealth belonging to slaveholders and distributed it "to the emancipated negroes and the needy leaders in the war of freedom." Strother thought the fictional titles that the raiders bestowed upon themselves revealed their deep delusions. "He, John Brown, was to be the commander in chief of the armies of the new government while among his immediate followers were several high officers of the anticipated state. Kagi was named as Secretary of State I think; Copell a good looking mulatto was to be a judge of the Supreme Court; Shields Green the negro barber was already elected a member of Congress, while upon the persons of the wretches who were slain on land and water were found regularly made out commissions, entitling them to the posts of Captain, Lieutenant, Honourable etc., etc."[48]

For Strother, the height of folly was the pikes. He drew Virginia slaves holding them likes shovels. The caption read, "Much obliged to dat ar possum wattomie for dese pike he gin us—dey's terrible handy to dig taters wid." The artist tried to diffuse the panic sparked by Brown's raid by underlining the stereotype of docile, ignorant slaves. Strother was doing more than making fun of blacks; he was trying to spread hope that Americans would stop focusing on looming warfare and seek productive rather than destructive things and thoughts. In an attempt to offset the apocalyptic visions swirling around the nation, Strother borrowed Isaiah's prophecy that "they shall beat their swords into ploughshares and their spears into pruning hooks."[49]

Disfranchised Prophets

HARPERS FERRY ALSO RAISED anxieties because it empowered dispossessed groups and threatened established institutions. The ease with which John Brown captured a federal armory shamed the government. The hysteria that Brown sparked among Virginians betrayed the manly façade that white southerners displayed. Beyond national and regional challenges, Brown's raid sparked racial, class, and gender upheavals that destabilized society at its bedrock. The grapevine that linked slave quarters transmitted news of the assault to remote corners of the plantation South. A former slave from Mississippi admitted, "We slaves knew very little about what was going on outside our plantations," but "it was impossible to keep the news of John Brown's attack on Harper's Ferry from spreading." Slaves and free blacks observed how whites feared John Brown and stoked widespread panic. Word of the raid reached Georgia slaves quickly. William Lovett wrote his fiancée on November 5, 1859, "I have bin in Trouble for the Last 2 weaks with the Niggers they have bin running away and fighting." Fears of an insurrection kept Lovett up at night: "I haven't had a nits rest in too weaks." Being in a precarious position after the attempted insurrection, slaves used ambiguous statements to unnerve masters without incurring their wrath. Slaves remarked to Amanda Edmonds, "Old Brown left a hard storm behind him." Edmonds could not tell whether they referred to the ominous weather that followed Brown's execution, particularly the dark Sabbath of December 4, or if a threat lurked behind their remark. When thirteen-year-old Susan Bradford Eppes heard about Harpers Ferry, the news turned her world "topsyturvy," because "we can trust none of the dear black folks who, before this, we had relied on at every turn." Eppes lived on a plantation in Florida. One slave, Frances, exploited the upheaval to threaten Eppes in a veiled way. One night Frances asked Eppes, "Do you understand what this is all about?" Eppes replied that she did not yet, but "we would know more after a few days." Frances laughed, "a crazy kind of laugh," and said, "Yes, you will; you white folks will know a heap you ain't never knowed before." Frances ran out of the room before Eppes could ask her what the remark meant.[50]

The false alarms and anonymous threats that people mailed to authorities at Harpers Ferry also used uncertainty to upend power. Local citizen Robert Conrad suspected that even the letters addressed to John Brown were intended for southerners. "We know that one favorite plan of the abolitionists is to alarm the country and agitate it as much as possible on this subject." Conrad noted that "all the rumors of armed bands . . . have been inquired into, and ascertained to be pure fabrications." Misinformation scared the public and preoccupied southern authorities who had to investigate each threat. The arsonists contributed to this hysteria whether they worked in concert with the anonymous writers or not. Conrad suspected that the fires in Jefferson County were started by a league of "the lowest class, white and black" stirred by Brown's attack to indulge "all the mischievous propensities of their nature." His theory seems plausible. The lower classes could have exploited the crisis to harm their wealthier neighbors with impunity. In peaceful times they would have been the first suspects for such crimes, but Brown's raid placed imaginary distant enemies before real local dissidents, in a sense cloaking the lower classes and giving them a chance to right a wrong or release some resentment.[51]

The crisis emboldened African American prophets to rejoice that John Brown had fulfilled their hopes and visions. When Osborne Anderson told an old slave mother about the impending raid, she said "liberating the slaves was the very thing she had longed for, prayed for, and dreamed about, time and again; and her heart was full of rejoicing over the fulfillment of a prophecy which had been her faith for long years." Frederick Douglass struck a prophetic tone by framing the raid as an Old Testament reckoning. "Like Samson, [Brown] has laid his hands upon the pillars of this great national temple of cruelty and blood, and when he falls, that temple will speedily crumble to its final doom, burying its denizens in its ruins." Other African Americans prophesied that Brown would inspire the slaves to start a race war throughout the South. Francis E. W. Harper saw the future in a dream. "I saw the green sward stained with his blood, but every drop of it was like the terrible teeth sown by Cadmus; they woke up armed men to smite the terror-stricken power that had invaded his life." A black army would assault slavery until it "tottered and fell amid the shouts of men who had burst their chains, and the rejoicings of women newly freed." Her dream ended when the day of atonement dawned, "and Freedom, like a glorified angel, smiled over the glorious jubilee." Black journalist Thomas Hamilton painted a darker future. He predicted if Nat Turner had led Brown's men, "the soil of Virginia and Maryland and the far South would by this time be drenched in the blood and the wild and sanguinary course of these men, no earthly power could stay." He imagined the Harpers Ferry crisis "will engender in its bosom and nurse into maturity a hundred Nat Turners." John Sella Martin, the first African American pastor of Tremont Temple in Boston, delivered one of the most beautiful, terrifying prophecies on the day of Brown's death. "It is thought by the slaves . . . that the meteors from the heavens are sparks that escape from the storehouse of the lightnings to strike upon the craters of volcanoes, and that is the cause of their eruption." Brown's death was a meteor that "has fallen upon the volcano of American sympathies." Though it may be dormant for a time, "it shall burst forth in one general conflagration of revolution that shall bring about universal freedom." Martin had escaped from slavery in 1856. When he preached a looming violence, his interracial audience cheered. Henry Highland Garnet was also born a slave, and on execution day, he preached bloodshed to a congregation in New York City. "In the signs of the times I see the dreadful truth, written as by the finger of Jehovah—"*For the sins of this nation there is no atonement without the shedding of blood.*" Echoing Brown's favorite scripture, Hebrews 9.22, Garnet believed that "the nation needed to see a picture of the future of slavery and its ends, and methinks God has been pleased to draw it in crimson lines."[52]

Harpers Ferry also inspired women to join public debates about the future. Abolitionist Lydia Maria Child said the event "renewed my youth and strength, and filled me with electricity, and one word of apology for slavery makes the sparks fly." She asked Governor Wise for permission to nurse Brown's wounds which triggered a heated exchange on the subject. Their debate drew so much attention during the election year that "a posse of Republicans" sought her out "to look at the woman who 'fired hot shot at Governor Wise.'" When Virginia authorities closed John Brown's execution to all but military personnel, they barred all women from the event. This gender discrimination irked Amanda Edmonds, who barraged officers who attended the execution with questions the day after Brown died. She reveled in the gory and sublime details of the execution. "After he was taken down, they cut his throat, boxed him up and sent his remains to his wife," she noted in her diary. "He was attended to the scaffold by a thousand five hundred soldiers, and their splendid brass bands. Oh what an awfully sublime a glorious, a charming scene. I almost wish that I was a man," she confessed, "that I could have been their [*sic*] to looked upon it."[53]

Women found other ways to join the event and debates it generated. When investigators identified Franklin Sanborn as one of the Secret Six, Louisa May Alcott volunteered in a vigilance committee that protected him. She also hosted Brown's widow and daughters at her home in July 1860. In January 1860, she published a poem about Brown's execution in the *Liberator*. Alcott urged northerners to die for freedom as Brown did when she prophesied about the effect of his martyrdom:

> That moment when the brave old man
> Went so serenely forth
> With footsteps whose unfaltering tread
> Re-echoed through the North.

Child prepared northerners for Brown's martyrdom by publishing her correspondence with Governor Wise and Brown while he awaited execution.[54]

Margaretta Mason, the wife of Virginia senator James Mason, replied to Child in a public correspondence that debated slavery's place in the Bible and the role of violence in American social movements. She censured Child for comforting Brown, "whose aim and intention was to incite the horrors of a servile war—to condemn women of your own race, ere death closed their eyes on their sufferings from violence and outrage, to see their husbands and fathers murdered, their children butchered, the ground strewed with the brains of their babes." Instead, Mason told Child to comfort the families of Brown's victims. In 1860, the American Anti-Slavery Society printed the women's correspondence as a tract that sold 300,000 copies. Such attention raised questions about the place for women in public discourse, an issue that an anonymous woman addressed in "A Woman's View of a Woman's Duty" the week after John Brown died. The author blamed women's partisan fervor for John Brown's raid. "They have urged an excitable, ardent and rash fanatic on to a bloody death, and instead of going on their knees and praying Almighty God to forgive this horrible sin, content themselves with writing letters for publication, or making sentimental journeys to their victim's prison." The writer condemned these "women of ardent vanity and mediocre minds." One of the most revealing episodes of self-empowerment among women was the Richmond boarding house prank. When they composed a phony threat, the women did not anticipate how seriously male authorities would receive it. Because the mayor, police, and local militia rushed to defend them, the women realized that they inadvertently wielded the power to summon local manpower. When they confessed authorship two days later, the women performed a service that expressed their apology for trespassing in the masculine sphere: they cooked and served their all-night defenders a special dinner.[55]

An array of evidence about John Brown's raid—diaries, letters, sermons, literature, military reports, interrogations, court statements, and public speeches—suggests how and why apocalyptic narratives swept the nation after Harpers Ferry. National media spread prophecies of race war and looming bloodshed. Northern sympathy for Brown and his men appalled southerners and deepened the sectional divide more profoundly than the failed assault. Despite the power of telegrams and steam-powered printing presses to assemble stories with a wide currency, local communication remained a powerful force in shaping rumors and prophecies. Anonymous threats, slave remarks, neighborhood gossip, fireside yarns, practical jokes, family correspondence, and private diaries coalesced in stories about tomorrow's surprise attack, a hard storm coming, and "Blood for Blood" revenge. These private streams of rumor and prophecy entered a public discourse about the horizon of expectation. Nineteenth-century technology accelerated and expanded the nation's antebellum rumor mill.

Wide Awakes and Minute Men

IN 1860, NO GROUP signified this acceleration of rumors and bellicose politics more than the Wide Awakes, a youth movement that stumped for Abraham Lincoln and electrified the nation. It began in March when five clerks carrying torches and wearing capes escorted a Republican speaker through the streets of Hartford, Connecticut. By November, the Wide Awakes were attracting hundreds of thousands of volunteers across the North. The militancy of the group distinguished it from other political movements. Wide Awakes wore shiny black uniforms, marched in step, carried torches, and organized by army ranks and orders. Their pamphlets teemed with military metaphors, transforming voters into soldiers, parties into armies, and ballots into weapons. Before the election they read the Civil War's most popular military manual, William Hardee's *Rifle and Light Infantry Tactics*. When Secretary of War Jefferson Davis adopted the rifle musket for the US Army in 1855, Hardee redesigned American tactics to address the expanded killing zone of the weapon. The Springfield .58 caliber rifle increased the accuracy of infantry from 100 to 500 yards. While other nations addressed the rifle's deadliness by thinning compact assault lines, Hardee took a more American approach—speed. He predicted that men would be safer in the rifle's killing zone if they moved faster. His manual increased the quick step to 110 paces per minute and the double quick to 165 steps. This innovation attracted the Wide Awakes, who wanted their parades to surprise spectators with speed and precision. Ulysses S. Grant himself trained Wide Awakes how to form and move like soldiers.[56]

Wide Awake rallies late at night, tramping through streets and materializing in town squares, unified Republicans and terrified their opponents. When William Seward stumped for Lincoln before fifty Wide Awake companies, he sensed how a new generation raised during the height of sectionalism would empower the Republicans. "The reason we didn't get an honest President in 1856, was because the old men of the last generation were not Wide-Awake, and the young men of this generation hadn't got their eyes open. Now the old men are folding their arms and going to sleep, and the young men throughout the land are Wide Awake." Virginian John Lawson followed the movement while studying medicine in New York City. "The whole Country north of Mason & Dixon line has been at a white heat if I may so express it, and New York City has been as it were incandescent with torchlight procession and party display." He told his cousin, when the time comes, "I should be found at the first blast of the trumpet occupying my position 'upon the tented field' aye in the very vanguard defending Southern rights and institutions." South Carolinian Grace Elmore found herself engulfed by marching Wide Awakes one night after going to the opera in New York. "'Twas a beautiful sight—but how I hated them all as they shouted 'Lincoln and Hamlin.'" For Elmore, the Wide Awakes were "the last insult this Yankee nation seek to put upon the downtrodden South." If they succeeded in electing Republicans, "the South will rise as one man and secede from this already detested Union."[57]

South Carolina responded to the Wide Awakes by forming Minute Men companies that stumped for secession. Minute Men identified themselves by wearing blue cockades on black felt hats. The cockade, a relic of revolutions past, also echoed the Nullification Crisis, when South Carolinians wore them to express support for their state's sovereignty. As election day approached, Elmore observed that blue cockades were "as plentiful as blackberries. No man feels he is a man unless his hat is turned up at the side with a blue rosette." Her brother, Albert, joined the Minute Men at the age of seventeen and started drilling because "we don't know when we will be wanted." When she objected that he was too young, Albert insisted, "I'm not too young to carry a gun, and I'm a better shot than most men." Later that day, Grace sat at her window, trying to realize the future "lying before me; my brother going to battle." "I tried to take it all in, and in imagination to a certain extent I did realize the horrors of war." Grace forced herself to imagine her brother and his friends "slain and left on the battle field." As she lay in bed that night, Grace expected "every sorrow that the war might bring to me. I saw my Mother in her old age shorn of her wealth, her two boys gone, her children scattered." Most Minute Men, like Albert Elmore, came from the slaveholding class and expressed a paramilitary vigilance against abolitionist raiders and Wide Awake agitators. Northerners scoffed at them. The *New York Herald* predicted, "Blue cockades would soon be as scarce as blue roses." When a young man wearing a cockade appeared in Lincoln's office weeks after the election, Springfield men berated him. One fellow challenged him, sneering that barking dogs never bite, while another bet him that he never owned a slave or a foot of earth. Lincoln was more accommodating to the young man, offering him a volume of the Joint Debates so that he could share Lincoln's true position with his fellow southerners. Lincoln remarked that perhaps he would be afraid to carry such writing back to the South, where holding a copy of *The Impending Crisis* or *Uncle Tom's Cabin* could get you killed. Insulted, the young man grabbed the book, said he would dare take it anywhere, and bolted from the room.[58]

Wide Awakes and Minute Men echoed John Brown's militant politics. They sought to shape the future by gathering arms, drilling men, and fomenting revolution. Their military titles and regulations reiterated Brown's provisional army and constitution. All three groups anticipated a future that they would fashion by being more organized, combative, and armed than the enemy. All three looked to the American Revolution for inspiration. Albert Elmore's company of Minute Men followed the example of the signers of the Declaration of Independence, pledging "our lives, our fortunes, and our sacred honor," to fight for independence. They believed that the people, led by their vanguard agitation, would drag timid statesmen into the future. In November 1860, Grace Elmore prophesied, "Politicians will shrink away in the background, and the mighty will of the people will be heard and so certain as day follows night shall that will proclaim Secession." She turned twenty-one that month.[59]

Arming for the Future

WHILE APOCALYPTIC NARRATIVES AFFECTED the presidential campaign, fears of a looming race war stirred southern militancy. From Virginia to Texas, vigilantes scoured the countryside for more John Browns. In Richmond, John Pegram wrote his younger brother, Willie, that he "never saw anything like the military and patriotic feeling now existing at the South. Before the Harpers Ferry outbreak this Regiment could not muster over three hundred and fifty men, now we have about seven hundred and fifty." The quality of the volunteers impressed Pegram more than the quantity. "Such men were never seen in any ranks as those that are in the first Regiment at this time," he boasted. They all wore new gray uniforms. William Johnston reported similar scenes in Galveston, Texas. "There is great military excitement in the city." He estimated that 2,000 soldiers patrolled the town and he inspected the fortifications. "They seem to be doing things up 'brown,'" he joked. Rumors surged through the city of an invasion from Mexico. Meanwhile Mississippi appropriated $150,000 to arm and revitalize its state militia. Counties deluged Governor John Pettus with requests for guns. Harpers Ferry stoked vigilance—a posture of fearful anticipation that charged the air with military spirit and excitement. Young men raced to join companies that would be ready for the looming race war. These southern regiments and arms that assembled to face the next John Brown in 1860 formed the heart of the Confederate army a year later.[60]

Americans across the nation sought Brown's pikes as relics of the future, harbingers of a revolution to end or defend slavery. Within months of the raid, about half of the Harpers Ferry pikes circulated the nation as personal souvenirs. A local clerk mailed one to Samuel Colt as a gift. The Baltimore & Ohio railroad sold pikes to passengers at the Harpers Ferry station until a company official ended "this pike trade" because it "only adds to the excitement." People sensed the looming war and wanted a piece of it. The Virginia legislature appropriated more than $500,000 to prepare for war. Turner Ashby witnessed the state's growing war spirit after Harpers Ferry. As part of the state militia that swarmed to Charlestown, he saw gray uniforms from Richmond mix with cerulean blues of Alexandria, buff and yellows from the Valley, and crimson coats of southwestern men. The assembled horsemen traded talk of fox hunting for discussions of military tactics. "Men are growing desirous to know, not how to cultivate, but how to defend their soil," he said. Andrew Hunter, Virginia's prosecutor against John Brown, understood the raid as "the beginning of a great conflict between the North and the South on the subject of slavery." He convinced Governor Wise to assemble a large military force not only "for the protection of the jail and the repelling of parties who were known to be organizing with the view of rescuing Brown and the prisoners, but it was for the purpose of preparing for coming events."[61]

Secretary of War John Floyd was at the center of this growing war storm. His father had been governor of Virginia during Nat Turner's insurrection. In 1831 the governor feared that Turner's revolt will "lead to much more disastrous consequences than is at this time apprehended by anybody." The elder Floyd read William Lloyd Garrison's *Liberator* after the attack and accused it of inciting slave revolts. "The first drops of blood, which are but the prelude to a deluge from the gathering clouds, have fallen," Garrison warned. The *Liberator* reprinted a jeremiad from its first issue, commanding, "Read the account of the insurrection in Virginia, and say whether our prophecy be not fulfilled."

Wo if it come with storm, and blood, and fire,
    When midnight darkness veils the earth and sky!
Wo to the innocent babe—the guilty sire—
    Mother and daughter—friends of kindred tie!
    Stranger and citizen alike shall die!
Red-handed Slaughter his revenge shall feed,
    And Havoc yell his ominous death-cry,
And wild Despair in vain for mercy plead—
While hell itself shall shrink and sicken at the deed!

"If this is not checked," Floyd predicted, "it must lead to a separation of these states." His son lived his prophecy. Weeks after Brown's execution, the younger Floyd used his cabinet position to transfer thousands of weapons from northern to southern arsenals. More than 100,000 muskets moved from Massachusetts to North Carolina, South Carolina, Georgia, Alabama, and Louisiana. Floyd collected crates of Harpers Ferry pikes and shipped them to a Texas armory where they eventually armed a Confederate regiment.[62]

Joseph Anderson, the owner of Tredegar Ironworks in Richmond, profited from the South's panic after Harpers Ferry. Days after Brown's execution Anderson wrote the governors of slave states. "The time has arrived when the South should be looking to her defences, and we offer our Foundry and our experience to your State, whenever she may require them, and will charge for our guns (iron and brass) shot and shells, the same price we receive from the Government of the United States." During the election campaign, Anderson anticipated a Republican victory and traveled north to acquire all the machines and employ all the artisans he would need to manufacture southern rifles for the looming war. When Lincoln won the election, southern states wrote to Anderson for munitions and guns. The largest order came from South Carolina, which requested mortars, shot, shell, and powder to accomplish "an incessant bombardment and cannonade of many hours duration." Tredegar worked day and night to fulfill the order.[63]

The Return of Henry Clay Pate

ON NOVEMBER 21, 1859, Henry Clay Pate visited John Brown in jail and demanded the return of his knife. Many southerners called on Brown and the vast majority of them enjoyed a polite exchange. Pate did not. Brown confessed that he had given Pate's knife to a friend. When Pate pressed him for a name, Brown refused. Gifts forge and strengthen social bonds, but in this case, Brown honored one man by disrespecting another. Brown and Pate understood this fact. When Pate confronted Brown in jail he sought more than his knife; he demanded restitution. By stealing Pate's knife, Brown had forged an unwelcome association with Pate. Returning the possession to its rightful owner was the only way to acknowledge the wrong, the only way to restore boundaries between them. Only the knife could sever Pate's subordinate affiliation with Brown. [64]

So much had changed since Pate had fought Brown in Kansas three years earlier. That border war for western territory tried to resolve the nation's future on its margins, far from eastern population centers. Fewer people would be caught in a vortex of territorial disputes. Drawing boundaries on a map seemed manageable by Congress. Now a race war threatened Pate's home state, where thousands of people could die in an insurrection. The federal government rescued Harpers Ferry where its own property was at stake. Would Washington be as quick to protect the property and lives of southerners living far from federal arsenals and interests? Bleeding Kansas set rival settlements against each other. A race war would envelop households in fire and blood.

If Brown would not provide restitution, Pate determined to find it, and his knife. He published a pamphlet calling for the return of his possession. "If Brown's friend will send my weapon to me, I shall be obliged to him," he said. Pate even offered to purchase it. Then he did a most remarkable thing. Most Virginians, like Edmund Ruffin and David Hunter Strother, denounced Yankee complicity and sympathy for Brown from the safety of the South. Clay Pate headed north. To restore his honor, he reversed Brown's course. If Brown could leave his home in New York and attack southern honor in Virginia, Pate could leave his home in Virginia and attack Brown's character in New York. Five days after Brown's execution, a time when church bells tolled and millions mourned the martyr, Pate denounced Brown in a speech at the Cooper Institute in New York City. According to Pate, "If everything Brown said and done were to be taken together, nothing characterizing a truly courageous man would be found." The North was also wrong about Pate. He was not the border ruffian that abolitionist rags portrayed but a newspaper editor and lawyer, a go-ahead man. [65]

Pate prophesied looming disunion, war, and anarchy. After Harpers Ferry, he warned, the South would no longer tolerate abolitionists. In 1850, anyone who dared to predict that Virginia approached emancipation would have been tarred and feathered. In 1860, a worse fate awaited such rascals. Brown epitomized hypocritical abolitionists, "holier than thou" prophets who "would revolutionize the Union, and set unwilling slaves free, without giving them any means for supporting themselves." The North's reaction to Brown's insurrection suggested that the region preferred slavery to die in a bloody race war than by peaceful means. A looming insurrection would murder many southerners, but it could not kill slavery. Abolitionists "might as well try to abolish death as to abolish slavery. It had existed from the beginning of the world, and those making a Don Quixote war on it, might just as well make a war on death." Pate urged "the North to come to the aid of the South in the present crisis" before it was too late. "If the abolitionist papers did not stop their incendiary articles in time," Pate prophesied, "a war between the North and South would come, and wo to all those who had occasioned it." Disunion would splinter the Union into many governments, and "this glorious federation would become the prey of anarchy and confusion." Pate predicted the same chaos that Lincoln prophesied on the same stage weeks later, but they pointed fingers in opposite directions. Pate accused abolitionists of fomenting insurrections, while Lincoln suspected secessionists of conspiring for disunion.[66]

Trying to recover his reputation and turn back the clock, Pate spent most of his lecture recalling the battle of Black Jack. When the *New York Herald* reported Pate's lecture, the paper called the battle "famous" and assumed "its details are doubtless familiar to all our readers." But Pate insisted that northerners had the details wrong, because abolitionist papers slandered him and misrepresented his surrender. Instead of being a coward or dupe who surrendered his posse to nine men, he capitulated to a superior force. According to Pate, Brown confessed in jail that his army outnumbered Pate's force by five to one odds. Pate drew a bird's eye map of the battle on a large blackboard. All of the confusion he felt in Kansas disappeared in New York amid straight lines and sweeping arrows. When he asked the audience for questions, a young man in a military overcoat shot from his seat and asked, "Do you think that if I were to go to Virginia I would be allowed to speak as you speak here tonight?" "Certainly, sir, you would," Pate replied, but everything about his lecture supported the accusation within the stranger's question. Pate and his fellow Virginians would not allow northern prophecies of border war, class war, or race war in the Old Dominion. The pointer Pate carried said as much. He stood before his heckler armed with a Harpers Ferry pike. The fact that his missing knife modeled the blade escaped him.[67]

4

Prophecies

WHEN MARINES DRAGGED JOHN BROWN unconscious from the engine house, Lieutenant J. E. B. Stuart stole his bowie knife, an English blade with a beautiful tortoise shell handle. Stuart alone could confirm Brown's identity. In 1856 he rode with Colonel Edwin Sumner into Brown's camp and released Henry Clay Pate's posse after Black Jack. Stuart hated Brown and wanted Harpers Ferry citizens to kill him. He singled out David Hunter Strother, an acquaintance and prominent local man, and suggested that Brown was "a man so infamous for his robberies and murders that if the people here knew his antecedents he would not be permitted to live five minutes." Street sounds from a gathering mob penetrated the cell and disturbed Brown. [1]

Strother was more interested in sketching than lynching Brown and complained that his subject was too bloody for an accurate portrait. When Stuart ordered someone to clean Brown's wounds, another wounded raider, Aaron Stephens, remarked, "If there is any manhood in you and you are not a set of old women you should immediately have him cared for." The raider was challenging the masculinity of the South and Stuart knew it. "You son of a bitch," Stuart snapped, "your treatment is to that of midnight thieves and murderers not of men taken in honourable warfare." [2]

Other southerners followed Stuart's example of belittling the raiders' intentions while gathering battle trophies from them. The Baltimore Greys investigated a rumor that arms were hidden in the surrounding mountains. Six hours later the militiamen returned to town with two wagons filled with hundreds of revolvers, rifles, torches, percussion caps, gunpowder kegs, and cartridges. No midnight thieves stockpiled weapons like this. The raiders' possessions substantiated their plans in ways that their statements could not. Stuart took a squad of marines to Brown's headquarters at the Kennedy farm. By the time they arrived, neighbors had already ransacked the place for souvenirs. Military maps and drilling manuals littered the farmhouse floor. When Stuart checked an outlying cabin, on the first floor he found crates filled with tent canvas, axes, hominy mills, men's clothing, and boots.

Climbing to the second story, he discovered counterpanes neatly piled three feet high. Above, in the loft, hundreds of spears lay across the floor and rested against the walls. Stunned, Stuart turned to a local man, John Unseld, who guided him to the location, and told Unseld to break the attic window and throw the spears down into the yard. Unseld did as he was told. While he was tossing pikes out the window, citizens reappeared and collected them before Stuart could cart them to town. Overwhelmed by the task at hand, Stuart allowed each person to take five spears. When that amount did not satisfy civilians or diminish the work ahead, he raised each person's quota to fifty. During the spree, white southerners shattered spear shafts to collect pocket-sized relics. [3]

Trophy hunters also vied for pieces of the insurgents. After Dangerfield Newby died, people cut off his ears as mementos, picked his pockets, and stole letters from his wife, Harriett Newby, a slave. Harriett hoped Dangerfield would buy her freedom and was "looking forward to the promest time of your coming." She feared her master planned to sell her. "Then all my bright hops of the futer are blasted," she said, "for if I thought I shoul never see you this earth would have no charms for me." Medical students from Winchester dug up the bodies of two raiders minutes after they were interred and carried them to anatomy class. When one of the raider's parents asked the faculty for their son's remains, the students refused to surrender the body. "This nigger that you are trying to get don't belong to the faculty," they explained. Southerners collected things to make sense of the raid, uncover its supporters, and predict its consequences. They also savored trophies that flaunted its failure. Relic hunters had long prized the remains of slave insurrectionists, so southerners' abuse of the black raiders' bodies fit within macabre rituals. Their craze for pieces of white raiders, however, marked deepening sectional hatred. Authorities had to conceal Brown's casket and use decoy hearses to throw off relic hunters. The body of his son Watson did not make it north until the 1880s. When it arrived, fingers and toes were missing. [4]

Southerners also grasped and circulated things from Brown's raid to alert their countrymen of looming war. Edmund Ruffin believed from the start that Brown invaded Virginia to wage civil war. In his opinion, Brown's invasion deserved a southern declaration of war, but the slave states lacked unity of vision and purpose. During the hysteria surrounding the raid, Ruffin acquired "one of the spears which Brown had brought to arm the slaves." Instead of recognizing civilized, defensive European pikes, Ruffin and other white southerners saw African spears, barbaric, offensive weapons. Ruffin appreciated the difference and exploited every chance to show his trophy to the public as a warning of imminent bloodshed. The federal bookkeeper who listed things captured after the raid counted "a large quantity of spears, sharp iron bowie knives fixed upon poles, a terrible looking weapon, intended for the use of the negroes." He gave one to his wife as a souvenir. John Wilkes Booth participated in Brown's execution as a member of the Richmond Greys and took a piece of the wooden box that Brown sat on during his ride to the gallows. Booth distributed splinters of it to his friends. His prized souvenir was one of Brown's spears. Major B. B. "Bird" Washington, a member of the Winchester militia and the great-great-nephew of George Washington, presented it to Booth as a token of friendship. The weapon brought him much pride. "I helped to hang John Brown," Booth wrote, "and while I live, I shall think with joy upon the day when I saw the sun go down upon one trator [*sic.*] less within our land."[5]

When Ruffin, a little old man clutching a seven-foot spear, attracted crowds in the streets of Charlestown, he got an idea. Ruffin asked military officials for fifteen pikes, one for each slave state, and planned to send one to each southern governor for display in the state house, where his trophies would "serve as a most eloquent and impressive preacher" in his absence. These arms would express a visceral power that surpassed his best writing. His plan resembled something Ruffin did during Andrew Jackson's Bank War, when he cleverly attached calls for financial reform to the backs of bank notes before returning them to circulation. With Ruffin's artful additions, each note would "instruct by its back as many persons as it cheats by its face," Ruffin quipped. He enjoyed appropriating the enemy's objects for his own ends. The label Ruffin attached to each spear ensured that they conveyed his message:

> To the State of ________.
> SAMPLE OF THE FAVORS DESIGNED FOR US BY OUR NORTHERN BRETHREN.
> The most precious benefit derived from the Northern States, by the Southern, if rightly using it, "out of this nettle *danger*, we pluck the flower *safety*."

Ruffin was addressing slave owners who received many samples for cloth, tools, and other items from northern manufacturers. In a sense, these samples were promises that northerners made to southerners. Businesses vowed to deliver to slaveholders in the future, in bulk, the same quality items. Ruffin wanted the master class to know that Brown's spear was the genuine article, the very thing that Yankees threatened to send south en masse. Brown's spears belonged to a long tradition of insurrectionary violence, but one critical fact distinguished them: white northerners financed and forged Brown's weapons. Ruffin's samples prophesied the civil war that Yankees would bring. Harpers Ferry pikes substantiated popular accusations that abolitionists incited slave revolts.[6]

The quotation Ruffin attached to the spear, "out of this nettle danger, we pluck the flower safety," suggests how he envisioned himself as a rebel leader. The line belongs to Henry "Hotspur" Percy, William Shakespeare's famous fire-eater in *Henry IV*. Nineteenth-century Americans considered Hotspur a tragic hero, a daring nobleman who died avenging his insulted honor on the field of battle. A military hero from the countryside, Hotspur represented to southern slave owners the older feudal order that rebelled against the king's more modern style of rule that courted the masses. After the current government used guile and deceit to usurp the throne from its legitimate heirs, Hotspur sought to restore justice and reconstruct the legitimate order by purging the nation of corruption in a bloody civil war. Anticipating enemy hordes arrayed against him, Hotspur vowed, "The mailed Mars shall on his altar sit/Up to the ears in blood."

In the scene Ruffin quoted, Hotspur conducted the same chore that consumed Ruffin, corresponding with sympathizers in an attempt to galvanize a rebel alliance. Looking abroad, he and other secessionists projected themselves as conservative prophets rebelling against a modern rule that transgressed timeless laws. Figure 4.1 depicts Ruffin dressed for rebellion. Like Hotspur, southern secessionists upended the present to restore a static, fictional past.[7]

During the secession crisis, Virginians did not accept Ruffin's gift. He asked Albert Rust to deliver a pike to the new governor, John Letcher, but although Rust sympathized with secession, he objected to "having any thing to do with the pike." He feared that its mere presence could spark another revolt. When Ruffin himself offered a pike to Letcher, he stressed how it was "sent from the North to arm slaves, and to be imbrued in the blood of the whites of the South." He asked Letcher to display it in the capitol building, "as impressive and abiding evidence of the fanatical hatred borne by the dominant party of the North to the institutions and people of the Southern States." Letcher ignored the request.[8]

South Carolinians welcomed the fire-eater's gift. When they seceded a year after Brown's execution, South Carolinians gave Ruffin a special seat at the proceedings and proudly displayed his spear. It stood at the front of the hall while every delegate from the state walked past it to sign the ordinance

Figure 4.1 Edmund Ruffin. National Archives, photograph no. 111-BA-1226.

of secession. The president of the convention, David Flavel Jamison, shared Ruffin's eagerness for bold action and his frustration at fellow southerners who expected things to get better on their own. Jamison publicly berated his fellow South Carolinians for not uniting against the abolitionists' threat a month before Brown's raid. "We are looking to some sudden turn of fortune we know not what to rescue us from the doom we have not the courage to avert," he fumed. A French historian enamored with the Revolution, Jamison urged manly anticipation at the secession convention. He told delegates "to dare! And again to dare! And without end to dare," a line first spoken by

Georges Jacques Danton during the French Revolution. In the same speech, Danton outlined a war strategy that appealed to warrior prophets like Ruffin and Brown: "One portion of our people will proceed to the frontiers, another will throw up intrenchments, and the third with pikes will defend the hearts of our cities."[9]

Histories of the Future

LOOKING ABROAD, SECESSIONISTS EMBRACED the mantle of revolutionaries because they aimed to anticipate the future and make it. How intoxicating the atmosphere of looming independence and war must have felt to Ruffin and other fire-eaters. "I trust to meet you next summer—under the shadow of a Southern Confederacy," wrote one secessionist to another at the beginning of 1860. "The mirage wraps you round," Laurence Keitt reported from the Confederate founding in Montgomery. When secessionists' visions started to materialize in 1860, people convinced themselves that the prospects looming on the horizon were real and achievable. "Sail on and you will meet the ship you saw in the air," Keitt observed. "The thirsting Pilgrim sees in the Arab desert, the palm trees and the fountains—not now—but one more day stride, and he is there." Southerners only had to anticipate the future, to progress toward it with courage and initiative, and their visions would come true. "*Forward* is the inexorable word in this world," he proclaimed, "forward, for the fountains and the palm trees." It did not occur to Keitt how his perspective distorted the looming futures he sought on the horizon.[10]

Looming events seemed so tangible to Ruffin in 1860 that he wrote a history of the future. In two months, he penned over three hundred pages that foretold secession, civil war, and southern independence. The *Charleston Mercury* printed the first chapters in serial form. He titled his book *Anticipations of the Future* and considered it "the most pleasant labor of the kind that I have ever performed." This weird book of predictions defies simple description. Because the story killed thousands of Yankees in every conceivable fashion, it was a work of wish fulfillment. Because it spread propaganda to affect the presidential election, it was campaign literature. Because it literally wrote the Confederacy into existence, it was a prescient piece of literary nationalism. Because Ruffin urged society to embrace an alternative vision of the future, his work was a prophetic text.[11]

In Ruffin's history of the future, the real trouble started in 1864 when William Seward replaced Abraham Lincoln as president. Southern radicals who expected Lincoln to attack slavery directly waited in vain for an excuse to secede. Lincoln was "praise-worthy, and respected for probity, wisdom, and firmness. . . . [V]iewing the Union as a whole, he served its general interest well, and maintained the dignity of the government." William Seward was different. He persuaded the Republican Congress to serve only northern interests. They raised tariffs and improved only northern canals and ports. They commissioned only Yankees as military officers and swelled the ranks with free labor scum. Meanwhile, Seward packed the Supreme Court with abolitionists who overturned the Dred Scott decision. The value of slavery in the Border South plummeted, because runaways knew this administration ignored the Fugitive Slave Law. In diplomacy, the government acknowledged the sovereignty of Haiti and Liberia. Haitians wasted no time sending a minister, "a stout, burly negro, of clumsy frame" who called himself the Duke of Marmalade. All this time, southerners shouted but did nothing. Without bold action to back their fiery language, southern statesmen looked fierce but fragile to men across the aisle from the North.[12]

In 1867, six states (New York, Ohio, Michigan, Minnesota, Kansas, and California) voted behind closed doors to split in two, thereby adding twelve abolitionist senators and giving Republicans the three/fourths majority needed to abolish slavery. In 1868, Seward won reelection unopposed. These events finally convinced six Deep South states to secede on Christmas Eve 1868. That night South Carolina captured Fort Sumter without a single casualty. Virginia and the Upper South remained in the Union, but they warned the federal government not to tread upon their soil. When Seward sent an army through western Virginia, the Old Dominion repulsed it and seceded. The rest of the South followed, except for Texas.

The Civil War erupted in the summer of 1868. Northern armies of abolitionists invaded the South. William Lloyd Garrison captained one group of 700 whites and blacks who sailed five ships to Maryland. Their cargo included 10,000 muskets and 5,000 pikes to arm the slaves. "If the plotters had known anything of negro human nature, they might have been sure that any such conspiracy, if confided to as many as fifty negroes, would necessarily be discovered and betrayed." Southerners knew Garrison was coming three days before he arrived. Concealed along the shoreline, defenders fired into Garrison's men after they disembarked. The Yankees who fought back died of gunshot wounds on the beach. Preachers and abolitionist lecturers who came along for the adventure fled for their boats and were stabbed to death in the surf. Southerners singled out Garrison, "the apostle of insurrection and massacre," and hanged him.[13]

A much larger abolitionist army led by Owen Brown, John Brown's son, invaded Kentucky. They butchered men, women, and children "after the infliction of still greater horrors." During their first night back in the South, Negro soldiers in Brown's army deserted in the hopes of returning to their former masters. Apparently, escaping to slavery was their motive for enlisting with the enemy. "Like all other northerners, Brown was entirely ignorant of the peculiarities of negro nature, disposition, and character." An army of white Kentuckians surrounded Brown's dwindling force, massacred the Yankees, rounded up the remaining Negroes, and returned them to bondage. Kentuckians hanged Brown and twenty-seven officers from a giant oak, leaving their carcasses for the birds. The executioners were a number of Negro prisoners "who, when invited, readily volunteered to perform the . . . duty, and appeared to enjoy" it.[14]

Meanwhile, conditions deteriorated on the northern home front. Without southern commerce, thousands of northern workers lost their jobs and took to the streets. At first, they organized hunger processions to show their strength. When the war worsened, 40,000 rioters attacked New York City. The government sent 4,000 regulars into the melee. One thousand fought desperately and died in the streets. Three thousand joined the mob. By nightfall the horde controlled the city and torched it. More than a million New Yorkers burned to death under "one raging sea of flame, rising in billows and breakers above the tops of the houses." Thugs attempted the same thing in Philadelphia, but reliable military forces slaughtered thousands by firing artillery shells into the crowds. A Boston mob proved more successful. In addition to plundering the city, they hunted down and lynched prominent abolitionists. In Washington, DC, the government fled the capital after Virginia and Maryland seceded. The United States set up a temporary seat of power in Albany, while the Confederacy claimed Washington for its own capital. The only noticeable change in the District was a new law expelling free Negroes. Most blacks stayed in the city, however, because they voluntarily returned to slavery.[15]

On September 20, 1868, the North requested a truce. The terms did not recognize southern independence, but it was an established fact nonetheless. The United States was so crippled by this short, destructive war that another wave of secession seemed imminent. In time, the West and mid-Atlantic would join the stronger Confederacy, leaving fanatical New England alone, poor, and irrelevant.

At first glance, *Anticipations of the Future* looks like a gory elaboration of Ruffin's Cassandra prophecy. As Ruffin pointed out in his diary, the central point of each piece was to "show how extreme oppression may be inflicted on the southern states, & their virtual bondage to the north [secured], without any infraction of the federal constitution." In both prophecies, Republicans employ the same trick of subdividing free states to reach the three-fourths majority needed to abolish slavery. But a closer reading of the novel reveals Ruffin's attempt to write the Confederacy into existence. Ruffin crafted literary nationalism by engaging other southern novels that forecasted secession and civil war. Privileging the nostalgia of southern literature eclipses the futurity and breathless anticipation that pervaded antebellum southern writing.[16]

Ruffin first got the idea to write *Anticipations of the Future* months after John Brown's raid when he picked up a copy of *Wild Southern Scenes* by John Beauchamp Jones. The book caught Ruffin's eye because "the subject promised something," the future. Jones presented "a *prospective* narrative of the supposed incidents & results of a separation of the Union." Here was a story that anticipated secession and civil war at a time when Brown's raid resurrected Ruffin's hope for the future. Imagine how disappointed Ruffin was when he reached the end of the book only to find disunion averted and sectionalism dissolved. "A very foolish book," Ruffin concluded, "which I regret having bought, or spent the time in reading." In Ruffin's opinion, Jones "shows little sagacity in his conceptions of future political consequences & events." For someone like Ruffin who followed political developments obsessively, *Wild Southern Scenes* was too true to its title. Jones spun harebrained scenarios, outrageous accidents, and unlikely characters that spoiled the potency of his prophecy. Perhaps the book's idea, Ruffin mused, "might be carried out to good purposes" by someone who scanned the political horizon scientifically. Three days later, Ruffin set himself to the task by writing the first seven pages of *Anticipations of the Future*.[17]

Jones's history of the future foretold a revolution that would exceed the French Reign of Terror. Northern authorities erected a guillotine in every city and township. Tribunals of Three investigated and executed people suspected of sympathizing with slavery and the South. Claiming the right of Revolution, a northern tyrant named Ruffleton assumed the title Lord Protector and planned an empire reminiscent of Rome. His Senate would consist of hereditary nobles drawn from the finest families. His subjects would identify themselves as Americans only; all state lines would be erased, all sectional affiliations would vanish within the new empire. His ambitions failed when Britain joined the war to finish off an old enemy. Stirred by the return of their revolutionary foes, American armies united, repelled the invaders, and reconstructed the Union.[18]

As Ruffin wrote *Anticipations of the Future*, he also consulted *The Partisan Leader* by Nathaniel Beverley Tucker, Ruffin's friend and distant cousin. A law professor at William and Mary, Tucker set the standard for southern histories of the future in 1836 when his book predicted that Martin Van Buren sought the presidency to secure northern dominion over the South. Like Ruffin, Tucker timed his publication in an attempt to influence the presidential election. Tucker warned that Van Buren conspired to turn the presidency into a dictatorship by creating a sectional majority party that would help him win an unprecedented third term of office. When Van Buren accomplished his plan, Virginia was the only southern state that supported his reelection. The rest of the South coordinated a swift secession movement and formed a separate nation. Instead of using political power to attack slavery, Van Buren and the North oppressed the South economically through taxes and tariffs that filled northern coffers. The Yankees also drained the federal treasury for personal gain. Here Tucker's prediction echoed the recent nullification crisis instead of the development of radical abolitionism in the North, still a small movement in 1836. Freed from northern tariffs, southerners embraced free trade markets and prospered. The Southern Confederacy preserved the legacy of the Revolution, the spirit of the Union, and the laws of the Constitution. Virginia dawdled, unsure about abandoning the nation it sired. Meanwhile, Van Buren turned the Old Dominion into a military base to launch attacks against the South and to intimidate Virginians into political submission. This tyranny convinced Virginians that the South was correct all along. When Van Buren sought and won a fourth term of office, Virginians refused to support him and launched a secession movement in the midst of Van Buren's statewide military camp. What ensued was a nasty guerrilla war that tested the allegiance of every Virginian and decided the fate of free government in America.[19]

Tucker predicted how a civil war that had roiled beneath the surface of American life for so long would boil over. In 1849, western Virginia, with its mountain gaps and natural fortresses, sheltered guerrillas intent on freeing their state from federal occupation. A West Pointer from Virginia, Douglas Trevor, abandoned his military commission after a painful period of indecision and became the partisans' brilliant commander. Douglas's older brother, Owen, remained in the federal army that subjugated his native state. For Tucker, the brothers' war theme implies more than allegiance tests and sectional conflict. By casting the younger family members as heroes and heroines, Tucker argues that younger Virginians would be more willing and able to restore the state's honor and rights than their cautious elders. The family patriarch, Hugh Trevor, is a virtuous statesman who has served the federal union too long to recognize its corruption and dissolve it. Hugh's younger brother, Bernard, upholds the same republican principles, but has devoted his life to serving Virginia, so he is more willing and able to ally with the true defenders of liberty when civil war erupts. Likewise, the next generation of Trevors demonstrates varying levels of devotion to the federal union depending on age. The oldest son, Owen, serves as Van Buren's henchman with hopes of winning promotion and power. The middle son, Douglas, struggles mightily with whether his duty lies with the federal army he swore to serve or the state he loves. The youngest son, Arthur, rushes to join the Virginia partisans when he is old enough to shoulder a musket.[20]

Antebellum southerners, like other Americans, lived during an era of changing temporalities. Instead of expecting cyclical decline and regeneration, many Americans anticipated inevitable advancement. William Trescot considered progress "the first principle of life." In religion, prospective millennialism eclipsed a retrospective biblical vision focused on original sin. In politics, thinkers shifted their focus from conserving civic virtues from the past to realizing national ambitions in the future. As someone who shook hands with George Washington and yearned for southern independence, Tucker exemplified both approaches to time. *The Partisan Leader* reconciles this tension and marks this shift toward the future by assigning different allegiances to Trevor men according to age. Tucker also relies on biblical allusions. He names Douglas Trevor's mountain hideout the Cave of Adullam, David's natural fortress during his war against Saul. Like David and Saul, Douglas and Owen are fighting a family feud for government power and virtue. In both cases, the younger rival fights a more just war, God blesses the younger man, and the elder dies. By defying primogeniture Tucker also alluded to an established Old Testament theme of God favoring younger sons. Youthful virtue rather than customary privilege will restore freedom and order to the world. Such biblical allusions grounded Tucker's vision of the future in providence and glories past while also lifting his anticipations toward progress and the notion that brave men and women could break the cycle of republican decay.[21]

These books by Ruffin, Jones, and Tucker provided blueprints for secession and war. To show how earnest they were, each prophet rejected conventions of nineteenth-century novels to discourage the impression that their work was fictional. Instead, they wrote histories of the future in the past tense that relied on "eyewitness" accounts. Tucker's history is written by a southern soldier who "fought" in the Civil War. When the narrative strays dangerously close to the nineteenth-century novel—during love scenes, for instance—the narrator interjects, "In this true history, I am unfortunately bound down by facts," and therefore have no time for romance. To drive home the point that his work is history, not fantasy, Tucker listed the publication date of *The Partisan Leader* as 1856 instead of 1836, when it appeared in print. Jones narrates the future's history from an omniscient perspective but concludes with the narrator waking from a nightmare. In effect, the writer dreamed the nation's future, awoke in the present, and reported the portentous events as a warning. Ruffin's familiarity with both books helped him to devise a simpler narrative strategy. He assumed the voice of a *London Times* correspondent reporting the war to Europe. Devoid of dialogue and written from the perspective of a neutral observer, *Anticipations of the Future* reads more like an edited collection of primary documents than a novel.[22]

Like historical memories, these historical anticipations told stories of another time that empowered the few, oppressed the many, and justified institutions and conditions in the present. Tucker, Jones, and Ruffin epitomized the region's prospective focus on time. Southerners remembered a past that affirmed their present identity, but they also anticipated a future worthy of remembrance, a future that avoided complacency, decay, and the anchor of past precedence. Tucker looked forward to "the magnificent future, and glorious destiny of a Southern Confederacy."[23]

Treating anticipations of the Civil War as the temporal partners to historical memories of the conflict is the first step to unlocking Ruffin's prophecy of blood. John Brown's pikes awoke visions of a new future within Edmund Ruffin. Reading Jones's novel showed Ruffin how he might lead the South to a new identity and future by narrating it in advance. His anticipations also justified possession not of land but slaves. As sectionalism intensified throughout the antebellum period, southern secessionists rewrote the region's past, present, and future in an attempt to shield the South from external criticism and internal dissension. Demonizing the North and predicting an apocalypse was important for convincing southerners to secede, but no less important were secessionists' efforts to order southern society so that each race, gender, and class banded together in the crucible of secession and war.[24]

All three books empower white men by showcasing their natural leadership during warfare. Each text projects a future made by white patriarchs who echo the visionary zeal of Patrick Henry, the republican virtue of George Washington, and the military genius of Francis Marion. Aristocratic blood distinguishes the southern heroes in each future epic. Jones gives his hero the most aristocratic name of all, Randolph, and models him after Washington by making him a president who takes to the field of battle as commander in chief. *The Partisan Leader* obsesses about class distinctions. In the opening scene, yeomen in buckskin materialize from the rugged terrain to encircle a handsome young rider. The stout frontiersmen belong to a partisan band and halt the rider to learn his identity before allowing him to penetrate their hideout. Though the youth lacks their skills as woodsmen and their experience as veteran soldiers, his "whole air would have passed him for a gentleman, in any dress and any company, where the constituents of that character are rightly understood." Social standing makes the stranger their superior from the moment his class is confirmed. The hero in *Anticipations of the Future* mirrors the partisan leader in Tucker's book. Both men are Virginia aristocrats trained at West Point who reluctantly resign from the army before assuming leadership of locals. Partisan bands reified the social authority of white patriarchs without relying on the military sanction of a distant government. These prophecies recalled the southern legacy of the American Revolution and anticipated the Confederate pantheon of Robert E. Lee, J. E. B. Stuart, and John Mosby. Such anticipations also prefigured the éclat white southerners would bestow upon shrouded riders of the Ku Klux Klan. Regardless of which time these visions address, chivalrous gentlemen ride to the rescue of local commoners and lead yeomen to victories over federal henchmen. Past, present, and future told similar stories that elevated white patriarchs by praising their inherent ability to save the South.[25]

While they empowered white men, southern literary nationalists gave white women minor roles at best in the future Confederacy. Women are absent or passive in all three histories of the future. Ruffin briefly mentions women as victims of merciless invaders and urges southern men to teach ladies how to shoot. The women in Tucker's prophecy are no more than courtship prizes, and when powerful men compete for female attention, Tucker dismisses this as an unfortunate digression from the important work of statecraft and warfare. The only powerful woman in all three works is Charlotte, the mystic in *Wild Southern Scenes*. Modeled after Cassandra, Charlotte knows the future and saves southerners from disasters, but even she is denigrated. Randolph says she would have made a great general if she had been a man. Instead of encouraging his daughter to emulate Charlotte's foresight and patriotism, Randolph repeatedly tells her to be like marble, immovable and statuesque during warfare. When Tucker, Jones, and Ruffin wrote a southern nation into existence they designed no public space for women.[26]

All three works justify slavery by arguing that blacks preferred bondage to freedom and would defend the southern institution against invading abolitionists. Black Confederates play a more decisive role in southern anticipations of the war than they do in Lost Cause memories of it. In Ruffin's work, loyal slaves save the South by informing their masters about the approach of northern armies. In Ruffin and Jones, blacks who joined enemy ranks reveal their true colors and switch to the Confederate side at pivotal moments to turn the tide in major battles. Slaves pull off a similar trick in Tucker's prophecy when they capture Yankee soldiers who wrongly assumed that black southerners would view federal troops as liberators. When the federal officer learns about the trick that slaves played on his men, he gasps, "Regular troops prisoners to negroes!" and asks how it is possible. The master replies, "The eagle is no match for the owl in the dark." Using their cunning, nocturnal ways, the slaves destroy US soldiers who fatally misjudge them. Tucker prophesied, "There is an exhibition to be made, which will have a good effect on friend and foe, —I mean an exhibition of the staunch loyalty and heart-felt devotion of the slave to his master." He expected that the Civil War would provide an opportunity for southerners to "show that that which our enemies, and some even of ourselves, consider our weakness, is, in truth, our strength." Jones projects the same role for black Confederates, prophesying that "the world will then see that our slaves did not augment our danger, or even embarrass us, when the enemy came into our country." He envisioned "more than two hundred thousand of our negroes" will be "doing valuable service in the construction of fortifications, and in collecting provisions and materials for our armies. And this they [will] do most cheerfully, and even beg to fight for us!" Such forecasts helped southern intellectuals solve what historian Eugene Genovese calls "the slaveholders' dilemma": how to square southerners' faith in freedom and progress with their defense of human bondage. Confederate prophets anticipated the slaves would be the South's wild card, the unexpected asset that clinches southern independence and propels civilization forward.[27]

Examining anticipations reveals common purposes shared by visions of the future and past. Because the future is as inaccessible as the past, forecasters participate in the same process of choosing details, plotting narratives, and granting meaning to a time that people practice when creating memories. Tucker, Jones, and Ruffin could have chosen myriad foreseeable events to fashion the future. Similar to the purveyors of southern memory, they stressed social, economic, and political "events" that spoke to contemporary concerns in 1860 and empowered southern white patriarchs. The subtitle of *Anticipations of the Future* baldly proclaims the purpose of Ruffin's history of the future: *To Serve as Lessons for the Present Time.* As such, anticipations and memories reveal more about the individual, society, and context that create them than about the time they depict. This insight stresses the primary reason the analytical category of historical memory is useful for interpreting cultural anticipations, but there is another way to understand visions of the future.[28]

The Prophetic Imagination of a Secessionist

RELIGIOUS STUDIES OF PROPHECY illuminate dimensions of futures past that remain obscured by inverting memory studies. At first glance, this idea seems dubious when applied to Ruffin's book. Ruffin opened *Anticipations of the Future* by flatly denying any prophetic power. Anticipations come from many sources; prophecies, by definition, have one, divine origin. Speaking to readers through the voice of reason, not God, Ruffin "designed to deduce correct conclusions [about the future] by sound reasoning" instead of relying on miracles or unfettered fantasy. But Ruffin's notification marked his place within, not beyond, a wide spectrum of prophetic thought in nineteenth-century America. Premillennialist Millerites and Mormons, postmillennial evangelicals, utopian perfectionists, spiritualists, providential boosters of manifest destiny, and secular champions of scientific progress all fixated on the future. Religion, particularly Protestant faiths, informed how nineteenth-century Americans imagined the coming era. Every stripe of prophetic imagination illuminated the past, present, and future in its own shade. But this spectrum of American prophecy also blended together in imperceptible places and ways. Sharp dichotomies of sacred and secular, religious and scientific, faded in the luminous and liminal world of American prophecy. Whether they relied on faith in providence or confidence in progress, nineteenth-century visionaries believed the future was discernible. When Avery Craven judged Ruffin's religion "a strange mingling of reason and faith," he described nineteenth-century American cosmology in general. Judeo-Christian expectations and practices preconditioned even the modern, rational forecasts of nineteenth-century southern intellectuals like Ruffin.[29]

A classic religious study, Walter Brueggemann's *The Prophetic Imagination* helps to make sense of Ruffin's work as a prophetic text. By stressing "the constitutive power of imagination," Brueggemann shows how prophetic scriptures spread "poetic scenarios of alternative social reality," a task strikingly similar to the goals of literary nationalists. He insists that prophets not only describe but also create alternative worlds through prose, verse, and symbolic action.[30] He defines prophetic imagination as a consciousness that topples power and liberates society by spreading alternative perceptions of reality. This definition obviously describes the works of Moses, Jesus Christ, and Martin Luther King Jr. It also depicts the labor of secessionists. The prophetic imagination of Edmund Ruffin and other "apostles of disunion" upended authority and freed a political minority by urging a radical alternative for the future. The prophetic imagination of Ruffin and his colleagues worked beneath causes and nationalisms to shape *how* the conflict was imagined and fought. "The task of prophetic imagination," according to Brueggemann, "is to cut through the despair and to penetrate the dissatisfied coping that seems to have no end or resolution." Secessionists like Ruffin faced the same mission. Heading into the election of 1860, the country despaired of finding a solution to sectionalism. Compromises unraveled. Men of action loathed the stale air of congressional debate. Secessionists imagined a way through the political impasse and beyond southern nightmares of racial equality and political impotency. Their prophecy also "cut through the despair and penetrated the dissatisfied coping" that marked Ruffin's life at this time. When he completed his book, Ruffin confessed, "I fear this writing of mine . . . would offer to a capable judge, indications of a failing mind." Harpers Ferry inspired a prophecy that gripped Edmund Ruffin until he shared it with the world.[31]

Brueggemann explains that prophets must accomplish three tasks to escape hopelessness and inspire change. First, speak concretely about the newness that awaits society and how it will redefine the world. Second, bring public expression to people's suppressed dreams. Third, offer enduring symbols that contradict and upend prevailing perceptions of reality. Ruffin attempted all three in *Anticipations of the Future*. His work described the new southern nation vividly and showed how it would change North America and the world. Throughout the book, he redefined America by inverting popular expectations. Slavery, not free labor, proves to be the stable, productive labor system in wartime. Negroes prefer slavery over freedom. New Orleans, not New York, becomes the commercial capital of North America. The Northeast, not the South, is politically ostracized. Washington, DC, is the capital of the Confederate, not the United, States of America. Ruffin ends the novel with New England, not the South, descending into an economic and political pit similar to conditions in Haiti. Brueggemann found similar inversions in the prophecy of Second Isaiah. He explained, "When the Babylonian gods have been mocked, when the Babylonian culture has been ridiculed, and when the dethroned king is re-enthroned, then history is inverted." The same can be said about Ruffin's work: when Yankee gods have been mocked, when Yankee culture has been ridiculed, and when masters return to power in Washington, then history is inverted.[32]

Second, Ruffin publicly expressed southerners' suppressed hopes and yearnings. He fulfilled southern dreams for prosperity, freedom, and peace, but only after he lashed northerners with a violent reckoning. US soldiers and sailors receive no quarter throughout Ruffin's war. Abolitionists are singled out and lynched by irate northerners. The prophecy fulfilled secessionists' guarantee of a short war by calling a truce after months of terrible destruction. In the preface, Ruffin promised southerners that the "means for safe and perfect defence, and for full retaliation . . . , for achieving independence, and for securing the subsequent preservation of peace, and unprecedented prosperity" are "as certain as can be any events of the future." Masters also wanted to believe that slaves preferred bondage, their "natural" condition. As a humanitarian sensibility spread throughout the Atlantic world, southern planters loudly professed that their slaves loved them. This deep yearning is the decisive factor in Ruffin's war: the Confederacy wins because masters understand the hearts and minds of black people.[33]

Third, Ruffin spread enduring symbols that contradicted prevailing perceptions of reality. Brueggemann argues that prophets spread hope by borrowing familiar signs from collective memory and projecting them into the future. Ruffin's prophecy evokes southern memories of the American Revolution, the fundamental symbol of America's challenge to "the regnant consciousness." The eight years when southern statesmen deliberate, form conventions, and appeal to the government for justice echo the decade when colonists sought redress from the king before declaring independence. Ruffin's war mirrors the scale and nature of the War for Independence. Armies of a few thousand campaign across the countryside while companies of minutemen rally to battles. His combat scenes replicate Lexington and Concord when "single marksmen [fired at the enemy] from every place of concealment." The novel also contains memories of the conflict that Ruffin knew firsthand as a veteran, the War of 1812. In Ruffin's war, armies burn cities and the government abandons Washington, DC, calamities that Americans had not experienced since their last war with Great Britain. By evoking these historical memories Ruffin tried to kindle southern nationalism by recalling a time when southern masters forged and defended their sovereignty against mighty, tyrannical powers.[34]

Ruffin and other Civil War Americans found meaning within their turbulent time by looking forward as well as backward. On a superficial level, each section's projections of the American Revolution can be read as attempts to legitimize secession or sanctify the Union. But beneath the surface of political rhetoric, their search forward and backward in time shows how people used the most relevant symbols, memories, and prophecies to orient a present that departed from the rest of their experience. In other words, prophecy and memory reinforced each other by addressing the crisis from opposite directions. Historian Elizabeth Varon argues that southerners practiced the same Janus-faced search for meaning during the political crises of the 1790s. She writes, "In every instance, Southern intimations of disunion looked backward and forward. They tapped anxieties and resentments about the founding itself, particularly anti-Federalist fears that government consolidation would undermine state sovereignty. But disunion talk also served warning that a new opposition party was consolidating, with a strong base among Southern and Northern agrarians alike, and would challenge the Federalists for control of the national government." The meeting of memory and prophecy gave meaning to the present.[35]

This interplay of remembrance and anticipation is evident when Ruffin's *Anticipations of the Future* is compared to "The Blackwater Guerrilla" (1851), a narrative he wrote about his grandfather's experiences during the Revolution. Relying on manuscripts he discovered when he moved to Coggin's Point Farm and interviews he conducted with old men who fought beside his grandfather, Ruffin wrote a family history of the Revolution to preserve the past for his descendants. Ruffin begins "Blackwater Guerrilla" by telling his family, "I am not writing a history." As his subtitle makes clear, this is an oral "tradition of revolutionary times." Locals shared legends of the Blackwater Guerrillas with their children and grandchildren by the fireside and recalled old adventures during Independence Day celebrations. The history of George Washington, Benedict Arnold, Lord Cornwallis and Lafayette, of Bunker Hill, Cowpens, and Yorktown may have filled the schoolbooks that local boys carried on their daily walks through the countryside, but their imaginations were fired by stories of shadowy partisans conspiring in the Blackwater swamp to strike the redcoats and vanish in the night. The land had changed some since the Revolution, but the swamp was still there.[36]

In both "Blackwater Guerrilla" and *Anticipations of the Future*, Ruffin spills considerable ink showing how conditions worsened because of the inaction of well-intentioned southerners. Both stories look back with regret on missed opportunities from a future vantage point when things are a mess. "Blackwater Guerrilla" tells a story of Virginia in 1780, five years into a terrible war. When the British military shifted its forces from North to South, local communities lacked the resources to resist. Men of military age were away serving in General Washington's army, crippled from that service, or dead. The community had given most of its arms to the cause, which left the home front vulnerable to marauding enemies. "The farms visited by the plundering parties were not only stripped of every portable article that could be useful to the robbers, & convenient for them to take away, but property of far greater amount & value, which they did not want, & could not remove, was often wantonly destroyed." The invaders were also emboldened by local Tories who revealed their sympathies now that the British occupied the area and seemed to be winning the war.[37]

People fled to the Blackwater swamps when marauders approached their houses. The landscape offered their sole refuge against invaders and neighbors who betrayed them. This state of affairs greeted Edmund Ruffin's grandfather when he returned from a tour of service as a captain of Minutemen. Owner and resident of Coggin's Point, Ruffin "found his house deserted, his slaves & other property left at every risk of loss, & his wife sojourning at the residence of a friends' family on the border of Blackwater swamp." Ruffin quickly formed a band of partisan rangers from men in the neighborhood, many of them too young for military service.[38]

On their first adventure, Ruffin led his men on a night raid against the British supply line. Ruffin's lieutenant ordered the partisans to give quarter to the British, but in the confusion of a night battle, the partisans slaughtered all but one man who found the protection of the lieutenant. Edmund Ruffin does not explain where his grandfather was during the massacre or why he failed to stop it. As if to excuse the atrocity, he notes that one of the dead was a large black man dressed in sailor's clothes. Ruffin's band suspected the man was a fugitive slave from Charleston who had joined the British to serve as their guide. Apparently not all slaves were as loyal to their masters as Edmund Ruffin wished to believe. In the end, the attackers captured a boat with supplies for Lord Cornwallis, one hundred knapsacks, and the camp equipment of a major. Ruffin's party divided the loot. They suffered no casualties and killed eleven enemy soldiers in addition to the black guide.[39]

Ruffin admits that partisan fighting did not conform to the rules of honorable warfare, but he excuses it by stressing the atrocious behavior of the enemy and by insisting that circumstances made guerrilla tactics the people's only option. When he compares this night raid to his grandfather's final action of the Revolution, Ruffin calls fighting at Yorktown "more dignified, though perhaps less useful service" than his leadership of the Blackwater guerrillas. Ruffin, Tucker, and Jones apply the same rationale for defending partisan warfare and promoting secession. Secession, like partisan warfare, may be irregular but it is acceptable, even honorable, when gentlemen resort to it to protect their property and rights from a merciless enemy. Under both conditions the natural born leaders of the South would rise to the occasion. For Ruffin, fighting against the threat of emancipation, racial equality, and race war justified the Blackwater massacre in 1780 and Virginia secession in 1860.

Revolutionary Times

LINKING THE AMERICAN REVOLUTION and secession suggests that hope animated southern fire-eaters. However, when southern radicals like Ruffin pushed for disunion they spread nightmares from another revolution. Haiti motivated secessionists as much as the spirit of 1776. At John Brown's trial, Andrew Hunter insisted that Brown "wanted the citizens of Virginia calmly to hold arms and let him usurp the government, manumit our slaves, confiscate the property of slaveholders, and without drawing a trigger or shedding blood, permit him to take possession of the Common wealth and make it another Hayti." During the campaign of 1860, Albert Bledsoe, an old friend of Lincoln, warned that black Republicans sought to reenact "the first act in the grand drama of Haytien freedom." Quoting Archibald Alison's popular history of the revolution, Bledsoe claimed, "The negroes marched with spiked infants on their spears instead of colors; they sawed asunder the male prisoners, and violated the females on the dead bodies of their husbands." Weeks after Lincoln's election, the Reverend Benjamin Palmer prophesied Louisiana's future if the state did not secede. "Sapped, circumvented, undermined, the institutions of your soil will be overthrown; and within five and twenty years the history of St. Domingo will be the record of Louisiana. If dead men's bones can tremble, ours will move under the muttered curses of sons and daughters, denouncing the blindness and love of ease which have left them an inheritance of woe." Secessionist commissioners prophesied racial equality, race war, and racial amalgamation if slave states remained in the Union. "If we fail," Stephen Hale warned, "the light of civilization goes down in blood, our wives and our little ones will be driven from their homes by the light of our own dwellings, the dark pall of barbarism must soon gather over our sunny land, and the scenes of West India emancipation, with its attendant horrors and crimes . . . [will] be re-enacted in their own land upon a more gigantic scale." Confederates reiterated these points when the war worsened and Lincoln proclaimed emancipation. James Thornwell hoped the South would "diffuse the very liberty for which Washington bled" by resisting the revolution for which Louverture died. Thus, he insisted, "We are not revolutionists; we are resisting revolution."[40]

In 1860, historical memories of Haiti inspired the prophetic imagination of South Carolinian Mary Howard Schoolcraft. In its final chapter, Schoolcraft's *The Black Gauntlet: A Tale of Plantation Life in South Carolina* forecasts a future more terrifying than the prophecies of Ruffin, Jones, and Tucker. According to Schoolcraft, the Harpers Ferry raid would inspire other "disorganizers" to choose violence over sectional compromise. "We will put weapons in the hands of the Africans," they said; "we will supply them with torches, swords, and pikes, instead of Bibles." Schoolcraft imagined how a slave revolt would engulf the South when a president belonging to the "Ethiopian equality party" took office. "The great outbreak of the French Revolution, in 1798, was not more sudden, desolating, and bloody." Aided by covert abolitionists, the slaves consumed the South in "fire, massacre, and barbarian cruelty and treachery" until "the extermination of the white race seemed inevitable." Only "the high spirit of the old cavaliers and gentry" saved white southerners from extinction. "Streams of African blood" stained the Mississippi river red. "In a few months a *million* of negroes were put to the sword." This recurrence of Haitian gore repulsed northern voters who ousted the abolitionists from power, but not until the South seceded, established the "United States South," and forged diplomatic and commercial treaties with Europe that empowered the South and ruined New England. Schoolcraft's southern confederacy renounced Thomas Jefferson's "false political apothegm" that all men are equal. She concludes her vision with judgment day. When God calls forth the souls of masters for a final reckoning, "each one of these slave-holders will approach the throne of God bringing thousands of redeemed African heathen in their train; and every one of them, masters and servants, will receive the plaudit, 'Well done, good and faithful servant; enter thou into the joys of thy Lord.' "[41]

Revolutions required an acceleration of events and movement along a new trajectory that was as social as it was political. As Karl Marx expressed it, "Every revolution dissolves the old society, and to that extent is *social*. Every revolution dissolves the old power, and to that extent is *political*." Marx, like Robespierre and Jefferson, insisted that successful revolutions benefited all humanity and not just the winners. By this logic, civil wars in modern times were not simply internal conflicts but world events. Their outcomes either forwarded or hindered all humanity. "We are passing through one of the greatest revolutions in the annals of the world," Alexander Stephens proclaimed during the Confederate founding. Stephens announced that the cornerstone of his new republic was racial slavery, and this government, the first of its kind, introduced a new chapter of political progress for the world.

"Looking to the distant future," Stephens prophesied, "all the great States of the north-west will gravitate this way, as well as Tennessee, Kentucky, Missouri, Arkansas, etc." In time "our destiny, and our high mission, will become the controlling power on this continent." George Bagby prophesied global domination for southerners' slaveholding republic. The "Republic of Virginia" would govern half of the world because of its reliance on African slavery. The other half would be ruled by Russian serfdom. In "Ethnogenesis," Henry Timrod celebrated the slaveholding republic by prophesying that it will "give labor to the poor,/The whole sad planet o'er." Timrod composed the poem in the future conditional tense, using the word "shall" fourteen times. George Mercer also reveled over "the grand mission before us; we must conquer the prejudices of the world and prove to Christendom that we are right—that our government is founded upon the truths of the Bible and the nature of man."[42]

Because of these stages of civilization, revolutions were not national events but global transformations ushered in by movements of ideas and the rebuilding of social structures and governments. Americans understood the looming revolution not only within their own revolutionary past but also within the international revolutions of their own time. After secession, this southern appeal to liberty garnered support but not recognition from the world. Across the political spectrum and around the world, people understood the looming civil war as a final test of the republican experiment. Liberals elevated the experiment as an unprecedented development that promised to break old cycles of political systems and encircle the globe with freedom and democracy. Conservatives derided the experiment as an unproven government destined to collapse as its predecessors had since ancient Rome. Both visions of revolution anticipated historic futures. The Civil War would secure either the future of democracy or slavery in the world.[43]

Ruffin's analogies to the Revolution and his decision to prophesy through a voice of reason illustrate a modern, anticipatory temporality. His view of time and prophecy contrasts with those of Judeo-Christian prophets who assert authority by expecting God's future. God's prophets do not reason or prove things; they reveal providence, God's cosmic hand on the future. The Enlightenment created a different type of prophet, the rational prognosticator who forecasts how humanity, not God, will make the future. These more secular prophets applied experience and knowledge from the past to glimpse an empty future in which men make tomorrow. Mississippian William Carey Crane called them "political prophets." Men who studied the "habits, tastes, aptitudes and idiosyncracies" of past civilizations to know how humanity will act "in the future under given circumstances" may seem prescient or gifted. But "the infallible connection of cause and effect is a law" that illuminates the visions of political prophets. "Given a cause, no prophet is required to predict an effect," because logic and common sense "predicate" all future outcomes. In 1860, Crane told Mississippians, "The political prophet may look forward to that august period, when the mere dream of our present political economists shall have been realized." [44]

The faith that Ruffin, Crane, and other secessionists placed in political prophecy echoed the logic that Thomas Jefferson articulated in the Declaration of Independence. That document exudes a rational approach to prophecy and history: "When in the course of human events it becomes necessary for one people to dissolve the political bands which have connected them with another, and to assume among the powers of the earth the separate and equal station to which the laws of nature and of nature's God entitle them, a decent respect to the opinions of mankind requires that they should declare the causes which impel them to the separation." In Thomas Jefferson's prophetic imagination, people make history and seize the future by relying on logic. For Jefferson, Ruffin, and Crane, the future belonged to reasoning men who act decisively.[45]

This anticipatory temporality ordered society for Jefferson, Ruffin, and other southern patriarchs. Neither Jefferson nor Ruffin deemed African Americans capable of intelligent, rational action and saw them as governed by superstition rather than reason. Masters frequently claimed that their slaves lacked a profound understanding of the past and the future; their bondsmen lived solely in the present. Instead of facing an empty future of limitless possibilities, slaves faced no future at all. By definition, the slave's future belonged to the master. In Ruffin's more sectional era, he denied that northerners relied on reason and a boundless future. For him there was no clearer sign that the South would prevail in a civil war than his conviction that reason and experience governed southerners while religious fanaticism controlled the North. This belief supported his prophecy that New England would descend into barbarism. Only reasoning men who learned from history and weighed the consequences of actions (and inaction) could design the future. Beyond childish slaves, a host of others lived beneath Ruffin's esteem because they lacked self-control and reason. Emotive women, drunken immigrants, fanatical Yankees, and vanishing Indians lived for the past or present but not the future. As William J. Grayson predicted in his epic poem, "The Hireling and the Slave," "Like their wild woods, before the Saxon's sway,/The native nations wither and decay. . . . Such, too, the fate the negro must deplore,/If slavery guard his subject race no more."[46]

Conceiving an open future that is foreseeable through deductive reasoning encouraged Ruffin to favor anticipatory action over reactionary expectations. Southern firebrands like Ruffin are often deemed reactionary men, but Ruffin's prophecy, his agronomy, and his strategy for immediate secession were proactive. When a South Carolina crowd serenaded Ruffin, he urged them to secede and provoke a war with the United States because "the first drop of blood spilled" would compel Virginia and every other slave state to South Carolina's side. By acting first, South Carolinians channeled the reactions of others. In *Anticipations of the Future*, Ruffin urged southerners to strike the first blow. He mocked southern Unionists and cooperationists who preferred to wait until northerners violated the Constitution. Such men were "submissionists" in Ruffin's opinion. The term teems with racial and gender connotations but it defines a passive mode of action, not a racial or gender ideology. John Townsend articulated this point when he asked, "Will the South remain a passive victim, and, like the timid sheep, allow itself to be bound whilst the butcher is preparing the knife for its destruction; or will she not rather throw off, at once, her degrading sloth and cowardice, and, summoning her ample powers, throw off a government which is about to be taken possession of by her deadly enemies?" Secession may bring civil war in its train, but Townsend preferred conflict to the "*folly of a timid submission*," which would seem peaceful in the short term while Yankees perfected their plans but, in the end, would doom southerners with "emancipation of their slaves; then poverty, political equality with their former slaves, insurrection, war of extermination between the two races, and death, or expatriation, to fill up the picture." Ruffin's novel makes the same argument by beginning with hundreds of pages that describe the South's tortuous passivity while the North artfully maneuvers toward abolition without giving southerners the clear insult they expect. Once the docile spell is broken, however, the South roars to life and crushes the North in a short, destructive war. Months of aggression accomplish a result that years of hesitancy nearly ruined.[47]

The prophetic imagination of Ruffin and other secessionists complicates our understanding of nineteenth-century nationalism. Benedict Anderson argues that nations created "imagined communities" by using clocks, media, railroads, and telegraphs to stress the simultaneity of time. People belonged in the same nation because they experienced the same present. Southern fire-eaters contributed to this illusion by circulating pamphlets and newspapers. Ruffin, for instance, helped to found the Association of

1860, a propaganda agency for secession. But the century's technologies and print cultures also expressed a restless, heterogeneous time that looked backward and forward for cause and effect, beginning and end. The Confederacy relied on history and prophecy to create its imagined community. Americans reflected each new development of the crisis through their understanding of past troubles and future forebodings. Newspapers made this process possible, and one of the most influential southern presses, Robert Barnwell Rhett's *Charleston Mercury*, published Ruffin's *Anticipations of the Future*. When each fictional chapter appeared in the *Mercury*, it looked and sounded exactly like the day's news. Ruffin and Rhett gave readers the impression that they were reading the future. During the secession crisis, *De Bow's Review* also published excerpts from *Anticipations of the Future* that stressed the "fidelity of slaves to their masters" during the looming revolution. By obscuring distinctions between present and future, news and prophecy, the secessionists molded collective consciousness and political action. They made secession and war appear inevitable.[48]

During his pilgrimages for disunion, Ruffin used symbolic actions as well as words to link secession to the American Revolution. Anticipating Lincoln's election, Ruffin sought a southern orator to play the part of Patrick Henry. He chose William Yancey and pointedly asked him in a long, pleading letter, "Will you be the Henry for this impending contest?" Ruffin assured Yancey, "Move in it at once, and I would stake my life on the venture that your success will not be less complete and glorious than that of your great example." As he toured the South, Ruffin wore a Virginia homespun suit to exhibit his support for southern independence. When he spotted South Carolina Minute Men wearing the blue cockade of past revolutions, he joined their ranks and had one sewn on his hat. After the South Carolina legislators voted to hold a secession convention, he convinced the editor of the *South Carolinian* to replace the state flag outside his press office with the Fort Moultrie flag as a "symbol of 'the expected Southern Confederacy.'" Whether consciously or not, Ruffin performed his prophecy throughout the South in ways that echoed Ezekiel's strenuous, public expressions of his prophecy. Ruffin's performance exuded a vigor and force that belied his age—the work of prophets and revolutionaries was physically demanding. In a real sense, secession was Edmund Ruffin's religion. He even dated his belief in disunion to a time when a revival swept his family, but not him, into evangelicalism.[49]

Orphaned from the Past

RUFFIN'S PAST SHAPED HIS prospective bent and imagination. When he marched to John Brown's scaffold, no frailty of body or mind betrayed his age among soldiers. At five feet eight inches tall and one hundred thirty pounds, his frame was economy incarnate. He did not smoke, drink, gamble, or chase women, ate only when necessary, and worked relentlessly. Only his most striking feature, a white waterfall of hair that poured down his neck and shoulders, marked his sixty-five years. At Harpers Ferry, Ruffin's legs remembered how to march in step, a task he had not performed since the War of 1812.

If financial hardships shaped John Brown's prophecy, family tragedy molded Ruffin's vision. Ruffin's mother died before he could remember her. She had been an orphan when she married George Ruffin, and her two brothers followed her to the grave during Ruffin's childhood. When Ruffin tried to fill his family tree in 1856 the only thing he knew about his mother was her name. His father's line was also ravaged by deaths. For three generations, a single Ruffin son survived to adulthood. This tenuous line of male heirs buried their wives and children in family plots. As an adult, Ruffin fought the miasmas that he believed killed his family with the same vehemence that he fought Yankees. As a boy, though, he was powerless to combat forces that killed his kin and deprived him of a family circle. Ruffin knew his paternal grandfather and his father, but the rest of his Old Virginia family and their legacy had vanished.[50]

Ruffin spent most of his childhood alone in his father's library. His closest friends were Shakespeare, Scott, Dickens, Brontë, and Eliot. Ruffin read all of Shakespeare's plays before his eleventh birthday. When he entered William and Mary at sixteen, Ruffin lived off campus and did not forge lasting friendships. He spent hours every week devouring newspapers and literary reviews. He also scoured scholarship, from Malthus on politics and Smith on economics to Davy on chemistry, Lyell on geology, and Gibbon on history. If death's pervasiveness had persuaded Ruffin to distance himself from others, a second round of family deaths reinforced this habit. When Ruffin was thirteen, his grandfather died and left his farm at Coggin's Point to him when he reached maturity. Three years later, when Ruffin was struggling to pass his first year of college, his father died. Ruffin found himself an orphan with no kin. A neighbor, Thomas Cocke, became his legal guardian.[51]

Ruffin's circumstances were not unusual in the early republic. Mortality rates encouraged millions of Americans to focus on the afterlife and devote their worldly work to reaching Heaven where they expected an eternal family reunion. Feeling adrift and rudderless, Ruffin sought solace and understanding in the Bible and at the Episcopal church he attended. But most scripture and doctrines failed his test of reasoning. Despite his best efforts, he did not believe in Heaven. Instead of an afterlife, he expected decomposition in the grave, a natural, cyclical returning to the earth that his guardian Cocke emphasized.[52]

When the United States declared war against Great Britain in 1812, it seemed that forces beyond his control would provide Ruffin what religion, education, and family had not—his future. He traveled to the militia muster in Prince George County and volunteered to serve in a company of the Fourth Virginia Regiment. Private Edmund Ruffin was eighteen when he marched to Fort Norfolk on the Chesapeake Bay, where he searched the horizon for enemies. At the beginning of 1813, the British Navy appeared in Hampton Roads shortly after Ruffin and his company returned home. Though military service did not give Ruffin experience in battle, it did impart some significant impressions. He witnessed how a naval blockade could stifle the southern seaboard and raid interior tributaries. From Hampton Roads the enemy quickly implemented a strong blockade that radiated across the Chesapeake Bay and up the James River. Their vessels carried marines who disembarked to raid the estates and communities on the shores and riversides. Ruffin recalled, "Along all these shores were the richest farms and the most dense slave population in Virginia; and wherever the British landed they were complete masters for the time, and usually the only white occupants of the place." According to Ruffin, the enemy stole slaves and other valuables, but the slaves were taken by force of arms, not by seduction or deception. From this he learned that when war came to the South, slaves would be loyal to their masters. Whenever the British threatened the tidewater counties, the militia called out the white male residents to face the threat. This left women, children, and property "all in the power of the slaves, and all in perfect security." Ruffin knew of no incident of the slaves destroying crops, stealing property, or harming people. Their presence, while the farmers and planters were off at war, ensured that the fields were maintained and the harvests collected. Far from being a threat to the South in time of war, slavery was a valuable asset.[53]

After returning from war, Ruffin convinced Cocke to grant him his inheritance: 1,582 acres and fifty slaves. He realized he knew nothing about farming. Instead of trusting the African Americans who had tilled the soil for generations, Ruffin turned to his father's books for advice. As a boy he had read Thomas Hale's *The Compleat Body of Husbandry*, a four volume, eighteenth-century English manual for country gentlemen. Hale began with a narrative history of agriculture that attributed every advance in farming to Europeans from ancient Romans to the modern British. He then dissected the whole business of farming from the ground up, beginning with soil management. Despite its claims to comprehensive knowledge, Hale's books proved "totally unsuited to this country." Then Ruffin turned to *The Arator*, celebrated essays by fellow Virginian, John Taylor. When Ruffin's farm continued to suffer, Cocke tried to convince him that his soil was static and sterile. Sure that Virginia's glory would never return, Cocke walked into the woods with a shotgun and committed suicide. Ruffin lost his best friend and only mentor.[54]

Instead of succumbing to despair, Ruffin fixated on the future. He started conducting experiments on his farm and keeping detailed records. He married Susan Travis and started a family. When nine of their eleven children survived childbirth, the future took on more significance, and the pressure to fix the farm increased. A proactive mindset informed by reason and experience guided Ruffin's agronomy. Through trial and error he discovered how marl prepared the soil for fertilizer. The same temporality and assertiveness animated his pursuits of secession and agronomy. In his famous essay on calcareous manure, Ruffin urged farmers to shake their passive dependence on old ways and seize a more prosperous future by saving southern soil from ruin. "If we may venture to leave the sure ground of practical experience," he wrote, "and look forward to what is promised by the theory of the operation of calcareous manures, we must anticipate future crops far exceeding what have yet been obtained." As an advocate of "book farming," Ruffin believed that planters who read the latest agricultural science and applied experimental practices on their plantations would revive the soil, yield greater crops, and thus become masters of a more prosperous future. Farmers who distrusted new approaches enslaved themselves to customs that doomed the land. In agriculture and politics, Ruffin dreamed of southern regeneration through independent reason and proactive agency.[55]

Ruffin hoped that his achievements would garner him fame and political power. All the ingredients seemed to be in place: manor born to an old family of Virginia gentlemen, married to a prominent family from Williamsburg, an accomplished planter and master of slaves, educated, refined, Episcopalian, with a dash of military service. These distinctions secured Ruffin a seat in the Senate of the Commonwealth, but he resigned before the end of his term. He lacked charisma and his nerves got the better of him. Ideas that were well formed, arguments that were perfectly arrayed, and phrases that were graceful and lucid in his mind spilled out of his mouth incoherently. He had vision but no voice. After his failed term in the state legislature, Ruffin pursued writing instead. He founded an agricultural journal, published books and pamphlets, and sharpened his quill in political propaganda. Still, in this age of oratory, men of influence were heard, not read. Ruffin remained a fringe figure, a radical reformer on the outskirts of politics. Avery Craven insightfully suggests that Ruffin's handicap merely excused a political failure predetermined by his temperament: too independent for parties, "too honest for intrigue, too stubborn to be manipulated, too sensitive to rebuff, he was not a successful politician." Exile on the political periphery freed him to focus on the future. He became a prophet.[56]

A Prophet Is Not without Honor

DURING THE SECESSION CRISIS, Ruffin stepped into the spotlight. He dropped the pseudonyms of an editorialist and the anonymity of a conspirator to appear in public as a national founder and an old man in uniform. He drew increased attention from friends and enemies and relished the fame that had eluded him all his life. Ruffin traveled across the South spreading his prophecy and encouraging its fulfillment. Northerners noticed how Ruffin borrowed religious practices to agitate for southern nationalism. *Frank Leslie's Weekly* featured a story about him, explaining that "the old man goes from Convention to Convention a political Peter the Hermit, preaching secession wherever he goes." According to legend, Peter the Hermit, a priest from Amiens, sparked the first Crusade by traveling across France prophesying a war to reclaim Jerusalem. Ruffin liked the article so much that he kept a copy in his scrapbook. He started to compare himself to Christ. On the night he preached secession to a serenading crowd in Columbia, South Carolina, he scribbled in the margin of his diary an observation Jesus had made, "A prophet is not without honor but in his country and among his own kin, and in his own house."[57]

The scripture proved truer than Ruffin cared to admit because his own children and household challenged his anticipations of the future. Three nights before the presidential election, his two eldest sons, Edmund Jr. and Julian, visited to debate the looming war. They feared Lincoln's election, hoped to avoid it, and counseled patience when facing the coming crisis. Their father was excited and impatient to fashion the future while it still seemed pliable. "I wish the question tested & settled now," he said. "If there is general submission now, there never will be future maintenance of our rights—& the end of negro slavery may be considered as settled." He regretted that voting in the election postponed his departure for South Carolina for three days. The impending fate of the South consumed Ruffin. "I can think of little else," he confessed.[58]

After Ruffin left for South Carolina, Edmund Jr. mailed his father sober assessments of the political mood in Virginia and urged caution. He estimated that Virginians were "opposed to secession 8 to 1, and to the exercise of it by our southern friends." The Old Dominion would not join a Southern Confederacy unless doing so averted bloodshed. Fears of "Civil & Servile War" consumed Virginians when Edmund Jr. discussed the future with them. "What I fear," Edmund confessed, "is that some of the Hot heads of the South will come into unnecessary collision with the Fed. Troops in some way." "Let the first blood be shed by Fed. arms," he counseled his father. Edmund Jr. urged Ruffin and South Carolinians "not [to] be hasty in an attack on the forts." "Try negotiation first, it may save a bloody civil war."[59]

Julian also stressed political divisions within the South and recommended restraint. The vast majority of men in his neighborhood opposed secession. Surveying the Upper South, he predicted "there is no hope of the border states going with the South now." Only "madness" by the Republicans could compel them to secede. Like his older brother, Julian thought that South Carolina was moving too quickly and rashly. He was disappointed to hear that federal workers in the state had resigned their posts. Customs officials and postmasters in particular would better serve the state by going back to work instead of resigning to flaunt their political allegiance. Worse, Julian heard a "rumor of a collision between some federal authorities & the citizens in relation to the removal of certain arms." Violent demonstrations by citizens "might lead to serious results." Julian warned his father, "Northern people are determined to fight." He hoped "all may end peaceably" but worried that secession would atomize North America. Looking to the future, he expected "the border states on each side of Mason & Dixon's line" would form a third nation between the extremists North and South. All sorts of contingencies and scenarios seemed possible during a chaotic winter. Ruffin's sons favored secession but they wanted the South to be sober, deliberate, and careful about the process. They had grave doubts about the unity of the slave states. They abhorred war and sought any strategy that might lead to peaceful disunion.[60]

Edmund Jr. and Julian presented a formidable argument against their father's prophecy, but the strongest, most outspoken disagreement with his anticipations of the future came from his daughter, Mildred Ruffin Sayre. Living in Frankfort, Kentucky, Mildred understood divisions within the South far better than her father. She read papers from across the country, including the Deep South, the Upper South, and the North, to gauge shifts in public sentiment about the future. While Ruffin traveled through South Carolina, Mildred read *Anticipations of the Future* and told her father, "It seems to me your predictions are coming to pass far in advance of the time appointed. But I am in hopes that the fighting part will not come to pass." Like her brothers, Mildred hoped the nation would avoid bloodshed. She and her sister Elizabeth both "hoped that all the Southern states would secede to-gether." She encouraged Ruffin to seek grace and trust providence instead of progress. "The things of this world, when they become so engrossing sometimes crowd out these better, pious feelings." She knew him too well. She sensed how worldly renown and anticipatory politics captivated him more than religion and eternal life.[61]

While Edmund Ruffin anticipated a war that led to southern glory and independence, Mildred expected the conflict would bring interminable suffering and uncertainty to the South. "The future looks very dark," she warned him. Though she sympathized with South Carolina's position, she feared "coming events." "I do not see how civil war is to be avoided," she told her father, "and oh, what sufferings & troubles and losses we shall all have to suffer in case of war." She prayed that God would spare the nation from bloodshed. Mildred understood why Ruffin "would enjoy exceedingly the exciting & stirring events that are taking place in the seceding states," but she saw nothing to celebrate. She heard dark portents of "so much suffering in those states that have withdrawn" from the Union, and "more than all, with civil war threatening" she could not "look to the future with any pleasure." Kentucky was deeply divided about the future. Her husband taught school and "a good many boys in his school [were] from Mississippi." Mildred considered it a sign of southern divisions that "the other boys call them foreigners." She would rejoice over secession "if the South were more united." Mildred planned to visit Ruffin in the summer, but "ere that time our whole country may be plunged in war, and I don't know what will become of us."[62]

In addition to cooperative secession, Mildred wanted the South to seek equal rights first through national conventions and last-minute compromises before resorting to disunion and risking war. Her father argued, "*Delay is Submission*." In his view, "not a day's postponement of action shall be allowed to the urgent arguments of friends (real or pretended) in favor of delay of secession." Mildred disagreed, "I fear that S.C. and some of the other southern states are hurrying our whole country into civil war," she told Ruffin. She warned him, "Public feeling will turn very much against S.C. if she hastens things." Mildred denounced the brash anticipations of South Carolina and could not "see why she should be in such a hurry to take Fort Sumter." Instead, "a great deal ought to be done, and ought to be borne before we plunge into a war, which will be the more violent for being between brothers, and the end of which we may never see." Her words proved prophetic. Most of the Ruffins, including Mildred, would not survive the war that their father was about to start.[63]

While his family awaited the looming war, Ruffin was in South Carolina fulfilling his prophecy. Staring at Fort Sumter in Charleston harbor, Ruffin was living his imagined future. It was the most gratifying experience of his life. During the summer of 1860, he had acquired detailed information about the harbor and fort from friends in the federal government. When rumors swirled that the Confederates would resist attempts to supply the fort's garrison on April 8, Ruffin raced to the Citadel, borrowed a musket, and boarded a steamboat to be in the harbor when his anticipated war began. Nothing happened. The following morning, he embarked with a boatload of volunteers for the Confederate batteries at Morris Island. The spectacle of an old man with long white hair clutching a musket and eager to fight drew a crowd and commanders of many regiments urged Ruffin to join their unit. He chose the Palmetto Guards because he anticipated that their position would be in the center of the looming battle. He was right. When drumbeats summoned men

Figure 4.2 Bombardment of Fort Sumter. Currier & Ives, Library of Congress, Prints and Photographs Division.

to their positions before dawn on April 12, 1861, Ruffin fired the first shot of the war. The shell struck the northeast parapet of Fort Sumter. As Figure 4.2 shows, Confederate batteries that ringed Charleston harbor opened fire. When Major Anderson surrendered, Ruffin carried the Palmetto Guards' flag at the ceremony. To mark the historic event, he gathered relics. Picking through the debris, he pocketed shell fragments and, when no one was looking, cut a swatch of fabric from the first Confederate flag to fly over conquered territory. History seemed to be happening exactly as Ruffin prophesied.[64]

5

Anticipations

WHILE FIRE-EATERS SPREAD HARPERS FERRY pikes for secession, abolitionists displayed them for liberation. Horatio Rust stamped his original pattern pike in honor of his old friend: "CAPT JOHN BROWN EXECUTED AT CHARLESTOWN, VA DEC 2 1859." When Brown's body arrived in New York City, P. T. Barnum offered $100 for his clothing and a pike. The undertaker, Jacob M. Hopper, kept Brown's clothes to promote emancipation. Hopper belonged to a Quaker family of abolitionists who ran the Underground Railroad and supplied the Harpers Ferry raid. The Hoppers gave William Lloyd Garrison one of Brown's twelve original pikes, and the pacifist prized it. Garrison noted that Virginia's motto, "*Sic semper tyrannis*," asserted the slave's right to kill his owner. Virginia's state seal showed a man conquering his oppressor by wielding a pike. Thomas Russell, the Massachusetts judge who sheltered Brown after he fled from Kansas, visited Brown in jail and carried home a pike. Philadelphia abolitionist James Miller McKim escorted John Brown's widow, Mary Brown, to and from Charlestown, received the pike that Brown's son Oliver carried, and gave it to Wendell Phillips. When a Virginia slaveholder mailed Phillips a lock of Brown's hair to flaunt the raid's failure, Phillips cherished it. McKim and Phillips were so convinced that Harpers Ferry relics could spark a war against slavery that they advocated touring John Brown's body across the North. Mary Brown refused.[1]

Visions of white northerners freeing black southerners through bloodshed recalled Harpers Ferry and anticipated the Civil War. Standing before Brown's casket, Wendell Phillips predicted that the Harpers Ferry raid, though a short-term failure, would kill slavery in the end. For years, Phillips disputed a popular charge that abolitionists lacked foresight. Critics argued that immediate abolition would cause long-term economic and political problems that reformers ignored when they advocated revolutionary change. Pointing to the aftermath of British emancipation in the Caribbean, proslavery advocates accused abolitionists of imagining emancipation as a moment instead of a process. Phillips countered that slavery deadened Americans' imagination of the future. Northern reactions to Brown's raid supported his point. After the execution, some Bostonians judged Brown foolish for wasting his life, just as their ancestors regretted Joseph Warren's death at Bunker Hill. Like Warren, Brown sealed the doom of despotism by sacrificing himself at the beginning of a long war for freedom. It only took time to see the truth. "History will date Virginia Emancipation from Harper's Ferry," Phillips predicted.[2]

Phillips prophesied a revolution for equality, while Edmund Ruffin forecasted Confederate independence. Both were certain that their side would win the looming war by relying on reason. "The North *thinks*—can appreciate argument,—it is the nineteenth century." "The South *dreams*—it is the thirteenth and fourteenth century," Phillips explained. For Ruffin, the South would prevail because practical experience guided its leadership while religious fanaticism consumed northerners. When Ruffin observed "Fanatics do not reason" in *Anticipations of the Future*, he doomed Phillips's cause. Phillips countered that passions clouded southern thinking about secession. He considered Ruffin's shot at Fort Sumter to be "the yell of pirates against the Declaration of Independence." Men like Ruffin raced to war because their motives and plans could not withstand a sober, reasoned inspection.[3]

Like Ruffin, Phillips relied on prophecy to frame the looming war. After the surrender of Fort Sumter, he read from the prophet Jeremiah to encourage Massachusetts men to march to war. "I proclaim liberty for you, saith the Lord, to the sword, to the pestilence, and to the famine." God willed the war to accelerate history and progress. Phillips anticipated that disunion would create "the very irrepressible conflict which they leave us to avoid." The southern nation would require native industrialists and merchants who would oppose slavery from within the Confederacy. Capitalism would kill slavery and raise a southern middle class in its wake. If the Revolution secured independence, the Civil War would guarantee equality. Emancipation would be the logical consequence of rash reactions by Edmund Ruffin and other fire-eaters. The secessionist's "declaration of independence is the jubilee of the slave." Phillips predicted that each cannon would speak better than a thousand abolitionists.[4]

Abolitionist forecasts shared a sense of anticipation that unfolding events offered a unique chance to purge the nation. As events quickened, northern fervor intensified faster than reformers anticipated. Deep South secession and the bombardment of Fort Sumter stirred public passions that abolitionists hoped to direct toward emancipation. On April 19, 1861, 100,000 New Yorkers rallied for war in Union Square, where they cheered defenders of Fort Sumter and applauded Oregon senator Edward Baker for promising to sacrifice 750,000 men in the looming war. Northern radicals interpreted such responses as a long-awaited public turn in favor of emancipation. McKim faced the future with breathless anticipation. "We never expected anything but *temporary* disunion," McKim explained, "We knew that collision would come, then abolition, and then we supposed re-union. But we are having all these together." Astute observers recognized that people were getting ahead of themselves. Enthusiasm in 1861 convinced Americans that they could sense how the drama would unfold. Abolitionist Eliza Wigham recognized the dangers of this sensibility. Society's confidence could not clarify the future. Because of their eagerness to realize anticipations, people overestimated the likelihood of things happening. They also underestimated the time it would take to fulfill them. The war spirit of 1861 even swept up Garrison. "I think dear Garrison's prophetic spirit has led him to believe that what he sees *will* come out of the present excitement *has already* come," Wigham said. Radicals like Ruffin, Phillips, and Garrison misjudged their control over the future. Millions of ordinary people, like those who crowded Union Square, also anticipated the looming war, and their collective imaginations and actions would eclipse the influence of reformers.[5]

Hearing the Future

BEYOND BEING A STATE of mind, anticipation was a sense and emotion. Anticipations aroused bodies, channeled thoughts, and consumed energy. Hearts pounded, breath quickened, and hair stood on end. When William Nugent anticipated the looming war in 1861, his emotions were "conflicting and nearly overwhelming." The "vindictive spirit" that consumed Nugent terrified him as a Christian. Sounds as well as sights aroused Americans' attention to looming events. The imagined outcome pleased some and terrified others, but whether people dreaded or dreamed of war in 1861, anticipating the future heightened feelings and consumed attention. The sounds that Civil War Americans recorded and the music they made echoed their anticipations.[6]

Sounds from the looming war came from different voices that overlapped in time, and people sought the direction of change above the noise and the tempo of change beneath it. Living through momentous events was a sensation akin to listening to new music. Each successive event was relational to the whole. Anticipation was an evolving grasp of the whole as each moment made that whole more complete by unveiling not only a new piece of it but also a new perspective from which people anticipated the next step in the process. Successive events—Lincoln's election, South Carolina's secession, Fort Sumter's surrender—were linked developments that showed the direction of looming war. Groups debated where the future was heading in 1861 but no one questioned that the year would be momentous. While events revealed the melody of history unfolding, the crowding of news quickened the pace and intensified the times, heightening awareness of the looming war.[7]

Sensory history helps to explain how the sounds of 1861 affected feelings about the future. Revolutions release a cacophony because people assert their right to be heard. During the presidential election and secession crisis, rising decibels in debates silenced opposing views and foretold impending war. In October 1860, Andrew McCollam tried to describe for his father the excitement swirling through sleepy Centenary College in Jackson, Louisiana. "You may imagine the clatter there is at meal time," he said, where, "the subject of politics is very much discussed." "Every street corner is the scene of an animated discussion . . . and on every side the ear is greeted with the lengthy harangues of embryo politicians." When the war came, Centenary's faculty closed the school for lack of students.[8]

Charleston became the epicenter of southern sound in 1861. A city known for its quiet order changed its acoustics once South Carolina seceded and prepared to shell Fort Sumter. If we could hear the city before the war began, historian Mark Smith explains, "It would resemble a mounting crescendo, the volume increasingly turned up until eardrums almost shattered." Men shouted secession in the streets, toasted the death of the Union, and serenaded fire-eaters like Ruffin until they gave impromptu speeches. Inside Fort Sumter, Abner Doubleday thought the "many threats and noisy demonstrations" anticipated war. When Charleston erupted with cannon fire, the symphony of war was literally deafening for Ruffin who lost hearing in both ears from manning a mortar. *London Times* correspondent William Russell was on the streets of Charleston after Fort Sumter fell and reported "crowds of armed men singing and promenading the streets." A military symphony echoed off buildings: "clanking spurs," rhythmic footfalls, "drummers beating calls." Russell recognized the tune of the times because he had heard it before, in Paris in 1848. George Templeton Strong heard the same sound in New York City the following day as the Sixth Massachusetts marched to Washington. The "immense cheering" swept him up. "My eyes filled with tears, and I was half choked in sympathy with the contagious excitement."[9]

Marching tunes heralded the future by filling the air with anticipations of forward movement. Standing still was intolerable in 1861. As John Pierpont explained in his poem "Forward!," God taught Union recruits that "the primal plan /of all the world, and man,/is Forward! Progress is your law—your right." Only despots wanted people to stand still; only tyrants enchained slaves. Freedom meant looking forward, coming forward, and moving forward. The most popular song in the Union army in 1861, "John Brown's Body," insisted that everyone and everything was "moving on." Alice Cary's "Song for Our Soldiers" urged Union volunteers to march to the center of the war and win it. Cary wanted the Union army to charge, shoulder to shoulder, into the South, find white southerners, tear them apart with cannon fire, then find black southerners, and break their chains. Frederic Hedge captured how synchronous northerners were with the music of war in "Our Country Is Calling," "Our heart-beat echoes the beating drum, /Our thoughts with the trumpet tally." "All knew that the more a man sings, the better he is likely to fight," one volunteer explained. "So we sang more than we slept, and, in fact, that has been our history ever since." Another recruit marveled while a city of tents "were all raised at the beat of a drum." The power of sound to synchronize and embolden the nation seemed limitless.[10]

Confederate music used similar tempos and themes to arouse men to fight. When Baltimore citizens attacked the Sixth Massachusetts one week after Fort Sumter, the bloody riot stirred Confederate hopes that Maryland would join the Confederacy and thus encircle the Union capital within rebel territory. Baltimore native James Randall heard about the riot while teaching in Louisiana. The news electrified him. Unable to sleep, he felt possessed by a spirit, and wrote the lyrics to "Maryland, My Maryland" in the middle of the night.

> I hear the distant thunder-hum,
> Maryland, my Maryland!
> The "Old Line" 's bugle, fife, and drum,
> Maryland, my Maryland!
> She is not dead, nor deaf, nor dumb;
> Huzza! She spurns the northern scum—
> She breathes! She burns! She'll come! She'll come!
> Maryland, my Maryland!

Newspapers spread the poem across the South, and Baltimore singers set it to the tune of an old college song. Their performances became so popular that federal authorities exiled the singers to the Confederacy. When rebel volunteers marched to war, Randall's song rivaled the popularity of "Dixie" because it expressed the relationship between sounds, allegiances, and anticipations. A Confederate veteran remembered how soldiers sang it "with a good deal of hope and vim." Randall and other Maryland secessionists hoped that their state was not out of step with the times. When the Army of Northern Virginia invaded the state in 1862, soldiers entered Maryland as liberators and sang the song with the earnest belief that its lyrics anticipated the future. This sensation of feeling the future unfold intoxicated raw recruits. When a South Carolina regiment received its battle flag, the sound was deafening as several bands played music and the men joined in singing. That night one of them confessed, "I felt at the time that I could whip a whole brigade of the enemy myself."[11]

The Seat of War

THESE ACOUSTICS OF 1861 excited Americans who anticipated the looming war as a unique chance to liberate society from the past and fashion the future. Forecasts of a ninety-day war full of fun and frolic, vows that one recruit could whip ten enemies, promises to drink all the blood spilled by secession, such sentiments anticipated a short, romantic war. These boasts also shared a popular feeling that people controlled the future and whoever reached the "seat of war" would make history. More than a synonym for warfront, the "seat of war" represented the abstract heart of the conflict where an open prospect beckoned to people who had the foresight and courage to reach it first. In May 1861, Mississippian James Kirkpatrick noted "a common enthusiasm and eagerness for the fray" among recruits deepened into "a rivalry among different organizations who should be first in the field." When Henry Shaw of the Second New Hampshire Infantry received orders to pack up and march into Virginia, he wrote a letter on the back of a map titled "Interesting Bird's Eye View of the Seat of War" and mailed it home. On the eve of the battle of Bull Run, Shaw wanted his family to preserve the seat of war under glass as proof that he was among the first to reach it. The war transformed the antebellum race of life into a race to the heart of the war's activity. Go-ahead men proved themselves by being the first to the fray. In Boston, Augustus Ayling heard rumors for weeks that his 29th Massachusetts Volunteers were headed "for the 'seat of war,'" and finally believed them when the men mustered on May 21, 1861, and received the materials of war: "knapsacks, haversacks, canteens, dippers, knives, forks, spoons, etc."[12]

The firing on Fort Sumter angered Philadelphian Ambrose Hayward. "My mind labors under a high state of excitement," Hayward told his brother. Rebel boasts to make slaves of northerners and unfurl "the Palmeto

[sic] Rag over the Capitol at Washington" incensed him. "I have a feeling at times of late, a kind of burning in my bosom since these troubles have commenced." He envied the first recruits. "They seem impatient for the field. Every one has a smile upon his face. you would suppose they were going . . . on a pleasure Excursion." Hayward volunteered on his twenty-first birthday. "I have loafed long enough," he told his father. "21 years ago I was an Infant in arms, now I am to arms in Infantry, Just as I expected." "The boys are all alive with Ecitement of moveing and i must join them," he explained to his sister. His company boasted a fine glee club, and Hayward found it "hard to write with 200 men surrounding me with their yelp singing." When Hayward received ammunition, it smelled like blood and sparked dreams of "driving the Rebels if we met them at the point of our Sword Bayonetts."[13]

A deeper look reveals that not everyone anticipated a ninety-day war. On April 11, 1861, the eve of the war, Arthur Carpenter wished for a long, terrible struggle to restore the republic's virtues. "I believe that a war of 5 or 10 years would be a great thing," he said. "It would purge our nation of some of its filth and dead heads, and then we should be ready to commence anew." Perhaps through the powers of regenerative violence the United States could last another eighty or ninety years. A twenty-year-old shoemaker's apprentice from Indiana, Carpenter imagined war as humanity's greatest meritocracy, a contest that exposed "fops and light brained scoundrels . . . in high places" and replaced them with natural leaders like him. "Big men seem willing to drink all the blood that will be spilled by this war," South Carolinian Jesse Walton Reid noted in June 1861. "I think they will have to be as big as they feel before they do so," he predicted. Politicians "may possibly be able to drink all they themselves have shed, but I fear they will not be able to take the whole bottle. Time will show." Reid understood that the fall of Fort Sumter did not whip or conquer the enemy. "That thing remains to be done hereafter, if at all." When Reid marched to Virginia he knew he might never return. In Ohio, James Garfield echoed Reid's predictions. He could "see no possible end to the war till the South is subjugated." "There can be no doubt that we are now entering upon a terrible and bloody war." Garfield was prepared to sacrifice a million lives for the Union.[14]

What anticipators had in common in 1861 was not what they forecasted but how they approached the future physically and mentally. Whether they envisioned a war that was short or long, bloodless or destructive, anticipators felt empowered by the possibilities of the conflict, stressed human agency, and raced toward an open future with urgency. In

January 1861, Governor Thomas Moore of Louisiana seized the federal arsenal in his state before Louisiana seceded. The day after Fort Sumter fell, Josiah Pender, the owner of the Atlantic House Hotel in Beaufort, gathered seventeen men, called them "Pender's Battery," and captured Fort Macon from a stunned Union sergeant. Like Moore, Pender anticipated the future—North Carolina remained in the Union for more than a month. Days later, Henry Clay Pate seized his second chance at military glory by forming "Pate's Rangers," a cavalry company of sixty men. He armed them with carbines that he fished from the wreckage of a sunken ship at Norfolk and joined Wise's Legion, an independent command created by former governor Henry Wise.[15]

Orlando Poe articulated the mindset behind such conduct when he headed to West Point in 1852. Poe sensed "a bright prospect before me" and "it rests with me alone whether it shall be bright" or "blackened forever." Similar beliefs intoxicated eighteen-year-olds, the largest age group in both armies during 1861. Going to war, they thought, would be a coming-of-age experience for them and the nation, and like Poe they imagined the future in stark polarities. Faith that the future offered them a unique opportunity to make history empowered youths and radicals on both sides. As Phillips expressed it, Lincoln was "in place" but Garrison was "in power." Abolitionists were "pioneers of a Christian future," and the war seemed to clear their path to that future.[16]

In 1861, Confederate leaders anticipated an exclusive opportunity to forge a nation in the fires of war. Henry Wise rejoiced, "It is a war of purification." He told recruits, "You want war, fire, blood to purify you; and the Lord of Hosts has demanded that you should walk through fire and blood—You are called to the fiery baptism and I call you to come up to the altar." He insisted, "The call is for action," not reflection or reason. "The man who dares to pray, the man who dares to wait until some magic arm is put into his hand . . . is worse than a coward." Wise urged southerners to "take a lesson from John Brown." "Get a spear. . . . Manufacture your blades from old iron, even though it be the tires of your cart-wheels." Make your own bowie knife, because "your true-blooded Yankee will never stand still in the face of cold steel." Wise wanted Confederates "to get into close quarters, and with a few decided, vigorous movements, always pushing forward, never back," they would assert sovereignty by sweeping away enemies that polluted southern soil. His call to arms articulated America's fascination with blades and close-quarter killing. In 1861, thousands of volunteers posed for portraits brandishing bowie knives.[17]

Professional soldiers anticipated how the looming war offered them a rare chance for meteoric promotion. In 1861, lieutenants and captains who had not distinguished themselves during peacetime clamored to become colonels and generals. General George McClellan wrote his wife, "By some strange operation of magic I seem to have become *the* power of the land." At age thirty-five, McClellan sensed his chance for greatness. In April 1861, Orlando Poe served as McClellan's staff officer. The general remarked to Poe that the looming war "is much better than managing Railroads and adding up columns of dollars and cents." Poe, who was trained as a topographical engineer, agreed. "There is something extremely exciting about all this. One feels as though he were really amongst men and likely to take a part in manly deeds." No more gazing at stars and winding chronometers for Poe. The future promised him "a struggle amongst men, where the supreme intellect must tell." Like Henry Wise, Poe forecasted, "This is a Holy war." He was equally confident that his was the side of "progress and truth."[18]

Anticipating Freedom

IN 1861, ENSLAVED AMERICANS who raced toward the war seeking freedom exemplified anticipations of an open future that beckoned to the bold. Millennialism, faith in Christ's imminent return, and Jubilee, an Old Testament prophecy of freedom, framed black anticipations of the looming war. As historian Matthew Harper explains, "It was a belief in the intersection of human history and divine history that gave African American believers a window on the future." Their time and God's time met when the war started. Slaves anticipated the conflict as divine reckoning for the sin of slavery and the fulfillment of prophecies by Jeremiah and other biblical figures. The war created unprecedented circumstances and opened opportunities for slaves to forge their future. Uncertainty enshrouded the present, but one fact was clear—masters like Edmund Ruffin had started a war they could not win without the help of slaves. How black southerners approached the war would affect its meaning and outcome. For anticipators in the slave quarters, the surest path to that future was the shortest one to the seat of war.[19]

On May 23, 1861, the day that Edmund Ruffin and other Virginians celebrated their state's ratification of secession, three enslaved men, Frank Baker, Shepard Mallory, and James Townsend, anticipated freedom and grasped it. While white Virginians toasted their entrance into the Confederacy, Baker, Mallory, and Townsend commandeered a boat and rowed four miles across the estuary to Fort Monroe. Twelve thousand Union soldiers garrisoned the old stronghold that guarded Hampton Roads and the naval approaches to Baltimore, Washington, and Richmond. Baker, Mallory, and Townsend had worked at Sewell's Point, digging artillery emplacements aimed at the Yankee fort. Their master, Confederate Colonel Charles Mallory, sensed the danger of leaving them within sight of the enemy and told them he planned to take them to North Carolina where they could work for the Confederate army at a safer distance from Yankees. All three men had families in the area and moving to another state held no appeal to them. Seeking a better future for themselves across the bay, they had no assurance that Union guards would allow them inside the fort. Rowing toward the Union pickets at night, the men risked being shot. If they made it inside the fort, there was no guarantee that Yankee officers would grant them asylum.[20]

Friends and family anxiously waited to see if the three men returned. A Massachusetts private stationed inside Fort Monroe recalled how the slave community responded to the news. "There was no known channel of communication between them and their old comrades; and yet those comrades knew, or believed with the certainty of knowledge, how they had been received." Soldiers asked the runaways if more were coming and the black men said, "If they were not sent back, others would understand that they were among friends, and more would come the next day." Scores of slaves followed. "Such is the mysterious spiritual telegraph which runs through the slave population," the soldier observed; "proclaim an edict of emancipation in the hearing of a single slave on the Potomac, and in a few days it will be known by his brethren on the Gulf."[21]

Harry Jarvis heard the news and seized the chance to escape his master, "the meanest man on the Eastern shore." Conditions on the plantation deteriorated "after the war come." The day his owner shot at him, Jarvis "reckoned I had stood it about as long as I could, so I took to the woods." Hunted by patrols and dogs for three weeks, Jarvis relied on friends for news and food. When his master posted men along the shoreline to catch him if he tried to escape to Fort Monroe, Jarvis waited until his master's birthday. "I knew they'd all be drinking and carousing night and day, and all the servants be kept home, so I took the opportunity to slip down to the shore in the night, got a canoe and a sail, and started for Fort Monroe." Out on the water, a storm raged over his little boat, but Jarvis was not afraid. "It was death behind me, and I didn't know what was ahead." What was ahead was Jarvis's future and he was determined to reach it that night. "I just asked the Lord to take care of me, and by and by the wind went down to a good steady breeze straight for Old Point."[22]

Jarvis arrived at Fort Monroe the next morning and told General Benjamin Butler he wanted to enlist. Butler said it was not a black man's war. Jarvis prophesied, "It would be a black man's war before they got through." While Butler envisioned a short, romantic war for the Union that would liberate black southerners to punish traitors, Jarvis anticipated a long, destructive war that would require black soldiers for victory. Not content to labor for the federal government in exchange for food and shelter, Jarvis wanted a uniform and pay. The future could not arrive fast enough for him. When he saw a man at Fort Monroe returned to his master, Jarvis decided it was time to move on. He "hired on to a ship going to Cuba, and then on one a going to Africa, and was gone near two years." He returned in 1863, when his prophecy was fulfilled, and enlisted in the Fifty-Fifth Massachusetts Infantry.[23]

In spring 1863, John Washington found freedom in Falmouth, Virginia, when cannon fire disrupted breakfast at the hotel where he worked. A Confederate cavalryman dashed into the room and reported the Yankees were coming. "In less time than it takes me to Write these lines, every White Man was out the house," Washington recalled. He and a group of African Americans went to the riverside, where they heard Union marching bands playing on the opposite bank. Union guards spotted them and crossed the river in a boat. When the soldiers asked them about the whereabouts of the rebel army, Washington presented them with Confederate newspapers. "I told them I was most happy to See them all that I had been looking for them for a long time." The soldiers assured him that he was free and could find work in their camp serving some of the officers. That night Washington realized he "had truly Escaped from the hands of the Slaves Master and With the help of God, I never Would be a Slave no more." He anticipated claiming every dollar earned by his labor and felt that "Life had a new joy awaiting me."[24]

From the beginning, Washington sensed that the war might offer him a chance for freedom, but he despaired at the spectacle of fresh recruits pouring into the Confederate capital. "Thousands of Troops was Sent to Richmond from all parts of the South on their way to Washington, as They Said. and So many troops of all description was landed there that it appeared to be an impossiability, to us, Colord people; that they could ever be conquord." Washington was literate and read the newspapers "and eagerly Watched them for tidings of the War." Literate slaves anticipated the future for friends and family by spreading the word of imminent battles and policies. The best news that Washington learned was "that Slaves was daily Making their escape into the Union lines." But the papers also convinced him that the Federal army would not reach Richmond in the foreseeable future. Instead of waiting indefinitely for liberators to arrive, Washington devised a plan to approach the Yankees. With a holiday pass, he traveled to Fredericksburg, Virginia, at Christmas 1861 and found a hotel where he could work as a steward and bartender. "My Master was not pleased when he heard of my intention to remain in Fredericksburg that year; he Seemed to think I wanted to remain too near the 'Yankees,' though he did not tell me these words."[25]

Washington gave himself credit for anticipating the war's possibilities and seizing an opportunity for freedom by going to the Union army; however, both he and Harry Jarvis believed that God worked behind the scenes to make their escapes possible. Washington remembered God freeing him from bondage on Good Friday. Whether his memory was accurate or not, it illustrates how African Americans believed in the confluence of God's time and human history. Matthew Harper argues, "Nineteenth-century black Protestants attempted to locate themselves within God's plan for human history—past, present, and future—by writing their own experience into biblical and supernatural narratives." At Fort Monroe, fugitive slaves told soldiers that the Book of Daniel foretold the Civil War and Union victory. Chapters thirteen to fifteen prophesied how the king of the north would come south, capture its most fortified cities, and destroy its best armies. As historian Kathryn Gin explains, enslaved people "used the core concepts of ultimate justice, ironic reversal, and future bliss to make sense of the world in which they lived, to critique its imperfections, and to rearrange its pieces in their imaginations of a better life."[26]

As Figure 5.1 depicts, when black southerners raced to Union lines, they revealed something that most Americans had not realized about the looming war: the future would unfold where fugitive slaves met federal authorities, not simply where Union soldiers fought Confederate troops. Assembled within Union lines, African Americans expressed their anticipations of the future through music. In summer 1861, a northerner visiting Fort Monroe heard a black man with a chorus of ten others singing in a tent. The melody was the sweetest minor he ever heard. Its peacefulness struck him. "There was no confusion, no uproar, no discord—all was as tender and harmonious as the symphony of an organ." He published the lyrics for northerners.

Through music, black southerners conveyed to northerners that their response to liberation would be orderly and solemn, not chaotic and bacchanal. When the Reverend Lewis Lockwood met with contraband at Fort Monroe for missionary work, they assured him that "some great thing was in store for them and their people," and substantiated their claim with music.

Figure 5.1 "Stampede of slaves from Hampton to Fortress Monroe," ***Harper's Weekly,*** **August 17, 1861. Library of Congress, Prints and Photographs Division.**

Go down to Egypt—Tell Pharoah
This saith my servant, Moses—
Let my people go.

Stunned by its sadness and hope, Lockwood stressed their music was "not boisterous; but in the gentle, chanted style." When he first published the great spiritual "Go Down, Moses," Lockwood showed that slaves understood emancipation as a sacred event that they had anticipated for decades in song.[27]

Private Edward Pierce of the Third Massachusetts Infantry heard African American music while stationed at Fort Monroe. When General Butler employed former slaves to construct earthworks around Hampton, Virginia, Pierce collected laborers, recorded their names, ages, and masters, provided them with tools, supervised their work, and procured their rations. He sought more than rudimentary information from these people. Pierce wanted to know their feelings, hopes, and projects. In their conversations and songs, Pierce heard blacks' universal desire for freedom. The solemnity of this desire struck him. Pierce anticipated that the war would give black men muskets and uniforms, and after listening to their spirituals, he trusted that African Americans would fight with power and dignity. Just as sound outpaces steam engines, "events travel faster than laws or proclamations," he explained. Their religious faith convinced him that black soldiers would not battle like ferocious savages. Instead, they would behave like citizens—better citizens than white southerners who betrayed their country. Scanning the horizon, Pierce predicted American slavery would die at its birthplace, Virginia's eastern shore. The event would mark the next chapter in human progress.[28]

When James Miller McKim visited Port Royal, South Carolina, another location where slaves found freedom early in the war, music affirmed the character and temporality of African Americans.

No more driver call for me,
No more driver call;
No more driver call for me,
Many a thousand die!

No more peck of corn for me,
No more peck of corn;
No more peck of corn for me,
Many a thousand die.

No more hundred lash for me,
No more hundred lash;
No more hundred lash for me,
Many a thousand die;

McKim first heard this song when six black soldiers from the 1st Regiment of South Carolina Volunteers rowed him from Hilton Head to Beaufort. Music synchronized their strokes, bounced off the waves, and echoed from inlets of passing islands. When they encountered a boat of friends on the water, their acquaintances asked what their clothing meant. "We's Uncle Sam's chil'n now; we's Uncle Sam's chil'n now; we's none of your fiel' hans'." McKim understood that the slave songs "tell the whole story of these people's life and character." They looked backward to celebrate the end of slavery and memorialize its victims while facing an open future with hope. It was the only song that McKim heard them sing in a major key.[29]

Thomas Higginson, one of John Brown's Secret Six, commanded a black regiment in South Carolina and shared McKim's wonder for African American music. Whenever he heard his men singing, Higginson strained to catch their words and raced to his tent to record them. For Higginson, music combined black history and prophecy. Their temporality expressed "nothing but patience for this life,—nothing but triumph in the next. Sometimes the present predominates, sometimes the future; but the combination is always implied." Songs like "This World Almost Done," "The Coming Day," and "We'll Soon Be Free" spread a millennial faith that everything, not just slavery, would soon end. Most of the songs Higginson heard relished the looming future as a time of peace, rest, and reunion with loved ones. Others prophesied a harrowing apocalypse. "Down in the Valley" imagined slaves running from lightning and fire through the valley of death to fulfill Jesus's promise of freedom during the second coming.

> We'll run and never tire,
> We'll run and never tire,
> We'll run and never tire,
> Jesus set poor sinners free.

When Higginson watched his regiment march, with every face fixed straight ahead, he saw "a regiment of freed slaves marching on into the future." "Ride in, Kind Savior" expressed black troops' anticipations that the future beckoned to them and God would see them through it.

> Ride in, kind Saviour!
> No man can hinder me.
> O, Jesus is a mighty man!
> No man can hinder me.
> We're marching through Virginny fields.
> No man can hinder me.
> O, Satan is a busy man,
> No man can hinder me.
> And he has his sword and shield,
> No man can hinder me.
> O, old Secesh done come and gone!
> No man can hinder me.

On New Year's Day, 1863, Higginson's camp celebrated emancipation by reading Lincoln's proclamation aloud and presenting the colors to the regiment. When the American flag appeared, an elderly black man starting to sing "My Country, 'tis of thee." Other black people joined him. When whites started to sing along, Higginson hushed them. "I never saw anything so electric; it made all other words cheap; it seemed the choked voice of a race at last unloosed." When the song ended, Higginson gave a speech, "but the life of the whole day was in those unknown people's song."[30]

When Lucy Garrison visited Port Royal, the sounds of slavery and liberation filled her with an urgency to record black music. Already, former slaves preferred not to sing songs that evoked painful pasts. She wanted to publish this music before it vanished. A classically trained pianist, Garrison had trouble transcribing the music's unexpected rhythms and unpredictable vocal flourishes. One of her colleagues in the project confessed that "the odd turns made in the throat, and the curious rhythmic effect produced by single voices chiming in at different irregular intervals, seem almost as impossible to place on the score as the singing of birds." Like birdsong, African American music traveled across the South, sounding the same refrain from Virginia tobacco fields to Louisiana sugar plantations. "It is said to have been sung for at least fifteen or twenty years in Virginia and Maryland, and perhaps in all the slave States, though stealthily, for fear of the lash; and is now sung openly under the protection of our government," Lockwood explained. The music proved that "the slaves are familiar with the history of the past, and are looking forward hopefully toward the future." His insight may seem obvious today, but during the Civil War it refuted popular notions that blacks lived for the present alone, insensible of history and prophecy, memory and ambition, like beasts of the field. As Frederick Douglass explained, slaves by definition had no future. Douglass recalled how his master "advised me to complete thoughtlessness of the future" to enforce dependence. When thousands of enslaved people like Douglass anticipated the future and seized it, they affirmed their humanity and freedom.[31]

Be Bold, Be Bold

THOUGH FUGITIVES AND VOLUNTEERS anticipated the future, they did not progress in unison. While volunteers sought the warfront to distinguish themselves as individuals, fugitives approached danger to protect their families. For volunteers, the war beckoned as an event that promised to fulfill childhood anticipations of glory on the battlefield. Antebellum schoolbooks devoted disproportionate space to America's military history. As boys, the eager recruits of 1861 learned that manhood could be affirmed by charging into the teeth of war. Eighty percent of the volunteers of 1861 were unmarried. By contrast, fugitives sought the warfront to affirm their family ties. They fled masters who planned to distance them from Union lines by scattering their loved ones into the Confederate interior. When runaways recorded their identities at Fort Monroe, they listed their family members, including spouses and children separated by the slave trade years ago.[32]

The anticipations of soldiers and slaves expanded the scale of the Civil War. More young men volunteered than the warring nations could manage; more enslaved people sought freedom than authorities could receive. Hundreds of thousands who enlisted generated copious paperwork. Hundreds of thousands of African Americans who ran toward freedom did not create a similar paper trail. Authorities pushed them from one camp to another without documenting them. When Confederate forces overcame Union camps, the people they re-enslaved did not receive the same level of attention from Union authorities as the soldiers who were killed, wounded, or captured in the same engagements. Nonetheless, by the middle of 1864 almost 400,000 former slaves reached Union lines. Historian Eugene Genovese estimates that this figure doubled by the final year of the war, when Union armies penetrated black majority counties in the Confederate interior. This traffic involved people running toward their future and not just escaping from their past. Brave souls anticipated liberty and risked death to seize it. Their collective courage expanded the war's meaning and dimensions. Some leaders imagined the war's eventual dimensions but none of them could achieve such levels by proclaiming freedom from above. Anticipations of the war from below, not decrees from above, realized the war's potential. The Civil War's magnitude stemmed from millions of young men and enslaved people who anticipated its potential.[33]

Ten years before the Civil War, Theodore Winthrop vented impatience for his future to begin in a poem titled "Waiting." After graduating from Yale in 1848, Winthrop wandered through European revolutions seeking a romantic cause, a war, to slake his ambition. "For such illumined moments I will grope," he wrote, "bearing my half-quenched hope." Winthrop paced the globe impatient for glory and undaunted by poor health. He rode the Oregon Trail, paddled Puget Sound, hiked the Adirondacks, trekked the coast of Maine, crossed the Isthmus of Panama, and found the headwaters of remote rivers in Nicaragua and California. During his adventures, he shot at Indians and jaguars, contracted smallpox, wrote travel volumes, and campaigned for John C. Frémont. Still, he failed to find his future.[34]

When civil war loomed after Lincoln's election, Winthrop saw an opportunity to become America's Thucydides. "We are making our history," he said, "hand over hand." In 1861, soldiers, civilians, and statesmen used the phrase "hand over hand" to express humanity's rapid progress into the future. An old sailing term akin to "hand over fist," both phrases referred to climbing a rope quickly, but "hand over hand" referred to forging time. Thomas Townsend agreed, "We are making our history hand over hand." To document everything, Townsend collected New York newspaper clippings in a massive scrapbook. His volume for 1861 exceeded 1,700 pages, and Townsend did not finish it until 1864.[35]

Winthrop joined the Seventh New York Infantry, a unit brimming with elite New Yorkers who shared his conviction that the path to victory beckoned straight ahead. They wore gray uniforms with white cross belts and bowie knives and enlisted for thirty days. The regiment was the first in the city to go to war. On April 19, they tramped down Broadway and Courtland under a "bower of flags," as Figure 5.2 depicts. Thousands of bystanders slapped their backs and pressed gifts into their hands. Sounds along the march raised Winthrop's anticipations. Cheering drowned out the music of marching bands and the rattling of gun carriages. Ladies' gloves and white handkerchiefs floated down from surrounding buildings. Winthrop thought, "It was worth a life, that march." The regiment boarded a ferryboat for New Jersey and then a train bound for Philadelphia, where Winthrop and a comrade received hard-boiled eggs from Quakers. Winthrop mocked their expectant posture toward the war and future. "The two ladies thee-ed

Figure 5.2 **"The Seventh Regiment Marching down Broadway to Embark for the War,"** ***Harper's Weekly*, May 4, 1861. Library of Congress, Prints and Photographs Division.**

us prayerfully and tearfully, hoping that God would save our country from blood." Such citizens meant well, but they were only beginning "to comprehend the fiery eagerness of men who live in historic times." Winthrop was a man of faith, but during the war fever of 1861, notions of providence averting bloodshed and resolving the crisis did not appeal to him.[36]

When the Seventh arrived in Washington, DC, the city was unprepared to quarter them, so men camped in the House chamber of the Capitol. "We appeared with bayonets and bullets because of the bosh uttered on this floor," Winthrop wrote. "Talk had made a miserable mess," and the Seventh promised to fix things with their actions. Surveying the Capitol's interior, Winthrop decided their first act should be "a little Vandalism." The room belonged to a "bygone epoch" when the departed Slave Power ruled with its "flavor of the Southwestern steamboat saloon." Winthrop judged the reign of planter aristocrats "an historic blank." A younger generation had arrived to fill that void and fulfill the promise of the Revolution. Orlando Poe felt the same way. "Now is the time when we want young and active men." Older men may be patriots "but after they have become loaded with years and honors, they become unfit for such an emergency as this." When the Seventh received orders to be ready to march, the men anticipated their destination. " 'Harpers Ferry!' says one, 'Alexandria!' shouts a second. 'Richmond!' only Richmond will content a third. And some could hardly be satisfied short of the hope of a breakfast in Montgomery."[37]

In published dispatches Winthrop anticipated a short, romantic war, but his private correspondence predicted a long, terrible conflict. He told *Atlantic Monthly* readers that Confederates "have not faith enough in their cause to risk their lives for it, even behind a tree or from one of these thickets, choice spots for ambush." With jaunty self-assurance, Winthrop described the Civil War as a half war and impatiently wondered if any blood would be shed. In private, he confessed, "I see no present end of this business. We must conquer the South. Afterward we must be prepared to do its polic[ing] on its own behalf, and in behalf of its black population, whom this war must, without precipitation, emancipate. We must hold the South as the metropolitan police holds New York. All this is inevitable." No clearer vision of the war and reconstruction was uttered in 1861, but his public statements remained romantic. In May, he described camp life to the public "as brilliant as a permanent picnic." That same month, he confessed to George Curtis, "I miss my Staten Island. War stirs the pulse, but it wounds a little all the time." His frail health was not holding up in camp. In public, Winthrop marveled at the North's rush to enlist and defend the Union, while Washington filled with uniforms of every hue. "It seemed as if all the able-bodied men in the country were moving," Winthrop observed. In private he admitted that these amateurs needed seasoning before they could save the country. "They must ripen awhile, perhaps, before they are to be named quite soldiers. Ripening takes care of itself; and by the harvest-time they will be ready to be cut down." What a chilling metaphor of looming carnage. Winthrop's anticipations of the future cannot be reduced to short war fantasy or long war realism. Many possibilities coexisted without contradiction.[38]

Winthrop and the Seventh answered Lincoln's April 15 proclamation for 75,000 men to "re-possess the forts, places, and property which have been seized from the Union" by secessionists. Some have misinterpreted this call as proof that even Lincoln underestimated the scale of the looming war. Contemporaries criticized Lincoln for not calling out 300,000 men or more. Stephen Douglas argued, "The shortest way to peace is the most stupendous and unanimous preparation for war." When Lincoln asked for only 75,000 volunteers, he followed the advice of General Winfield Scott, who anticipated that a massive muster would present the government with more men than it could manage and provoke the Upper South to secede. Others insist that Lincoln's call for ninety-day enlistments illustrates his faith in a short war. However, a 1795 militia law limited the service term of volunteers to thirty days after the assembling of Congress. When Lincoln's proclamation called Congress to a special session on July 4, it thus limited the enlistments to about ninety days. To convene Congress earlier would have shortened the volunteers' service; to postpone Congress's return would have slowed mobilization by depriving Lincoln of the legislature's help.[39]

Lincoln did not stop building the military after his April 15 proclamation. Four days later, he declared a blockade of the Confederate coast. In early May, he increased the regular army and navy and urged governors to muster their remaining volunteers for three years instead of three months. Lincoln understood that the government could do nothing to discourage the eager waves of recruits. He told New York governor Edwin Morgan, "The enthusiastic uprising of the people in our cause, is our great reliance; and we can not safely give it any check, even though it overflows, and runs in channels not laid down in any chart." When Congress met on July 4, Lincoln asked them for "at least four hundred thousand men." Like many Americans, Lincoln hoped that 1861's swarm of war anticipators would win the war for his side. "The people will save the government," he predicted, "if the government itself, will do its part, only indifferently well."[40]

When the Seventh finished its term of service and mustered out, Winthrop transferred to Fort Monroe to serve as General Butler's secretary. The move satisfied his eagerness to travel straight to the seat of war. "By Liberty! but it is worth something to be here at this moment, in the center of the center!" Winthrop exclaimed. "Here we scheme the schemes! Here we take the secession flags, the arms, the prisoners! Here we liberate the slaves—virtually." Winthrop was anticipating events. The garrison had not captured flags, weapons, or prisoners yet. Fort Monroe was already an emancipation magnet, and the slaves who reached the stronghold were "virtually" free.[41]

In early June, a runaway named George Scott left the safety of Fort Monroe to scout the Confederate position eight miles away. Scott had escaped his master two years earlier and lived in a nearby cave until freedom beckoned at the fort. No one knew the area better. A rebel sentry spotted him spying on the Confederate camp, but Scott returned safely to the fort with a detailed description of the enemy's strength and location near Little Bethel and Big Bethel. With Scott's intelligence in hand, Winthrop and Butler devised a plan to march through the night, attack at dawn, and capture the smaller enemy force. The slave, the volunteer, and the general were convinced that they knew what was ahead. With initiative, anticipation, and daring, they would seize victory. "We hope to bring in field-pieces, prisoners, horses, and burn a church or so. If I don't come back, dear mother, dear love to everybody."[42]

Winthrop's plan called for two separate regiments, one from Newport News and another from Camp Hamilton, to coordinate midnight marches, ferry across Hampton creek, repair and cross the New Market bridge, meet on a country road, and surprise the enemy at Little Bethel and then Big Bethel before dawn. Rockets fired from Newport News would help the columns synchronize their movements. The Fifth New York infantry, a well-drilled Zouave unit, would provide the column that Winthrop accompanied from Fort Monroe. He anticipated a swift, romantic charge into the center of the enemy's position. The march was "to be rapid, <u>but not hurried</u>." "If we find the enemy and surprise them," Winthrop ordered, "men will fire one volley, if desirable, <u>not</u> <u>reload</u>, and go ahead with the bayonet." If the assault captured the enemy stationed at Little Bethel, the plan ordered men to "push on to Big Bethel and similarly bag them." Winthrop anticipated burning or exploding both enemy fortifications, seizing any field pieces, and using them to repel a pursuit from the enemy's main body "if he has any." Winthrop decided that the Zouaves did not need new rifles, because "most of the work will be done with the bayonet, + they are already handy with the old ones." With rockets, bayonet charges, Zouave uniforms, and the element of surprise, Winthrop anticipated a dashing thrust to victory. When they marched out of Fort Monroe, Winthrop and Scott led the column side by side. Winthrop insisted that his fugitive scout needed a "shooting iron." Butler gave him a revolver. Scott said he could smell a rebel soldier farther than a skunk.[43]

Winthrop's plan would have tested the abilities of veterans. The columns lost synch when one of them encountered a "squad of negroes" who "inquired anxiously the way to 'the freedom fort.'" Orders stipulated that the troops would wear white armbands to identify each other in darkness and battle. It did not work. Inexperience and a spectrum of uniform colors caused confusion. Winthrop, for example, still wore his gray uniform from the Seventh New York Volunteers. When the second column caught up with the first, the vanguard emerged from the night beside the road and fired into them. The volley wounded twenty-one men and erased the element of surprise. Once officers regained order, they knew their mission was compromised and met to decide whether to continue or return to the fort. Winthrop convinced them to press forward. The march took longer than expected and Confederates had hours to prepare for their arrival. When the Union force finally reached the enemy well after dawn on the following morning, the men were tired, thirsty, and hungry. Around noon, Winthrop made a reconnaissance of the enemy's position with a private. A shower of bullets forced them to lie down behind a fallen tree.[44]

The rush of battle had sapped Winthrop's strength but not his determination to reach the center of the war. If he could only sleep for five minutes, Winthrop said he would be all right. He calmly told his comrade that he would see the inside of that enemy trench before he returned to Fort Monroe. When ordered to retreat, Winthrop instead stood up on the log and urged the men to "come on." A North Carolinian shot him through the chest. His ability to march forward to the future ended yards from the Confederate line. Winthrop had anticipated this death ten years earlier in his poem "Waiting."

Let me not waste in skirmishes my power,—
In petty struggles,—rather in the hour
Of deadly conflict may I nobly die!
In my first battle perish gloriously!

He was the first Civil War officer killed in battle.[45]

In 1861, Americans defined courage as boldness—forwardness. Heroes did not stand still and await the war, they anticipated it, ventured to its center, and, if necessary, died to ensure their nation's future. In June, after the bloodless bombardment of Fort Sumter and before the carnage of Bull Run, Theodore Winthrop embodied this courage for Unionists and Confederates. The poem "Bethel" memorialized him by closing every verse with the same command, "Column! Forward!" "The gallantry of Maj. Winthrop is the subject of universal admiration both with the federal and rebel forces," reported the *New York Tribune*. Both sides valued his body and possessions as relics of the looming war. Confederates collected his sword, pistol, and watch as trophies and sent them to loved ones in North Carolina. They buried his body where it fell, and when Winthrop's mother sought her son's remains and watch, Confederate Colonel Daniel H. Hill took it upon himself to fulfill her requests.[46]

When he hunted down the watch and sent it to Butler, Hill expressed Confederate anticipations of the future. He praised "Young Winthrop, who fell while gallantly leading a party in the vain attempt to subjugate a free people." For Hill and his troops, Winthrop's watch foretold the fate of all Yankees who invaded the South—the time it marked was their deaths. Hill believed in "the retributive justice in God's governance of the universe." Anyone who studied history has "seen the destroyer and desolater of countries himself ruined and left desolate." It was only a matter of time.[47]

Louisiana soldier William Clegg agreed. On July 4, Clegg observed the holiday by pronouncing the old Union dead. The United States "is a failure & was but an experiment." After the victory at Bethel, Clegg walked the battlefield, smelled great pools of blood, saw where Winthrop fell, and drew a map of the first major Confederate victory. Surely the event proved that God favored the newer American republic. But independence would require untold years of sacrifice, just like the first American Revolution. In October 1861, when Clegg saw the American flag flying over the enemy's position, he echoed Hill's sentiment. That proud banner now waved over despotic armies "in the futile attempt to subjugate a free enlightened & brave people." While he thought about the old flag, enemy squads burned nearby homes. Black clouds darkened the horizon.[48]

After Winthrop's death, a journalist entrusted with his earthly affairs recalled a conversation he overheard between Winthrop and Butler before the expedition left the fort. "Be as brave as you please," said Butler, "but run no risks." "Be bold, be bold—but not too bold," replied Winthrop, quoting the English fairy tale of Mr. Fox. In the story, Lady Mary, unwilling to await her future, sought a glimpse of it by traveling to her fiancé's castle the day before her marriage to Mr. Fox. She discovered his fortress deep in the wood, and its gate read, "Be bold, be bold." She opened the gate and marched up to the door, which said, "Be bold, be bold, but not too bold." Undaunted Mary forged ahead, into the hall, up the stairs, to another door, where she read, "Be bold, be bold, but not too bold,/Lest that your heart's blood should run cold." Mary was most daring. She opened the door and walked into a gallery strewn with bodies and skeletons of young ladies covered with blood. There she hid from her lover while he hacked the finger off a fainted maiden to steal her diamond ring. The severed digit flew into Mary's lap, but in his rage, Fox did not see it happen. Mary ran home, and the next day, when Fox arrived to sign their marriage contract, Mary confronted him with the severed finger. Her brothers cut him to pieces.[49]

The fairy tale of Mr. Fox conveyed a moral for soldiers and slaves in 1861. Like Lady Mary, Winthrop ventured to his future and found the unexpected. They both waded through the blood of youths like themselves, but Winthrop did not heed his own advice. Instead of racing back to his castle he pushed too far ahead. His remains and possessions, like the lady's severed finger and ring, became harbingers of what awaited the boldest anticipators of the future at the seat of war. Be bold, be bold, but not too bold—the same advice applied to African Americans. Butler's contraband policy rewarded slaves who displayed an anticipatory position toward the future. Be bold enough to run to Union lines and bold enough to work for the federal army, but not too bold. Don't ask for a uniform and musket, like Jarvis did. Be bold enough to labor for the Union but not so bold as to ask for freedom.[50]

Courting War

THOUSANDS OF YOUNG WOMEN anticipated the looming war. They read, spoke, and wrote about political developments in spite of social conventions that deemed such topics unfeminine. They urged their husbands and brothers to volunteer and march to war. Men who stayed home risked dishonoring themselves and their families. Women stitched battle flags for local companies, sometimes made from their wedding gowns, and gave stirring speeches when they presented the banners to men. Some women wished they could become soldiers. "What I would give to be able to go in our Army!" Margaret Williams told her brother. "Hardships and fatigue I would endure without a murmur or complaint, and when engaged in battle I would never show quarter." In April 1861, Louisa May Alcott confessed, "I've often longed to see a war, I've often longed to be a man." She yearned "for a battle like a warhorse when he smells powder." For the first time in her life, Sarah Morgan regretted being a woman because she could not fight. All the real men "are off at the seat of war." Those still at home were "only trash." Morgan asked God why she was "made with a man's heart, and a female form, and those creatures with beards were made as bewitchingly nervous?" Some women approached the war by volunteering as nurses in army hospitals. "The height of my ambition was to go to the front after a battle," Alcott wrote. She worked in a hospital and watched several surgeries, "feeling that the sooner I inured myself to trying sights, the more useful I should be."[51]

Abolitionist Abby Hopper Gibbons raced to the war in 1861. Raised a Quaker, Gibbons renounced pacifism and embraced John Brown's violent plans to kill slavery. In 1856, she served as the president of the Kansas Aid Company in New York City and helped Henry Ward Beecher ship weapons to the territory. When George Stearns urged her to donate funds to raise and equip a "secret force" led by Brown, she did not hesitate to contribute to the cause. Weeks before the Harpers Ferry raid, Brown visited Gibbons and shared his plans. She knew it was folly, told him so, and asked how he would treat southern women and children. Brown promised not to touch a hair on their heads. After his defeat, she acquired a pike and displayed it in her parlor to memorialize his friend. There it stood when men sacked her house during the draft riots of 1863.[52]

When war erupted, Gibbons headed to the capital to work as a nurse for the United States Sanitary Commission. Not satisfied to stay in Washington, "the dirtiest, most God-forsaken hole in the universe," she headed to hospitals closer to the warfront in Virginia and Maryland. Gibbons was proud to count herself among "those who have time and means to do the needful, and have the *will*." She urged women who could not work at the front to "knit, knit, knit" for the soldiers. Passing through Harpers Ferry on her way to "The Slaughter House," a makeshift hospital for amputees in Winchester, Virginia, Gibbons overheard soldiers singing "John Brown's Body" over and over again. [53]

The Civil War disrupted thousands of engagements and weddings, including Lizzie Gaillard's plans to marry in Columbia, South Carolina, on January 15, 1861. "The 16th finds me still Lizzie Gaillard and very uncertain as to when I shall be anything else," she wrote a friend in Virginia. Her wedding was postponed indefinitely because of the "threatening and <u>warlike</u>" atmosphere. "Is it not strange how uncertain are all human anticipations?" she asked. Since secession weeks earlier, Gaillard and everyone she knew focused on the future. Though people showed few outward expressions of passion, she sensed "the excitement is deep." Everyone seemed determined to die rather than submit to Black Republicans. She was "almost crazy" to know whether the federal government would let her state go in peace or compel it to fight. All six of her brothers had volunteered, including one who had returned a year early from studying in Germany. When she thought about them and her fiancé, Gaillard hoped that South Carolina might avoid "the horrors of civil war," but she was confident of victory if the Yankees were foolish enough to fight. The stolid patience of North Carolina and Virginia dumbfounded her. "Why will she not move?" Gaillard asked her friend about Virginia. She understood why Virginians hesitated to leave a nation they created, but her "hot South Carolina blood" would not allow her to reflect on such things. The past was past and she only cared for the future and looked with pride and hope toward her new republic. Why not take Fort Sumter now? Every man in South Carolina was a soldier, all the preparations for attacking the fort were in place, and still Jefferson Davis waited.[54]

When Lincoln's call for troops triggered Virginia's secession, Caroline Davis praised her state for assuming a leading role in the Confederacy and the war. She heard a rumor that Lincoln asked Governor John Letcher to refrain from sending out more troops, "wishing to make the impression that hostilities will cease," Davis surmised, "but things have gone too far now." She imagined colorful companies of armed men sprouting along Virginia's border and throughout the Confederacy to defend southern rights. The image thrilled her. Time seemed to accelerate with each piece of momentous news. April 1861 passed with a flash. "We are indeed living pages of History now! What is to be the end of all, + who is to be the recorder?" Davis anticipated her diary would chronicle amazing things.[55]

Not satisfied to wait for war news to arrive, Davis jumped into the war effort by stitching pants for a local company. The women hardly completed the job when orders arrived and the company marched to war. When her brother volunteered, Davis worried about him succumbing to the temptations of camp life if the war lasted for an indefinite period of time. She preferred that he were in "actual engagements" instead of resting in camp. Thoughts of where and when the first battle would be fought consumed her. Newspapers said Confederate troops encircled Richmond. "No one knows Gen Lee's plans," but Davis sensed "there is to be a bloody fight somewhere + soon." She felt a "fevered restlessness" that seemed to "forebode something" momentous would happen. Though she tried to convince herself that she was not superstitious, Davis could not shake the feeling that her body felt looming events. When newspapers reported the victory at Bethel, a battle where two of her cousins fought, Davis felt physically attuned to how "change succeeds change in our country's history + in the history of many of us." She believed "the hand of Providence is with us" and would defend and save southerners from the unrighteous war being waged against them.[56]

In Boston, Lucy Larcom felt "a soldier-spirit" rising within her when she associated with volunteers during the first weeks of the war. American flags canopied the streets. Patriotic anthems echoed off storefronts festooned with goods arranged in red, white, and blue patterns. For the first time in her life this quiet, religious schoolteacher carried her heart into a crowd and felt pleasure. She sensed the conflict deepening and thanked God that no wavering divided the North. "We are transformed into an army, ready for battle at a moment's warning." Larcom wanted a war terrible enough to kill slavery. "I would rather the war should last fifty years, than ever again make the least compromise with slavery, that arch-enemy of all true prosperity, that eating sin of our nation." When she heard Charles Sumner speak on the war, his calm demeanor surprised her. "We are all expecting orators to speak as we feel,—intensely." History was approaching its climax. In the beginning, Puritans of the Old Colony brought liberty to America, while aristocrats of the Old Dominion imported slavery. Centuries after this original sin, reckoning and atonement came to America. Traveling home after Sumner's speech, Larcom passed a soldiers' camp. Rows of white tents rested in the shadow of autumn hills as blue lines of men marched and countermarched. She knew the picturesque scene concealed "what war is." How could women know war when they only read about it in newspapers, knitted socks for regiments, and sewed quilts for hospitals? "There is more for women to do than to be lookers-on." When the war turned against slavery, Larcom vowed to close her school, march to the center of the conflict, and teach the contraband.[57]

Brothers' War, White Man's War

REGARDLESS OF WOMEN'S ANTICIPATIONS, American society defined the looming contest as a brothers' war. Benjamin Butler and Harry Jarvis disputed whether the war was white or black, but they assumed without question that it was a man's concern. During the secession crisis, Virginian Green Berry Samuels promised his fiancée, Katherine Boone, that he would talk with her before he made a decision about the future. After Fort Sumter, Samuels joined the army without consulting her. "If there is any object in this world that must be contemptible in the eyes of every true woman," Samuels reasoned, "it is a cowardly man." Men made the future, while women awaited it. Masculinity favored enterprise, action, and foresight. Femininity preferred patience, inactivity, and intuition. "You must try in this day of terrors to overcome the timidity of your woman's nature," Samuels told Boone, "and await the result of this crisis with the heroic spirit of the women of the Revolution." He left for war without seeing her.[58]

Samuels's duty as a man and citizen bound him as a defender of Boone and the Confederacy, the symbolically feminine nation-state. Confederates symbolized their new nation as feminine, meaning men who rushed to war could reconcile their ambition and excitement for adventure with their manly and civic duties. Samuels told Boone, "The life of every honorable man is not his own but belongs to his country and if I know your disposition you would rather lose a Lover on the field of battle fighting for his country than secure a husband who was afraid to go." The war clarified Samuels's relationship to Boone while it complicated their courtship.[59]

Samuels doubted the Civil War would be a lark that solidified his engagement to Boone in time for a fall wedding; instead, he predicted a terrible bloodletting without end. "No tongue can tell, no imagination paint the frightful calamities that will befall our unhappy country," he predicted in April 1861. When Boone learned of Samuels's enlistment, she shared with him her hopes "that this unhappy war would soon draw to a close." "God alone knows what will be the result," he replied. Like thousands of other recruits, Samuels imagined an "unnatural" brothers' war. "Is it not awful to think that brothers must shed each others blood?" he asked. As units poured into Harpers Ferry, their spirit was intoxicating. "You can form no idea of the enthusiasm existing among all ranks here," he wrote to Boone; "there seems to be but one feeling, undying hostility to the North and the determination to fight to the death." Samuels knew that the enemy was "concentrating powerful masses of troops at Washington," and he anticipated an enormous battle soon.[60]

While anticipations of a brothers' war animated Samuels, fears of a race war moved John Boykin and his neighbors in Antioch, Georgia. After Fort Sumter, they formed the Ben Hill Volunteers because "our slave population is large and we are a good way from LaGrange our county site." Boykin explained to Governor Joseph Brown that his company wanted "muskets or some arm(s) for drilling purposes" more than they wanted a swift transfer to the battlefront. A display of firepower could scare local slaves who might otherwise exploit the turmoil of war to revolt. In 1860, the census taker counted 6,223 whites and 10,002 slaves in Troup County, a place bordering the black belt and Alabama. When Antioch men heard nothing from the governor for almost a month, Boykin sent a second request for guns. This time he suggested that the volunteers might borrow arms from a local military academy because "the school is pretty much suspended." Boykin pleaded with Brown, "Please let us hear at once from you on the subject of arms—we are anxious for them." The Volunteers joined for only twelve months because "they could not well leave home for an undefinite time [*sic*]." Within weeks, the excitement of the war changed their minds. "At the last company meeting," Boykin informed Brown, "a member moved that the company should 'go in for the war' when two thirds or more were in favor." Boykin had no doubts that his men would "resolve to offer our services for the war" at the next company meeting on June 22, "and be ready at any moment to march to the seat of war." [61]

The Ben Hill volunteers followed a pattern of mobilization that countless communities experienced in the spring of 1861. National events—the surrender of Fort Sumter or the president's call for volunteers—coupled with local contexts (in Antioch's case a large slave population) to compel men of action into forming local companies. At first these companies were self-appointed and self-regulated. Bound by state militia laws, the men who filled these units could be intensely local in their concerns and identities. The tide of war swept most of these volunteers into larger affiliations that fed nationalist goals and feelings. Within weeks of forming to patrol the slave population and maintain local order, the Ben Hill volunteers became Company F, 4th Georgia Infantry, and enlisted in the Confederate army. Similar transformations occurred simultaneously across the South. Railways could not accommodate the flood of men and supplies that funneled toward the "seat of war." The Antioch men took passenger trains from Atlanta to Wilmington, North Carolina. At Wilmington, however, the only available cars for Richmond were freight cars, so the volunteers entered their new capital packed like the raw material of war that they were.[62]

Contrasting the Ben Hill Volunteers' mobilization with the experiences of the Cincinnati Home Guards illustrates how race affected the ways that men could anticipate and enter the war. When Confederate cavalry under General John Morgan threatened Cincinnati in August 1862, black citizens of the city called a meeting and organized the Home Guards to defend the city. White Cincinnati responded with mockery and intimidation to the Home Guards's offer to help. The police demanded the keys to the building where the volunteers met and compelled the group to take down the American flag that flew over their recruiting station. The officers explained, "We want you damned niggers to keep out of this; this is a white man's war."[63]

When Morgan's raiders approached Cincinnati in September 1862, the same police who scoffed at the Home Guards forced them into building fortifications for the city. They treated the blacks roughly, impressing them into military camps at the point of bayonets. Peter Clark, a local African

American leader, understood the racial discrimination inherent in their actions. "Permission to volunteer would imply some freedom, some dignity, some independent manhood." Compelling black men to dig defenses for white soldiers, whether done by Unionists in Cincinnati, Ohio, or Confederates in Yorktown, Virginia, underlined the assumption that black people were resources, not actors, in this war. When Union General Lew Wallace learned of this incident, he organized the Home Guards into a Black Brigade and appointed officers. As with the Ben Hill Volunteers, larger events swept the local companies into national armies, but race determined how this process unfolded and what the government expected from men.[64]

While authorities urged white volunteers to march to the front lines with anticipation, officials told black volunteers to wait calmly for the war to come to them. When Captain James Lupton presented the American flag to the Black Brigade, he urged them to "be loyal to duty, be obedient, hopeful, patient." He promised, "Slavery will soon die, the slaveholders' rebellion . . . will shortly and miserably perish," but Lupton did not want the Black Brigade to rush into the conflict and claim responsibility for victory. Black men should receive freedom and rights from white liberators instead of asserting freedom and rights on their own. The brigade's colonel, William Dickson, stressed this point when the brigade disbanded. He praised them not for their bravery, patriotism, or anticipatory zeal to defend their homes, but for "the accustomed patience of your race" and for laboring "cheerfully and effectively." Dickson understood that his men "have learned to suffer and to wait," but he urged them to continue this practice instead of seizing initiatives and making history. "Go to your homes with the consciousness of having performed your duty—of deserving, if you do not receive, the protection of the law."[65]

The volunteers ignored Dickson's advice. When the federal government finally accepted black regiments in 1863, members of the original Cincinnati Home Guards joined Massachusetts regiments and marched to the front. Peter Clark understood why these men risked slavery and death in the South instead of staying home and waiting for society to recognize their sacrifices and rights. "They wish to be numbered among the children of the nation, to be invested with the privileges wherewith she endows her sons, to feel the heart throb when gazing upon the country's flag; to say with proud joy: we too are American citizens! Is this too much to hope for?" Clark looked forward to a day "when free black children shall sing songs of Liberty and Union, over the tombs of John C. Calhoun and Preston S. Brooks."[66]

Civil War anticipations of a "white man's war" contradicted history. Black soldiers had fought with George Washington during the Revolution,

Andrew Jackson at the battle of New Orleans, and John C. Frémont during the Mexican War. When free blacks organized companies and offered their services to the government, they challenged white anticipations of the war. In Cleveland, African Americans rooted their vision of the war in historical precedents and resolved "that today, as in the times of '76 and the days of 1812, we are ready to go forth and do battle in the common cause of the country." In New York City, black men who anticipated a chance to join the US army began drilling in a public hall. White supremacists, including police, lashed out against these black initiatives. The chief of police in New York City ordered blacks to disperse their organization and warned them that he could not protect them against mob violence. During the antebellum period, the rise of "whiteness" as a racial identity spread from labor groups to militia companies, even in liberal states like Massachusetts. When the war came, Boston blacks petitioned the legislature to strike "from the militia law of the State the odious word 'white,' by which they are now precluded from being enrolled." Realizing that they faced more racial discrimination in 1861 than their ancestors had at the start of previous wars, many African Americans dreaded a conflict that would erase the modest gains of antebellum reform.[67]

The story of Jacob Dodson illustrates why African Americans foresaw declension and dreaded rising racism in 1861. Weeks after Fort Sumter surrendered, Dobson, a black veteran who had fought with John C. Frémont in the Mexican War, volunteered to assemble a black company to defend Washington, DC. In the 1850s, Dodson successfully petitioned Congress for military service pay. Even southern filibusters, like John Quitman, supported Dodson's Mexican War service record. But the Civil War was different. If he had white skin, Dobson's qualifications would have garnered him an officer's commission. Instead he received a blunt rejection. Secretary of War Simon Cameron replied, "This Department has no intention at present to call into the service of the Government any colored soldiers." Cameron addressed him as "Jacob Dodson (colored)."[68]

The experiences of black volunteers sparked a debate among African Americans: should free blacks approach the war with proactive anticipation or cautious expectation? Black southerners debated whether to seize the initiative, escape bondage, and seek their future in the Union army or wait for the war and the Union army to come to them. Black northerners also faced a dilemma between anticipating and expecting the war. Blacks who foresaw a white man's war that would intensify racial hatred and discrimination urged African Americans to take an expectant posture toward the conflict and wait for signs of a better future before rushing to join a fight that was not theirs.

This position was most popular before the bombardment of Fort Sumter electrified northern war sentiments. None of the candidates in the election of 1860 championed the rights of free blacks nor the emancipation of enslaved ones. When the Deep South seceded, many free blacks welcomed disunion. "He that is able to read this nation's destiny, can see and decipher the handwriting on the wall," wrote a correspondent of the *Anglo-African*, a prominent black newspaper. Secession of the slave states would free the federal government from its obligations to protect the vile institution and move freedom's border from Canada to the Mason-Dixon line. Anticipating secession in a speech on December 3, 1860, Frederick Douglass said, "I shall be glad of the news, come when it will, that the slave States are an independent government." After disunion, Douglass imagined "men could be found at least as brave as a [William] Walker, and more skillful than any other filibusterer, who would venture into those States and raise the standard of liberty." Douglass prophesied that "a Garibaldi would arise who would march into those States with a thousand men, and summon to his standard sixty thousand, if necessary, to accomplish the freedom of the slave."[69]

When war fever in 1861 inspired northerners to fight a "white man's war" for the Union, some blacks urged their race to wait for the conflict to change in their favor before committing their lives to an errant cause. "No regiments of black troops should leave their bodies to rot upon the battlefield beneath a Southern sun, to conquer a peace based upon the perpetuity of human bondage," wrote a correspondent to the *Anglo-African*. "Our policy must be neutral," he said, "ever praying for the success of that party determined to initiate first the policy of justice and equal rights." A black man from Troy, New York, agreed: "We have nothing to gain, and everything to lose, by entering the list as combatants." William H. Parham, a black teacher in Cincinnati, heard about the police crackdown against the African American Home Guards in his city and said he opposed black military activity all along. "It being their fight I assure you they are welcome to it, so far as I am concerned." Even hopeful advocates in the *Anglo-African* preferred waiting for signs of a better cause ushered in by providence before diving into the fray. "Colored men whose fingers tingle to pull the trigger, or clutch the knife aimed at the slave-holders in arms, will not have to wait much longer," the newspaper prophesied. The worsening war would force the Union to address black rights and accept black arms. Wait until "the government shall be willing to accept our services."[70]

Others disagreed and took an anticipatory stance from the start of the war. Alfred Green, a black teacher in Philadelphia, opposed patience and prayer in 1861. "This inactivity that is advocated is the principle that has ever had us left behind, and will leave us again unless we arouse from lethargy and arm ourselves as men and patriots." Green urged black men to organize in spite of white opposition, and he was thrilled to witness black men drilling "in the regular African Zouave Drill, that would make the hearts of secession traitors, or prejudiced northern Yankees quake and tremble for fear." "God will help no one that refuses to help himself," Green insisted. "If ever colored men plead for rights or fought for liberty, now of all others is the time." He warned if blacks squandered this opportunity, "we will be left a hundred years behind this gigantic age of human progress and development." Seizing the initiative would prove black manhood while anticipating emancipation would prove black "foresight in the midst of all these complicated difficulties."[71]

Free blacks who favored anticipation and enterprise stressed progress instead of providence as the driving force behind history. An editorial in the *Anglo-African* predicted that the war was "but another step in the drama of American Progress. We say Progress, for we know that no matter what may be the desires of the men of Expediency who rule, or seem to, the affairs of the North,—the tendencies are for liberty." Leaders like Secretary of War Cameron may appear to have the power to exclude people like Dodson from military service, but such politicians could not control the war. As the conflict deepened, the North tended toward liberty in spite of its racism. "May the cup be drained to its dregs, for only thus can this nation of sluggards know the disease and its remedy." The editorialist urged African Americans to put aside expectant postures that relied on providence in favor of anticipatory positions that focused on the "progress of this struggle." "Out of this strife will come freedom," he assured. "Public opinion purified by the fiery ordeal through which the nation is about to pass, will rightly appreciate the cause of its political disquiet, and apply the remedy," the abolition of slavery.[72]

Time and Military Strategy

THE DEBATE BETWEEN ANTICIPATION and expectation that stirred African Americans in 1861 also tested governments that year and the same outcome prevailed: anticipation trumped expectation. Visions of the future shaped policy and strategy in Washington and Richmond because Americans had little experience or education to prepare for the looming war. No American had ever commanded a mass army. The most experienced officer on either side, General Winfield Scott, had led a force of only 14,000 men in Mexico. Born in 1786, Scott was too old to take the field. None of the younger officers who had served under him had experience leading a brigade, let alone an army. Beyond their lack of experience, Americans knew little about military theory and strategy. West Point educated soldiers in engineering and mathematics more than in strategy and administration. The officers who would lead Union and Confederate armies in 1861 had spent most of their military careers chasing Native Americans and building forts. They had never organized a staff, supplied a mass army, formed a grand strategy, or directed a corps in combat. As a result, anticipation instead of experience shaped Union and Confederate plans when the war began. A comical circumstance underlined both governments' anticipatory approach to the war: neither side had accurate maps of the eastern half of the continent. Before the war, American topographers had focused on the unorganized expanses of the far West, the place where the nation imagined its future would be. In 1862, General Henry Halleck tried to command a department in Missouri with "no maps other than the general ones in book-stores" he found in St. Louis. Union generals in the eastern theater lacked accurate maps of northern Virginia until 1863. With their eyes trained on the horizon in 1861, Americans did not know where they stood, but they raced forward anyway.[73]

Winfield Scott's vision for the Civil War was exceptional for taking an expectant posture: he hoped to win the war not by conquering the enemy in battle but by avoiding bloodshed and waiting for peace. Invading armies might conquer the Confederacy after three years and hundreds of thousands of casualties, Scott predicted, but the outcome would not be a clear victory. After a "frightful" destruction of southern life and property, the Union would gain "fifteen devastated provinces! not to be brought into harmony with their conquerors." The South would require policing "for generations by heavy garrisons" at quadruple the cost that the government could extort from the region through duties and taxes. Accomplishing this feat would kill American democracy because the president would assume the powers of a "Protector or an Emperor" to execute the laws.[74]

As a Virginia Unionist, Scott sensed that southern resistance would stiffen with each Union advance. Marching into the region would confirm secessionists' predictions of northern coercion and undermine southern Unionists' attempts to reassert local control. After the bombardment of Fort Sumter, Lincoln's call for volunteers to quell the rebellion had triggered a second wave of secession that swept Scott's native state into the Confederacy. If the threat of federal activity swayed southern allegiance, the realization of such threats would sever the Union forever. Worse still, the amateur qualities of the invading armies would court disaster. Scott knew from experience in the Mexican War that undisciplined volunteers provoked the populace by looting and destroying civilian property. Raw recruits were also prone to being ambushed in enemy territory and routed by determined defenders. These obstacles could only be overcome in time. The North needed time to recruit, train, and supply its forces. The South needed time to calm down. The longer both sides avoided hostilities, the better for the Union. Waiting to act would deprive southern nationalists of historical events to found their Confederacy and give southern Unionists time to reorganize and appeal to the people. Even nature would reward inactivity. Waiting until winter to head south would save federal forces from deadly diseases that thrived in the Deep South during warmer months.

After Fort Sumter fell, Scott shared his strategy with Lincoln. He planned to avoid a catastrophic war by blockading the Confederacy into submission. Shutting the secessionists off from Europe would deprive them of necessary supplies and eliminate the threat of foreign intervention. Scott's strategy relied on a principal federal strength and exposed a critical Confederate weakness: the Union navy could be strengthened by northern shipbuilding, while the Confederacy had no navy and few facilities to make one. While the navy closed Confederate ports along the Atlantic and Gulf coast, Scott envisioned "a powerful movement down the Mississippi to the ocean." He imagined a massive expedition of twenty steam-powered gunboats, forty transports, and sixty thousand men. The army would be composed of regulars and three-year volunteers who trained for four and a half months, meaning the expedition could not embark until mid-November 1861 at the earliest. This combined force of freshwater navy and army personnel would eliminate every enemy outpost along the Mississippi, occupy positions to maintain open lines of supply and communication, and capture and hold New Orleans until the Confederacy surrendered.[75]

Scott identified the key flaw in his strategy. "The greatest obstacle in the way of this plan," he said, was not Confederate advantages of holding interior lines of supply and communication, nor the enemy's local knowledge of the land and passion to defend it, but rather "the impatience of our patriotic and loyal Union friends." Northern anticipations of the war would challenge his approach. Scott predicted that amateur soldiers and political generals "will urge instant and vigorous action, regardless, I fear, of the consequences." After the fall of Fort Sumter, northern volunteers yearned to invade the South and punish the rebels for treason. Newspaper editors demanded an annihilating war. "Every advantage possessed should be held; every step should be forward; no concession should be made to any who stands in the way of the vigorous prosecution" of the war. A Philadelphia paper insisted, "Send the strong regiments forward to the ultimate points of decisive action without an hour's delay.—A blow as terrible as the nation's vengeance can make it should fall on Charleston." Governors across the North pleaded with Lincoln to allow them to raise more regiments than he requested. Turning back legions of eager men would dampen patriotism and lower morale during the nation's greatest crisis. "On to Richmond," not "Wait for Washington," was the northern rallying cry. Scott witnessed this war fever and feared the people would be "unwilling to wait."[76]

His prophecy proved correct. The people would not wait for passions to cool, troops to train, supplies to assemble, and blockades to tighten. Anticipations of war swept the nation in the spring of 1861 and the old general was out of step with the times. As historian Russell Weigley notes, Scott was "a museum piece, a soldier of an age gone by whose perceptions of war and strategy had little influence on most of the very graduates of West Point whose service in Mexico he so fulsomely praised, because the young graduates inhabited a new world of very different values from Scott's, the military world of Napoleon." Napoleonic warfare, with its mass armies, revolutionary zeal, and decisive battles, appealed to the volunteers and younger regular officers who would fight the Civil War. This anticipatory fervor is illustrated in the derisive nickname that people gave to Scott's strategy, the "Anaconda policy." Yearning for offense and speed, the nation could not have picked a less heroic metaphor for Scott's vision: who would prefer to crawl around the enemy and squeeze him to death?[77]

Scott circulated his strategy as a response to George McClellan who proposed an aggressive, anticipatory plan of action weeks after Fort Sumter. McClellan argued that Union forces "should not remain quietly on the defensive." Instead, he advocated invading the heart of the Confederacy with 80,000 men. McClellan would cross the Ohio River, march up the Kanawha Valley, destroy secessionist forces in Virginia, and capture the new Confederate capital of Richmond. The only difficulty he anticipated was "crossing the mountains," but he "would go prepared to meet them." If setting foot in Kentucky enflamed secessionist resistance there, McClellan planned to switch his course for Nashville. "Were a battle gained before reaching Nashville," he predicted, "the strength of Kentucky and Tennessee" may be "effectually broken." Then his triumphant army would proceed to Montgomery, "aided by a vigorous movement on the eastern line toward Charleston and Augusta." At some undetermined point in the bowels of the Deep South, the Union's eastern and western armies would converge and secretly march on "Pensacola, Mobile, or

New Orleans." McClellan believed that his plan would "relieve the pressure on Washington" and "bring the war to a speedy close."[78]

McClellan shared the anticipatory zeal of volunteers who raced to enlist so that they could march to the seat of war, win the decisive battle, and return home heroes. Like the fresh recruits, McClellan was eager for a war he anticipated would make his future. He based his vision of the looming war on his observations of the Crimean War. When he described the qualities of a great commander, McClellan articulated an anticipatory view of war while deriding the "slow and blundering" positions of expectant leaders who applied "half-way measures" and waited for war to come to them. Great generals "keep constantly in view the object of the expedition, and . . . press rapidly and unceasingly towards it." For McClellan this meant focusing on cavalry tactics (he devoted separate chapters to Russian, Prussian, Austrian, French, English, and even Sardinian horse soldiers) and his anticipatory view of military command.[79]

When the Civil War began, publisher J. P. Lippincott seized an opportunity to sell McClellan's report as a prophetic manual written in the 1850s for the volunteers of 1861. "The citizen soldier, whose patriotism alone takes him to the field, will here find the best precepts in his newly-adopted profession," Lippincott claimed. "It contains his own theoretic views and rules, now to be carried out in practice," Lippincott promised. "It is—as it were—his own military history written, unconsciously, in advance." The subject of McClellan's report is not a prophetic "military history" of the Civil War. He anticipated three future wars: Indian wars, invasions by foreign powers, and US border wars with Canada, Mexico, and the West Indies. What it offered volunteers in 1861 was a glimpse of their future commander's ethos and temporality: McClellan appears in his pages like a soldier captivated by the romance of cavalry movement, the ghost of Napoleon, and the minutia of military life. The *North American Review* admitted lacking the expertise to evaluate the volume but nonetheless praised McClellan's "scientific precision" and "careful judgment." Reading the book bolstered "the confidence of enlightened and cultivated men" in McClellan, "whom, under Providence, our national future so essentially depends."[80]

When Scott received McClellan's plan to lead 80,000 men into the heart of the Confederacy, he forwarded it to Lincoln with an attached commentary that eviscerated every aspect of it. Scott realized that McClellan imagined raising his mass army from the three-month volunteers Lincoln had requested after the bombardment of Fort Sumter. "Their service would expire by the time he had collected and organized them," Scott explained. Besides this error in time, McClellan's plan ignored the sober realities of war apparent to an expectant, defensive strategist like Scott. "A march upon Richmond from Ohio would probably insure the revolt of Western Virginia, which if left alone will soon be five out of seven for the Union," Scott predicted. Worse, "the general eschews water transportation by the Ohio and Mississippi in favor of long, tedious, and break down (of men, horses, and wagons) marches." By marching toward the center of the Confederacy, McClellan planned "to subdue the seceded States piece-meal instead of enveloping them all" with a blockade that required fewer men and resources.[81]

When Scott concluded that northern anticipation and eagerness for war was "the great danger now pressing upon us," he did not recognize the assumption that Confederates would wait to be enveloped. While northern men called for an offensive strategy, southern recruits also yearned to take the war to the enemy. If the Union faced political pressures to recover the South, the Confederacy encountered greater political pressure to assert its sovereignty. Whether or not Union armies invaded the Confederacy, rebel forces itched to "liberate" slave states on the border, particularly Maryland, Kentucky, and Missouri. The border war of Napoleonic proportions that Jones prophesied in 1860 loomed large in 1861.[82]

The debate between anticipatory and expectant strategies that occurred in Washington also affected Richmond. A West Point graduate, President Jefferson Davis planned a defensive strategy reminiscent of George Washington's conservation of manpower, but southern anticipations thwarted his designs as thoroughly as northern excitement quashed Scott's ideas. Many factors undermined Davis's plan to outlast the enemy by being passive and avoiding costly campaigns. During the Revolution, Washington faced an enemy that relied on manpower and material reinforcements from across the sea. The Confederacy fought a foe whose numerical advantages were nearby and could easily attack any weak spot in Confederate defenses. The scale of the Civil War was so much larger than that of the Revolution that when armies occupied territory, the citizens suffered in ways they did not during British occupation. The Confederacy was more densely populated than the colonies and needed the economic resources of all areas to beat the Union. Basically, a porous defensive position would be disastrous for Confederate politics and economics. The ghost of John Brown haunted the Confederate perimeter. All along the border, including the coastline, southern politicians and citizens feared midnight assaults by abolitionist hordes bent on rape and insurrection. Historians criticize the Confederacy for spreading its manpower too thinly across the South, but that token rebel presence was necessary to keep distant white southerners loyal to the new nation and to frustrate black southerners who might exploit the turmoil of war to revolt.[83]

The greatest obstacle to Davis's passive, defensive plan was Confederate anticipations of an offensive war that would whip the enemy and conquer peace. Confederate enthusiasm for war reached its zenith in the summer of 1861 when Richmond planned its war strategy. The people did not want to stand still and await an enemy invasion. "The idea of waiting for blows, instead of inflicting them, is altogether unsuited to the genius our people," argued the *Richmond Examiner*. Southerners wanted to determine where the battle would be fought and won, and many of them wanted to fight on northern soil. Newspaper editors argued that one Confederate army campaigning in Ohio or Pennsylvania was worth more than all the fortifications the young nation could build to guard its borders. Their tone was anticipatory and confident in the ultimate success of their arms.[84]

Many Confederate officers, particularly Robert E. Lee, P. G. T. Beauregard, and Thomas Jackson, articulated an offensive strategy that would strike the enemy when he least expected it and force him to fight on ground of the Confederates' choosing. This vision of the war required an anticipatory mindset: the Confederates would imagine the coming campaign, intuit the enemy's movements, and seize the initiative. Lee knew that this aggressive strategy risked heavy casualties but he feared a long, destructive war that bled the Confederacy to death more than he dreaded costly campaigns that gave the Confederacy a chance to win the war. As Lee explained, "We must decide between the positive loss of inactivity and the risk of action." Lee understood that his strategy would take years to work. Popular predictions forecasted Confederate independence after a single, decisive victory. Anticipating that the Union would not quit after early defeats, Lee hoped to win the war before the enemy could harness its superior strength to best advantage, but it would take time. According to historian Emory Thomas, "When Lee made rare remarks about the prospects of the Confederacy in the impending war, he told people what they did not want to hear." Lee thought forecasts of a ninety-day war were delusional. Thomas Jackson agreed. Anticipating the looming war in January 1861, Jackson wrote a northern relative that the people of Virginia would "defend it with a terrific resistance—even to taking no prisoners." Like McClellan, Jackson was an early advocate for a war that plunged into the heart of enemy territory with disciplined armies that destroyed enemy forces and occupied political and economic centers. Jackson dreamed of bringing the war to northerners in the shortest amount of time possible.[85]

The Most Anticipated Battle of the War

BOTH NATIONS' ANTICIPATORY STRATEGIES collided at the battle of Bull Run. After months of mobilizing, drilling, and marching, armies of eager volunteers met across Bull Run creek on July 21, 1861. When more than 36,000 men engaged each other, the contending forces marked the largest battle in the history of the continent. All told, General Irvin McDowell's Union army of roughly 50,000 men was the largest in American history. Trusting in their size and impatient to press forward, Unionists anticipated that McDowell's ranks would progress unimpeded to Richmond, even if it experienced an occasional setback or defeat along the way. All of Washington anticipated victory. Citizens and politicians drove to the battlefield with picnic baskets to watch history unfold. Confederates also anticipated triumph. Railroads raced thousands of troops from the Shenandoah Valley to site of the conflict. Impatient to receive telegrams from the front, Jefferson Davis rode to the battle too. It was the most anticipated event of the war.[86]

Edmund Ruffin would not miss it for the world. Carrying cheese, crackers, blankets, and shoes, he raced to join his Fort Sumter comrades, the Palmetto Guards. Everything seemed to be unfolding just as he had anticipated in *Anticipations of the Future*, including the enemy's barbaric behavior. When he heard rumors of Yankee atrocities, Ruffin accepted them as fact. He wanted the Confederacy to pursue the strategy that worked in his history of the future: guerrilla warfare without quarter. Merry sounds around campfires, laughter, and martial music convinced him that he belonged to a great army, a band of knights. The finer elements of the South had stepped forward to make history.

But events moved faster than Ruffin could manage. His body ached from sleeping on the ground and his new shoes tortured his feet. As the Palmetto Guards raced from one position to the next, Ruffin fell behind. He asked to ride on artillery caissons and caught up with his company but was too tired to be of service. At Charleston he could man a position and participate in the bombardment as well as younger men. Bull Run exposed any delusions Ruffin had about his body's ability to fight like an eager volunteer. If the Guards charged a position, he could not keep up and join the fight. If they retreated, he would fall behind and risk being captured. Nonetheless, when the battle erupted Ruffin was determined to be at the center of it.[87]

On July 21, the enemy did not attack the Guards position and Ruffin sat impatiently listening to history happening on the next ridge. It galled him to be "confined to one spot all day, between a high hill & thick woods, where nothing could be seen." When the music of war crescendoed, he followed the rolling thunder and climbed a hill. Ruffin "became so excited with the sounds of the firing" that he deserted his post to reach the seat of war. A battery of artillery spotted him and carried him forward to a vantage where he spied a ragged blue line retreating. The old man gratefully accepted an offer to fire a shell at the invaders. It exploded among men scurrying to cross a bridge. Ruffin watched as panicked survivors fled from the carnage he caused. After the battle, he walked to the spot where his shell landed, collected battle trophies, and counted the dead. Only three bodies remained. Disappointed, Ruffin convinced himself that he killed or wounded at least fifteen Yankees. He predicted that the victory at Bull Run "would be virtually the close of the war." In *Anticipations of the Future*, Ruffin imagined northern armies bleeding to death in costly invasions of the South. Union aggression would cause "the impossibility of conveying reinforcements and supplies to the seat of war." Then, as northern society descended into anarchy, troops would be needed to suppress insurrections at home. He was impatient for that end. Ruffin even wished for death while the spirit of 1861 climaxed: if only a cannon ball had painlessly killed him at Bull Run, just as he had done to his enemies. Nothing would be better for his legacy than to die like John Brown, a willing sacrifice at the dawn of his cause.[88]

At Bull Run that distinction fell to Francis Bartow. A Georgia lawyer and politician, Bartow did not flinch from secession and war because he considered Lincoln's election as dangerous to southern lives and institutions as Brown's raid. "Let age bring its wisdom and experience, manhood its matured strength, and youth its ardor, and thus with a clear conscience in the sight of man and God, march forward on our mission." The time for calm deliberation had passed. During the secession winter he confessed, "I see no safety, no honour, no fidelity in any other step, than the quick advance, through fog through doubt, through darkness into the glorious field of action." While serving as a Georgia delegate to the Confederate Provisional Congress in Montgomery, Bartow resigned to be among the first Confederates in battle. At Bull Run he helped to reverse the tide of battle. A horse was shot out from under him. He found another and pressed forward. "Boys, follow me!" he hollered, waving his cap, when a shell fragment struck his heart. Bartow's wife received news of his death the next day. She sent word to his mother but did not have the heart to finish the letter. Her sister concluded the note, saying, "Let me beg you to remember that he died the most glorious death that man can wish for, and that in that death he has left you a spotless name, an inheritance the noblest and richest that man can leave." He was the first brigade commander killed in battle during the war.[89]

Civil War Americans did not descend into a war that was unexpected in length and bloodshed. Instead, they realized a horrible conflict that many of them had anticipated from the start. Winthrop, Ruffin, Samuels, Jarvis, Garfield, Reid, Gaillard, Larcom, Bartow, and thousands of other people sensed the war's magnitude. The atrocity rumors that swirled through both armies before and after Bull Run reveal that both sides expected the worst from the other. Their biggest miscalculation in 1861 was not the length or nature of the war but rather humanity's ability to control it. Every eager soul who sought the center of the war thought that he could better himself and his country by anticipating the future and making history. Individual initiatives did little to alter the titanic struggle. But together the anticipations of thousands of volunteers and runaways affected the war's scope and direction. Only time would reveal their influence, however, and many people were desperate to make history by moving forward to the heart of the struggle. Like Ruffin at Bull Run, these Americans came to realize that the heart of the war was impossible to reach, if it even existed.

6

Expectations

WHEN THE WAR CAME, Henry Clay Pate's bowie knife belonged to a gentleman in Massachusetts. Pate suspected Samuel Gridley Howe, the husband of Julia Ward Howe and a member of the Secret Six. Howe was a good guess, but evidence points toward another man. Unlike most friends who betrayed Brown in the initial aftershock of the attack, this man praised him. He argued that Brown's raid shocked Americans because they were too accustomed to wielding weapons in ignoble affairs: dueling, waging foreign wars, killing Indians, and hunting fugitive slaves. Urgent to change northerners' initial reaction to the news, he repeated his speech in Worcester and Boston. "I think we should express ourselves at once, while Brown is alive," he told a friend. When Frederick Douglass declined to appear at a Boston rally for Brown, this man took his place on the program. Newspaper summaries of his speech edited out its boldest points. James Redpath asked him to provide a definitive account of Black Jack for his book about Brown and dedicated the volume to him. His name was Henry David Thoreau.[1]

If this provenance is true, death cut short the lives of most men associated with the knife. Brown gave the blade to his son Frederick, the wild rider at Black Jack, perhaps to recognize his role in winning the battle. Another member of Brown's party stole the knife from Frederick and "traded it off" before Frederick's death in Kansas. At dawn on August 30, 1856, Frederick left a friend's house to care for their horses. Walking down the road, he stopped when two riders approached. "Good morning," Frederick hollered. He recognized Martin White, a Methodist minister. "I know you," White said, "and we are foes." The minister shot Frederick through the heart. To settle matters, two of Brown's sons set off to kill White while Brown hunted for Pate's knife. After an exhaustive search, he "traced the knife through several parties, and finally got it."[2]

When Thoreau first met Brown in 1857, he asked to see Pate's knife and admired it. Black Jack and the Harpers Ferry raid inspired Thoreau as principled acts of heroism against great odds. The looming civil war did not. Days before the firing on Fort Sumter, Thoreau confessed to a friend, "I do not so much regret the present condition of things in this country (provided I regret it at all) as I do that I ever heard of it." Reading newspapers compelled him to ponder "deeds of darkness" on the horizon. Two days before the war, Thoreau wrote, "Blessed are they who never read a newspaper, for they shall see Nature and through her, God." Months later tuberculosis started to take his life. Thoreau fled to Minnesota hoping that inland air would clear his lungs. Death came for him in May 1862. His neighbor, Bronson Alcott, visited Thoreau on his last day. Alcott found his friend "lying patiently & cheerfully on the bed he would never leave again." Thoreau told Alcott, "It took Nature a long time to do her work" but he was almost gone. "Now comes good sailing," Thoreau said, and then he died. He was forty-four.[3]

Death took Henry Clay Pate two years later on the Telegraph Road north of Richmond. When Brigadier General George Custer's cavalry threatened to raid the Confederate capital on May 11, 1864, Colonel Pate's Fifth Virginia horse soldiers dismounted and waited for the enemy beside an abandoned inn named Yellow Tavern. Repeating what he did at Black Jack, Pate sought cover for his men in sunken wagon ruts and gullies. It was a strong position. An open meadow beside the road ended in a curtain of dark woods. After Pate placed skirmishers and sharpshooters, pickets reported the enemy dismounted and coming forward in three, solid lines. The first row stepped out of the woods when an aide-de-camp from General J. E. B. Stuart found Pate and ordered him to hold the position "at all hazards." Pate's grey eyes stared at the man vacantly. The aide repeated the order, thinking Pate had not heard him over the din of battle. Pate said nothing, but his face paled. The order was a death sentence. When the enemy filled the meadow, Pate's advanced lines fell back into the road. Looking at the men of the Fifth Virginia while he galloped from the scene, the aide sensed "it was a trap and they knew it."[4]

The enemy broke Pate's right flank. He ordered his men across the road and into a ditch on the opposite side. When Pate managed to check Custer's advance, Stuart witnessed this momentary success and rode over to commend him. A lot had happened between the two men since their first meeting in Kansas on the day Brown stole Pate's knife. When the Civil War gave Pate a second chance to spill blood for sovereignty, he raised a cavalry battalion by assembling riders from across Virginia. He dreamed of an independent command called "Pate's Rangers" that would rely on the local knowledge of men from every corner of the Old Dominion to harry the enemy and disappear into the night. Before Pate could realize his dream, Stuart ordered Pate's men added to his cavalry and placed a crony, Thomas Rosser, in command of

Pate and his troops. After Pate's surrender at Black Jack, nothing could convince Stuart that the border ruffian had an ounce of military talent. Furious, Pate feuded with Stuart and Rosser, ruining his chance for promotion. Instead of fighting during the peak of Confederate glory in 1862–1863, Pate was relieved of duty and court-martialed twice by Rosser. When he finally cleared his name in 1864, Pate raced to the front for a chance at vindication. His feud with Stuart ended at Yellow Tavern when the general rode up and praised him. "You have done all that a man could do. How long can you hold this position?" Stuart asked. "Until I die, General," Pate answered.[5]

He kept his promise. When the enemy swarmed his position, Pate stood above his men on the bank of the road encouraging them to hold fast. "One more round, boys, and then we'll get to the hill," he yelled. A soldier asked Pate if they should surrender. After Black Jack he could not. While Pate waved his hat to rally his survivors, a bullet smashed his right temple. He fell dead in the road. In his official report, Custer announced the death of "the notorious Col. Henry Clay Pate."[6]

Stuart saw Pate's end through field glasses before he met his own. "Pate has died the death of a hero," he said, and then a bullet tore through his side. Sensing that the wound was mortal, Stuart urged his men to secure a victory, saying, "I would rather die than be whipped." The night before, Stuart had told his friend, Major Andrew Venable, that he "never expected to live through the war" and would rather be dead than conquered. Now he asked Venable if "the death pallor" showed on his face. "I hope not," Venable replied. Expecting the end, Stuart bequeathed his possessions. He gave Venable his gray horse, asked that his personal effects be sent to his wife, arranged the transmission of his official papers to Richmond, explained that he promised his spurs to Mrs. Lilly Lee of Shepherdstown, Virginia, and wanted his son to have his sword. He did not mention the bowie knife he took from Brown at Harpers Ferry. Stuart asked Doctor Charles Brewer if he would survive the night. Brewer doubted it. Stuart called Venable to his side. "You know that Pate and myself have had unkind feelings toward each other," he said. He told Venable that Pate's death at Yellow Tavern was "one of the most gallant and heroic acts of the war." According to Stuart, when he complimented Pate, the former enemies shook hands under fire. "I want you Major to let his friends know," Stuart said. "I am going fast now," he said. "I am resigned; God's will be done." Stuart was buried in Hollywood cemetery in a plot directly above Pate's grave.[7]

Edmund Ruffin heard about Stuart's death while he prepared for his own. For a month he battled a mysterious illness that left him dizzy, feverish, shaky, and wracked with pain. He lost appetite and sleep. When his symptoms decreased so did his strength. Friends and neighbors paid their last respects. When tremors ceased to trouble his hand, he resumed his diary to stay current on the latest campaigns and forecast their consequences. The prospect of dying before the war ended terrified him. Rumors about the clash at Spotsylvania Court House convinced Ruffin it was "the greatest & bloodiest battle of this war of great & bloody battles, & that Grant had been decisively defeated." He thanked God. But Lee's army was like Ruffin's body. Victories against the invaders sapped strength that could not be replaced. The "relative conditions of our worn-down army & of the enemy's" portended "an end to our so-far obstinate resistance & defense."[8]

That night he wrote a letter to his sons, titled "My Last Directions." He expected to "die soon & suddenly, & almost without any immediately previous warning." Ruffin wanted his body placed in a plain, pine coffin without drapery or dressings. He forbade any attempt "to separate the coffin from contact with the filling mass of earth." No "means shall be used to retard the earliest nearest approach & later joining of 'earth to earth,' which is inevitable, & cannot occur too soon." One of the sons he addressed, Julian, was dead, a recent casualty of the unprecedented destruction of 1864. When a telegram brought Ruffin the news, his children tried to shield their father from the terrible truth that his boy had been decapitated at Drewry's Bluff.[9]

Dread

THIS FINAL CHAPTER FOCUSES on expectations of death, destruction, and Armageddon. It returns full circle to the original meaning of the knife with a coffin-shaped handle. When possessions outlived their owners, their mute endurance acted as surrogates for the dead. The vacant chair at the family table, the shirt that retained a scent, such things represented the presence of the departed, for a while. The associations that possessions acquired when families accumulated them were as tenuous as their lives and fortunes. Stories about things faded and changed as generations perished or objects were stolen or lost. Time erased the meaning that people ascribed to things, but the objects remained.

Forces impersonal, perhaps supernatural, controlled things. When the war acquired its own momentum and killed thousands, it undercut Americans' confidence that they made history by anticipating events and fashioning the future. The destructive indecision of military campaigns challenged people's faith in perpetual progress. Facing uncertainty, some

Americans looked to God and expected providence to design tomorrow and provide a meaningful ending to the war. Others doubted that the Almighty was responsible for such carnage and waste. For doubters, the war defied linear narratives toward civilization or the millennium. Whatever fate awaited America, people sensed that the war's outcome would arrive in its own time and on its own terms.[10]

Instead of anticipating a glorious war that would revitalize the nation, thousands expected a ruinous conflict that would spin out of control. The short war myth, the persistent idea that all Americans anticipated fun and frolic in 1861, silenced men and women who expected the war's terrifying dimensions and dreaded the future. When Fort Sumter fell, college student Andrew McCollam wrote, "There can be no doubt that the most destructive and bloody war has been inaugurated at Charleston, which this country has ever witnessed, and every citizen coming under the militia law will eventually have to go." Most important, the short war myth ignores the expectations of women and African Americans. Women across the nation expressed dreadful predictions about the war's destruction and length in their private writings. "Dante never saw more clearly the tortures of the damned than I have the possibilities of the Future," Grace Elmore wrote. She imagined her brother dead on the battlefield, her mother shorn of wealth in old age, her family scattered. Untold thousands of women envisioned similar tragedies.[11]

Such expectations were not exclusive to women. If mothers and wives dreaded a long, destructive war from the beginning, African Americans prayed for a conflict that would endure long enough to kill slavery. Blacks hoped for a cataclysm that other Americans dreaded. Thousands of people who expected the worst confessed their fears in letters and diaries. Moderates from across the country warned their leaders that the extremism of secessionists and abolitionists stoked passions that would escalate into a harrowing war. Even men who volunteered in 1861 feared the coming struggle. Chandler Gillam of the 28th New York glimpsed the looming war in July 1861 when his regiment passed through Harpers Ferry. He visited the spot where John Brown was hanged, counted bullet holes in nearby buildings, and sifted through the ruins of an arsenal burned by departing Confederates. "Such is the fortunes of war," he warned his wife, "<u>death and destruction</u>." In nearby Martinsburg, Virginia, Holmes Conrad pleaded with his sons not to enlist. "No one knows but my wife how I tried to keep them from this war," he told a friend. Both boys joined and died together at Bull Run. "How do I stand it, having now <u>no sons</u>?" Conrad survived them by convincing himself, "God meant to take them in His own way." Instead of imagining war as a revolution shaped by the people, these Americans saw war as a storm driven by impersonal forces. At best, God orchestrated the reckoning. At worst, chaos prevailed.[12]

Just as looming death fostered expectations in a person, wars spread waves of expectations through nations. War paused, altered, or ended life. None could escape one of those fates, and all prayed for a resumption of prior projects. William Wilkins of Michigan yearned to know his future, which "the God of Battles only knows." After a terrifying scrape through the streets of Winchester, Virginia, he wrote his wife how he wished to "daguerreotype to you the feelings of my own heart." "Whatever fate befalls, keep up as before the same strong, trusting, hopeful heart, and rest assured that in God's good time I shall be returned to you in safety." When the unexpected battle enveloped him, Wilkins resolved to live a higher, purer life if God would protect him from the storm. "I never felt God's sustaining grace, and His guiding and strengthening hand so forcibly" as at Winchester.[13]

Francis Donaldson felt a similar experience during a midnight raid in October 1861. Officers ordered the men to approach the enemy in silence, but Private Joseph Pascoe broke the tension by jesting and damning God. Donaldson warned him, "Be careful that the Almighty God, whom you have just asked to damn your soul, don't take you at your word." He urged Pascoe to be quiet: "You, among others of us, may be called suddenly to meet this God above [that] you so grossly defy, so cease your cursing and act as a man." Gunfire interrupted them, lighting the woods opposite from Donaldson's column. "My heart was paralyzed with a dreadful fear and my hair stood on end," he confessed. "Whether it was that I was unable to move, I cannot say, but I stood still in the middle of the road for a moment and looked right into the flaming tongues of fire." Someone knocked Donaldson to the ground and covered his body. It was Pascoe, shot dead through the throat. "How awfully swift the avenging hand of the almighty," Donaldson told his brother.[14]

Iowa private Scott Boyd was too shocked to move during his first battle, Shiloh. When his brother, Cyrus, tried to revive him, Boyd said he could go no further. Certain that the future was theirs to fashion, the brothers had volunteered with their local Wide Awakes. Shiloh changed their thoughts of the future from eager anticipations to dreadful expectations. Gazing at strips of flesh hanging from flowering trees, Cyrus asked, "Can there be anything in the *future* that *compensates* for this slaughter?" Soldiers like Boyd, Wilkins, and Donaldson entered military life with anticipations of traveling to the seat of war, making history, and forging the future through manly activity. Instead, war seized them, made them wait, and suspended their fate and the future in anxious expectation. Because he served in his division's headquarters, Wilkins anticipated being at the center of things. However, he and other men were "doomed to be inactive spectators" while the war "pours in upon us from every quarter." Like a flare illuminating an enemy assault, expectations exposed an inevitable fate that froze people in their tracks. The future arrived in unpredictable bursts like telegraphs and gunfire. In December 1861, Sarah Preston expressed this temporality when she expected a terrible battle to begin. "For the last two weeks we have been kept in constant excitement not knowing what hour might bring a telegram that we had been attacked."[15]

Not everyone who expected the war sensed approaching death. Many dreaded anarchy. Others feared a financial collapse and saw a panic looming on the horizon. People who sympathized with the opposite region, like New York conservatives and Virginia Unionists, feared that warring parties dragged them and the nation into a senseless struggle. Others expected nothing specific but felt a sickening feeling about the war and knew, by premonition, that it controlled their fate and their family's future. All who had these visions of the looming war shared a dreadful feeling that the future rushed toward them, and they were powerless to avoid it. Even people at the center of activity, like Abraham Lincoln's private secretary John G. Nicolay, confessed, "Events are crowding so thickly upon us that it is impossible to calculate their present or future importance." New Yorker George Templeton Strong expressed the same feeling. "We are living a month of common life every day," he said. At different points in the conflict, all sorts of Americans felt this way—from generals and statesmen to common soldiers, from women at home to refugees on the road, from former slaves to Wall Street speculators.[16]

Letters from the Brink

WHEN THE CIVIL WAR loomed, ordinary people shared dreadful expectations in letters to politicians. Perhaps Stephen Douglas received more of this mail than anyone. He was the only presidential candidate who campaigned nationally. A talented northern statesman with southern ties, Douglas was widely considered a man who could resolve the crisis. From the Harpers Ferry raid through the secession crisis, people from Maine to Mississippi flooded him with letters. Their predictions give a glimpse of the wide spectrum of visions Americans had about the future. Significantly, these prophecies cannot be reduced to a party line or sectional bias. Moreover, they shifted with major events: the future looked different after Harpers Ferry, different again during the 1860 campaign, different in another way after Lincoln's election, and altogether different after secession.[17]

Citizens who wrote Douglas expected a long bloody war and proposed numerous ways of avoiding it. Southerners were particularly alarmed. "For Heavens sake try to avoid the awful calamity now plain in sight," pleaded an anonymous writer from Alabama.[18] William Cunningham, also from Alabama, thought civil war would be "so dark" and destructive "that I for one, would prefer not to . . . speak of its consequences and effects." Nonetheless Cunningham warned Douglas "if the Fight is ever commenced it will last always or end in extermination so far as the South is concerned for they never will be whipped back into the Union." He urged Douglas to broker a peace that reimbursed the Union for lost property and established diplomatic ties between the two nations.[19]

Many writers looked to the past, most commonly to the Revolutionary era, for a glimpse of the future. Citing David Ramsey's history of the American Revolution, Thomas Gibson of Illinois argued that "our once glorious union is at this time similar to [the] troubles of . . . 1775." At the outbreak of the Revolution, colonial friends in Parliament had warned that Britain could never conquer America. They urged the king to "withdraw the troops from Boston immediately" and seek a peaceful way to resolve the crisis. Gibson pleaded with Douglas not to make the same mistake as the British. In Gibson's opinion, people who compared Lincoln's position to Jackson's during the nullification crisis were making a terrible mistake. Coercing Charleston, the hotbed of secession, was like coercing Boston, the center of independence. The results would be the same: a long, unwinnable war.[20] Another Illinois citizen looked to the Constitutional Convention for his prophecy. He argued that the federal government "has no constitutional power" to negotiate with secessionists, so the citizens must "call a National Convention" of all the states to either "satisfy the disaffected and induce all to remain in the Union" or find "a means of adjustment" that compensated the United States for losing the South. A horrible war was "inevitable" if Lincoln's government faced secession alone, because "the only arbitrament permitted to it is the sword." In short, the people had to save the government from itself just as they had during the Constitutional Convention of 1787. He insisted, "There could be nothing dishonorable" or illegal "in such a course." "Our government . . . is itself one of mutual agreement of the people. Why should we be monarchically tied down to mere governmental forms in such a crisis as this?" he asked.[21]

Others told Douglas that politics caused the nation's troubles, so the country should look elsewhere for a solution. These writers used economics, religion, and even gender to explain the crisis. A New Yorker warned Douglas that the economic and social bonds of slavery would draw the Upper South into the Confederacy, creating a formidable enemy. He noted that secession had already increased the price of cotton, thereby giving the South an extra $35 million, "the strongest possible encouragement for a maintenance of their position, and a corroboration of their theory that Cotton is King." He warned Douglas, "It is a common error, dear sir, with Governments, alike with individuals, to under-value the strength and resources of opponents." He predicted that "a manufacturing impulse will be stimulated and fostered throughout the whole South," despite its meager shipping and industry.[22] J. L. Napier of Mississippi thought religion caused "the horror that now stares us in the face." Black Republicans fomented a "northern crusade of the higher law, [that] proposes to confiscate [slaves] as a matter of faith." Napier predicted a "long dark and dreary future" of religious fanaticism and blood. He compared America's future to Europe's dark past of religious warfare.[23] William Morton of Georgia thought disunion was permanent, but war could be avoided if Mary Lincoln urged her husband to seek peace. According to Morton, "Mrs. Lincoln has more influence than all the politicians. Napoleon the 1 did well when he had the sensible Josephine to advise him. . . . Mr. Buchanan's failure [as president] was for want of a sensible wife." "Peace will be preserved and the two governments . . . will work in harmony" if Mary Lincoln could convince the president that "no force can ever affect reconstruction." Only the sensible counsel of a loving wife could save the country from a long civil war.[24] These Americans were not innocently anticipating the best but vocally expecting the worst. As one writer put it, there was "great diversity of opinions as to the best course to persue, every one seems to have a different notion about the future and it is putting on a biblical appearance."[25]

John Crittenden received similar messages while he tried to broker a sectional compromise in December 1860. For all of these writers, averting civil war was men's work. "In such a crisis," W. G. Fullerton told Crittenden, "it becomes every citizen to give his best thoughts to his country, and if I succeed in inducing you to read the following, I will have done my duty." Fullerton marked his message "private" and urged Crittenden to "read it yourself," because he believed "a little spark may kindle a great fire and something you read herein may start a train of thought in your more experienced, comprehensive, and powerful mind, which may lead to the development of a plan resulting in the salvation of our union." The men who wrote Douglas and Crittenden expected great things from their leaders. A confidential correspondence between patriots would inspire big men to find a solution to the nation's troubles. As one correspondent explained, "It is the duty, and should be the endeavor of every true and enlightened Statesmen and patriot to exercise a wise forecast."

Communication could clarify the crisis, ease section tensions, and generate a fair compromise. "Our greatest danger," C. B. Haddock told Crittenden, "arises from the mutual ignorance of the South and the North of each other's real feelings and purposes. Until this ignorance is corrected and some better mutual understanding is had, the public mind cannot be quieted."[26]

Proposals to avoid bloodshed by redrawing the map inspired many Americans who felt caught between the radicalism of New England abolitionists and Deep South secessionists. James Robb wanted Crittenden to convene a Constitutional Convention in Louisville and invite delegates from only the border states: Maryland, Virginia, Kentucky, Tennessee, Missouri, Pennsylvania, Ohio, Indiana, and Illinois. By barring extremists from both sections, sober statesmen could craft moderate amendments and then promise to ally all of the border states with whichever region swore to support the compromise. Maryland governor Thomas Hicks agreed that "patriots, pure men, must stand up and beat back the powers of darkness." Hicks sensed that extremists sought to precipitate secession and war by stirring passions and silencing reason. "Stave off a collision," he advised Crittenden; "let the people have two weeks more for reflection and they will take the matter in hand. Then, farewell to the efforts of fanatics, for these 'dry brush piles' North and South, fired with the Lava of Hell will be extinguished." N. P. Tallmadge feared that the time for debate "seems to be passed, and passion alone reigns triumphant." On the day he expected South Carolina to secede, Tallmadge was "an attentive and anxious spectator of passing events." He feared that disunion and civil war would atomize the nation into four or five squabbling republics "never again to be united." None of the dire predictions of disunion he heard matched the horrific ending that loomed ahead. "The most searching and penetrating eye cannot reach them—the most vivid imagination cannot paint them. All of the real or fancied wrongs, on the one side or the other, are as nothing, absolutely nothing, compared with the dire calamities which must inevitably overtake us."[27]

Reading the mail of Stephen Douglas and John Crittenden reveals how letters conveyed expectations of the looming war. Their correspondence expressed widespread emotions that led to very different solutions to the crisis. Grief versus indignation over the dissolved Union shaped divergent reactions to what loomed ahead and how to face it. Alarm hardened into anger in some people while for others it settled into anxiety. The point is not to quantify emotions and count whether more people imagined a long, dark war or a short, glorious one. No amount of research can sustain such overgeneralizations. The point is that Americans sensed a crisis beyond their control and shared their premonitions with leaders who may have had the power to stop it. "You may think it presumptious in an obscure individual like myself addressing you," James Robb told Crittenden, "but my anxiety for the preservation of the Union is my apology." Such appeals reinforced antebellum notions that correspondence was a form of prayer. People who prayed—or wrote Douglas and Crittenden—believed their thoughts traveled reliable paths to reach a distant power that might work on their behalf. Civil War correspondence was an act of faith.[28]

Artist and Apprentice

THE LOOMING WAR TERRIFIED Samuel F. B. Morse who did everything within his power to avoid it. The spirit of 1861 sickened him. "I should as soon think of rejoicing that one of my sons has killed the other in a brawl," he wrote a friend. Though he considered himself a nationalist, Morse confessed that his "sympathies are strongly with the South, especially the Christian slaveholder." He had fond memories from his early days as a portrait painter in Charleston, and his wife's family had ties to the South, particularly her brother who owned a sword-making company in New Orleans. His sentiments were not unusual in New York City where many people made fortunes trading southern cotton. The mayor floated an idea to declare New York a neutral port to retain its southern commerce. During the secession crisis, Morse founded the American Society for Promoting National Unity and hosted meetings in his parlor. He hoped the organization could convince secessionists to remain in the Union by proving they had friends in the North. The "precipitancy" and "passion" of the hour maddened Morse. "I am persuaded that if time were taken calmly to ascertain and to prove the real sentiment of the North towards the South, it would be found in indignant rebuke of these troubles of our peace." Passions trumped logic and politicians exploited the atmosphere to elevate their positions. "It is easy to raise a storm by those who cannot control it," Morse warned.[29]

When the Confederacy formed in February 1861, Morse blamed Republicans for driving a wedge between the sections. "We are now the Untied and no longer the United States," he jibed. Expecting a ruinous war, Morse marveled that Republicans were "shutting their eyes and ears to the actual condition of things." Morse read and approved of the Reverend James H. Thornwell's secession pamphlet, "The State of the Country," for its expectant posture and reliance on God. Thornwell explained, "When it was perceived that the tendency of events was inevitably driving the South to disunion, a condition from which she at first recoiled with horror, then she began to cast about for considerations to reconcile her to her destiny. Then, for the first time, was it maintained, that, instead of being a loser, she might be a gainer by the measure which the course of the Government was forcing upon her." Morse felt certain that the Republicans' "irritating hints and acts of coercion" compelled Thornwell and other southerners to secede.[30]

The future presented Morse with no country. He could not go South and felt repulsed by the North. "I am tempted, and may yield to the temptation, to seek a home in more peaceful Europe." The thought stunned Morse, a man who had despised and distrusted Europe his whole life. "To flee for safety from the toasted land of freedom, to despotic Europe! What a change! What an anomaly!" While both sides prepared for war, Morse paid an emissary to meet with Abraham Lincoln and Jefferson Davis. When these missions failed, Morse suspected a European conspiracy was destroying America. Morse's God was not behind this war, and if the sectional leaders could not stop the madness, then an infernal cabal must be running things. To alarm the nation, he published another conspiracy theory, *The Present Attempt to Dissolve the American Union, A British Aristocratic Plot.* Morse warned that British abolitionists were orchestrating disunion and civil war to destroy American slavery and eliminate the United States as a looming international challenger to Great Britain. "Where are the people?" Morse raged; "why do they sleep when incendiaries have fired the house?"[31]

Morse's former art student, David Hunter Strother, shared his fears that a cabal pushed the nation into a long, destructive war. While the New Yorker blamed abolitionists and British conspirators for the impending bloodbath, the Virginian blamed secessionists. "The people averse to the war at first have been cheated & forced into it by leaders who have not the capacity to maintain it successfully, nor the wit to invent a respectable reason for it." The Confederacy was founded on "fraud, injustice & violence. Its declarations to the world are contradictory, irrational and contemptible." Counter to the spirit of the age, an oligarchy dedicated to slavery "has not the sympathy of a single civilized nation." Confederates might crush local resistance for a while, but their power was not permanent.[32]

Like Morse, Strother thought it was madness to embrace the looming war with anticipation and precipitate action. He watched Virginia militia sack Harpers Ferry before the people had ratified secession. While the armory burned, Strother sat down to sketch the scene. Violence eroded order, confusion reigned, and Strother wondered if conservative critics like Thomas Macaulay were right about America—the first major trial was dissolving the republic into anarchy. While thinking about the future, Strother noticed that the American flag had disappeared above the arsenal, replaced by the flag of Virginia. He stared at the flag and shuddered at the consequences. Against his will, Strother's citizenship had shifted from a nation that spanned the continent to a broken fragment. The moment recalled feelings that overwhelmed him while visiting Mount Vesuvius. Standing on the rim of the volcano, Strother peered "down upon the sea of smoke that concealed every thing around and beneath, when a sudden breeze rolled the clouds away and for a moment my eyes beheld the hideous gulf that yawned below. A pit whose sulphurous horrors and immeasurable depth were revealed only by the glare of lurid flames and boiling lava—whose appalling aspect paralyzed the senses like the grasp of a nightmare."[33]

Strother could not shake awful premonitions about the looming war that froze him in dreadful expectation. While his father traveled to Washington to offer his services to Abraham Lincoln, Strother married Mary Eliot Hunter and tried to forget about the impending crisis by starting a home in Berkeley Springs. When Virginia finally voted on the ordinance of secession in May, the results were a formality, but Berkeley Springs voted for the Union. Local militia mutinied when Virginia authorities dragged them into the Confederate army. When rebel recruiters knocked on Strother's door, he answered it with a loaded gun. In July, when the Union army concentrated in northern Virginia to prepare for the battle of Bull Run, Strother offered his services as a local advisor but did not enlist. While following Union troops on the march, he watched slaves welcome soldiers as liberators. Strother overheard an older slave ask "if this was not the army that was come to set them free?" A soldier from Boston answered, "No, my man, we have come here solely to execute the laws." Bewildered and disappointed, the black man watched the army pass in silence, then sighed and saluted. To Strother, he looked like someone "awakened from a long cherished dream."[34]

Strother could sympathize with the feeling. He sensed that the war exceeded everyone's power to harness it: the soldier on the march, the expectant slave, the new president, and Strother himself. In the end, the war compelled him to fight. Confederates harassed and jailed his father, who died from the trauma. When Strother's sister wrote him a letter with the sad news, Confederates intercepted it and kept it as a trophy. In the winter of 1862, an emaciated rebel deserted to Union lines carrying Strother's letter as a token of good will. Union sentries took the letter to headquarters, where William Wilkins read it. He telegraphed Strother the fate of his father so that the forwarded letter would not surprise him. What "a sad commentary on the unhappy state of our poor country," Wilkins wrote his wife. "What grateful feeling we should have," for extremists who wanted " 'stiff-backed men who would consent to no compromise' and who thought 'the state of the country required a little blood letting.' " Strother joined the Union army and shared his knowledge of the Shenandoah Valley with General Phillip Sheridan. When Union forces burned the valley in 1864, Virginians blamed Strother for the destruction.[35]

Women Waiting

MANY WOMEN SHARED THE dire expectations of Morse and Strother but lacked their access to power. While voters hoped to affect the future by appealing to leaders through the mail, women often waited for the future to arrive in the mail. The war compelled men, from home front to headquarters, to receive the future in letters, reports, and telegraphs, but the burden of correspondence fell heavily on mothers and wives. Any message from the war could darken the future, but not receiving word felt worse—it trapped women in anxious expectation. Perhaps Charlotte Forten, an elite, black northerner, expressed this feeling best. When word that a steamer with mail arrived, Forten decided she "wasn't going to expect any more." She was "disgusted" with the mail for disappointing her so often. "Nevertheless, I *did* expect despite myself," she confessed. Hope for letters filled Forten despite her efforts to quash it. When a slave went to the steamer in search of mail, Forten's heart beat fast while awaiting his return. "Calm outwardly, but what a flutter of expectation within," Forten never imagined she would "become so *insane* about letters." The war intensified expectations by separating people, elevating perils, and disrupting the regularity of the post. Nothing was certain except suspenseful waiting.[36]

Women sensed this when their men left silence in their wake. "The sounds that broke the stillness of the night were to me the groans of the wounded," wrote Grace Elmore after her brother joined the South Carolina Minute Men. "I harrowed my heart with every sorrow that the war might bring to me." In June 1861, Carrie Fries of North Carolina thought women's "hardest struggle is after the excitement of preparation is over and they are left to await the future as best they can." Fries sewed uniforms for departing volunteers, but after the men left, "the loneliness is really painful, you can form no idea of it." The day her brother and uncle left for war, Kate Stone sensed "the weary days of watching and waiting that stretch before us!" Stone understood that volunteers could anticipate the future, march toward it, and buoy their spirits with new scenery, excitement, and the satisfaction of performing duties. The war compelled women who stayed behind to expect the future. Fate would come when either men returned or news of their deaths arrived.[37]

As they awaited the future, thousands of women watched political events unfold with deep anxiety and relied on religion to understand personal and national trials and peer over the horizon. In April 1861, Kentuckian Fanny Broderick confessed to her sister, Mary Collins, "The future appears so dark that we cannot feel the same interest in anything that we did." When the looming war convinced her "how uncertain every[thing] is," Broderick feared approaching evils that could not be averted. "Passion instead of reason rules now." Their other sister, Lizzie, considered the looming war a sign from God. "It seems to me that this must be the close of the 'thousand years' when Satan should be let loose upon the earth and these are his last dying throes, his struggles for victory." She did not bother reading the secular newspapers because they concentrated on the fleeting present. Instead she read religious presses that focused on the unfolding future. Lucy Larcom of Massachusetts expressed a similar apocalyptic vision when Lincoln won in November 1860. "I have lived a good deal in the past week, and the world has been doing a great business" she wrote in her diary. "Freedom takes long strides in these better days. The millennium is not so far off as we feared."[38]

After Fort Sumter fell, Eliza Fain of Tennessee expected a terrible war. "Never before in our country's history have we been called to witness such dark foreboding hours," she wrote in her diary. Fain prayed, "Where, O where infinite eternal all wise God is it to cease. Are we bent on self destruction—is there no help with thee O my father in these dread hours to stay this overwhelming calamity." In May her husband and two sons left for war. Fain had given birth to thirteen children. High mortality rates for mothers and babies in the Old South turned pregnancy into a time of dreadful expectation. Fain's sister died after giving birth to her first child at age nineteen. The hopes, fears, and dangers associated with pregnancy and childbirth encouraged women to expect a future that was beyond their control, arrived unexpectedly, and changed the course of their lives. Social norms reinforced this expectancy. From courtship to motherhood to widowhood, life encouraged women to wait for the future to arrive in the form of a gentleman caller, a marriage proposal, an end to mourning periods. Motherhood in particular meant trepidation mixed with joy. After escaping epidemics and accidents to reach maturity, Fain's family now faced an unexpected danger. Warfare assaulted and scattered families that Fain and countless other women had risked their lives to create.

"The sacredness of the home circle has been invaded," she wrote, "perhaps never again to be as it has been; our family altar has been broken down."[39]

When women imagined the war, they envisioned its arrival in their dooryards and its power to take their men from home and kill them. The war's power over women's future was more evident than women's power over the war. Men across the nation imagined how they would travel into the future, reach the center of the war, and affect its outcome. That was an anticipation of honor and glory in the heady, public world of politics and battlefields. Women felt more stationary and powerless before an approaching war, an impersonal force that only God could avert. In New Orleans, Lucy Blair waited with "heartrending suspence" to hear if her loved ones survived the battle of Bull Run. "Every dispatch was watched with trembling." She wished she had wings to carry her to the battlefield "now that loud mouthed cannons had hushed" and prayed God "will check his children in their mad course of distruction." Over time the war both underlined and undermined women's dependency and immobility. By sending men away, the war fixed thousands of women at home in anxious expectation of word from loved ones. But the absence of men forced new responsibilities on women that affected their temporality. They had to anticipate future needs and provide for them instead of expecting the men to do things. And when the war reached home in the form of approaching armies, southern women took to the roads.[40]

Fain expected the Civil War in East Tennessee would become "a most dreadful calamity," and she was right. Despite her faith in slavery, she feared her slaves might turn against her and beseeched God to quell "a rebellious spirit in our blacks." The ruin Fain feared came to pass. Guerrilla warfare consumed her world, and she became a target of Tennessee Unionists. On April 5, 1865, the enemy arrived at her home at dawn. When she opened the door, a Unionist neighbor, William Sizemore, stood before her. "Good morning Mrs. Fain, I am here and intend to tear you up and burn your house down." They burst open doors, emptied her smokehouse, cellar, and springhouse, stole her silverware, and took her horse and saddle. The war took her most cherished property, her slaves. She chastised a Unionist neighbor for supporting emancipation, because "there was nothing good in it." Instead of elevating black souls, freedom "was calculated to excite pride, haughtiness of spirit and every feeling contrary to the word of God."[41]

Through prayer, Fain and others expressed an expectant posture toward the war and the future. Indeed, her God had already made the future, sealed her enemy's fate, and would unfold time through providence. Fain asked God to protect her family in battle and gave thanks "when a kind Providence directs the balls aimed at them in another direction." When a winter storm passed over her sons' prison camp and blew down trees, giving the prisoners additional fuel against harsh elements on Johnsons Island, she believed "the hand of God supplied my prisoner boys with fuel." When she wasn't praying for God to fulfill her expectations, Fain prayed to Him to thwart the enemy's. On the day of Lincoln's second inauguration, she prayed, "O Lord defeat the plans of these wicked men and bring all their expectations to naught." As the conflict escalated beyond anyone's control, even warring governments prayed. National days of thanksgiving and prayer increased with the mounting carnage. The unprecedented scale of these wartime church services convinced some Americans that the side that prayed the most would win the war. As a southern woman explained to her northern aunt, "If you only knew how many fervent prayers went up from this Southern Confederacy for help against the invading foe and a speedy honourable peace, you would know it was impossible to conquer a people whose trust is in the help of God."[42]

Harriet Beecher Stowe expected the war would invade her family circle and prayed for intercession. Her son Fred had been one of the first to volunteer in the spring of 1861 when he joined Company A of the First Massachusetts. As she said goodbye to Fred, Stowe met his chaplain, J. M. Crowell, who promised to protect him from danger. Crowell wore a sword and assured Stowe it was not ornamental. After her son fought at Gettysburg, Stowe waited for more than a week to hear his fate. As Figure 6.1 depicts, northern women like Stowe received the future in the mail. The letter that finally arrived was written in a strange hand. "Dear Madam, Among the thousands of wounded and dying men on this war-scarred field, I have just met with your son, Captain Stowe." The letter was from chaplain Crowell, and Stowe braced for the next sentence. Fred was "in the hands of good, kind friends." A shell fragment tore into his right ear, and the chaplain could offer no assurance that he would recover. He only said that Fred "is quiet and cheerful, longs to see some member of his family," and anxious that his family should know his fate. Fred Stowe survived the wound but came home an alcoholic. Chaplain Crowell's sword proved incapable of protecting Stowe from the sins of camp, let alone the perils of battle.[43]

Stowe understood the war as God's reckoning upon the South. For centuries this place scattered black families. Now God dispersed white families. For centuries this land denied black men a future, treated them like beasts to be bought and killed. Now God deprived white men of a future, treated them like fodder to be drafted and slaughtered. The oppressors annihilated a race for generations. Now God destroyed the enslavers' race in

Figure 6.1 **"News from the War,"** ***Harper's Weekly*****, June 14, 1862. Library of Congress, Prints and Photographs Division.**

no time at all. Leaders could not stop this devastation. "Never have public men been so constrained to humble themselves before God and to acknowledge that there is a Judge that ruleth in the earth," Stowe said. In Virginia, where American slavery began, God's work was terrifying to behold. "Verily his inquisition for blood has been strict and awful." A blind passer-by traveling through the Shenandoah Valley could not mistake His meaning. For Stowe, the war refuted the anticipations of Edmund Ruffin and confirmed the warnings of another Virginian. "The prophetic visions of Nat Turner, who saw the leaves drop blood and the land darkened, have been fulfilled. The work of justice which he predicted is being executed to the uttermost."[44]

Ruination of the South required northern martyrs, and Stowe tried to avert her mind from "this vision" of innocent souls destroyed to avenge the slavers' sins. "I feel I need to write in these days, to keep from thinking of things that make me dizzy and blind, and fill my eyes with tears so that I cannot see the paper." Think of childhood merriment and household things, she told herself, but the deaths of local boys crowded her mind. "It is not wise that all our literature should run in a rut cut through our hearts and red with our blood." But Stowe could not think or write of anything else.[45]

Julia Ward Howe shared Stowe's vision of the war and used religion to frame her expectations. She transformed the anticipatory marching tune, "John Brown's Body," into the expectant psalm, "Battle Hymn of the Republic." The original song was a Yankee joke about an eager recruit of 1861. Sergeant John Brown of the Second Massachusetts Infantry was a short, singing Scotsman who suffered wisecracks because of his martyred namesake. "This can't be John Brown—why John Brown is dead," his comrades would jest. The battalion rewrote a popular revival song, "Say Brother Will You Meet Us on Canaan's Happy Shore," into a marching tune that teased the poor sergeant. When they marched eagerly toward the seat of war in 1861, the battalion spread the song from Boston to Broadway. Howe returned the song to its religious roots when lyrics interrupted her sleep one night. In Howe's version, God, not a soldier, marches on to war. His judgment for the sin of slavery caused the war and conducted it. The gathering armies of 1861 merely testified to His presence and performed his bidding: "He is trampling out the vintage where the grapes of wrath are stored;/ He hath loosed the fateful lightning of His terrible swift sword; / His truth is marching on." Howe's poetry expressed how untold numbers of women prophesied the war from the beginning. Instead of anticipating a glorious, short war that would be won and lost by men on the field of battle, women doubted when the war would end, dreaded its destructive power, and understood the struggle as God's reckoning that would unfold according to His time and design.[46]

Telegraphing the Future

THE FIRST PERSON TO see things unfold was often a new kind of prophet—the telegraph operator. Like prophets of old, telegraph operators "saw" the future by hearing it and used a special language to read invisible signs and translate their meaning for society. The war put the skills of telegraph operators in high demand. When Washington, DC, requested the best operators that the Pennsylvania Railroad could spare, Andrew Carnegie

Figure 6.2 Signal Telegraph Machine and Operator—Fredericksburg. Morgan Collection of Civil War Drawings, Library of Congress, Prints and Photographs Division.

personally escorted his four best men to the capital. One of them, David Homer Bates, recalled the stress of waiting for arriving dispatches. His title, "operator," privileged the slim fraction of time he spent tapping message on the machine, as Figure 6.2 shows. "Listener" was a more accurate description of his work. He and other operators spent endless hours straining to hear approaching news. As Quartermaster General Montgomery Meigs testified, "I have seen a telegraph-operator in a tent in a malarious locality shivering with ague, lying upon his camp cot with his ear near the instrument, listening for messages which might direct or arrest movements of military armies." Operators embodied the tortured position that the war imposed on all Americans: all they could do was wait for the war to unfold.[47]

Civil War expectations imprisoned Bates. At the start of the war he worked at the Navy Yard near Washington, DC. Authorities placed an armed sentry outside the door to his solitary telegraph office. No one was permitted to disturb the operator. "These orders were obeyed literally, and for four days I was virtually a prisoner," Bates recalled. The guard passed meager meals to him. Bates waited and waited. Unable to stand it any longer, on the fifth day he locked the door, opened a window, and escaped. When he returned and unlocked the door, the sentry appeared and said he would shoot Bates if he repeated the stunt.[48]

The strain of waiting for the future to arrive took its toll on men in the telegraph office. The first superintendent of telegraph operators in the War Department, John Strouse, worked himself to death. He began the war in poor health and did not last a year. The second superintendent resigned instead of facing the same fate. The third, Major Thomas Eckert, was a titan, physically and mentally. As a young man he traveled from Ohio to New York City to see Morse's invention in person and then built his own telegraph from memory when he returned home. At the start of the war, Eckert escaped Confederate warrants for his arrest as a spy. When a War Department clerk bought cheap iron pokers, Eckert proved their inferiority by breaking them over his flexed forearm. Only men like Eckert survived as telegraph operators. Like fortune tellers and spiritualists, operators mediated worlds, a position that overtaxed their bodies and minds.[49]

Bursts of sound interrupted tense expectations when a telegram arrived over the wire. The message came, one letter at a time, punctuated by dramatic pauses. As the operator transcribed the dispatch from Morse code to English, he capitalized words that he deemed important, because the message did not appear in distinct thoughts and sentences. Instead of unfolding in order with syntax, the message arrived as a matrix of words with five, six, or seven columns and lines. These blocks of text included "blind words," extra text intended to confuse enemy interceptions. A keyword in the message revealed the order and direction in which the matrix should be rewritten and transmitted. "For instance," Bates explained, "a certain key-word would represent the combination of seven columns and eleven lines and the route would be up the sixth column, down the third, up the fifth, down the seventh, up the first, down the fourth, down the second." The meaning of the message emerged by following this trail and then discarding blind words and keywords. The future arrived as nonsensical garble and the operator literally deciphered it.[50]

Uncertainty prevailed because even decoded messages contained ambiguous clues about the future. The truncated prose of telegrams could torment a recipient. A telegraphic messenger woke Oliver Wendell Holmes the night after Antietam to announce: "Captain Holmes wounded shot through the neck thought not mortal at Keedysville." The message haunted Holmes for days. Was his son's wound "*Thought not* mortal, or *not thought* mortal," he wondered. As the doctor rumbled south on a train, locomotion stirred thoughts about the wound. "Windpipe, food-pipe, carotid, jugular, a great braid of nerves, each as big as a lamp-wick, spinal cord." A bullet *through* the neck ought to kill at once. For days Holmes had only the same twelve words from the telegram to interpret his son's fate.[51]

The speed of telegraphy could transmit the trauma of a battle unfolding. On April 13, 1861, James Garfield and other Ohio state senators adjourned to huddle around a telegraph operator while news from Fort Sumter arrived. Garfield tried to describe the "terrible excitement and suspense" he felt. For hours on end, everyone was captive to the silent oracle, waiting for the future and speculating about it. To pass the time, Garfield wrote a letter describing the unfolding battle. "An hour ago a telegraphic dispatch announced that the war steamers had crossed the bar amid a storm of fire from the batteries, and that a flag of distress was hung out from the walls of Sumter, and that the whole interior of the fort was enveloped in dense smoke, indicating that it had taken fire from the red-hot shot from Moultrie," he wrote. The senators spread a large map of Charleston harbor across the table and Henry B. Carrington, adjutant general of Ohio, described the scene. Garfield could "almost see the battle."[52]

Telegrams about the surprise attack of the Confederate ironclad *Virginia* produced a similar sensation among Abraham Lincoln's cabinet. The telegraph operator seemed to see the naval action in real time and relay its effects and emotions.

> She is steering straight for the Cumberland—the Cumberland gives her a broadside—She keels over—Seems to be sinking—No, she comes on again—She has struck the Cumberland and poured a broadside into her—God! The Cumberland is sinking—

After the *Virginia* sank the *Cumberland*, burned the USS *Congress*, and ran the USS *Minnesota* aground, it threatened to steam up the Potomac and shell the capital in forty-eight hours. While the city raced to block the river, Lincoln and his cabinet stood in the War Department telegraph office in suspense waiting for word of the approaching ship. When a telegram from Major General John Wool reported that the USS *Monitor* arrived and "will proceed to take care of the *Merrimac*," the suspense of expecting the Confederate warship in Washington was replaced by the suspense of awaiting the results of the first ironclad battle in history.[53]

Lincoln, who expected the future by temperament, haunted the telegraph office. Most days he left the White House, walked to the War Department, and sat at Eckert's desk, waiting for the future to unfold. "I believe I feel trouble in the air before it comes," he told his aide John Hay in September 1863 after spending a night in the telegraph office reading dispatches from the front. While battles raged, Lincoln punctuated tortuous silences with short messages, like "Colonel: What news?" During the summer of 1862, he sat at Eckert's desk and wrote on foolscap. Like the operators, Lincoln wrote in short bursts and long pauses. Arriving telegrams interrupted his work, but the silence of the place provided a better writing space than the White House. Each night, Eckert locked Lincoln's writing in his desk drawer without reading it. Once while writing, Lincoln looked out the window and spotted a giant spider web between the windowsill and portico. Eckert joked that the operators called the colony of spiders "Major Eckert's lieutenants" and assured Lincoln that they would report soon. "Not long after a big spider appeared at the cross-roads and tapped several times on the strands, whereupon five or six others came out from different directions." When Eckert and his men looked at the web, they saw operators and wires transmitting messages. Lincoln did not share what he saw in the web. Maybe he saw the war with its web of contingencies touching everywhere and restricting everyone. Perhaps he saw how slavery ensnared the nation. Sitting in the telegraph office, waiting for the future in 1862, Lincoln was writing the Emancipation Proclamation.[54]

It seems paradoxical that Lincoln, the Great Emancipator, attributed unfolding events to God or Fate. If any individual could claim control of the war, it was the president. Yet he explained, "I claim not to have controlled events, but confess plainly that events have controlled me." When the war entered its third year, "the nation's condition is not what either party, or any man, devised or expected," Lincoln said. "God alone can claim it." Historians have attributed Lincoln's fatalism to a number of factors: melancholy, folk culture, the deaths of loved ones, republican jurisprudence, and the war. All these factors and more influenced him, but his temporality preconditioned how he understood things. Because he lived time with expectancy, sensing how the future approached him like waves reaching a shore, Lincoln focused on external forces, invisible elements that affected people and made history.[55]

With victory imminent at the start of his second term, Lincoln still favored expectations over anticipations of the future. "With high hope for the future," he ventured "no prediction in regard to it." Instead Lincoln recalled how the war consumed everything four years ago. "All thoughts were anxiously directed to an impending civil war. All dreaded it, —all sought to avert it." And yet "the war came." The sentence did not assign blame to either section for causing the war, but it also expressed expectancy. The war came to the present, because God willed it. Harriett Beecher Stowe believed the Union fought on God's side. Northerners like her son sacrificed their futures to help God punish southerners. Lincoln had a different vision. His God waged a separate war for "His own purposes." The entire nation was guilty of slavery, and God was chastening both sides "until every drop of blood drawn with the lash shall be paid by another drawn with the sword." Lincoln knew people were "not flattered by being shown that there has been a difference of purpose between the Almighty and them. To deny it, however, in this case, is to deny that there is a God governing the world."[56]

Could Prospect Taste of Retrospect

EMILY DICKINSON SHARED LINCOLN'S expectancy but denied that God orchestrated the war. She felt the future like a fated bullet. It approached her with lethal speed. The dreadful suspense of waiting for its arrival was worse than the future itself, worse than death. Suspense "does not conclude," as death does. Instead it "perishes—to live anew." The future replaced one suspense with another, like the telegram that announced the arrival of the *Monitor*. Waiting for the war's future felt like "annihilation—plated fresh/ with Immortality."[57]

Dickinson's insights about expectation, written in 1863, contrasted with society's anticipations in 1861. Eagerness for victory was like beating drums and blaring bugles—it thrilled for a while but could not last. Beating drums and hearts stopped, blaring bugles and lungs ran out of breath. More Americans would have expected the future in 1861 if they had paused amid aggressive anticipations and pondered war's certain outcomes: death and destruction.

What is to be is best descried
When it has also been—

Could Prospect taste of Retrospect
The tyrannies of Men
Were Tenderer—diviner
The Transitive toward.
A Bayonet's contrition
Is nothing to the Dead.

Dickinson's expectations in "My Triumph lasted till the Drums" challenged Walt Whitman's anticipations in "Beat! Beat! Drums!" Written in 1861, Whitman's poem resounded with the year's threats and marches.

Make no parley—stop for no expostulation,
Mind not the timid—mind not the weeper or prayer,
Mind not the old man beseeching the young man,
Let not the child's voice be heard, nor the mother's entreaties,
Make even the trestles to shake the dead where they lie awaiting the
hearses,
So strong you thump O terrible drums—so loud you bugles blow.

Whitman celebrated flag-waving patriotism in 1861 and sang the sounds of war. He imagined the poet "as one carrying a symbol and menace far into the future,/ crying with trumpet voice, Arouse and beware! Beware and arouse!" The warrior poet promised, "I'll put the bayonet's flashing point, I'll let bullets and slugs whizz." In 1861 Whitman did not shy from war's destruction.

I'll pour the verse with streams of blood, full of volition, full of joy,
Then loosen, launch forth, to go and compete,
With the banner and pennant a-flapping.[58]

After nursing dying soldiers in Washington hospitals for years, Whitman's drumming slowed to a dirge. In the "The Wound-Dresser," he confessed the error of his early war chants.

(Arous'd and angry, I'd thought to beat the alarum, and urge
relentless war,
But soon my fingers fail'd me, my face droop'd and I resign'd
myself,
To sit by the wounded and soothe them, or silently watch the dead;)

Waiting for death in anguished expectation replaced marching to war with eager anticipation. When war worsened and deaths mounted, Whitman's poems darkened and tired. He kissed the dead goodbye, spoke of prophecy and reconciliation, marked the slower tread of returning soldiers, and felt a veteran's recurring nightmares of battle. Perhaps by 1865, after sitting beside so many deathbeds, Whitman would have agreed with Dickinson that we dwell not in a home but "in Possibility." We live in the future, "impregnable of eye," and search the heavens for any sign of paradise.[59]

The contrast between Whitman's anticipations and Dickinson's expectations echoed a shift in Civil War music from the stirring marches of the early war to the melancholy ballads of the late war. The transformation of "John Brown's Body" into the "Battle Hymn of the Republic" expresses this change, but other tunes substantiated the shift. Instead of celebrating volunteers marching to war, "Tenting Tonight" depicted soldiers "wishing for the war to cease" after battle. Instead of looking forward to the seat of war, the song stressed, "many are the hearts looking to the right, to see the dawn of peace." Walter Kitteridge, a member of the Hutchinson Singers, wrote the song when he was drafted into the Union army in 1863. While the marching tunes of 1861 focused on departing soldiers, the music of the late war centered on anxious loved ones waiting at home. In 1863, Charles Carroll Sawyer inscribed "Weeping Sad and Lonely" to "Sorrowing Hearts at Home." "Weeping, sad and lonely, Hopes and fears how vain! Yet praying; When this cruel war is over, Praying that we meet again!" "Oft in dreams I see thee lying On the battle plain, Lonely, wounded, even dying, Calling, but in vain." "While our nation's sons are fighting, We can only pray." Over a million copies of the song sold during the war. Like "Tenting Tonight" it was popular with both nations. Late war music expressed more than weariness and grief. It acknowledged that wars exceed human agency. By 1863, massive religious revivals in both armies and nations articulated the same thing. For a time, the war turned Americans' dominant temporalities from anticipations to expectations.[60]

Dickinson believed the conflict escaped human control and thought of war as something natural, terrifying, and destructive—a storm. In 1862, she described war as natural as the bloody western horizon before nightfall. A year earlier, amid early war anticipations, painter Frederic Church imagined the American flag in a red sunset. His painting, *Our Banner in the Sky*, conveyed an assuring message from God that the Union would prevail. Prints of the painting sold well across the North. Dickinson saw something different on the horizon—a gory battlefield. She described a landscape slick with solid blood. Soldiers appeared in rigid formation, fated to die, their role in the unfolding drama was "Due." Like actors and the sun, men bowed and disappeared at the appointed time.[61]

The telegraph first arrived in Amherst, Massachusetts, in 1861, when Edward Dickinson, Emily's father, brought it to town as president of the Amherst & Belchertown Rail Road. In October a telegram arrived with word that the widow Adams had lost both of her sons. Frazar Stearns, an Amherst soldier and friend of Emily's brother, signed it. Six months later, a telegram brought news of Stearns's death. For Dickinson, as for Lincoln, the telegram delivered the future in unexpected bursts, but instead of carrying the fates of armies it reported the deaths of friends with electric indifference.

> The Future—never spoke—
> Nor will He—like the Dumb—
> Reveal by sign—a syllable
> Of His Profound to Come—
>
> But when the News be ripe—
> Presents it—in the Act—
> Forestalling Preparation—
> Escape—or Substitute—
>
> Indifferent to Him—
> The Dower—as the Doom—
> His Office—but to execute
> Fate's—Telegram—to Him—

For Dickinson, the future spoke in Morse code—sudden, cryptic, and devastating. The power of telegraphy fascinated Dickinson so much that she appropriated its language in her poetry. Her lines, like telegraphy, compressed language to a spare economy that permitted multiple meanings and puzzled readers. Dashes replaced punctuation and marked bursts of communication instead of delineating phrases and thoughts. Capitalization stressed important words instead of dividing sentences.[62]

Dickinson learned about the electric potential of telegraphy to mediate between unseen worlds from Edward Hitchcock, president of Amherst College and theorist of the "universal telegraph." She also read Hitchcock's *The Religion of Geology*, and her poem "The Chemical conviction" reiterates Hitchcock's explanation of how resurrected bodies will avoid incineration when God consumes the world in fire. Hitchcock used experiments on magnetism conducted by Baron Reichenbach and recently translated into English to argue that every soul bears a unique electric pulse or *odyle.* Reichenbach and Hitchcock believed that sensitive beings received thoughts electrically, through telepathy, just as telegraph operators and spiritualist mediums communicated with unseen forces. Dickinson grasped the spatial and temporal dimensions of Hitchcock's work when she observed, "The Brain—is wider than the Sky." Individual thoughts surpassed the horizon. When the Civil War loomed in 1861, Emily Dickinson imagined herself able to sense the energy of other souls. Letters seemed charged with the *odyle* of other souls. They traveled great distances to convey the feelings of an absent mind. "A Letter always feels to me like immortality," Dickinson told Thomas Higginson, "because it is the mind alone without corporeal friend." She sensed "a spectral power in thought that walks alone" through telegraph wires or postal routes. Thousands of letters from the front arrived after the death of the writer, conveying the thoughts of ghosts.[63]

Society believed that women were better suited to communicate with souls in this world and beyond the veil of death. Like a telegraph operator, Dickinson composed her poems suddenly, dictating them on whatever scrap of paper was at hand. Literary scholar Jerusha Hull McCormack explains that Dickinson's "use of the dash—by which the words are themselves held in suspense, as if even she, as author, were unable to predict where they would fall next—renders the act of composition itself as a kind of drama." She presents herself as a medium and operator. Julia Ward Howe described inspiration as if she received a telegraph from God and raced to transcribe it. When she composed "Battle Hymn of the Republic," Howe "sprang out of bed, and . . . scrawled the verses almost without looking at the paper." While male telegraph-operators worked in public, female mediums and fortune tellers worked in the home. They were not creators but transmitters of another voice.[64]

Family Men Leave Their Future Behind

THE WAR COMPELLED THOUSANDS of men to fight even though they preferred peace. Ujanirtus Allen, a Georgia planter and slave owner, expected a long war and dreaded it from the start. When he volunteered, Allen left behind his home with thirteen slaves, his wife, Susie, and their newborn child, a boy they had not yet named. While other men foresaw their future in the war, Allen hoped his future was at home. Intensely curious to know what was next and how it would affect him and his family, Allen yearned for a clearer vision of the future. "Oh that I was gifted with the eyes of prophecy that I might looke beyond the vail that o'er shadows the mystic future," he wrote. Unable to make sense of the present, let alone the future, Allen felt no destiny, only a sinking feeling that the war would outlast every politician's promise.[65]

Allen and his comrades entered Richmond on July 22, 1861, the day after a glorious victory at Bull Run. Awash with rumors of the battle, the new capital celebrated. Allen did not join the party. "I live and move in a kind of trance, that I cannot describe or you conceive," he told to his wife. Street corners buzzed with reports that Confederates inflicted casualties at a ten to one ratio. People laughed at rumors that humiliated the Yankees. One story told about enemy officers who were so confident of victory that they "checked their baggage to Richmond," including "a good supply of fine wines and brandies" to toast the surrender of the Confederacy. Another said that "a letter arrived at the post office . . . directed to Gen. [Winfield] Scott." Allen chuckled, "I guess President Davis will take care of it for him." Many rumors claimed to be reactions from Union prisoners who were filing into the city day and night. "Some say that the only truth that Lincoln told them was that they would be in Richmond in July." The most famous Union prisoner was Congressman Alfred Ely of Rochester, New York. "Poor fellow," Allen quipped, "he came out to see us whipped, and was taken prisoner. I am told that he cries like a child." Allen could have taken all these sunny reports as proof that his premonitions of a long war were false. He could have sent such information home as confirmation that he would be home to celebrate their first Christmas as a family.[66]

Instead, Allen doubted the validity of rumors and stressed that the enemy had fought hard. "What I tell you is from good authority," he wrote home. "Many of them were well drilled and armed. They pitted about 10,000 regulars against our West wing among their other men. They thought they were invincible." The awesome splendor of military activity in Richmond impressed Allen, but he knew that similar scenes were taking place in Washington, and neither side was invincible. "Both parties are making all the preparations for a mighty strugle," and he anticipated that "when they do come in contact thare will be such a din of arms that the whole universe will tremble." The sheer size of each government's war effort raised doubts in Allen's mind that the conflict could end soon. "This war will not end until Lincoln's resources are all gone; money, men and credit," Allen prophesied. "I do not believe that the pride of the North will yield unless compelled to. How long it will be, I do not know." Allen conceded that "a great many leading men [predict] that we will conquer a peace in a few months," and he admitted that the Confederacy might shorten the war if it won the next string of battles. But if the Union won the next campaign, Allen expected, "the war will be long and bludy." "It is the opinion of many prominent men that [the war] will finish before Christmas. Some think that the pride of the Northern people will not suffer them to acknowledge our independence soon, not under several years." Allen counted himself in the second group.[67]

Expecting to fight for an indefinite period, Allen started requesting winter clothes for his men during the summer of 1861. "If the people do not provide for them they will certainly suffer," he predicted to his wife. Allen wanted "blankets shoes etc. from home" so that his men would be ready for the colder weather of Virginia winters. Over time his view of the war's horizon darkened. "I fear this war will become one of extermination," he confessed. "I can not divine the future. I know of nothing that I can say only Hope! Hope!! Hope that golden chain that ever binds us to the future, dazeled by whose beauty we forget the present with all its harsh realities." Hope could not erase Allen's darkest anxieties of Confederate defeat. He envisioned enemy hordes, "led on by fanaticism and lust for 'beauty and booty'" planning to "scatter misery, desolation and want in its path." "Defeat with us is utter ruin. We would be disfranchised, dishonored, murdered and our property taken away from us. The might of man is unable to conceive the desolation that would cover our country." Killed at Chancellorsville, Allen did not live to see his prophecies fulfilled. His wife saved his letters for the future, so that their son would know his father.[68]

John Hilton, corporal in the 111th Pennsylvania Infantry, also had a family at home and feared he would never see them again. Born and raised in England, he did not share the war fever that swept thousands into the ranks in spring 1861. Instead, Hilton enlisted in fall 1861 hoping to collect a bounty as the war ended. A year later cannon fire interrupted him while he wrote home. Under the stress of impending battle, Hilton wrote his wife that he was uncomfortable, in danger, and uncertain about the future. His comrades suspected that "the rebels are getting the worst of it" and would soon surrender. Hilton hoped it was true. Perhaps a great battle would break the rebellion and bring peace. Hilton closed by sending his love and adding the postscript "the order is given to march don't know where." He was headed to Antietam.[69]

After fighting for eight hours straight and firing about 120 rounds, Hilton's hopes for a short war shattered at Antietam. He "dropped 2 or 3 grey backs" to avenge the deaths of friends. Throughout the battle, comrades noticed him loading his gun and laughing hysterically. Twice his regiment fixed bayonets and repulsed Confederate charges. "Such a sight of dead bodies I never saw before," he confessed. Being ten years older than most of his comrades, he dreaded a long conflict and doubted his stamina for it. A childhood injury to his ankle dogged him on long marches. Chronic diarrhea weakened and embarrassed him. He debated how much information he should share with his wife. Hilton did not want to discourage or scare her with the truths he learned about the war or his worsening health. Instead he chronicled his regiment's service, sent his son pictures of camp, and asked for money and letters. Though short on paper, Hilton often left space unwritten on his final page. Either he did not know how to express his experiences or chose not to. He needed time and quiet to find the composure to gather his thoughts. "I am expecting the word fall in every minute you see so we have to write in a hurry," he explained before he headed to Antietam. Four days later he found time to assure his family that he was safe.[70]

His letter never arrived. For three weeks Mary Hilton waited to hear if her husband survived the bloodiest day in American history. She sent him a letter at the end of September but still no reply came. In it she tried to express her deepest worries and stressed how much the children missed their papa. When word from her husband finally arrived in October, Mary was relieved but John Hilton's sister, Jane, scolded her brother. "Your good letter was received in due time and you don't know how very glad we all were to hear from you," she began. Jane believed God spared John Hilton at Antietam, but she wrote, "I feel afraid that something will happen to you at some time." From her perspective, his odds of survival looked grim. "What if you should fall as thousands of others have done?" she asked. "Do you not go to battle with the visions of your little family before you and oh how dreadful it would be if you should be taken away from them through this unholy war." Freeing the slaves did not sanctify a war that Jane Hilton considered "very unjust and wicked" because it "slaughtered" thousands "every day." A family friend named William Wood had recently died, leaving behind a wife and children. Jane predicted, "If William could have been spared he bid fair to become a rich man at some future day." Instead he was a corpse. The war stole William Wood's future, and for what? Like thousands of other women, Jane Hilton did not imagine the war as a romantic time of heightened emotions and heroic deeds. The war killed husbands and fathers. It erased the fortunes, happiness, and bonds of families. Mothers, wives, and sisters dreaded the war's threat to their loved ones in arms. Social pressures made it difficult for women to express their reservations publicly, but privately they vented concerns in diaries and letters. Men did not want to receive demoralizing letters, but they had no choice. Jane felt she had to speak her mind. "I wish you had not volunteered," she said.[71]

John Hilton left the army three months later. By then the winter war he dreaded had come. Defeat at Fredericksburg and slogging through miles of mud left him disheartened and sick. He saw men and horses killed by the march and feared he would be the next to fall. Hilton doubted any amount of fighting could stop it. If Antietam could not end the war, what battle could? The war had gained its own life and momentum. Only extermination could end it and no bounty was worth that conclusion. Many comrades had lost hope and some deserted. Unlike most of his war letters, Hilton crammed the final page in packed prose to share his fullest sentiments. He closed by telling his wife "I often imagine that I am with you but it is only like a dream to pass away."[72]

Hilton sought and received an honorable discharge. A sympathetic surgeon diagnosed him with rheumatism. Years after the war, John Hilton told people that he left the army after he suffered a heart attack. Instead his heart was no longer in the war. He lied to folks that he was discharged in January 1865 instead of January 1863 and claimed that the papers for his promotion to captain were already made out when the heart attack forced him out of the army. When cannons ceased to roar, he became active in veterans organizations, went to regimental reunions, became a Republican, and on his deathbed saluted a portrait of his comrades. His obituary identified him as Captain John Hilton. This final coda about Hilton's memory of the war suggests the relationship between his anticipations, experiences, and memories of the conflict. The war did not fulfill John Hilton's hopes, but his memories of it did. When the war outlasted his endurance, Hilton found a way home and through his recollections fashioned a war and service record that verified his imagination. Only by understanding the war that he expected and experienced can the war he remembered be understood.[73]

Should I Stay or Should I Go

THE EXTRAORDINARY CIVIL WAR diary of Aquila Johnson Peyton, a Virginia schoolteacher, gives a glimpse of the internal dialogue untold numbers of men had when they did <u>not</u> rush to war. While most of his peers started diaries to chronicle their part toward the unfolding drama, Peyton kept one to document his excruciating, inner war over whether or not to enlist. Tangled emotions and excuses mixed with conflicted reasoning and social pressure on every page. Peyton hoped religion would chart his future course. His favorite scripture was Proverbs 3: 5–6, "Trust in the Lord with all thine heart; and lean not unto thine own understanding. In all thy ways acknowledge him, and he shall direct thy paths." When he asked God whether or not he should enlist, Peyton received no answer.[74]

Like his peers, Peyton yearned to prove his manhood. His heroes rose early, walked erect, "self-possessed at all times," punctual, silent, and vigorous. Each New Year he resolved to be like them. When he turned twenty-four in 1861, the war offered a new path toward Peyton's ideal, but soldiering conflicted with his sensibilities. Peyton was pious, quiet, and studious. To him, soldiering signified two things: sin and death. "We know not how soon the grave may close over us," he warned himself. He doubted his mettle to march and fight and feared that his soul remained unworthy of salvation. The Yankees were not his worst enemies; he was. "My heart is so desperately wicked, and I am so prone to forget God and to fix my affections on things on earth, that death has great terrors for me."[75]

Before he could decide how to face the future, the future faced him at every turn and mocked his indecision. As war loomed, the future encroached upon Peyton's life by invading the spaces where he lived, worked, and prayed. Meanwhile others—his parents, brother, prayer circle, students, and friends—urged Peyton to enlist. Young men who faced the war with passive expectations instead of aggressive anticipations risked humiliation, and Peyton knew it. In 1859, when a fever swept through the community and took the life of a young man, Peyton read the Psalms to prepare himself for death. In 1861, when secession and war loomed on the horizon, he read Jeremiah and Ezekiel to hone his prophetic imagination.

The future arrived in Peyton's church in January 1861. At a prayer meeting, the preacher addressed the state of the nation and encouraged pious expectancy and prayer. Men of the congregation, however, urged manly anticipation. After the service Peyton participated in "a warm political discussion" outside the church with two men about secession. Peyton preferred to wait and see how Republicans ruled, but his debaters pushed for immediate secession. The emotional exchange bothered Peyton, and he vowed not to be "drawn into so excited and violent a discussion again." Ten days later, citizens held a political meeting inside the church. The meeting passed resolutions in favor of secession and nominated William Barton to represent the county in the upcoming secession convention. Peyton did not vote for or against the secession resolutions, but he did vote for Barton. After the meeting, he noticed that someone had raised a flag with fifteen stars above the general store. The following week Peyton found himself in another political argument, except this time he advocated immediate secession.[76]

The future came to his schoolhouse after Fort Sumter fell. "The war we have been expecting has commenced," he feared. When many of his students left to join a juvenile company called the Mount Herman Young Guards, Peyton closed his school for a week to consider his options. Unready to rush to war, he joined a home guard of older men and the local militia. Rumors swirled that the militia would assemble to be drafted into Confederate service. Peyton's "feelings were far from pleasant" when he headed home for the muster. At the courthouse he learned that his brother, John, had joined a volunteer company. He admired the colorful appearances of assembled companies but did not feel compelled to join one. When friends joined his brother's company, Peyton was melancholy "that our most amiable, intelligent, + useful young men, the object of the most tender affections and most ardent hopes, must be exposed to destruction along with the most despicable." Edmund Ruffin and other war hawks pointed to elite southerners in the ranks as a sign of inevitable victory and the justness of their cause. Peyton saw it as a waste of promising lives. He reopened his school, though most of his scholars were not present. "War is the absorbing subject of thought and topic of conversation with all," he despaired.[77]

In May, Peyton tried to achieve his manly ideal without enlisting. No more "putting the hand about the face or head, speaking fiercely or impatiently to my pupils, and humming tunes continually when alone." He promised to rise early and walk and sit erect. Peyton enjoyed drilling with the militia and home guard but felt "averse to camp life, or to trying my fortune in the field." When the militia mustered in late May, the colonel announced that he needed one hundred men out of the assembled 800 to form a volunteer company. Peyton's "feelings were, in consequence, of a very unpleasant nature." When only two men stepped forward, the colonel threatened to draft the remainder if more men did not volunteer. Before he left the courthouse, Peyton "had a strong notion of volunteering," but did not. Instead he took "a fresh interest" in his students. While he planned to continue teaching, Peyton also vowed to exercise more to "prepare myself as much as possible for a soldier's life." His watchwords, "Patience" and "Energy," illustrate how expectations and anticipations pulled him in opposite directions.[78]

The community watched Peyton struggle and tried to convince him to enlist. In April, when local men advised him to join a volunteer company in Orange, he "did not feel inclined to." In May, when he consulted with his students' parents, some urged him to close the school, but he did not.

In June, his religious mentor urged him to volunteer. "He says he does not wish unduly to influence me, but gives it as his opinion that it would be best for me to join the company John is in." Single men ought to volunteer, the mentor explained, "and those who have families be allowed, if possible, to remain at home." Peyton valued the old man's advice but could not bring himself to follow it. When he asked his parents if they thought he should volunteer, Peyton's father encouraged him to visit his brother's company along the Potomac. Peyton left the next day. The picket guard that greeted him was a friend from home. He had dinner with the captain of the company. That night, in camp, Peyton could not sleep. In the morning he returned home without enlisting. Weeks passed. His father escorted him back to John's camp. His brother assured him that he preferred military life to being at home. Peyton went home. In town he met another friend who had joined his brother's company. The man said John wanted him to join his unit. Peyton did not.[79]

While his honorable alternatives to enlistment diminished, Peyton prayed, "Oh Lord, 'cause me to know the way wherein I should walk.'" Whenever he felt "a disposition" to join his brother's company, "considerations that make it seem improper" surfaced. "I must decide soon," he admitted. Peyton wanted to volunteer but feared he lacked the vigor and stamina of a soldier. Being kicked out of the army as a weakling would be worse than never enlisting at all. Whenever eagerness to enlist overwhelmed him, Peyton reasoned, "what we are most eager to do is generally wrong." Eagerness stemmed from pride, a sin. He convinced himself that the militia performed a vital service, protecting the defenseless from slave revolts.[80]

The victory at Bull Run finally convinced Peyton to join the army. "After some reflection, I consented, with some fear, however, to have my name put down" as a member of Company I of the 30th Virginia Infantry, his brother's regiment but in a different company. Peyton had his measurements taken for a uniform, received a short furlough, and visited with his family. He also went to see a citizen who had witnessed the battle. Peyton was entranced by his account of it. The man showed him a musket he took off a dead Yankee. Women knitted him socks and a sleeping cap. As he marched to war, Peyton hoped that God's "ways are invariably ways of pleasantness; all his paths are paths of peace." Wherever the future took him, he vowed, "to walk in dependence upon God." The enemy had expected to continue their progress to Richmond, but the Confederates won a "decisive victory." "We should return thanks to God, whose over-ruling hand gave it to us." Upon enlistment, Peyton ended his war diary. His battle with himself was over.[81]

In New York, Lawrence Van Alstyne's internal conflict over enlisting lasted longer than Peyton's struggle. Because his diary began when he made up his mind to volunteer in August 1862, Van Alstyne barely mentions how private battles of 1861 consumed him. "I was a long time making up my mind about it," he admitted. "To be honest about it, I don't feel much of the eagerness for the fray I am hearing so much about." "This one could go, and that one, and they ought to, but with me, some way it was different." For a long time, Van Alstyne resented how the war obstructed his future prospects. "There was so much I had planned to do, and to be." The war could wait, he reasoned. "I was needed at home, etc., etc." Like Peyton, Van Alstyne would settle his mind about enlisting for a while, "only to have it come up to be reasoned away again." But his sense of duty dogged him. "Each time my reasons for not taking my part in the job seemed less reasonable. Finally I did the only thing I could respect myself for doing;—went to Millerton, the nearest recruiting station, and enlisted."[82]

Volunteering did not ease his anxiety about the future. When he told people about his enlistment, they acted as if he were heading to the gallows. Pity, evident on every face, gave Van Alstyne a feeling that he was attending his own funeral. His parents were the worst. "They had expected it, but now that it has come they felt it, and though they tried hard, they could not hide from me that they felt it might be the last they would see of their baby." Being delayed in a nearby camp prolonged the agony of leaving home. "The sooner we go the more patriotism will be left in us. Too much of it is oozing out through the eyes." Each day brought someone's family to camp for a final, tearful goodbye. "No doubt for many it is a last good-bye." Van Alstyne cried for them and thanked God that his parents had enough sense to stay away.[83]

When steamboats and railroads finally whisked him to war, Van Alstyne kept his diary assiduously, because "events crowded upon each other so fast." The little book in his pocket did more than make sense of the looming war; it helped Van Alstyne discover himself. "I am some other person," he confessed. When the war interrupted his plans, it made him uncertain about himself and the future. "My aims and ambitions are new;—that is if I have any." Van Alstyne feared, "I seem to have reached the end. I can look backwards, but when I try to look ahead it is all a blank," like the pages of his diary.[84]

Overwhelmed, Van Alstyne turned to a religious book he had read, *Robert Dawson; or, the Brave Spirit*, by Helen Cross Knight. The most famous passage in the book details how Robert, a farm boy, must drive cows to pasture one morning despite torrents of rain. Hiding in bed, Robert tries to reason with his father that none of the other boys work in bad weather.

His father, an invalid, explains, "You must meet the shower just as you must meet all obstacles. It will be only a few drops at a time! Can you not do that, Robert? Make up your mind, now, and act like a man." When Robert worked, the chant "Only a few drops at a time" made the shower seem lighter and the journey shorter. Remembering the event as a man, Robert understood that his father taught him how to approach the future. Life presented unknown obstacles, but it does no good "to grumble about them and magnify them." We cannot know "what shall be on the morrow," but the Bible teaches that each day is sufficient for the evils that come. " 'Only a few drops at a time, Robert,' " Van Alstyne wrote in his diary. "The days are made of minutes, and I am only sure of the one I am living in. Take good care of that and cross no bridges until you come to them." By taking things one day at a time, Van Alstyne kept a diary to ease his uncertainty about the future.[85]

Unfortunately, by detailing the war as it unfolded, the diary made Van Alstyne the regimental expert on its past but left him in the dark about its present and future. "I am quite an authority on the times and places we have visited and am often called in to settle some disputed question, but my notes all look backwards and are good for nothing when asked about the future." Rumors of distant battles, gossip about impending orders, conjectures about where they would march and camp, speculations about when they would be paid, hopes for the next mail, every detail about the present and future hid behind uncertain knowledge, bureaucratic muddle, and military secrecy. "Only a few drops at a time" offered little consolation within the fog of war.[86]

In January 1864, Van Alstyne yearned for a furlough. Stationed in New Orleans, his regiment heard rumors that they were bound for Matagorda Island off the coast of Texas. If true, the order to march might come any moment and thwart his hopes for a furlough. Desperate to know what would be written on the blank pages of his diary, Van Alstyne visited a fortune teller. The woman took him into a dimly lit room and spread a common deck of cards across a table. She told him that he recently received a letter from a family member that troubled him. This reminded him of a letter from his father. Then she predicted, "I was going on a journey and would start in nine days. That it was partly by water and partly by land, but mostly by water." This made him think of both possibilities, either his furlough home or his regiment's expected move to Matagorda. Her final prediction pointed to the latter when she said he would "meet with a great disappointment soon." What could that mean except that his furlough would be denied? Visiting the fortune teller only worsened his anxiety. When his friend said another fortune teller in the area had a better reputation but charged five dollars instead of one, Van Alstyne was tempted to see her. "If they should agree I would have to own up they knew something, and if they disagreed I would throw the whole thing off my mind, that is, if I can."[87]

For a week he fretted and hoped that either his furlough or the regiment's orders would arrive before he felt compelled to spend the five dollars. When he could stand it no longer, he left camp without a pass to visit Madam Black, the "Great Indian Astrologist." Instead of reading cards, she asked for the day and month of his birth and closed her eyes as if going to sleep. Then she "gave me as good a history of my past life as I could have told her." Van Alstyne was "tempted to run away and leave my future as it had always been to me, a closed book." He held his breath while she continued. Madam Black repeated what the other soothsayer said. He would soon take a trip in some vague direction. "Aside from a chat we had on other subjects, that was all I got for my $5." He considered the whole thing a swindle. The next morning his colonel called for him and asked what he was doing yesterday away from camp and handed him an official-looking document. Heart pounding, Van Alstyne opened the envelope and found his furlough.[88]

Future Dreams

SOME AMERICANS WHO FACED the future with an expectant point of view believed their dreams offered signs of what was coming. Perhaps the world offered signs of the future, and people strained to receive them. Because seeing the future required a different sense than sight, people put faith in dreams. God visited prophets of the Old and New Testament at night in their dreams. Samuel, Daniel, Zachariah, and Paul received visions in the dark, an apt description of prophetic imagination. Emily Dickinson sensed that her dreams were more truthful than her vision.

> Let me not mar that perfect Dream
> By an Auroral stain
> But so adjust my daily Night
> That it will come again.

A dream, like the future, comes unexpected. The dream selects us as God singles out prophets or bullets choose casualties.[89]

When John B. Jones predicted the war in his 1859 novel, *Wild Southern Scenes*, he claimed to have dreamed it. When his dream came true in 1861, Jones had an apocalyptic nightmare about the war. Nature's dark omen, a comet, flashed across the heavens that June and inspired his vision. The dream featured a "great black ball" looming in the heavens. "It obscured the moon. The stars were in motion, visibly, and for a time afforded the only light. Then a brilliant halo illuminated the zenith like the quick-shooting irradiations of the aurora borealis." Men ran in every direction, screaming like women. As he watched the moon dissolve, Jones "thought of the war brought upon us, and the end of the United States Government." He and his family witnessed "the end of all things sublunary" without fear or remorse. When he woke, Jones tried to return to sleep, "curious to prolong the vision, but sleep had fled." Whatever was coming, Jones took comfort in the fact that he had faced it without panic.[90]

From the beginning he expected a long, bloody war. During the bombardment of Fort Sumter, Jones sat with Henry Wise, the former governor of Virginia, awaiting the news. Wise spotted a bayoneted musket in the corner of the room. He criticized the weapon "as inferior to the *knife*." Southerners would need extensive drilling to perfect wielding such a modern weapon, "but they instinctively knew how to wield the bowie-knife." "If a great war should ensue," Wise predicted, "it was not the improved *arm*, but the improved *man*, which would win the day." Southerners with bowie knives and ancient flintlocks would overrun "the popinjays of the Northern cities" because of superior character. Three days later, Jones learned that some of those popinjays wanted to kill him. A mob carrying a rope to hang Jones appeared at the Philadelphia office of his proslavery newspaper. Finding him gone, they destroyed the place, tore down his signs, chopped them up, and wore splinters in their hats as trophies. He understood that such men would stop at nothing to destroy the South. When Lincoln called for 75,000 men to suppress the rebellion, Jones took the proclamation to Wise and told him Lincoln's volunteers were "merely the videttes and outposts of an army of 700,000." Wise would not believe it. "He had not witnessed the Wide-Awake gatherings the preceding fall," as Jones had. For Jones, the battles of 1861 were "the pattering drops that must inevitably be succeeded by a torrent of blood!"[91]

Jones worked for the Confederate War Department, where he waited for the future to unfold in telegrams. He articulated the stress of expectations best during the resumption of active campaigning in 1863. On May 2, he wrote, "The awful hour, when thousands of human lives are to be sacrificed in the attempt to wrest this city from the Confederate States, has come again. Now parents, wives, sisters, brothers, and little children, both in the North and in the South, hold their breath in painful expectation." Telegraph operators announced the battle had begun that morning. All day, Jones heard the low rolling thunder of distant cannons. "A great battle seems inevitable," he thought. It was Chancellorsville.[92]

Some dreams fulfilled wishes that people could not make true. When Van Alstyne waited for his furlough to be approved, he dreamed about the paperwork passing through each step of the bureaucratic process and reaching headquarters. Before he could see whether officers had approved his request, he woke up sweating. Sallie Lovett of Georgia often dreamed that her husband, a soldier, was sleeping with her, only to wake up with a "breathless pillow" in her arms. "Honey I don't know what I would do with my self if I was to see you coming I think I would run plum out of my skin to meet you I would be so glad to see you I want you to come home soon as you can and see what I will do." Some nights Lovett dreamed that she awoke to realize that the war was only a nightmare.[93]

The dreams of Virginia Hammett illustrate a spectrum of hopes, fears, frustrations, and fates. Hammett first felt anxious expectations about the war when Union forces appeared at her Virginia home in April 1862. After that, expectations about "the invaders" filled her with dread. She never knew when the enemy would return, how long they would stay, and what they would do to her and her family. The enemy used her home as their headquarters and hospital, consumed her food, burned her fields, stole her possessions, threatened her father, and fought battles in her yard. A year and a half of such war sapped her energy and strained her sanity. "In dreams my mind is still full of war," she said. While asleep, "I see advances, repulses, skirmishes I see the army marching, camping, deploying in line of battle and doing all manner of things that armies do." Her dreams focused "in breathless anxiety" on the moment before "the booming of the first gun," that instant of expected, inevitable carnage recurred in her mind again and again.[94]

She often dreamed of danger approaching her. As a child she was picking cherries when a herd of cattle charged her. Hammett fled to dark woods, where the beasts did not see her and ceased their pursuit. Cattle terrified her for the rest of her life. During the war, they haunted her dreams. "I have awaken many times half frightened out of my wits by those phantom cattle," she observed in 1864. In nightmares she ran from them "with all my speed," climbed trees, and jumped fences to escape being trampled to death. In a similar dream during the fall of 1864, a squad of Yankee cavalry prowled around her house before dawn, doing more damage than she could see. Hammett spied a dozen Confederate soldiers resting nearby and "apparently unconscious of the close proximity of the Yankees." She ran from the house to alarm them. "Fly from here to the woods," she told them, "conceal yourselves while you can," just as she and her friends had sought sanctuary from the stampede. The soldiers ignored her. After such nightmares, Hammett tried to convince herself not to believe in dreams "as prognostic of the future." However she admitted, "I have dreamed of wants, persons, plans and things" that later came true.[95]

Hammett resented how the war confined her space and controlled her future. She yearned to travel, but the war often denied her even an afternoon visit to see neighbors. When occupying armies limited her movement, she journeyed in her sleep. She dreamed of visiting relatives in Missouri. One night she "stood on a portico in the city of Galveston Texas, [and] gazed out upon the bay." Another night she wandered the streets of Rome and visited the pope. In the fall of 1863, she traveled to Palestine in her dreams, pressing her feet with awe and reverence into the sacred soil and marveling at the ancient wonders of Jerusalem. She went to Europe to see "the vine clad hills of France." She even crossed into enemy territory, threading "the mazes of some northern city," "whirling away on a railroad through Wisconsin," and "gazing upon some wide waving prairie of the west." When the war imprisoned her on the family farm, she would "run, jump fly and swim" in her dreams.[96]

Her most persistent dreams yearned for hidden knowledge about the future. She frequently dreamed of receiving letters that she could not finish reading. A gust of wind or a stream would carry the letter out of sight. The light would go out, or the words would disappear from the page. At other times, mail arrived covered in black, and Hammett assumed it contained news of a death. Who was writing her, how would the letter affect her future? Whenever Hammett received these phantom letters in her sleep, she yearned to know, but never did. In a similar vein, she repeatedly dreamed that she lived in a house with an attic "about which there is some awful mystery, it is haunted or something." She felt "the most intense curiosity to penetrate its mysteries" but failed to enter the room every time. Climbing the long, winding staircase to the attic door provided too much time for something to happen and halt her progress. Sometimes she could find no one to go with her. Other occasions a light went out and darkness trapped her in the stairwell. Sometimes fear paralyzed her at the attic door. During such moments, she told herself "this is all nonsense living in a house in which there is a room I have never entered and afraid to do so." Still she could not move.[97]

In late 1864 she dreamed that the future appeared in person at her door. After a troop of Yankee cavalry left her yard, Hammett noticed an elegant woman standing at the door. Consumed by the enemy's destruction of her property, Hammett paid little attention to the visitor, assumed she was a Yankee, and finally received her with cool indifference. "She said she had come to repay me for all the losses and suffering the war had cost me, I assured her this was impossible." The woman introduced herself as Madame Fate. When the lady asked Hammett to take a walk, she tried to refuse but "had neither the will nor the power." They traveled over desolate fields where armies camped and passed over well-beaten roads as if they were floating. After a long journey, they came to Fate's residence, a weird structure—half house, half tent. Hammett explained that she must start for home, that her family would be uneasy about her absence. With a strange smile, Fate said, "you can't go you are my prisoner!" Shocked and angered, Hammett asked by what authority the lady captured her. "By the authority of Fate," she replied. "The past and all former associations and connections must be forgotten by you," the woman explained, "I intend you shall marry my son."[98]

Fate brought Hammett a husband, but she objected to the arrangement. She assumed Fate's son was a Yankee soldier. He resembled a Union officer, Captain Herbert Dilger, a German who visited Hammett earlier in the war and gave her his photograph. Dilger joined the enemy because he believed the Union was the best government on earth, "an asylum for the oppressed of all the world," and the Yankees convinced him that the rebellion was "a little thing which could be easily suppressed." Since then, Dilger had met and admired southerners like Hammett and wished he were back home in Germany. She cherished his likeness and kept it pressed between the leaves of her diary. "I think he was altogether the most beautiful human being I ever saw," she confided. Like Dilger, Fate's son had dark hair and eyes, looked younger than his age, and claimed noble blood. Fate spoke with a foreign accent. She explained to Hammett that her son did not have "a drop of Yankee blood in his veins." "My son is one whom a princess would not refuse," Fate assured her. Listening to Fate, Hammett felt her will to resist ebb. She cast one long look "back to the past to home and family" and felt that she must stay. Dinner was announced, Fate led Hammett to an adjoining room where her future husband waited, wearing a foreign uniform. The stranger received her with gentle kindness and calm assurance that he already knew she was to be his wife. Hammett began to accept Fate and her son and prepare to live the remainder of her days with them. Then she woke. Hammett never married.[99]

Lincoln treated dreams with a mixture of rural superstition and intellectual detachment. The Separate Baptist Church, where his parents were members, believed so firmly in predestination that it opposed missionary work. If God had already determined the fate of all souls, no amount of proselytizing could change the outcome. His father, Thomas Lincoln, was haunted by dreams and told his son that they came true. Thomas recalled a dream that came to him for years. In it he walked a narrow path that took him to a strange house. Inside sat a woman by the fire paring an apple, and in the firelight Thomas could see every feature of her face. He suspected that the woman would become his wife. According to Thomas, the dream returned again and again until he found the path while awake, followed it to the house, stepped inside, and met his future wife paring an apple.[100]

Lincoln searched his dreams for signs of the future. During the summer of 1863, while Mary and their son Tad were away in Philadelphia, Lincoln had a nightmare about a small pistol he allowed the boy to keep. He sent Mary a telegram: "Think you better put 'Tad's' pistol away. I had an ugly dream about him." In 1865, aboard the *River Queen* on a trip down the Potomac, he dreamed that the White House was on fire. Twice Lincoln wired Washington to see if everything was safe. Sensing that fate could befall him at any minute, Lincoln relied on dreams and telegraphy to try to avoid an approaching future. [101]

Mysterious forces propelled Lincoln in his dreams. In slumber, he was borne by the war toward its death and destruction. When battle reports arrived from Murfreesboro at the end of 1862, Lincoln dreamed of corpses in a field, midnight gunfire, and crowds reading casualty lists in the capital. His most portentous dream occurred on April 13, 1865. As members of the cabinet arrived for a meeting the next day, they asked if any news from General William Sherman had arrived by telegram. General Grant, who was present, said "he was hourly expecting word." Lincoln agreed, saying he "had no doubt" the news would "come soon, and come favorable, for he had last night the usual dream which he had preceding nearly every great and important event of the War. Generally the news had been favorable which succeeded this dream, and the dream itself was always the same." Secretary of the Navy Gideon Welles asked about the dream. "It related to your element, the water," Lincoln said. "He seemed to be in some singular, indescribable vessel, and that he was moving with great rapidity towards an indefinite shore." The dream preceded Fort Sumter, Bull Run, Antietam, Gettysburg, Stones River, Vicksburg, and Wilmington. Grant interjected, "Stones River was certainly no victory." Nonetheless, Lincoln insisted that the dream preceded major events. Lincoln confessed that he had this strange dream again last night. "We shall, judging from the past, have great news very soon," he predicted. Lincoln met his fate that night at Ford's Theatre.[102]

Matthew Jamison, a lieutenant in the Tenth Illinois Infantry, believed that future dreams "flashed upon the penumbra of our slumber world for a definite purpose; prophetic they are, and savor of admonition, instruction, inspiration." Most dreams follow "in line with the current of our lives," relate idle nonsense about the present, and vanish from memory. The future dream, "the token of a coming day," sticks with us. Jamison's portent interrupted his sleep ten years before the war. "A marching column of troops intercepted my progress in the slumber world, led by cavalry, followed by infantry, artillery and trains—a formidable array that threatened to trample me like a leaf under the horses' hoofs." The spectacle, unlike anything Jamison had witnessed in life or art, became too familiar to him during the war. People may challenge the truth of his nightmare or laugh at their own future dreams, but "no intelligent man questions the visions that crossed the disk of Abraham Lincoln's slumbers—that wonderful, startling portent of tremendous events."[103]

An Assassin's Fate

WHEN THE WAR CAME, John Wilkes Booth expected horrible things. "God, what a dismal future have we before us," he lamented. Booth detested politicians and prognosticators who looked to the future with a casual air, "who lightly think and say. There's naught to fear. all will be bright soon. As if the future was but to morrow." Booth challenged anyone to "look towards that aweful page and say to himself there, there is peace & happiness waiting to embrace us. Who, who is there, my friends that does not shudder when he contemplates what a few years may bring to light." At the brink of catastrophe, Booth refused to yield the future to anything—not fate, leadership, or even God. "It is time for all good citizens who are, or would be conservative to their country, in, this, her hour of need to come to action." He prophesied financial ruin, famine, and destructive war.[104]

Though he urged his countrymen to anticipate the war and forge the future, Booth lacked the will to fight. A Confederate sympathizer in a Maryland family of Unionists, Booth convinced himself that he avoided the war for his mother's sake. But he practiced an expectant behavior that he derided in others. In 1860, people who "stand Idly by hoping to save a country by *fast* and *Prayer*" were delusional, he said. In 1864, he admitted, "For four years have I waited, hoped and prayed, for the dark clouds to break" until "All hope is dead, my prayers have proved as idle as my hopes." He cursed himself a coward and despised his own existence for playacting during the greatest drama in American history. After Lincoln's reelection, Booth sensed "uncontrollable fate, moving me for its ends," and hoped "to do what work I can for a poor oppressed downtrodden people. May that same fate cause me to do that work well."[105]

He vowed to kill Lincoln when he heard the president talk about enfranchising black men. "This country was formed for the white not for the black man," Booth argued. Expecting racial equality, Booth hoped his actions would thwart the progress that John Brown had tried to precipitate at Harpers Ferry, and he was proud of his role in the capture and execution of Brown. "I thought then, *as now*, that the abolitionists, were the only traitors in the land, And that the entire party, deserved the fate of poor old Brown." Now the Republican Party pursued the same ends that inspired Brown and "what was a crime in poor John Brown is now considered (by themselves) as the greatest and only virtue, of the whole Republican party." "Strange transmigration, *vice* to become a *virtue*," Booth mused, "simply because more indulge in it." Booth could not bring all Republicans to justice, as he had helped to punish Brown for treason, but he could execute the head of the party. He followed Brown's example, assembled a motley crew of devoted followers, hatched a wild plan to alter the course of history, and resorted to violence to realize it.[106]

Things did not go as Booth planned. Though he accomplished his task in Ford's Theatre, his co-conspirators failed. Worse, the nation responded to his deeds with unexpected fury. Everyone turned against him "for doing what Brutus was honored for, what made Tell a Hero." Fate hunted him through swamps and woods, chased him with dogs and horses, as if he were a runaway slave. Wet, cold, starving, and despairing, Booth wrote his last diary entry, "To night I try to escape these blood hounds once more. Who who can read his fate. God's will be done. I have too great a soul to die like a criminal. Oh may he, may he spare me that and let me die bravely." Cornered in a barn, Booth refused to surrender when his pursuers set it on fire. One of the posse shot him through the spine and dragged him out of the building where he died. His end seemed foretold in one of his most popular performances, a reading of John Whittaker Watson's poem, "Beautiful Snow,"

Once I was pure as snow—but I fell:
Fell, like the snow-flakes, from heaven—to
Hell:
Fell, to be trampled as the filth of the street:
Fell, to be scoffed, to be spit on and beat.

After his death, Booth's body received the same treatment as Brown's. Authorities concealed it from relic hunters and quietly sent it to his family. When it arrived, his spinal column, where the bullet killed him, was missing. The vertebrae reappeared in the Army Medical Museum, ironically housed in Ford's Theatre.[107]

Jubilee

NO AMERICANS EXPECTED THE war with more hope and patience than the African Americans whom Booth sought to subjugate. When the war came, thousands anticipated its power to end slavery and raced to Union armies to gain freedom. Yet millions waited beyond the reach of the federal government, praying that the future would arrive on their plantation. Edwin White's 1861 painting, *Thoughts of the Future*, challenged popular histories and memories of that fateful year. Instead of approaching events with eager anticipation and racing to the seat of war, a lone black man sits at home and awaits the future with newspaper in hand beside an empty fireplace. A color print titled *Hayti* is the only decoration in the room. Its placement on the back of the door guaranteed two things. Only people welcomed into the home could see this celebration of black independence. And black militancy would be the last thing this man saw whenever he left home to enter public life. The work captures the tensions that African Americans felt between anticipating the future by seizing the initiative in public and expecting change to come in private. White society preferred that blacks await progress with silent expectations. In 1862 the first owner of the work retitled it *Thoughts of Liberia, Emancipation*. The prospect of African Americans receiving freedom from white benefactors and colonizing Liberia appealed to society more than the thought of black citizens seizing freedom in a revolution like Haiti's and upending America. Liberia has overshadowed Haiti's presence in the painting ever since.[108]

As in white society, gender affected how enslaved people anticipated or expected the war. Enslaved men moved beyond the boundaries of plantations more frequently and, thus, were better prepared to anticipate the war and move toward it. By running errands, visiting loved ones on other plantations, piloting boats, or hauling goods, black men traveled, albeit in circumscribed routes, throughout the South. At the start of the war, these men knew paths to Union forces better than women. Moreover, the Union army preferred black men as laborers (and later recruits), whereas it viewed women and children as encumbrances.[109]

The story of Louisa and Archer Alexander illustrates how enslaved women expected the war to come to them. In November 1863, Louisa received a letter from Archer, her husband, with the good news that he had earned enough money to purchase her freedom. Archer had escaped to St. Louis during the war. Elated, Louisa took the letter straight to her master, Jim Hollman, and asked if he would sell her. "He flew at me, and said I would never get free only at the point of the Baynot," she said. After the incident, Hollman kept Louisa within his sight, night and day. He raged against Lincoln, calling him a rascal, and swearing "if he had hold of Lincoln he would chop him up into mincemeat." Louisa despaired of seizing her future and sensed that freedom would have to come to her. Local friends sympathized with her plight but hesitated to cross Hollman. In the end, Louisa imagined only one way to freedom. She pleaded with Archer to "get soldiers to take me from the house." Unless the future came to her, Louisa felt certain she would remain Hollman's slave. "I had good courage all along until now," she said, "but now I am almost heart-broken."[110]

Other slaves endured forced migrations away from Union forces and prayed that freedom would overtake them during removal. Meanwhile, thousands of masters compelled enslaved men to follow them to war as body servants, and the Confederate government impressed thousands of black men, free and enslaved, to labor for the war effort. For these slaves, the future seemed to brush past them. When Union forces approached islands and enclaves along the Atlantic coast during the first years of the war, masters evacuated inland. When federal armies invaded Virginia, Tennessee, and Mississippi, masters marched their slaves southward. Texas was the final destination for thousands of black refugees. Elivira Boles of Mississippi endured a forced march to Texas in the final year of the war. While Louisa Alexander's master tried to intimidate her by insulting the Yankees, Boles's owner tried to scare her away from the enemy. He "tol' us de Yankees 'ud kill us iffen dey foun' us." Her master waited until the end to evacuate, giving Boles no notice that they would leave and no time to collect her things. Then he raced them to Texas. "We was a dodgin' in and out, runnin' from de Yankees." The pace proved too much for Boles's child. "I lost my baby, its buried somewhere on dat road." The same roads that led to freedom for some slaves prolonged bondage for others or marked their graves.[111]

When the approaching war carried their freedom, blacks sensed that the future confirmed their prophecies. Solomon Brantley, an enslaved blacksmith and cook, witnessed so much cruelty on a South Carolina plantation that he feared he was running out of time. He tried to empty his mind of painful memories, to work and live in the present and for the future, but terrifying visions cracked the mental discipline he had acquired in a lifetime of slavery. "I prayed the Lord to help my people out of their bondage. I felt I could not stand it much longer."[112]

If freedom did not arrive soon, Brantley expected to go mad. Witnessing torture tested his sanity. Brantley watched a woman suffer a flogging while lying face down with her hands and feet tied to stakes. When she cried out, her master kicked her in the mouth. After he exhausted himself, he went inside, returned with sealing wax, melted it, and dropped it onto her lacerations. When the wax hardened and he regained his strength, the master flicked off the wax with a riding whip. The separation of families also tested Brantley's mind. Brantley lost his wife and two sons when their master sold them away. Killing time in bondage proved more difficult when he no longer had family to return to in the slave quarters.[113]

When the war came, Brantley interpreted the conflict as God's answer to his prayers. "In Secesh times I used to pray the Lord for this opportunity to be released from bondage and to fight for my liberty." Good fortune gave him work as a cook on a steamboat, but he knew he could not stay. God had answered his prayer and Brantley felt compelled to do his part. "I could not feel right so long as I was not in the regiment." In August 1863, he enlisted in the 21st US Colored Troops. He died of typhoid fever in 1864.[114]

Long awaited, emancipation rewarded African American prophecies. Freed people sang about their fulfilled expectations. "Tis good for to have some Patience, / Patience, patience, / Tis good for to have some patience, / To wait upon de Lord." "Neber see sich good times afore," a freedman told abolitionist John Miller McKim. "Too good to last, massa; too good to last." McKim noticed that the only joy present in African American music expressed hope for the future. "Have a little patience," "God will deliver," these and similar refrains filled their music with expectations. McKim concluded that slavery heightened African Americans' spiritual senses. "As persons deprived of one sense acquire greater susceptibility to those that remain," bondage robbed blacks of a secular education and they adapted by expanding their expectations and deepening their sacred hopes and feelings. When freedmen told McKim that they regularly heard and talked with God, he believed them.[115]

Emancipation confirmed their faith and temporalities because freedom answered their prayers. "The children of Israel was in bondage one time, and God sent Moses to 'liver them. Well, I s'pose that God sent Abe Lincoln to 'liver us," a former slave said. The Reverend Peter Randolph explained, "Many of the old people had prayed and looked forward to this day, but like Moses they were permitted to see it afar off, and not enter it." Secessionists had insisted that slaves would murder and rape white southerners if freedom came. "But instead of that, they were praising God and the Yankees for life and liberty." When Union forces liberated the slaves of Wilmington, North Carolina, in 1865, Charles, a black religious leader of the Front Street Methodist Church, read Psalm 9 to a gathering of former slaves. "When my enemies are turned back, they shall fall and perish at thy presence. For thou hast maintained my right and my cause; thou satest in the throne judging right. O thou enemy, destructions are come to a perpetual end: and they hast destroyed cities; their memorial is perished with them." The leader continued by affirming that "the expectation of the poor shall not perish for ever." Charles urged his listeners to take down their Bibles and study the psalm on this day of Jubilee.[116]

Whether they accepted it or not, some white southerners understood the prophetic imagination of black people. When the white pastor of Front Street Methodist heard Charles speak, he realized how his black congregation sensed the war. "To these colored people this was their great jubilee. They had just crossed the 'Red Sea' dry-shod. In their estimation Pharaoh's hosts had been engulfed in ruin—gone down in a sea of blood!" When word of Lee's surrender reached an Alabama plantation, blacks gathered at their church to sing of Daniel in the lion's den who was "Safe now in the promised land," and praised God that "By and by we'll go home to meet him./ Way over in the promised land." Their confident voices presented a different vision for a white listener who "seemed to see the mantle of our lost cause descending." Beneath the social, political, and economic upheavals of 1865 swirled a temporal disorder: the expectations of black southerners eclipsed the anticipations of white southerners.[117]

The War against Edmund Ruffin

THIS TEMPORAL TURNABOUT HARRIED Edmund Ruffin. His slaves escaped as soon as the enemy approached, something he did not anticipate. "The number, & general spreading of such abscondings of slaves are far beyond any previous conceptions," he admitted. The war exposed Ruffin's delusions that slaves preferred bondage to freedom and, for the first time in his life, Ruffin armed himself against the likelihood of a slave revolt. When the Union army approached in May 1862, Ruffin expected slaves to rise up against him. "We prepared & loaded our fire-arms—& for the first time I even locked my room (which is also an out-door,) & closed & fastened the very frail window shutters, when I went to bed." Even his black overseer, Jem Sykes, joined the exodus when Union soldiers arrived.[118]

While his slaves turned against him, so did the war Ruffin worked so hard to create. In 1861, Ruffin had lived at the battlefront, firing the first gun at Fort Sumter and helping to thwart the enemy's advance at Bull Run. In 1862, one of his slaves took Ruffin's position at the seat of war. William, a carriage driver, fled, joined the Union army, and served as a knowledgeable scout when the enemy returned to the area in 1862. The Peninsula campaign ruined Ruffin's future because the enemy's approach compelled him and his family to abandon three of their plantations. Ruffin, a man who had personified precipitate action when he rushed toward the conflict by volunteering at Harpers Ferry, Charleston, and Bull Run, became a refugee fleeing from the war. The enemy hunted him as an outlaw and ringleader of secession. For three years, he and his family traveled across Virginia seeking a haven from the enemy for themselves and their remaining slaves. Ruffin realized that the fame he achieved in 1861 endangered his family when the war reached his homes in subsequent years.[119]

The material culture of the war turned on him too. At Harpers Ferry, Fort Sumter, and Bull Run, Ruffin collected and circulated battle trophies to realize his prophecy; now the enemy looted his things to signify the doom of secession. During the course of the war, the enemy destroyed all three plantations that Ruffin evacuated. They liberated slaves, trampled fields, burned fence rails, confiscated animals and grain, wrecked machinery, girdled trees, broke windows and doors, slashed furniture, looted his library, and carried off his private papers as relics. Graffiti on the walls read, "You did fire the first gun on Sumter, you traitor son of a bitch." "Old Ruffin, don't you wish you had left the Southern Confederacy go to Hell (where it will go) and had stayed at home," asked another vandal. The war turned things upside down. The glory that Ruffin so confidently anticipated failed to materialize. Instead, the looming war ruined him and stole his future. His children had warned him of this fate before he fired the first shot. Edmund Jr., Julian, Elizabeth, and Mildred had all predicted doom. By 1865, only his namesake survived.[120]

In 1861, Ruffin read a play that foreshadowed his fate, *The Dream* by Joanna Baillie. Monks in a fourteenth-century monastery reported a recurring dream of a shadowy nobleman with an injured arm beckoning to a yawning grave. A plague ravaged the community at the time, and the monks divined that the ghostly nightmare called for a penitent to lift the pestilence. When a column of soldiers passed by, the monks convinced them to draw lots to select someone to perform a mild penance. The fate befell their general,

Osterloo, a brave fighter who faced the task with uncharacteristic fear. Years earlier he had murdered the man with the broken arm who now haunted the town. When the monks learned of this, they decided Osterloo must die to right his wrong and lift the curse. The sentence stunned the general. No enemy ever witnessed him flee from battle, but Osterloo cowered before the monks and tried to escape his fate. Imminent death transformed him from a hero to a coward.[121]

Changing from a man of action to a sentenced prisoner shifted his temporality from anticipation to expectation, and everyone noticed the profound difference in his physical condition. "What a noble fellow this would be to defend a narrow breach, though he shrinks with such abhorrence from a scaffold. It is a piteous thing to see." His strength, vision, and voice vanished. The warrior who had sent so many men to their final accounting faced his own reckoning with terror. "An unseen world surrounds us: spirits and powers, and the invisible dead, hover near us," he feared. "Any thing that can be endured here is mercy compared to the dreadful abiding of what may be hereafter." When friends tried to rescue him, Osterloo regained his energetic anticipatory self and charged at the guards. "I have arms in my hand now, and my foes are before me!" he hollered. Overpowered and conducted to the scaffold, Osterloo sank in despair and died of fear before the executioner wielded his axe. After his death, Osterloo's soldiers returned to the monastery and refused to believe that their fearless leader had died of fright. He feared no man in battle when he actively charged into the future, but when forced to pause and wait for his approaching fate, the hero shriveled up and died.[122]

Ruffin wished to see *The Dream* performed on stage; instead, he watched the moral of Baillie's story unfold in his own life. Like Osterloo, fate robbed Ruffin of his anticipatory stance, forced him to await death, and sapped his vitality. When his time was up, would Ruffin face the end like Osterloo or John Brown? The question haunted him.

Epilogue

SHADOWS

IN 1892, HORATIO RUST gave his antebellum relics, including his John Brown pike, to Frank Granger Logan, a wealthy Chicago grain merchant and avid collector of Civil War memorabilia. Martyrdom for freedom unified Logan's collection. Visitors to his mansion at 2919 Prairie Avenue marveled at objects associated with Lincoln's assassination: a knife engraved "A Lincoln" that was in the president's pocket when he was murdered, a locket containing Lincoln's hair, his final autograph given to private secretary Charles Forbes that fateful night, and the black coat he wore to the theater. A zigzag slash from the buttonhole to the left armpit marked where someone cut open Lincoln's coat thinking he was shot through the heart. Much of the left sleeve was missing where a previous collector had cut out relics and presented them to subsequent presidents.[1]

Logan called his collection an "Emancipation Cabinet." During the Renaissance, European collectors gathered *Wunderkammern*, "wonder cabinets" that assembled sacred relics, natural curios, precious art, and technological marvels. Over time, wonder cabinets passed from one possessor to another and eventually landed in institutions, as John Ashmole's impressive cabinet came to rest at Oxford University. When Charles Willson Peale brought the tradition to America, his collection eventually became America's first museum. These earlier wonder cabinets placed mastodon bones beside the hair of a saint, famous paintings beside mechanical inventions, because all wonders celebrated God's creativity. Wonder cabinets gathered relics to preserve sacred pasts and fulfill humanity's covenant with God for the future. The nineteenth century changed things. By the antebellum period, Americans collected relics they associated with human progress instead of divine providence. Nineteenth-century museums separated natural history from human history, art from science. Logan's Emancipation Cabinet marked this cultural shift, honoring a national achievement instead of praising God's work.[2]

Rust understood how Americans treasured historical relics and capitalized on it. As a federal agent to Native Americans in California, he took Indian relics from his subjects, assembled wonder cabinets, and sold them to the University of Chicago, Stanford University, and other institutes of higher learning. But his favorite wonders came from the Browns. After the Civil War, Rust helped John Brown's children settle in Pasadena, California. He started marketing his Brown trophies after Owen Brown, the last living Harpers Ferry raider, died in 1889. In 1892, Rust advertised John Brown autographs, promising to sell them to eastern dealers for $15 to $20 a piece. He timed his advertisement to coincide with the Columbian Exposition in Chicago, because his Brown memorabilia, along with the rest of Logan's Emancipation Cabinet, was on display there inside the Harpers Ferry engine house where John Brown made his last stand. As Figure E.1 shows, locals advertised the structure as "John Brown's Fort" to attract tourists before it reached the fair. Organizers bought the building for $20,000 and spent an additional $40,000 disassembling, moving, and reconstructing the fort in Chicago for the event. In his guide to the exposition, John Flinn urged people to visit the building at 1341 Wabash Avenue to stand inside "this almost sacred relic of days just preceding the civil war." There people saw the sword that Brown captured from Lieutenant "Fort Scott" Brockett at Black Jack, the bowie knife that Owen Brown carried at Harpers Ferry, and an original pike made

Figure E.1 John Brown's fort, Harpers Ferry, West Virginia. Library of Congress, Prints and Photographs Division.

by Charles Blair in Collinsville, Connecticut. After the war, antebellum relics of the looming crisis acquired the historical value that people like Rust had anticipated for them.[3]

The meaning of Rust's relics changed when Logan acquired them and associated them with Lincoln's things. Instead of representing the diverse looming wars these things had projected—a frontier scrap, a class war, a slave insurrection, a revolution, or Armageddon—the pike recalled a simpler time when John Brown and Abraham Lincoln died for the same thing, black liberation. Rust also donated John Brown's field glasses from Bleeding Kansas so that tourists at the Exposition could "look upon the glass through which John Brown, the Liberator, looked into the future, and helped to read aloud the Emancipation Proclamation." The *Chicago Tribune* published a pamphlet about Logan's cabinet that explained, "These relics have a unity of meaning and interest." In hindsight, John Brown and Abraham Lincoln were "the author and finisher respectively of Emancipation, and the alpha and omega of American personal freedom."[4]

If the things on display could have testified for themselves, they would have told a different story. Brown's violent abolition and Lincoln's legal emancipation pursued different objects and ends. Contrasting temporalities shaped how each man viewed the future and understood his place in the world. If Brown could have seen the Emancipation Proclamation through his field glasses, he would have denounced it. Lincoln's plea that enslaved Americans refrain from revolt would have outraged Brown, who believed God formed the coming world through the bold actions of men like him who were willing to shed blood to advance freedom.

Brown was a founding member of the Radical Abolitionist Party, a group that failed to elect a single candidate. At the party's first meeting in October 1855, Brown read from Hebrews 9.22: "Without the shedding of blood there is no remission of sin." He asked the assembly to finance and equip his military operations in Kansas. Reading letters from two of his sons already in Kansas, Brown reported the aggressions of southern filibusters and the need for a manly northern response. The next day Gerrit Smith presented Brown with seven muskets with bayonets, seven revolvers, seven broadswords, and $60 that the meeting collected. The money paid for things like the binoculars that Brown carried. In 1855, the Radical Abolitionists agreed that violence was "the only course left to the friends of freedom." When Richard Hinton recalled that fateful meeting, he praised Brown for being "a free hand, untrammeled by compromise or party restraint, that 'feared God so much that it did not fear men.'" Only a visionary who stood above political bargains could see that God was returning the world to the furnace to be forged and reshaped by uncompromising hands.[5]

The Exposition also displayed the shawl Lincoln wore during his Cooper Union speech, in which he denounced the Harpers Ferry raid weeks after Brown's execution. Lincoln distanced himself from the dead raider by insisting, "John Brown was no Republican." He challenged Brown's claim to know God's plan and how to precipitate it on earth. Cloaked conspirators do not carry out divine providence with sharp actions like Harpers Ferry. Instead, parties, compromises, and laws make history at a rate that seemed too slow for impatient radicals like Brown but nonetheless transformed the Union while preserving democracy. In Lincoln's view, a circumspect and careful approach to change was more likely to discern and follow God's mysterious ways than an arrogant and reckless race to the future that Brown promoted. Government advanced the interests of the people by relying on reasoned debate, not religious violence.[6]

Ex Post Facto Prophets

AFTER THE CIVIL WAR, Americans forgot how they expected it. The broad antebellum horizon, with its diverse speculations, rumors, prophecies, anticipations, and expectations, shrank in hindsight. Society replaced its complex imaginations of looming border wars, economic clashes, racial strife, revolutions, and Armageddon with a simple myth that claimed no one knew the war would be long and bloody. After the fact, Americans convinced themselves that everyone had looked forward to a lark. According to this short war myth, the war would be a brief, bracing adventure that invigorated the nation. Before bloodshed, thousands of people did anticipate a romantic war, but thousands of others expected the worst. The short war myth overshadowed the dread that women felt. It ignored the dire warnings of conservatives and border men who sensed the approaching destruction. It erased the hopes of millions of African Americans who prayed for a cataclysm to kill slavery.

For many reasons, people's postwar memories differed from their antebellum forecasts of the conflict. The trauma, power, and duration of the event changed the world and how people viewed it. Understanding and articulating these changes must have been difficult for survivors. "I cannot believe I am the same person that was ever so lighthearted & hopeful in the future," wrote a widow in October 1865. "What a scene we have passed through in the last four years," she told her uncle. "I cannot dwell upon the past but with the most painful emotions." By focusing on the most mistaken predictions of 1861, people admitted they did not know the future as well as they imagined. Centering on the war's enthusiastic anticipators also privileged the perspectives of millions of volunteers. The short war myth honored the heroism of recruits who marched to war as boys in 1861 and returned home as men in 1865. The Civil War became a coming-of-age story about the people who fought it and the nation that endured it.[7]

This process of revision and mythology is evident on a personal scale by contrasting individuals' memories of the looming war with their anticipations of it. At the start of the twentieth century, Henry Adams recalled, "Not one man in America wanted the Civil War, or expected or intended it." Fire-eaters wanted secession but, according to Adams, even they anticipated peace. "Not one, however clever or learned, guessed what happened." As an old man, Adams described the atmosphere in America when he returned from Europe in 1860. In hindsight, the nation had rushed toward a war that no one believed in at the time. He remembered a procession of Wide Awakes passing his front door. "Military in all things except weapons," with torches aloft, long lines of men stretched along the hillsides from Quincy to Boston, where they met Henry's father, Charles Adams, a Republican congressman. Adams followed his father to Washington to work as his private secretary during the secession winter.[8]

Henry Adams's expectations of the war were more ominous than his memories of it. When war loomed, Adams wrote a series of editorials about the crisis from his vantage point in the nation's capital. "Almost everyone has talked of certain civil war; of streets drowned in blood, and of the city a prey to the flames," he reported on New Year's Day, 1861. Rumors of secessionist plots to sack the capital terrified residents, many of whom fled. Women wept when they talked about it. Even Adams believed the worst. "So many striking events have been crowded into the last few days that it is hard to keep the account," he confessed. "The sound of war in Washington" impressed him. Drumming filled the city as troops drilled, and even timid leaders like President Buchanan spoke in bellicose tones. He sensed the nation on the precipice of war. A single "telegraphic word" from Charleston or Washington would "set a host of bayonets in motion." When that telegram arrived in April, Adams wanted no part of the carnage. He followed his father to Great Britain and the diplomatic service.[9]

August Kautz never shied from warfare. A graduate of West Point, veteran of the Mexican War, and regular army officer who fought Native Americans before and after the Civil War, Kautz devoted his life to military service. In the Civil War he served as a cavalry officer in the eastern and western theaters.

Like many regular army officers, he was stationed in the West when the war began. In 1861, he left Washington territory, took a steamer to Panama, crossed the isthmus, and boarded a vessel bound for New York. When he arrived on August 2, Kautz entered a city still reeling from the Union's rout at Bull Run. In his postwar memoirs Kautz recalled, "I was not the least surprised and had predicted that the attacking force on either side would be sure to meet with reverses until the troops became veterans." Kautz continued to Washington, DC, where he found regular officers and volunteers clamoring for promotion. He recalled in his memoirs that these men "did not seem to reflect upon the responsibility they were seeking, as though the war was going to be a holiday affair and the care of thousands of lives was a task of easy execution." Looking back on the moment as a veteran and career officer, Kautz thought, "When I reflect upon what it cost the country in blood and treasure before these Holiday heroes found their proper position I am astonished that no precautions are taken by our legislators to guard against such experience in the future."[10]

Kautz's memoir presents a more prophetic and sober view of the looming war than his wartime journals contain. He correctly recalled August 2 as the day he reached New York harbor and encountered northern humiliation after Bull Run, but his wartime experience of the event lacked the professional detachment he expressed after the war. Instead of predicting that the offensive force was fated to fail for lack of experience and discipline, Kautz was impressed by the scale of the battle. His journal recognized Bull Run as "the greatest battle ever fought on this continent." His Washington journal entries praised General George McClellan for imposing order and discipline, but Kautz did not criticize "Holiday heroes" for seeking promotion. At the time, he was engaged in the same quest for a high command. These discrepancies between Kautz's memories and his anticipations of the war may be reconciled. Perhaps he predicted defeat for the Union's raw recruits before Bull Run but dared not express that view even in his diary. Maybe he sensed a frenzy in Washington during the rush to promotion but needed hindsight to identify "Holiday heroes" and understand their significance. Regardless of the reason, Kautz's writings illustrate a larger pattern of shifting stories that changed how Americans described the looming war for generations to come.[11]

By 1866, David Hunter Strother noticed how American memories of the looming war differed from anticipations of it. An accomplished writer, Strother spotted how postwar authors—he labeled them "ex post facto prophets"—foreshadowed the tragedy by contrasting their prescience about the future with society's naiveté at the outset. Instead of recalling a single, enthusiastic cheer for the looming war, Strother remembered "a confusion of tongues" in 1861 that rivaled the tower of Babel. He published a series of articles in *Harper's New Monthly Magazine* that tried to document his personal war as a Virginia Unionist. Despite his good intentions, even Strother employed the short war myth to frame his memories of the war. In his fourth installment for *Harper's*, titled "Expectancy," Strother claimed that society's hopes for a ninety-day war died at the battle of Ball's Bluff. "The war which had burst upon many like a thunder-clap from a cloudless sky . . . was now developing into a reality whose proportions and consequences it was bewildering to estimate." Like the "ex post facto prophets" he criticized, Strother remembered naïve Americans who "flattered themselves that the conflict would be 'sharp and short.' "[12]

Strother's war journals tell a different story. Instead of focusing on lost hopes of a short war after Ball's Bluff, Strother's entries for that period looked to the future and lost hope for Reconstruction. "If the Federal Government succeeds in crushing the armed front of the Rebellion," he asked, "what hope is there of a permanent maintenance of law & order among a people who seem to have lost all perceptions of right & wrong?" He doubted that America's mild, inefficient, and whimsical republic could forge and maintain the forceful and steady military rule that the postwar South would require. Instead of reflecting on how these profound wartime thoughts resonated with events in 1866, Strother erased his Reconstruction predictions from his war memories. By recollecting the end of early war innocence in 1861 instead of the start of Reconstruction forebodings, the Virginia Unionist contributed to sectional reconciliation at the expense of historical accuracy and racial justice.[13]

Postwar novelists used the short war myth to frame the war as a tragedy. Writing fourteen years after Appomattox, Henry James argued that the war dealt "a fatal blow to that happy faith in the uninterruptedness of American prosperity." The war generation had "eaten of the tree of knowledge," and the postwar American "will be a more critical person than his complacent and confident grandfather." The Civil War revealed the world as "a more complicated place than it had hitherto seemed, the future more treacherous, success more difficult." [14]

James wrote these lines in a biography of Nathaniel Hawthorne, a severe critic of the war whose insightful wartime writings challenge James's portrait of simple, happy, antebellum Americans. Hawthorne hated the thoughtless patriotism and groundless certainty he witnessed in 1861. Instead of anticipating a short, romantic war at the outset, Hawthorne expected "we are . . . at the beginning of a great war—a war, the issue of which no man can predicate." Visiting Harpers Ferry, Hawthorne derived "intellectual satisfaction" when he considered the hanging of John Brown. The misguided prophet deserved to die for his "preposterous miscalculation of possibilities," his reckless faith that a handful of men could free the slaves without civil war. "No human effort, on a grand scale, has ever yet resulted according to the purpose of its projectors," he warned.[15]

Mark Twain employed the short war myth in his firsthand account of the war's beginning in Missouri. His essay, "The Private History of a Campaign that Failed," is a cracker-barrel tale about the Marion Rangers, boyhood friends who anticipated a "holiday frolic" that would last "about three months." His description of the company echoed James's portrait of antebellum Americans: "young, ignorant, good-natured, well-meaning, trivial, full of romance, and given to reading chivalric novels and singing forlorn love-ditties." Twain recalled feeling "full of unreasoning joy" when the war came. The prospect of soldiering opened a new horizon for him. "In my thoughts that was as far as I went; I did not go into the details; as a rule, one doesn't at twenty-four." While playing soldier, Twain and his friends shot a solitary rider and watched the man die, gasping for air and calling for his wife and children. The experience sickened Twain, and he left the war.[16]

In 1861, Twain, who then went by the name Samuel Clemens, expected a different war than the holiday that he remembered. At twenty-four, he focused on Samuel Baldwin's *Armageddon*, not on vague ideas about new adventures. When he faced the looming war, he saw the end times and fled to Nevada. After the war, it was easier for him to fabricate a short war story for himself than to admit his antebellum faith in Baldwin's wild millennialism. In 1869, James Wood Davidson dismissed Baldwin's book in his anthology, *The Living Writers of the South*. "The day for such theorizing . . . such arrogance of exegesis, is probably past forever," Davidson announced. "This rhetoric about the Whore of Babylon and Spread Eagleism might have found patient hearers" in the past, "but the present age understands too well the relationship between the parent wish and the progeny thought to take to these proofs of prophecy." The Civil War caused a theological crisis that divorced Americans from the certainties and "excessively Biblical" thinking of Baldwin and other antebellum believers. Seers of sacred truths like Samuel Baldwin lost legitimacy after the cataclysm, and Twain was not alone for distancing himself from them.[17]

Beyond expressing the war's chasm between antebellum and postwar life, the short war myth appealed to Americans because it reconciled the North and South. Neither side could be blamed for causing the war if everyone misread its portents. No one bore responsibility for its death and destruction if all imagined a short, bloodless frolic in the beginning. Twain's story appeared in *Century* magazine's "Battles and Leaders of the Civil War," a popular memoir series that sought sectional reconciliation (and a handsome profit) by responding to America's heightened interest in the war on its twenty-fifth anniversary. Twain's story reconciled the sections by insisting that "Bull Run material" filled both armies. Green recruits with romantic notions and youthful innocence pervaded the ranks before war changed them. Those eager anticipators were prevalent, but Twain simplified his own past by claiming to be one of them.[18]

Century showcased the memoirs of generals, but series editors included reminiscences from ordinary soldiers to appeal to a wider readership. The generals' accounts were fact-checked by War Department clerks who were simultaneously producing the *Official Records* of the war. While such scrutiny worked for verifying the content of an order or the location of a brigade, the War Department was less effective when checking memories penned by the rank and file. Nothing in the *Official Records* could substantiate or question customary elements in a private's account: how he anticipated the conflict, why he volunteered, his first impressions of military life, and how he felt during his first battle. As a result, common soldiers enjoyed greater freedom of expression than their former generals. Twain's account was not the most fictional contribution from small-fry veterans. *Century* published P. D. Haywood's "Life on the 'Alabama', by One of the Crew" in 1886, only to discover later that Haywood, whose real name was James Young, never served on the famous ship. Generations of historians have accepted "Battles and Leaders" and the *Official Records* without pausing to question the motives and methods behind their production.[19]

The short war myth gained a consensus among historians and literary critics after World War I. Scholars compared the wars' origins and blamed blundering generations for starting them. Tragic, needless wars ensued because naïve nations imagined romance and adventure as they waded into a sea of blood. Historians argued that both wars matured and modernized society, while literary scholars insisted that bloodshed instilled realism and irony in literature. College curriculums started dividing "early" and "modern" American history and literature at 1865. In 1915, during the fiftieth anniversary of the Civil War and the middle of World War I, literary scholar Fred Lewis Pattee wrote that the Civil War gave birth to American "literary independence" from Europe. He pointed to Walt Whitman's *Drum Taps* and Abraham Lincoln's "Gettysburg Address" as examples of "new forces" emanating from "that mighty struggle." American letters matured by drawing deep pathos and sparkling realism from the soul of the great conflict.[20]

Though it appears in countless monographs, syntheses, and textbooks, the short war myth is more of an analytical device than knowledge. Pick up any American history textbook and you're likely to find Civil War recruits eager for a war they imagined would be short and fun. The blind enthusiasm of volunteers serves as a substitute for all American visions of the looming war, because the myth provides a simpler antebellum counterpoint for stories about the war making America more pragmatic, realistic, secular, or modern. Evidence abounds that antebellum Americans imagined wars that exceeded the Civil War in power and duration. People expected Armageddon, forecasted racial extinctions, predicted revolutions bloodier than the French, and even wished for a long, destructive war to purge America.[21]

The short war myth also prevails because of its seductive narrative. It ensures the deep, poetic structure of Civil War history. As historian Hayden White explains, scholars seldom recognize, let alone challenge, such devices, because they form the "accepted paradigm" through which we view the past and tell its stories. Bruce Catton used the short war myth to great effect in his popular *American Heritage* centennial history of the war in the 1960s. "This may or may not have been the end of America's golden age," Catton wrote, "but it was at least the final, haunted moment of its age of innocence." Ken Burns employed the short war myth with equal skill in his documentary film series, *The Civil War*, a work that has influenced how millions of Americans understand the conflict. We have accepted the myth as assumed knowledge for so long that we fail to see how it flattens the horizons and imaginations of Civil War Americans.[22]

The Scroll of the Mystical Future

IMPOSING AN AGE OF innocence on Civil War Americans obscures more than it reveals about them. The conflict did not start innocently and darken over time. It was messy, complicated, and uncertain in people's minds before it began. Likewise, the war did not modernize American society in a linear fashion. Early war anticipations that trusted progress over providence were more "modern" than late war expectations that prayed for mercy and divine intervention. Civil War Americans did not respond to new futures and changing temporalities in a unified way. Some people understood the cultural shift from anticipations to expectations as a permanent change in American thinking that fostered fatalism, pragmatism, and realism. For others, the future's tumult was a traumatic event that they coped with by erecting myths, memories, and monuments to a dead time. Sectionalism further divided American temporalities. Postwar northerners and westerners celebrated iconic cowboys and rags-to-riches men who gazed at the horizon with anticipation. In the South, the future of Reconstruction felt imposed by others. White southerners who mourned a lost cause and black southerners who struggled for equality against unjust odds expected a future affected by fate and external powers.[23]

Anticipations and expectations continued to battle for supremacy in America's imagination after the Civil War generation departed in the twentieth century. As each present dreamed and dreaded tomorrow within its culture and circumstance, a kaleidoscope of futures appeared, collapsed, and reformed over time. Technological and medical advances, space exploration, and social movements raised anticipations of progress. World wars, systemic prejudice, and economic depressions challenged America's faith in perpetual progress. Anxious visionaries felt the tempo of history accelerating, and immigrants introduced diversities that splintered American temporalities. Moving forward remained the national mission, but "forward" beckoned in competing directions. Capitalist anticipations abounded after the Cold War. When a seer prophesied the end of history in 1993, he announced human fulfillment, not Christ's return, as the millennium closed. Then the terrorist attacks of September 11, 2001 revived old fears of cloaked powers, zealotry, and doom. Utopian anticipations soared during Barack Obama's presidency and apocalyptic expectations followed Donald Trump's election eight years later. As historian Jill Lepore put it, "dystopias follow utopias the way thunder follows lightning."[24]

Civil War Americans could have understood their descendants' futures without the gift of prophecy. The war exposed the allure and folly of futurism, but they could not impart such wisdom to us. The pace of life quickened for them too, and, like us, they felt adrift on a sea of time. A pocket-sized invention, the telegraph, offered them instantaneous information that promised more knowledge than it delivered. Immigrants and refugees unsettled their futures. Unreason and dread poisoned their politics, and a cadre of wealthy Americans exploited the chaos to defend hidebound economic interests. Looming dangers terrified ordinary people who despaired of avoiding cataclysmic futures while others ignored the threat out of ignorance or selfishness. Even the worst nightmares in future times—human extinction caused by nuclear war, climate change, or pandemic—would have been relatable to nineteenth-century Americans who awaited Armageddon.

If we cast aside short war anticipators and focus our attention on other Civil War prophets, the history of the future offers new lessons. For African Americans, the Civil War ended an age of wickedness, not innocence, and their memoirs of the conflict have always offered alternative visions of the future. Instead of anticipating a frolic when the war began, slaves expected an answer to their prayers. Recalling his life enslaved to the Brent family in Richmond, Virginia, Thomas Johnson remembered anxiety, rumors, and biblical interpretations rippling through the black community as antebellum events unfolded. Despite learning to spell and write in secret, Johnson thought "the door to freedom seemed as much closed as ever" in the 1850s. A large map of the United States hung in his master's dining room. While cleaning the room, Johnson would study the names of every city along the rail line from Richmond to Boston. "Often I wondered whether I would ever see these cities, where all were free." Instead of using literacy to seek freedom in the North, Johnson employed it to find consolation in religion. Christianity promised him "the home beyond, where there was 'perfect rest,' and freedom, and peace, where there would be no slavery." This future "was almost daily before me," Johnson recalled, but finding religion seemed as difficult as reaching the North.[25]

Abraham Lincoln's candidacy in 1860 convinced Johnson and other slaves that their deliverance was at hand. "The slaves prayed to God for his success, and they prayed very especially the night before the election," Johnson recalled. Lincoln's election signaled the beginning of a great war orchestrated by the Almighty, who had heard the cries of oppressed people and would deliver them from bondage just as He had saved the Hebrews in Egypt. As his reading improved, Johnson shared the news he gathered from newspapers and the Bible with his fellow slaves. They considered both sources to be equally relevant to their present condition and future freedom. As Johnson explained, "Many of the coloured people believed that the 11th chapter of Daniel referred directly to the war," especially verses thirteen to fifteen:

> For the king of the north shall return, and set forth a multitude greater than the former, and shall certainly come after certain years with a great army and with much riches. And in those times there shall many stand up against the king of the south: also the robbers of thy people shall exalt themselves to establish the vision; but they shall fall. So the king of the north shall come, and cast up a mount, and take the most

> fenced cities: and the arms of the south shall not withstand, neither his chosen people, neither shall there be any strength to withstand.

When the sounds of Union artillery drew closer during the Peninsula campaign in 1862 and the siege of Petersburg and Richmond in 1864–1865, "the slaves were joyful and expectant." Every prophecy they read in Scripture was coming true.[26]

Freedom finally arrived when the Union army entered Richmond on April 3, 1865. "That scene of years ago comes up vividly before me at this moment," Johnson wrote at the turn of the century. Men and women wept and praised God. Black people danced in the streets, played instruments, climbed trees, yelled at the top of their lungs, and gave impromptu speeches to gathering crowds. "The long night of affliction in the house of our bondage had passed," Johnson said, "that deeply desired and hoped for and prayed for time had come." When Johnson remembered the Civil War, he explained its origins as a divine reckoning. "The innocent blood of murdered men and women and children had cried unto God from the ground, and He in His own time, which is always the right time and best time, and in His own way, which is the very best way, answered that cry." Johnson told people he was born three times: in 1834 as a thing, mere chattel; in 1857 as a Christian; and in 1865 as a free man. People are not responsible for their own births. History and providence blessed Johnson.[27]

Women recalled diverse futures too. Mary Chesnut labored to transform her wartime journal into a postwar work that questioned comforting myths that southerners told about the Confederacy and its war. Her husband, South Carolina senator James Chesnut, had celebrated secession by promising to drink all the blood that would be spilled by it. Mary never shared his confidence. In 1861, events crowded too quickly for her to anticipate the future. She dreaded the looming war but as the wife of a prominent secessionist could not escape its vortex. Edmund Ruffin promised to send her a Harpers Ferry pike. A doctor mailed her handcuffs that Union soldiers reportedly brought to Manassas. Chesnut doubted that the relics foreshadowed Yankee defeat. "Trophies for future generations," she called them.[28]

When defeat doomed the Confederates instead, Chesnut marveled at southerners who reconciled themselves to fate by starting anew with memories. She could not accept the short war myth because she felt differently when the war began and had recorded the forebodings of ardent secessionists in 1861. The war upended everything, but that did not mean antebellum southerners should be pardoned for their miscalculations and mistakes by claiming that no one expected the war would be long and bloody. Southerners had to own up to their errors. "Nearly all of my sage prophecies have been verified the wrong way," she admitted; "every insight into character or opinion I have given as to men turned out utter folly." Chesnut confronted southern myth and memory of the war by recalling the incoherence of the war years—its rumors, uncertainties, and chaos. Dreams, sounds, scraps of conversation interrupted her diary entries. Chesnut never finished her project. After her death, publishers edited her work so that it conformed to southern memory and postwar literature. They titled it *A Diary from Dixie*, though Chesnut had hated the song and disliked how the word represented her world.[29]

A wondrous vision of futures past came from an unlikely source, a traveling pianist and mystic named Jesse Shepherd. In 1869 at age twenty, Shepherd amazed Parisians with otherworldly sounds. Untrained and unable to read music, Shepherd improvised performances with massive hands that spanned an octave and a half. As his reputation grew, he met famous composers and gave recitals to royalty in Russia, Prussia, and Britain. A showman with rouged lips and manicured hands, Shepherd also performed séances. Though he claimed to be a mystic, some considered him a charlatan. In 1887, San Diego gave Shepherd a city block and enough money to build the Villa Montezuma, a Victorian palace with turrets and stained glass.[30]

Once his castle was finished, Shepherd left it for a literary career in Europe. He adopted the penname Francis Grierson in honor of his relative, Civil War general Benjamin Grierson. When he first published essays on mysticism in French, he caught the attention of Maurice Maeterlinck who judged Grierson "the supreme essayist of the age." Cosmopolitanism gave his work wider currency and a more stylish appearance, but beneath its avant-garde exterior, Grierson's mysticism echoed Edward Hitchcock's universal telegraph. "There is a psychic and magnetic correspondence through all things," he wrote. At first glance, the universe seems random, but sensitive souls could see beyond the veil of chance and discern "the law of phenomenal relativity." All thoughts and motives endured forever as unseen electrical waves pulsing through space. Clairvoyants comprehended how "the hieroglyphs of Modern Theosophy were written as by an invisible hand on the scroll of the mystical future."[31]

Unfortunately, as the twentieth century unfolded, its materialism and science threatened to extinguish the psychic consciousness that the nineteenth century had fostered to read the universal telegraph and discern the future. Grierson felt trapped in a fin-de-siècle world that closed humanity's awareness of the future. Even worse, twentieth-century Europe seemed to be slipping toward annihilation. A long era of peaceful mysticism seemed to be ending. In 1913, he prophesied world war in *The Invincible Alliance*. Germany worried him the most. "If the Prussian in 1870 was a fighting automaton with a will wound up like a clock, what would he be now after forty years of drill, and discipline far more reasoned, far more desperate." Living in England, Grierson watched society sleepwalking toward a looming war. People accumulated wealth, assumed control of their future, lived year to year in "chronic apathy" and "mock security." In "The Doom of American Democracy," Grierson predicted that the United States would not escape the fate of Europe. America derived its Gilded Age splendor from war profiteering during the Civil War, and the nation's capitalists would mire the nation in the coming conflict to enrich themselves. Americans were so focused on progress and material gain that they would misread the portents of their imminent destruction. For Grierson, warfare was never an engine for social good. Instead, it corroded national character and principles. In the looming war, "the so-called Christian nations . . . will throw off their masks and engage in an Armageddon of slaughter."[32]

When Grierson sensed a looming war, the shadows of futures past haunted him. Forty years of cosmopolitan life in European capitals did not dim Grierson's memory of how Americans approached the Civil War. As a boy, he heard rural seers prophesy looming bloodshed on the Illinois prairie. In *The Valley of Shadows*, he remembered how the unbroken vistas of Sagamon County trained settlers' gaze on the western horizon. He recalled a "bowie-knife man" from Bleeding Kansas who bragged, "I've put daylight through more'n one Abolitionist," and threatened to hang any man who wasn't "solid on the nigger question." His parents helped conduct runaways across the Underground Railroad. Grierson never forgot the fear in fugitive faces or the aggressive bearing of posses hunting for them. He attended the final Lincoln-Douglas debate at Alton. Rumors swirled that Lincoln would be mobbed if he repeated anti-slavery statements he had made in northern parts of the state. People expected the "irrepressible conflict" to begin, and Grierson remembered anxious expressions on the audience members' faces. Everyone "gazed upward at the group of politicians on the balcony like wrecked mariners scanning the horizon for the smallest sign of a white sail of hope." What young Grierson saw that day seared his memory: a homely pillar of a man with penetrating eyes and an earnest voice, Lincoln "infused into the mixed and uncertain throng something spiritual and supernormal." Douglas's wit, sophistication, and theatrics could outmatch any antebellum politician, but Lincoln won the crowd because he appreciated their dark premonitions about the future.[33]

Grierson wrote *The Valley of Shadows* to recover the expectations that ordinary people felt when the war loomed. Though hard work preoccupied Illinois farmers, laboring in the field prepared them to feel an unfolding, unnamable fate. "The prairie was a region of expectant watchfulness," he said. Standing in a sea of limitless grass, settlers appreciated how distant forces stirred the air. Gales churned undulating blades, clouds shadowed horizons, dark vapors consumed valleys. Camp meetings reinforced premonitions of silent powers, unspoken urgency, and looming trials. People believed things happened not by human motive but through "an impelling impulse." For the farmers, "the appearance of 'Uncle Tom's Cabin' was not a reason, but an illumination; the founding of the Republican party was not an act of political wire-pulling, but an inspiration; the great religious revivals and the appearance of two comets were not regarded as coincidences, but accepted as signs of divine preparation and warning." Grierson wrote his memoir to restore this vanishing orientation to the future, the mystical, expectant temporality shared by people on the Illinois prairie. The hurly burly of city life, the go-ahead bustle of capitalism, the strident confidence of science, all these forces in modern days threatened to extinguish an older way of approaching time, an ancient posture attuned to receiving signs in silence and reading portents in the sky. Grierson conjured this fading temporality in *The Valley of Shadows* by explaining how prairie silences gave voice to antebellum forebodings.[34]

Grierson showed how Sagamon's antebellum settlers approached the looming war with intelligence and religious faith instead of ignorance and enthusiasm. When forecasting their future, people of southern Illinois drew from a wide spectrum of political views and social backgrounds. Grierson remembered neighbors who went to church with him, "Old Whigs, Know-nothings and Democrats, Republicans, militant Abolitionists, and outspoken friends of slave-owners." When Donati's comet first appeared in 1858, during Lincoln and Douglas's senatorial campaigns, people predicted the end of the world. As the threatening body hurtled closer and closer, people considered it a sign of looming civil war. To interpret the comet, the minister of Grierson's church read Isaiah, chapter 19, verse 20: "And it shall be for a sign and for a witness unto the LORD of hosts in the land of Egypt: for they shall cry unto the LORD because of the oppressors, and he shall send them a savior, and a great one, and he shall deliver them." God had opened the roof of heaven to show people what was coming, and the minister warned, "Destruction 'll overtake them thet's on the wrong side in this here fight!" He told the congregation that the people crying for deliverance were the slaves and that the Lord called one of their own, Abraham Lincoln, to deliver them. This political endorsement in church angered proslavery settlers who stormed out of the chapel. It entranced Grierson, who still felt "the electric thrill" of that moment decades later. His father agreed with the minister and rural seers: "It certainly does look as if some great change would soon come over the country." Some took to religion for consolation, while others warned of civil war. His neighbor, Zack Caverly, assured people that the comet would pass without dropping from the sky, but the nation's politicians, lawyers, and hordes of settlers would bring the world to an end just the same.[35]

To read the future in the twentieth century, Grierson invented the "psycho-phone," a machine designed to receive universal telegrams transmitted to posterity by the dead. If Samuel Morse's device carried news of the present across electric currents, Grierson's invention conveyed messages from the future through mystic channels. The first message Grierson received on his device came from Ulysses Grant on September 9, 1920. In a brief report, Grant warned Grierson that the Panama Canal was insecure. Months later, inspectors found weaknesses in its fortifications. "The psycho-phone waves," Grierson assured readers, "are as definite as those received by wireless methods." For eight months, the dead prophesied to Grierson through his invention. Thomas Jefferson forecasted the future of American democracy. Elizabeth Cady Stanton explained what was in store for American women. Henry Ward Beecher prophesied a new Puritanism. Alexander Hamilton spelled out the forces that precede revolutions. Abraham Lincoln prophesied the future of Mexico and North America. No one except Grierson listened. Death came for him six years later in Los Angeles. At the end of a piano performance, he sat still, eyes shut, massive hands resting on the keys. Grierson often ended recitals with similar dramatic pauses before acknowledging his audience. This time he was gone.[36]

Though *The Valley of Shadows* received favorable reviews, it did not attract many readers. When Bernard DeVoto edited a new edition of the book after World War II, he recognized that Americans could better appreciate Grierson's expectant temporality in the 1940s than they did when the book first appeared in 1909.

> Twice since then our hearts have been sifted out before the judgment seat. Twice we have lived through the oncoming of a great war. Twice we have lived in a trance of doubt and foreboding, feeling time carry us on toward the dark event which we seemed unable either to understand or to affect—till out of blindness and paralysis of the will we came to resolution, understanding, and action.

Edmund Wilson praised Grierson as a "millennial" who evoked the "mood of apocalyptic expectation" that pervaded the antebellum frontier. Though Wilson and DeVoto proclaimed *The Valley of Shadows* a classic work of American letters, Grierson and his writing remain relatively unknown.[37]

The End of Edmund Ruffin

CONFEDERATE SURRENDER SHATTERED Edmund Ruffin's prophecy and threatened his selfhood. Because expectations precede all events, even unexpected ones, what people dread or dream about the future preconditions their perceptions and memories. Projects and possibilities structure life stories, and Edmund Ruffin embodied this point. His prophetic imagination shaped his reality by presupposing the war's scale, decisive factors, and outcomes. The alternative reality he expressed in *Anticipations of the Future* affected how Ruffin interpreted events and acted during the conflict. When the war erased Ruffin's future, it radically redefined his life's work. He told William Yancey before secession, "I would stake my life on the venture," and he did. Things did not go as planned. Defeat robbed Ruffin of his anticipated future as a national founder. Worse, the war disproved his claims to read the future through reason. How Ruffin approached time and understood the workings of the world died with the Confederacy.[38]

When the war changed his future, Ruffin concluded that God had never answered his prayers. For twenty-five years he offered daily prayers and "strove to silence & smother . . . discouraging doubts" that talking to God was pointless. "The passage of events," the deaths of his children, financial ruin, and Confederate defeat ended his daily prayers. "I do not think that any particular prayer of mine, even for the most laudable & unobjectionable object, (so far as I could judge,) has ever been granted, or that any effect was produced that I could [have] supposed was aided by my prayers." Ruffin did not blame God for the "incomprehensible results" of the war, and he accepted no responsibility for them. Instead he vented frustration at fellow southerners for not supporting the Confederacy. He concluded his diary. "I here declare my unmitigated hatred to Yankee rule—to all political, social & business connection with Yankees—& to the Yankee race." Ruffin wished he "could impress these sentiments, in their full force, on every living southerner, & bequeath them to every one yet to be born!" Instead of approaching the future with reason as he had advocated all his life, Ruffin raged against the ending he did not see and could not accept.[39]

Looking to the future, Ruffin tried to prophesy one last time. He predicted a "far-distant day shall arrive for just retribution for Yankee usurpation, oppression, & atrocious outrages—& for deliverance & vengeance for the now ruined, subjugated, & enslaved Southern States!" Too old to participate in this vague reckoning to come, Ruffin chose not to meet his fate. His contempt for the present mixed with his proactive bent to form a lethal combination. Unwilling to become a burden to his children and a subject to Yankee rule, Ruffin took control of his future. Sitting in his private room at his son's house, Ruffin waited for visitors to depart, noted the time on his watch, 12:15 PM, bequeathed the timepiece to his grandson, rested his chin on the barrel of a shotgun, and pulled the trigger.[40]

After the shot echoed through the house, Ruffin found himself alive and unchanged in the room. A misfire. Even the clearest actions failed to produce predictable results. Alarmed by the sound, women in the house raced outside to find Edmund Jr. instead of entering Ruffin's room, where they expected to find a headless corpse. Their fear gave Ruffin time. John Brown had stood still upon the trapdoor for fifteen minutes waiting for death. Now Ruffin endured an unexpected delay. He reloaded. Sounds of commotion approached. Before his son reached the doorknob, Ruffin fired again and met his end.[41]

Notes

PROLOGUE

1. John Thompson Brown to his wife, November 27, 1859, J. Thompson Brown Papers, 1833–1870, Virginia Historical Society, hereinafter, VHS.
2. November 18, 1859, entry, Robert A. Granniss diary, 1858–1861, VHS; "An Onlooker" to Henry Wise, November 15, 1859, "The John Brown Letters: Found in the Virginia State Library in 1901," *Virginia Magazine of History and Biography* 10, no. 1 (July 1902): 28.
3. William Kauffman Scarborough, ed., *The Diary of Edmund Ruffin*. Vol. 1, *Toward Independence, October, 1856–April, 1861* (Baton Rouge: Louisiana State University Press, 1972), 348, 361, 363.
4. As physicist Robert Greenler explains, "The maximum refraction effect is about equal to the angular diameter of the sun; so when you see the sun setting on the horizon, it may be, geometrically, totally below the horizon: It is like being able to see around the corner." Gleenler, *Rainbows, Halos, and Glories* (Cambridge: Cambridge University Press, 1980), 153–54.
5. Edmund Ruffin, "Remarks on the Soils and Agriculture of Gloucester County," *Farmers' Register* 8 (1838): 189–90.
6. Eugène Minkowski, *Lived Time: Phenomenological and Psychopathological Studies*, trans. Nancy Metsel (Evanston: Northwestern University Press, 1970); Martin Heidegger, *Being and Time*, Joan Stambaugh, trans. (Albany: State University of New York, 1996); George Lakoff and Mark Johnson, *Metaphors We Live By* (Chicago: University of Chicago Press, 1980); David Carr, *Time, Narrative, and History* (Bloomington: Indiana University Press, 1986).
7. "expectation, n. 1," etymology of "anticipation" and "expectation," OED online, November 2016, Oxford University Press. There are eight definitions of anticipation, and not until the last one is it a synonym for expectation: "the action of looking forward to, expectation."
8. Daniel Walker Howe, *What Hath God Wrought: The Transformation of America, 1815–1848* (New York: Oxford University Press, 2007), 285–327.
9. Catherine Clinton, *Harriet Tubman: The Road to Freedom* (New York: Little, Brown, 2004); Michael Burlingame, *Abraham Lincoln: A Life*, vol. 1 (Baltimore: Johns Hopkins University Press, 2013).
10. Bell Irvin Wiley, *The Life of Johnny Reb: The Common Soldier of the Confederacy* (Baton Rouge: Louisiana State University Press, reprint 1994), 19; Shelby Foote, *The Civil War: A*

Narrative, vol. 1 (New York: Random House, 1958), 63; James M. McPherson, *Battle Cry of Freedom: The Civil War Era* (New York: Oxford University Press, 1988), 333.

11. Chesnut was quoted in Drew Gilpin Faust, *This Republic of Suffering: Death and the American Civil War* (New York: Knopf, 2008), 3. Many historians point to Abraham Lincoln's call for 75,000 ninety-day volunteers to quell the rebellion as proof that even the people in charge misjudged the scale of the coming war after Fort Sumter. Lincoln's call for ninety-day militiamen illustrates his knowledge of federal law, not his mishandling of the crisis. A 1795 law restricted the president's calling of troops while Congress was not in session. See David Herbert Donald, *Lincoln* (New York: Simon and Schuster, 1995), 296. For an example of this misunderstanding, see Harry S. Stout, *Upon the Altar of the Nation: A Moral History of the Civil War* (New York: Viking, 2006), 61.

12. Johannes Fabian identified a similar tendency in anthropology. "Time, much like language or money, is a carrier of significance, a form through which we define the content of relationships between the Self and the Other." Johannes Fabian, *Time and the Other: How Anthropology Makes Its Object* (New York: Columbia University Press, 2014), xxvii; Carolyn Dinshaw, *How Soon Is Now? Medieval Texts, Amateur Readers, and the Queerness of Time* (Durham, NC: Duke University Press, 2012), 137; Bruno Latour, *We Have Never Been Modern*, trans. Catherine Porter (Cambridge, MA: Harvard University Press, 1993); Jonathan Boyarin and Martin Land, *Time and Human Language Now* (Chicago: Prickly Paradigm Press, 2008); Roxanne Panchasi, *Future Tense: The Culture of Anticipation in France between the Wars* (Ithaca, NY: Cornell University Press, 2009); Reinhart Koselleck, *Futures Past: On the Semantics of Historical Time*, trans. Keith Tribe (Cambridge, MA: MIT Press, 1985); Frank Kermode, *The Sense of an Ending: Studies in the Theory of Fiction* (New York: Oxford University Press, 2000); Philip Smith, *Why War? The Cultural Logic of Iraq, the Gulf War, and Suez* (Chicago: University of Chicago Press, 2010); Walter Brueggemann, *The Prophetic Imagination* (Minneapolis: Fortress Press, 2001); David Huron, *Sweet Anticipation: Music and the Psychology of Expectation* (Cambridge, MA: MIT Press, 2008). Writing the history of the future has its own rewards and challenges (committing to a single verb tense is difficult), but this work must be done if we hope to understand how a period and culture felt to the people who lived it. As an analytical category, prophecy links religious studies to history by showing how the prophetic imagination of the Civil War era shaped American thoughts and actions about a host of things, including politics, economics, society, and war. As such, my work joins an ongoing effort by historians to combine nineteenth-century religious history with cultural, intellectual, and political history of the period. In addition to Koselleck's work, scholarship that proposes histories of the future include Jon Cowans, "Visions of the Postwar: The Politics of Memory and Expectation in 1940s France," *History and Memory* 10, no. 2 (1998): 68–101; Panchasi, *Future Tense*; Barbara Adam, "History of the Future: Paradoxes and Challenges," *Rethinking History* 14, no. 3 (2010): 361–78.

13. William James, *The Varieties of Religious Experience: A Study of Human Nature* (New York: Longmans, Green, 1903), v; Jason Phillips, "John Brown's Pikes: Assembling the Future in Antebellum America," in *War Matters: Material Culture in the Civil War Era*, ed. Joan Cashin (Chapel Hill: University of North Carolina Press, forthcoming).

14. Lorraine Daston, ed., *Things That Talk: Object Lessons from Art and Science* (New York: Zone Books, 2008), 9; Phillips, "John Brown's Pikes."

15. Bill Brown, *A Sense of Things: The Object Matter of American Literature* (Chicago: University of Chicago Press, 2003); Bruno Latour, *Reassembling the Social: An Introduction to Actor-Network-Theory* (New York: Oxford University Press, 2005); Jane Bennett, *Vibrant Matter: A Political Ecology of Things* (Durham, NC: Duke University Press, 2009); Phillips, "John Brown's Pikes."

CHAPTER 1

1. Henry Clay Pate, *The American Vade Mecum: or, the Companion of Youth, and Guide to College* (Cincinnati: Morgan, 1852), 78, 3; Franklin Benjamin Sanborn, *Recollections of Seventy Years*, vol. 1 (Boston: Gorham Press, 1909), 103–4: "a magnificently mounted Bowie-knife, presented to Pate by his friends in Virginia, when he started out to subjugate the wicked abolitionists who had presumed to migrate to Kansas, and there oppose negro slavery. To me also, in the evening after, as we sat by my fire in the Channing house, Brown related the story of this capture, and when he mentioned the knife, I said, 'What became of that?' Brown gravely pulled up the right leg of his kerseymere trousers, above the top of his high boot, and drew from that crypt the sheathed knife which Pate had worn in another part of his outfit."
2. Stephen B. Oates, *To Purge This Land with Blood: A Biography of John Brown* (Amherst: University of Massachusetts Press, 1984), 143–44.
3. Salmon Brown to William E. Connelley, May 28, 1913, Boyd B. Stutler Collection, West Virginia State Archive.
4. Oates, *To Purge This Land with Blood*, 153.
5. Henry Clay Pate, *John Brown, as viewed by H. Clay Pate* (New York: The author, 1859), 34.
6. Four Missouri men were dead and many more were wounded. Two of Brown's men were badly wounded. Salmon Brown, "After the Battle of Black Jack," Record Id: 710, MS05-0025 A-F, Boyd B. Stutler Collection, West Virginia State Archive.
7. David S. Reynolds, *John Brown, Abolitionist: The Man Who Killed Slavery, Sparked the Civil War, and Seeded Civil Rights* (New York: Vintage Books, 2005), 186–87.
8. Peter R. Silver, *Our Savage Neighbors: How Indian War Transformed Early America* (New York: W. W. Norton, 2009); Reinhart Koselleck, *Futures Past: On the Semantics of Historical Time*, trans. Keith Tribe (New York: Columbia University Press, 2004). For the intersection of western visions and material culture in the nineteenth century, see Elliott West, *The Contested Plains: Indian, Goldseekers, and the Rush to Colorado* (Lawrence: University Press of Kansas, 1998); Virginia Scharff, ed., *Empire and Liberty: The Civil War and the West* (Oakland: University of California Press, 2015). In the nineteenth century, "filibuster" commonly referred to an unauthorized military campaign and the adventurers who waged it. Most of these actions targeted foreign soil, especially in Latin America, to expand the Union. This chapter shows how the war for Kansas was a filibuster fought in the same style and by some of the same men who invaded Latin America for glory and plunder.
9. Henry David Thoreau, "Walking," in *Wild Apples and Other Natural History Essays*, ed. William Rossi (Athens: University of Georgia Press, 2002), 69–70; Donald Worster, *Rivers of Empire: Water, Aridity, and the Growth of the American West* (New York: Pantheon,

1986), 3; Bernard DeVoto, *The Course of Empire* (Boston: Mariner, 1998), 404; Fulmer Mood, "Notes on the History of the Word 'Frontier,'" *Agricultural History* 22, no. 2 (April 1948): 78–83.

10. Daniel Walker Howe, *What Hath God Wrought: The Transformation of America, 1815–1848* (New York: Oxford University Press, 2007), 304–12 (Hegel quoted on page 305); Alexander Campbell Fraser, ed., *The Works of George Berkeley, D. D.*, vol. 3 (Oxford: Clarendon Press, 1871), 232; Thomas M. Allen, *A Republic in Time: Temporality and Social Imagination in Nineteenth-Century America* (Chapel Hill: University of North Carolina Press, 2008).
11. Koselleck, *Futures Past*, xviii; Anders Schinkel, "Imagination as a Category of History: An Essay Concerning Koselleck Concepts of Erfahrungsraum and Erwartungshorizont," *History and Theory* 44, no. 1 (February 2005): 51.
12. Michael O'Malley, *Keeping Watch: A History of American Time* (New York: Penguin, 1990), 27–31; Koselleck, *Futures Past*, 266, 206; Mark M. Smith, *Mastered by the Clock: Time, Slavery, and Freedom in the American South* (Chapel Hill: University of North Carolina Press, 1997). O'Malley stresses associations between industry and linear, progressive time on one hand and agriculture and cyclical, static time on the other. These associations shaped how nineteenth-century Americans understood time, but we don't want to assume that farmers did not embrace invention and progress. Consider the temporalities of Thomas Jefferson and Edmund Ruffin. Koselleck dates the saddle time from 1750 to 1850. While that century may have been the center of the conflict, a broader era of competing temporalities began earlier in Europe and continued well past 1850 in America.
13. Benedict Anderson, *Imagined Communities: Reflections on the Origin and Spread of Nationalism* (New York: Verso, 2006); Allen, *A Republic in Time*, 4; West, *Contested Plains*, 57–58; Koselleck *Futures Past*, xviii. Some scholars, most prominently Benedict Anderson, have argued that this modern temporality strengthened nationalism by making time homogenous. The profusion of clocks, telegraphs, railroad schedules, and national media supported the illusion that people experienced events simultaneously and thus belonged to one "imagined community" that moved forward together. Other scholars, like Koselleck, insist that time became more fractured after the Enlightenment. Greater tensions between millennial and secular, natural and clock time arose. As nations expanded, they included a wider spectrum of ethnicities, religions, and cultures that dreamed of different times and gazed at disparate horizons. Anticipations of progress caused more conflict than consensus where national borders widened. While Anderson's interpretation links homogenous time to the rise of nation-states, Koselleck's relates heterogeneous times to the increase in civil wars.
14. Alexander Hamilton, James Madison, and John Jay, *The Federalist, on the New Constitution, Written in the Year 1788* (Hallowell: Glazier, Masters and Smith, 1837), 29, 24, 35.
15. Robert V. Bruce, "The Shadow of a Coming War," in *Lincoln: The War President*, ed. Gabor Boritt (New York: Oxford University Press, 1992), 7; Thomas P. Slaughter, *The Whiskey Rebellion: A Frontier Epilogue to the American Revolution* (New York: Oxford University Press, 1986), 57.
16. Howe, *What Hath God Wrought*, 149.

17. Glover Moore, *The Missouri Controversy, 1819–21* (Lexington: University of Kentucky Press, 1943), 93 (first and second quotations), 94 (third), 50 (fourth and fifth); Henry Clay to Horace Holley, February 17, 1820, in James F. Hopkins, ed., *The Papers of Henry Clay*, vol. 2 (Lexington: University of Kentucky Press, 1961), 780–81.
18. Moore, *The Missouri Controversy*, 94 (first quotation); *Annals of Congress*, 16th Congress, 1 Session, 177 (second and third quotations); *Annals of Congress*, 15th Congress, 2 Session, 1205 (fourth and fifth quotations); Elizabeth R. Varon, *Disunion! The Coming of the American Civil War, 1789–1859* (Chapel Hill: University of North Carolina Press, 2008), 43–44; Michael Woods, *Emotional and Sectional Conflict in the Antebellum United States* (New York: Cambridge University Press, 2014).
19. Henry Clay to Leslie Combs, February 5, 1820, in Hopkins, *Papers of Henry Clay*, 2:74; Clay to Martin D. Hardin, February 5, 1820, Hopkins, *Papers of Henry Clay*, 2:775; Moore, *The Missouri Controversy*, 93.
20. Thomas Jefferson to John Holmes, April 22, 1820, in *The Portable Thomas Jefferson*, ed. Merrill D. Peterson (New York: Penguin Books, 1975), 567–69; Peter S. Onuf, *Jefferson's Empire: The Language of American Nationhood* (Charlottesville: University Press of Virginia, 2000), 113–14.
21. Howe, *What Hath God Wrought*, 158.
22. Peterson, *The Portable Thomas Jefferson*, 567–69.
23. John Quincy Adams diary, November 29, 1820, in Charles Francis Adams, ed., *Memoir of John Quincy Adams: Comprising Portions of His Diary from 1795 to 1848* (Philadelphia: J. B. Lippincott, 1875), 210.
24. Edward Everett, "Brethren, the Time Is Short," 27–28, Edward Everett Collection, Massachusetts Historical Society.
25. Ibid., 29, 32. Everett was no abolitionist. Six years later, when Everett was a member of Congress, William Lloyd Garrison criticized him for swearing to take up arms against any slave revolt. Robert H. Abzug, *Cosmos Crumbling: American Reform and Religious Imagination* (New York: Oxford University Press, 1994), 139.
26. Peterson, *Portable Jefferson*, 317–18; Onuf, *Jefferson's Empire*, 53; Allen, *Republic in Time*, 34.
27. Emma Willard, *An Address to the Public, Particularly the Members of the Legislature of New York, Proposing a Plan for Improving Female Education* (Middlebury, CT: Copeland, 1819), 29 (first and second quotations); 29; Willard, *History of the United States, or, Republic of America* (New York: Barnes, 1845), 364 (third); Willard, *Last Periods of Universal History* (New York: Barnes, 1855), 528 (fourth); Willard, *History of the United States, or, Republic of America* (New York: Barnes, 1855), 469 (fifth, sixth).
28. Howe, *What Hath God Wrought*, 312–15.
29. Doctrine and Covenants 87, quoted in Orson Pratt, ed., *The Seer* 2 (April 1854): 241. This prophecy was written during or after the Nullification Crisis, but Smith repeated it in the 1840s. Mormons reprinted it throughout the antebellum period. It appeared in *The Pearl of Great Price* (p. 35) in 1851. The Mormons' brand of American exceptionalism surpassed that of most of their contemporaries, but even they insisted that the republic could not escape the cataclysmic bloodshed that would usher in the millennium. John L. Brooke, *The Refiner's Fire: The Making of Mormon Cosmology, 1644–1844* (Cambridge: Cambridge University Press, 1994).

30. Allen, *Republic in Time*, 53; Thomas Jefferson to John Adams, January 11, 1816, in Peterson, *Portable Jefferson*, 552; John O'Sullivan, "The Great Nation of Futurity," *United States Democratic Review* 6, no. 23 (November 1839): 426; Schinkel, "Imagination as a Category of History," 43; Jefferson to Adams, August 1, 1816, in Lester J. Caperton, ed., *The Adams-Jefferson Letters: The Complete Correspondence between Thomas Jefferson and Abigail and John Adams* (Chapel Hill: University of North Carolina Press, 1987), 477.
31. Allen, *Republic in Time*, 53; John Taylor Hughes, *Doniphan's Expedition: Containing an Account of the Conquest of New Mexico* (Cincinnati: J.A. and U.P. James, 1850), 38.
32. Abraham Lincoln, "A Speech in the United States House of Representatives on the Mexican War, January 12, 1848, in Roy Basler, ed., *The Collected Works of Abraham Lincoln*, vol. 1 (New Brunswick: Rutgers University Press, 1953), 439–42.
33. Samuel D. Baldwin, *Armageddon: Or, The Overthrow of Romanism and Monarchy; the Existence of the United States Foretold in the Bible, Its Future Greatness; Invasion by Allied Europe; Annihilation of Monarchy; Expansion into the Millennial Republic, and Its Dominion over the Whole World* (Cincinnati: Applegate, 1854), 476 (first quotation), 162 (second), 61 (third); Phillips, "John Brown's Pikes." In 1856 Joseph Berg of Philadelphia published a prophecy that responded to Baldwin's. See Berg, *The Stone and the Image, or, the American Republic, the Bane and Ruin of Despotism. An Exposition of the Fifth Kingdom of Daniel's Prophecy and of the Great Wonder in Heaven of the Apocalypse* (Philadelphia: Higgins and Perkinpine, 1856). Berg doubted that Armageddon would be fought on American soil, but he shared the spread-eagle expansionism of Baldwin's prophecy.
34. Pate, *John Brown*, 36; Brown to wife and children, everyone, June 1856, in Zoe Trodd and John Stauffer, eds., *Meteor of War: The John Brown Story* (Maplecrest, NY: Brandywine Press, 2004), 84–88, quote 87–88.
35. "Terms of Surrender: John Brown, Articles of Agreement for the Exchange of Prisoners following Battle of Black Jack," John Brown Collection, Box 1, Folder 16, item number 4272, Kansas Historical Society (accessed online at kansasmemory.org, May 18, 2015); Sumner quoted in Oates, *To Purge This Land with Blood*, 155; Phillips, "John Brown's Pikes."
36. Alex Hawes, "In Kansas, with John Brown," 1881–1882, bound in Boyd B. Stutler, John Brown Pamphlets, vol. 4, p. 70, Boyd B. Stutler Collection, West Virginia State Archives; Phillips, "John Brown's Pikes"; Simon J. Harrison, "War Mementos and the Souls of Missing Soldiers: Returning Effects of the Battlefield Dead," *Journal of the Royal Anthropological Institute* 14 (2008): 785. For more Civil War scholarship that takes things seriously, see Simon Harrison, "Bones in the Rebel Lady's Boudoir: Ethnology, Race and Trophy-Hunting in the American Civil War," *Journal of Material Culture* 15 (2010): 385–401; Joan Cashin, "Trophies of War: Material Culture in the Civil War Era," *Journal of the Civil War Era* (September 2011): 339–67; Michael DeGruccio, "Letting the War Slip through Our Hands: Material Culture and the Weakness of Words in the Civil War Era," in *Weirding the War: Stories from the Civil War's Ragged Edges*, ed Stephen Berry (Athens: University of Georgia Press, 2011), 15–35; Megan Kate Nelson, *Ruin Nation: Destruction and the American Civil War* (Athens: University of Georgia Press, 2012); Virginia Scharff, ed., *Empire and Liberty: The Civil War and the West* (Berkeley: University of California Press,

2015); Brian Luskey and Jason Phillips, "Muster: Inspecting Material Cultures of the Civil War," *Civil War History* (June 2017): 103–12; Cashin, *War Matters.*

37. Bruno Latour asks a question that plagued Kansas settlers: "*How many participants* are gathered in a *thing* to make it exist and to maintain its existence?" Bruno Latour, "Why Has Critique Run Out of Steam? From Matters of Fact to Matters of Concern," *Critical Inquiry* 30 (Winter 2004): 246; Phillips, "John Brown's Pikes."

38. Bruno Latour and Peter Weibel, *Making Things Public: Atmospheres of Democracy* (Cambridge, MA: MIT Press, 2005); Bruno Latour, *Politics of Nature: How to Bring the Sciences into Democracy*, trans. Catherine Porter (Cambridge, MA: Harvard University Press, 2004); Jane Bennett, *Vibrant Matter: A Political Ecology of Things* (Durham, NC: Duke University Press, 2010). Latour calls this process *dingpolitik*, or thing politics. The dominant paradigm in political and military science still relies on *realpolitik*, which insists that material concerns (usually simplified as economic self-interest) motivate political movements and military actions. When belligerents calculate that the material gains from warfare will exceed their losses, they fight. Latour and other new materialists refuse to reduce politics to rational power plays in which humans objectify the material world without being affected in turn by the things that surround them. Latour stresses this dynamic between things and politics by noting that the root of republic, *res-publica*, means public matters (or things). Western thought has reduced modern politics to human ideas and actions, but in its ancient origins, representative government was an assembly of people and things. For more, see Phillips, "John Brown's Pikes."

39. Amy S. Greenberg, *Manifest Manhood and the Antebellum American Empire* (New York: Cambridge University Press, 2005), 11–13. Stephen Berry argues for the sectional differences between northern "civilized manhood" and southern "civilizing manhood. " Stephen W. Berry, II, *All that Makes a Man: Love and Ambition in the Civil War South* (New York: Oxford University Press, 2004). These two models for masculinity were most popular among middle-class white men. Other conceptions of manhood thrived in the antebellum era. For a striking example, see Jeff Forret, *Slave against Slave: Plantation Violence in the Old South* (Baton Rouge: Louisiana State University Press, 2015).

40. Michael Zakim, *Ready-Made Democracy: A History of Men's Dress in the American Republic 1760–1860* (Chicago: University of Chicago Press, 2003), 203; Steven Shackelford, *Blade's Guide to Knives and Their Values: The Complete Handbook of Knife Collecting* (Iola, WI: Krause, 2009), 307; Phillips, "John Brown's Pikes."

41. William C. Davis, *Three Roads to the Alamo: The Lives and Fortunes of David Crockett, James Bowie, and William Barret Travis* (New York: Harper Collins, 2009), 210; Phillips, "John Brown's Pikes."

42. Shackelford, *Blade's Guide to Knives and Their Values*, 307; Davis, *Three Roads to the Alamo*, 213–16 (quotations on 216).

43. John Hope Franklin, *The Militant South, 1800–1861* (Urbana: University of Illinois Press, 2002), 36; John Russell Bartlett, *Dictionary of Americanisms: A Glossary of Words and Phrases Usually Regarded as Peculiar to the United States* (Boston: Little, Brown, 1859), 46; Shackelford, *Blade's Guide to Knives and Their Values*, 307.

44. Davis, *Three Roads to the Alamo;* Oates, *To Purge This Land with Blood,* 123; Alan Nevins, *Ordeal of the Union*, vol. 2, *A House Dividing, 1852–1857* (New York: Charles Scribner's Sons, 1947), 433; William Henry Trescot, *An American View of the Eastern Question*

(Charleston: John Russell, 1854), 3; George Frederick Holmes, "Relations of the Old and the New Worlds," *De Bow's Review* 20 (May 1856): 529; Phillips, "John Brown's Pikes."

45. Pate, *The American Vade Mecum*, 75; T. H. Gladstone, *The Englishman in Kansas: Squatter Life and Border Warfare* (New York: Miller, 1857), 251–53, 262; Phillips, "John Brown's Pikes."
46. Gladstone, *The Englishman in Kansas*, 262–63; Phillips, "John Brown's Pikes."
47. Theodore Dwight Weld, *American Slavery as It Is* (New York: American Anti-Slavery Society, 1839), 188–90.
48. Nicole Etcheson, *Bleeding Kansas: Contested Liberty in the Civil War Era* (Lawrence: University Press of Kansas, 2004), 76–77.
49. Ibid., 76 (Lawrence quote), 39 (Thayer and Kansas emigrant quotes); Ronald G. Walters, *Antislavery Appeal: American Abolitionism after 1830* (New York: W. W. Norton, 1984), 29 (Higginson quotation); Kristen Oertel, *Bleeding Borders: Race, Gender, and Violence in Pre-Civil War Kansas* (Baton Rouge: Louisiana State University Press, 2009), 52.
50. Northerners also used women to conceal ammunition and gunpowder under their skirts. Thus, crate politics exploited gender norms to transport weapons. See Oertel, *Bleeding Borders*, 77.
51. George B. Cheever, *God against Slavery: And the Freedom and Duty of the Pulpit to Rebuke It, as a Sin Against God* (New York: Joseph H. Ladd, 1857), 189.
52. Ibid., 190–91. Italics in original.
53. Walter L. Fleming, "The Buford Expedition to Kansas," *American Historical Review*, 6 (1900): 38 (first quotation), 39 (second and third), 40 (fourth and fifth), 43 (sixth); Pate quoted in Alfred Thayer Andreas and William G. Cutler, *History of the State of Kansas* (Chicago: A. T. Andreas, 1883), Part 31.
54. Tony Horwitz, *Midnight Rising: John Brown and the Raid That Sparked the Civil War* (New York: Henry Holt, 2011), 48; David Atchison, "Speech to Pro-Slavery 'Soldiers,'" May 21, 1856, Richard Hinton Collection, Box 1, Folder 6, Kansas State Historical Society; Etcheson, *Bleeding Kansas*, 104–5.
55. Gladstone, *The Englishman in Kansas*, 40–41, 113. Gladstone expressed revulsion at border ruffians wearing free state clothing, but the Missourians were following an old ritual of wearing victims' clothing. British soldiers practiced the same ritual in Havana in 1762. See J. M. Mancini, "Siege Mentalities: Objects in Motion, British Imperial Expansion, and the Pacific Turn," *Winterthur Portfolio: A Journal of American Material Culture* 45, no. 2/3 (Summer/Autumn 2011): 125–40; Joan Cashin, "Material Culture in the Civil War Era," *Journal of the Civil War Era* (September 2011): 344.
56. Edward Payson Bridgman and Luke Fisher Parsons, *With John Brown in Kansas* (Madison: J. N. Davidson, 1915), 16.
57. James M. McPherson, *Battle Cry of Freedom: The Civil War Era* (New York: Oxford University Press, 1989), 148.
58. "Majority Report: Alleged Assault upon Senator Sumner: House of Representatives Report No. 182," in *Reports of Committees of the House of Representatives, Made during the First Session of the Thirty-Fourth Congress, 1855–56*, 3 vols. (Washington: Cornelius Wendell, 1856), I, 137, 44; Elizabeth R. Varon, *Disunion! The Coming of the Civil War, 1789–1859* (Chapel Hill: University of North Carolina Press, 2008); William W. Freehling, *The Road to Disunion*, vol. 2, *Secessionists Triumphant, 1854–1861*

(New York: Oxford University Press, 2008); Manisha Sinha, "The Caning of Charles Sumner: Slavery, Race, and Ideology in the Age of the Civil War," *Journal of the Early Republic* 23, no. 3 (Summer 2003): 233–62; Michael E. Woods, "Tracing the 'Sacred Relicts': The Strange Career of Preston Brooks's Cane," *Civil War History* 63, no. 2 (June 2017): 113–32.

59. "Majority Report: Alleged Assault upon Senator Sumner," 61.
60. Ibid., 89.
61. Ibid., 103.
62. Ibid., 100.
63. Ibid., 115 (first and second quotations), 116 (third and fourth), 118 (fifth and sixth), 119 (seventh through tenth).
64. Ibid., 23–26; William E. Gienapp, "The Crime against Sumner: The Caning of Charles Sumner and the Rise of the Republican Party," *Civil War History* 25, no. 3 (September 1979): 220; Freehling, *Road to Disunion*, 82; Varon, *Disunion!*, 268.
65. "Majority Report: Alleged Assault upon Senator Sumner," 60, 56, 49.
66. Ibid., 75.
67. Ibid., 31–32, 53–54; Woods, "Tracing the 'Sacred Relicts."
68. Oates, *To Purge This Land with Blood*, 130, 133–37.
69. William Howard Russell, *My Diary North and South*, I (Boston: Burnham, 1863), 165; Rachel Shelden, *Washington Brotherhood: Politics, Social Life, and the Coming of the Civil War* (Chapel Hill: University of North Carolina Press, 2015).
70. Russell, *My Diary North and South*, II (London: Bradbury and Evans, 1863), 8–10.
71. Ibid., 11–13.
72. J. S. Buckingham, *The Slave States of America* (London: Fisher and Sons, 1842), vol. 1, 408; James H. Lanman, "American Steam Navigation," *Hunt's Merchants' Magazine and Commercial Review*, 4 (New York: Freeman Hunt, 1841), 124; Walter Johnson, *River of Dark Dreams: Slavery and Empire in the Cotton Kingdom* (Cambridge, MA: Harvard University Press, 2013), 76–77.
73. Edmund Flagg, "The Far West, 1836–37," in *Early Western Travels, 1748–1846*, vol. 26, ed. Reuben Gold Thwaites (Cleveland: Arthur H Clark, 1906), 64; Baird, quoted in Johnson, *River of Dark Dreams*, 77, also see 104–5. For steam power changing American temporalities, see Arthur Cunynghame, *A Glimpse of the Great Western Republic* (London: Richard Bentley, 1851), 177: "the constant struggle which is here going on, as to who shall "go a-head" at the greatest speed, certainly engenders an amount of selfishness."
74. Alfred Bryant, *Millennarian Views: With Reasons for Receiving Them* (New York: M. W. Dodd, 1852), 221. Lord quoted in Robert Whalen, "Calvinism and Chiliasm: The Sociology of Nineteenth Century American Millenarianism," *American Presbyterians* 70, no. 3 (Fall 1992): 172 (note 37); Herman Melville, *The Confidence Man: His Masquerade* (New York: Dix, Edwards, 1857), 179–80; James T. Lloyd, *Lloyd's Steamboat Directory, and Disasters on the Western Waters* (Cincinnati: James T. Lloyd, 1856), 213, 228–29; Johnson, *River of Dark Dreams*, 108–9, 111–12.
75. As historian Walter Johnson explains, the pilot's task was "coordinating the senses and the flow of time, through the use of memory, observation, deduction, prediction, reaction," Johnson, *River of Dark Dreams*, 96.

76. Samuel Clemens to Orion Clemens, April 26, 1861, in *Mark Twain Letters, I: 1853–1866*, ed. Kenneth M. Sanderson, Edgar Marquess Branch, and Michael B. Frank (Berkeley: University of California Press, 1988), 120–21.

CHAPTER 2

1. Russell quoted in Franklin B. Sanborn, ed., *The Life and Letters of John Brown: Liberator of Kansas, and Martyr of Virginia* (Boston: Roberts Brothers, 1891), 508–10; Stephen B. Oates, *To Purge This Land with Blood: A Biography of John Brown* (Amherst: University of Massachusetts Press, 1984), 177; Jason Phillips, "John Brown's Pikes: Assembling the Future in Antebellum America," in *War Matters: Material Culture in the Civil War Era*, ed. Joan Cashin (Chapel Hill: University of North Carolina Press, forthcoming).
2. Brown and Stearns quoted in Sanborn, *The Life and Letters of John Brown*, 508–10; David S. Reynolds, *John Brown, Abolitionist: The Man Who Killed Slavery, Sparked the Civil War, and Seeded Civil Rights* (New York: Alfred A. Knopf, 2005), 222; Phillips, "John Brown's Pikes."
3. John Brown's notes for a speech copied in Franklin B. Sanborn, *Recollections of Seventy Years*, I (Boston: Gorham, 1909), 108. Thoreau quoted in Sanborn, *Recollections*, 112; Tony Horwitz, *Midnight Rising: John Brown and the Raid that Sparked the Civil War* (New York: Henry Holt, 2011), 63; Sandra Harbert Petrulionis, *To Set this World Right: The Antislavery Movement in Thoreau's Concord* (Ithaca: Cornell University Press, 2006), 120–23.
4. Simon J. Harrison, "War Mementos and the Souls of Missing Soldiers: Returning Effects of the Battlefield Dead," *Journal of the Royal Anthropological Institute* 14 (2008): 774–90; Harrison, "Bones in the Rebel Lady's Boudoir: Ethnology, Race and Trophy-Hunting in the American Civil War," *Journal of Material Culture* 15 (2010): 385–401; Joan Cashin, "Trophies of War: Material Culture in the Civil War Era," *Journal of the Civil War Era* 1, no. 3 (September 2011): 339–67; Michael DeGruccio, "Letting the War Slip through Our Hands: Material Culture and the Weakness of Words in the Civil War Era," in *Weirding the War: Stories from the Civil War's Ragged Edges*, ed. Stephen Berry (Athens: University of Georgia Press, 2011), 15–35; Phillips, "John Brown's Pikes."
5. *The Logan Emancipation Cabinet of Letters and Relics of John Brown and Abraham Lincoln* (Chicago: Chicago Tribune, 1892), 13.
6. James Redpath, *The Public Life of Captain John Brown* (Boston: Thayer and Eldridge, 1860), 193; Blair quotes from his testimony in "Mason Report," *U.S. Senate Select Committee Reports*, 1859–1860, II (Washington: no publisher, 1860), 121–29; *The Logan Emancipation Cabinet*, 11. Rust also paid postage for Brown to ship the weapon to him. Phillips, "John Brown's Pikes."
7. *The Logan Emancipation Cabinet*, 20; Horwitz, *Midnight Rising*, 66; Phillips, "John Brown's Pikes."
8. Bruno Latour, *Reassembling the Social: An Introduction to Actor-Network-Theory* (New York: Oxford University Press, 2005); Scott Reynolds Nelson, *A Nation of Deadbeats: An Uncommon History of America's Financial Disasters* (New York: Vintage, 2013), 139–40, 142.

9. Alison quoted in "Alison's History of Europe," *The American Whig Review* 2 (February 1845): 156; Phillips, "John Brown's Pikes." According to John Keegan, "The pike, or thrusting spear, was a simpler tool of war, and in the hands of hardy and fractious peasant communities from areas where the knightly class was small, such as Switzerland, could be wielded to oppose a dense barrier to cavalry attack, as long as the pikemen kept their nerve in the face of a charge." During the fifteenth century, Swiss pikemen asserted their superiority against mounted knights in a series of battles that fostered Switzerland's reputation as the motherland of mercenaries. The Swiss pike thwarted Hapsburg overlords and "destroyed Burgundian power for good." See John Keegan, *A History of Warfare* (New York: Knopf, 1993), 329.
10. Hinton Rowan Helper, *The Impending Crisis of the South: How to Meet It* (New York: Burdick Brothers, 1857); James Oakes, *Freedom National: The Destruction of Slavery in the United States, 1861–1865* (New York: W. W. Norton, 2013); Robert E. Bonner, *Mastering America: Southern Slaveholders and the Crisis of American Nationhood* (Cambridge: Cambridge University Press, 2009); John D. Majewski, *Modernizing a Slave Economy: The Economic Vision of the Confederate Nation* (Chapel Hill: University of North Carolina Press, 2009); John F. Kvach, *De Bow's Review: The Antebellum Vision of a New South* (Lexington: University Press of Kentucky, 2013).
11. Scott Sandage, *Born Losers: A History of Failure in America* (Cambridge, MA: Harvard University Press, 2005); Nelson, *A Nation of Deadbeats*; Edward E. Baptist, *The Half Has Never Been Told: Slavery and the Making of American Capitalism* (New York: Basic Books, 2014).
12. Wolfgang Schivelbusch, *The Railway Journey: The Industrialization of Time and Space in the Nineteenth Century* (Berkeley: University of California Press, 1986); David Jaffee, *A New Nation of Goods: The Material Culture of Early America* (Philadelphia: University of Pennsylvania Press, 2010); Daniel Walker Howe, *What Hath God Wrought: The Transformation of America, 1815–1848* (New York: Oxford University Press, 2007).
13. James H. Moorhead, *World without End: Mainstream American Protestant Visions of the Last Things, 1880–1925* (Bloomington: Indiana University Press, 1999), 2. As literary critic Frank Kermode explains, the century was marked by "the age of perpetual transition in technological and artistic matters and an age of perpetual crisis in morals and politics." See Kermode, *The Sense of an Ending: Studies in the Theory of Fiction* (New York: Oxford University Press, 2000), 28.
14. David M. Henkin, *The Postal Age: The Emergence of Modern Communications in Nineteenth-Century America* (Chicago: University of Chicago Press, 2006), 3.
15. Kenneth Silverman, *Lightning Man: The Accursed Life of Samuel F. B. Morse* (New York: Da Capo, 2003), 236; John Brown to Mary Brown, March 7, 1844, in *Meteor of War: The John Brown Story*, ed. John Stauffer and Zoe Trodd (Maplecrest, NY: Brandywine Press, 2004), 49–50.
16. Edward Hitchcock, *The Religion of Geology and Its Connected Sciences* (Glasgow: William Collins, 1851), 331 (first and second quotations), 341 (fourth and fifth quotations); Charles Babbage, *The Ninth Bridgewater Treatise: A Fragment* (London: John Murray, 1838), 112. Babbage built his theory of time on the work of Pierre-Simon, Marquis de Laplace, and included an excerpt from Laplace on probability in an appendix.
17. Hitchcock, *The Religion of Geology*, 331, 341.

18. Babbage, *The Ninth Bridgewater Treatise*, 117–18, 119.
19. Frances Power Cobbe, ed., *The Collected Works of Theodore Parker*, vol. 2, *Sermons, Prayers* (London: Trubner, 1879), 48; Laura Elizabeth Howe Richards, Maud Howe Elliott, and Florence Howe Hall, *Julia Ward Howe, 1819–1910* (Boston: Houghton Mifflin, 1915), 173–74; Julia Ward Howe, *Later Lyrics* (Boston: J. E. Tilton, 1866), 41.
20. Brown quoted in Oates, *To Purge This Land with Blood*, 55; Poe quoted in James Gleick, *Time Travel: A History* (New York: Pantheon, 2016), 15. Cushman quoted in Alex Nemerov, *Acting in the Night: Macbeth and the Paces of the Civil War* (Berkeley: University of California Press, 2010), 22, 17; James Russell Lowell, *Miscellaneous Poems* (Boston: Ticknor and Fields, 1857), 159; Paul Gilmore, *Aesthetic Materialism: Electricity and American Romanticism* (Stanford, CA: Stanford University Press, 2009).
21. James Gleick, *Chaos: Making a New Science* (New York: Penguin, 1988), 23. For a different comparison of the butterfly effect and the telegraph effect, see Nemerov, *Acting in the Night*, 22.
22. Hitchcock, *The Religion of Geology*, 22; Richard Hofstadter, *The Paranoid Style in American Politics and Other Essays* (New York: Vintage, 2008), 29, 31; Daniel Wickberg, "What Is the History of Sensibilities? On Cultural Histories, Old and New," *American Historical Review* 112, no. 3 (June 2007): 678.
23. Jill Lepore, *A Is for American: Letters and Other Characters in the Newly United States* (New York: Knopf, 2002), 140, 154; William G. Thomas, *The Iron Way: Railroads, the Civil War, and the Making of Modern America* (New Haven, CT: Yale University Press, 2011), 2; Henry W. Bellows, *A Sequel to "The Suspense of Faith," Addressed to His Own Congregation, Sunday Sept. 25, 1859, on the Reopening of All Souls' Church, after the Summer Vacation* (New York: D. Appleton, 1859), 44, 46; Nemerov, *Acting in the Night*, 17.
24. Silverman, *Lightning Man*, 51; Lepore, *A is for American*, 142.
25. Samuel Morse, *Foreign Conspiracy against the Liberties of the United States* (New York: Leavitt, Lord, 1835), 97; Silverman, *Lightning Man*, 139–41.
26. Gregory Orr, *Poetry as Survival* (Athens: University of Georgia Press, 2002), 17.
27. Silverman, *Lightning Man*; Lepore, *A is for American*.
28. Walt Whitman, "To a Locomotive in Winter," *Leaves of Grass* (Boston: James R. Osgood, 1881–82), 359; Mark M. Smith, *Mastered by the Clock: Time, Slavery, and Freedom in the American South* (Chapel Hill: University of North Carolina Press, 1997); Thomas, *The Iron Way*, 2–3; Howe, *What Hath God Wrought*, 564.
29. Whitney quoted in David Haward Bain, *Empire Express: Building the First Transcontinental Railroad* (New York: Penguin, 2000), 8.
30. Bain, *Empire Express*, 8; Thomas, *Iron Way*, 1.
31. Diary entry, November 7, 1833, Charles Francis Adams, ed., *John Quincy Adams, Memoirs*, vol. 9 (Philadelphia, 1874–79), 29.
32. Ibid., 30–31.
33. Ibid.; Thomas, *Iron Way*, 4; Michel Chevalier, *Society, Manners and Politics in the United States* (Boston: Weeks, Jordan, 1839), 289.
34. Henkin, *The Postal Age*, 40.

35. Sandage, *Born Losers*, 71; Chevalier, *Society, Manners and Politics in the United States*, 309; Philip Hone diary, May 22, 1837, in *The Diary of Philip Hone*, vol. 1, *1828–1851*, ed. Bayard Tuckerman (New York: Dodd, Mead, 1889), 260.
36. John Russell Bartlett, *Dictionary of Americanism* (Boston: Little, Brown, 1859), 171; Silverman, *Lightning Man*, 186–87.
37. Joseph N. Balestier, "The Annals of Chicago: A Lecture before the Chicago Lyceum, January 21, 1840," *Fergus Historical Series*, no. 1 (1876): 26; Sandage, *Born Losers*, 97; Phineas Taylor Barnum, *The Life of P. T. Barnum, Written by Himself* (London: L. T. Holt, 1855), 280.
38. Howe, *What Hath God Wrought*.
39. *New York Herald*, December 9, 1859, 2; Henry Clay Pate, *John Brown, as Viewed by H. Clay Pate* (New York: The author, 1859), 36; Henry Clay Pate, *American Vade Mecum, or the Companion of Youth, and Guide to College* (Cincinnati: Morgan, 1852), 31, 32.
40. James Fenimore Cooper, *Home as Found*, vol. 2 (Philadelphia: Lea and Blanchard, 1838), 117.
41. George E. Baker, ed., *The Works of William H. Seward*, vol. 4 (New York: Redfield, 1884), 290–92; Lincoln, "A House Divided," June 16, 1856, in *Collected Works of Abraham Lincoln*, ed. Roy P. Basler (New Brunswick: Rutgers University Press, 1953), 2:461–62; George Bancroft, *Literary and Historical Miscellanies* (New York: Harper and Brothers, 1855), 311.
42. Washington Irving, "Rip Van Winkle," *The Sketch Book of Geoffrey Crayon* (New York: C. S. Van Winkle, 1819); Robert Levine, *A Geography of Time: The Temporal Misadventures of a Social Psychologist* (New York: Basic Books, 1997), 9.
43. Alexis de Tocqueville, *Democracy in America*, vol. 1 (New York: George Adlard, 1839), 360; Horace Greeley, ed., *The Writings of Cassius Marcellus Clay* (New York: Harper and Brothers, 1848), 46 (quote), 202–6. Christopher Phillips argues that the Ohio River did not present a stark divide within the border West until the Civil War. See Phillips, *The Rivers Ran Backward: The Civil War and the Remaking of the American Middle Border* (New York: Oxford University Press, 2016).
44. Eric Foner, *Free Soil, Free Labor, Free Men: The Ideology of the Republican Party before the Civil War* (New York: Oxford University Press, 1970), 41, 51, 53; Frederick W. Seward, ed., *William H. Seward: An Autobiography* (New York: Derby and Miller, 1891), 266, 776, 806. Frederick Law Olmsted, *A Journey in the Back County* (New York: Mason Brothers, 1861), vii. For Thayer's plan, see George W. Smith, "Ante-Bellum Attempts of Northern Business Interests to 'Redeem' the Upper South," *Journal of Southern History* (May 1945): 177–81.
45. Harriet Beecher Stowe, *Uncle Tom's Cabin* (London: John Cassell, 1852), 207; Ronald Walters, *The Antislavery Appeal: American Abolitionism after 1830* (Baltimore: Johns Hopkins University Press, 1976), 115; Nathaniel Peabody Rogers, *A Collection from the Newspaper Writings of Nathaniel Peabody Rogers* (Concord, NH: John R. French, 1847), 272 (block quote); Nathaniel Peabody Rogers, *A Collection from the Miscellaneous Writings of Nathaniel Peabody Rogers* (Manchester, NH: William H. Fisk, 1849), 246; Heather D. Curtis, "Visions of Self, Success, and Society among Young Men in Antebellum Boston," *Church History* 73, no. 3 (September 2004): 613–34.

46. Franklin Sanborn, ed., *The Rights of Man in America* (Boston: American Unitarian Association, 1911), 172; Josiah Quincy, *Address Illustrative of the Nature and Power of the Slave States, and the Duties of the Free States* (Boston: Ticknor and Fields, 1856), 31, 28, 32; Brown quoted in Horwitz, *Midnight Rising*, 47.
47. Edward L. Ayers, *What Caused the Civil War? Reflections on the South and Southern History* (New York: W. W. Norton, 2005), 139; Smith, *Mastered by the Clock*.
48. David Herbert Donald, *Lincoln* (New York: Simon and Schuster, 1995), 80; Basler, *Collected Works of Abraham Lincoln*, 1:109.
49. Basler, *Collected Works of Abraham Lincoln*, 1: 108–10.
50. Ibid., 112–14.
51. Michael Burlingame, *Abraham Lincoln, A Life*, vol. 1 (Baltimore: Johns Hopkins University Press, 2013), 76 (Lincoln quotes from this page); Joshua Rothman, *Flush Times and Fever Dreams: A Story of Capitalism and Slavery in the Age of Jackson* (Athens: University of Georgia Press, 2012), 9.
52. Lincoln, "Message to Congress in Special Session," July 4, 1861, in Basler, *Collected Works*, 4:438; Sandage, *Born Losers*, 220–22.
53. Paul Finkelman, ed., *Defending Slavery: Proslavery Thought in the Old South* (New York: Bedford/St. Martin's, 2003), 67; Frank Byrne, "The Literary Shaping of Confederate Identity," in *Inside the Confederate Nation: Essays in Honor of Emory M. Thomas*, ed. Lesley Gordon and John Inscoe (Baton Rouge: Louisiana State University Press, 2006), 87; George William Bagby, "The Union: Its Benefits and Dangers," *Southern Literary Messenger* 32, no. 1 (January 1861): 3–4.
54. George Bagby, "Manifest Destiny of the World—Its Republic and Its Empire," *Southern Literary Messenger* (September 1859): 207–9; Matthew Karp, *This Vast Southern Empire: Slaveholders at the Helm of American Foreign Policy* (Cambridge, MA: Harvard University Press, 2016).
55. Finkelman, *Defending Slavery*, 59–60, 86–87, 194; Beverley Tucker, *The Partisan Leader* (New York: Rudd and Carleton, 1861), 55. Hammond's speech shows how competing speculations formed in dialogue, not isolation. Free labor advocates embraced his "mudsill" insult and formed "mudsill clubs" that rallied for Abraham Lincoln during the 1860 campaign. Abolitionist and proslavery forecasters relied upon an angry, intellectual exchange to sharpen their visions of the future. See Margaret Abruzzo, *Polemical Pain: Slavery, Cruelty, and the Rise of Humanitarianism* (Baltimore: Johns Hopkins University Press, 2011).
56. David F. AllmendingerJr., ed., *Incidents of My Life: Edmund Ruffin's Autobiographical Essays* (Charlottesville: University Press of Virginia, 1990), 174, 197, 198; Allmendinger, *Ruffin: Family and Reform in the Old South* (New York: Oxford University Press, 1990), 61; Benjamin R. Cohen, *Notes from the Ground: Science, Soil, and Society in the American Countryside* (New Haven, CT: Yale University Press, 2009), 93.
57. Hugh Buckner Johnston, "Josiah Pender," in *Dictionary of North Carolina Biography*, vol. 5, *P-S*, ed. William S. Powell (Chapel Hill: University of North Carolina Press, 1994), 62–63. William Kauffman Scarborough, ed., *The Diary of Edmund Ruffin*, vol. 1, *Toward Independence, October 1856–April 1861* (Baton Rouge: Louisiana State University Press, 1972), 318–19.
58. Scarborough, ed., *Diary of Edmund Ruffin*, 1: 318–19.

59. Ibid., 320, 319.
60. Ibid.
61. Ibid., 632.
62. *Callimachus and Lycophron, with an English Translation by A. W. Mair, Aratus with an English Translation by G R Mair* (London: William Heinemann; New York: G P Putnam's Sons, 1921), 497.
63. W. Sewell, trans., *The Agamemnon of Aeschylus* (London: Longman, Brown, Green, and Longmans, 1846), xxxi.
64. John B. Jones, *Border War: A Tale of Disunion* (New York: Rudd and Carleton, 1859), 44 (first and second quotations), 46.
65. Finkelman, *Defending Slavery*, 59, 60, 87; Jones quoted in Byrne, "The Literary Shaping of Confederate Identity," 84; Fitzhugh quoted in James M. McPherson, *Battle Cry of Freedom: The Civil War Era* (New York: Oxford University Press, 1988), 196.
66. Elliott West, *Contested Plains: Indians, Goldseekers, and the Rush to Colorado* (Lawrence: University Press of Kansas, 1998), 7; McPherson, *Battle Cry of Freedom*, 190.
67. Nelson, *Nation of Deadbeats*, 141–45.
68. Ibid.
69. Nicholas B. Wainright, ed., *A Philadelphia Perspective: The Diary of Sidney George Fisher Covering the Years 1834–1871* (Philadelphia: Historical Society of Pennsylvania, 1967), 279; John L. Huston, *The Panic of 1857 and the Coming of the Civil War* (Baton Rouge: Louisiana State University Press, 1987), 11, 16.
70. Huston, *The Panic of 1857*, 37; Sandage, *Born Losers*, 29; *Niles' Weekly Register*, January 9, 1819, quoted in Samuel Rezneck, "The Depression of 1819–1822: A Social History," *American Historical Review* 39 (October 1933): 28–47; Foner, *Free Soil*, 24; Frederick Jackson, *A Week in Wall Street* (New York: Frederick Jackson, 1841), 130–31, 136.
71. Sandage, *Born Losers*, 22; John Corrigan, *Business of the Heart: Religion and Emotion in the Nineteenth Century* (Berkeley: University of California Press, 2002); George Barrell Cheever, *God against Slavery: And the Freedom and Duty of the Pulpit to Rebuke It, as a Sin against God* (New York: Joseph H. Ladd, 1857), 57.
72. Finkelman, ed., *Defending Slavery*, 85–86.
73. Ibid., 82–83; Scarborough, *Diary of Edmund Ruffin*, 1:195–96; Karp, *This Vast Southern Empire*.
74. John Stauffer, *The Black Hearts of Men: Radical Abolitionists and the Transformation of Race* (Cambridge, MA: Harvard University Press, 2001), 114–15; Phillips, "John Brown's Pikes."
75. Stauffer, *Black Hearts of Men*, 122–23; Abraham Joshua Heschel, *The Prophets* (New York: Harper and Row, 1962), 190; Oates, *To Purge This Land with Blood*, 49; Phillips, "John Brown's Pikes."
76. Hitchcock, *The Religion of Geology*, 331; Reynolds, *John Brown, Abolitionist*; George W. Light, *Keep Cool, Go Ahead, and a Few Other Poems* (Boston: G. W. Light, 1851), 33–35; Stauffer and Trodd, *Meteor of War*, 102–3.
77. *King James Bible*, Judges, 7: 3,18; Charles Wesley, "Blow Ye the Trumpet, Blow," United Methodist Hymnal, Number 379; Stauffer and Trodd, *Meteor of War*, 77; Oates, *To Purge This Land with Blood*, 72–73.

CHAPTER 3

1. "Mason Report," *U.S. Senate Select Committee Reports*, 1859–1860, II (Washington: no publisher, 1860), 128; Stephen Oates, *To Purge This Land with Blood: A Biography of John Brown* (Amherst: University of Massachusetts Press, 1984), 286; Boyd Stutler to Donald B. Webster Jr., May 3, 1959, Boyd B. Stutler Collection, West Virginia State Archive; Jason Phillips, "John Brown's Pikes: Assembling the Future in Antebellum America," in *War Matters: Material Culture in the Civil War Era*, ed. Joan Cashin (Chapel Hill: University of North Carolina Press, forthcoming).
2. Kagi to sister, August 13, 1858, Richard Hinton Collection, Kansas State Historical Society; John Stauffer and Zoe Trodd, eds., *Meteor of War: The John Brown Story* (Maplecrest, NY: Brandywine Press, 2004), 100–101.
3. Osborne Anderson, *A Voice from Harper's Ferry* (Boston: the author, 1861), 32; Brown quoted in Oates, *To Purge This Land with Blood*, 289. For the perspectives of Brown's raiders, see Tony Horwitz, *Midnight Rising: John Brown and the Raid That Sparked the Civil War* (New York: Henry Holt, 2011).
4. William Shakespeare, *Macbeth*, Act 5, Scene 9; William French, "What 'May Become a Man': Image and Structure in Macbeth," *College Literature* 12, no. 3 (Fall 1985): 191–201; Grimké quoted in Theodore Dwight Weld, *American Slavery as It Is: Testimony of a Thousand Witnesses* (New York: American Anti-slavery Society, 1839), 23; Phillips, "John Brown's Pikes." For more on the practice, see Adam Rothman, *Slave Country: American Expansion and the Origins of the Deep South* (Cambridge, MA: Harvard University Press, 2005), 115; David Brion Davis, *Inhuman Bondage: The Rise and Fall of Slavery in the New World* (New York: Oxford University Press, 2006), 217.
5. Anderson, *A Voice from Harper's Ferry*, 8; Phillips, "John Brown's Pikes."
6. Anderson, *A Voice from Harper's Ferry*, 31 (italics in original). Brown quoted in David S. Reynolds, *John Brown, Abolitionist: The Man Who Killed Slavery, Sparked the Civil War, and Seeded Civil Rights* (New York: Alfred A. Knopf, 2005), 306; Phillips, "John Brown's Pikes."
7. John Brown, "League of Gileadites," January 15, 1851, in John Stauffer and Zoe Trodd, eds., *The Tribunal: Reponses to John Brown and the Harpers Ferry Raid* (Cambridge, MA: Harvard University Press, 2012), 8–9; Phillips, "John Brown's Pikes." For the gendering of slaves by reformers, see Bruce Dorsey, *Reforming Men and Women: Gender in the Antebellum City* (Ithaca, NY: Cornell University Press, 2002), 136–94.
8. Harriet Beecher Stowe, *Uncle Tom's Cabin: A Tale of Life among the Lowly* (London: George Routledge, 1852), 263–64; Martin Robinson Delany, *Blake; or, The Huts of America: A Corrected Edition*, edited by Jerome McGann (Cambridge, MA: Harvard University Press, 2017); quotes in Martin R. Delany, *The Condition, Elevation, Emigration, and Destiny of the Colored People of United States* (Philadelphia: published by the author, 1852), 37–38.
9. Stauffer and Trodd, eds., *Meteor of War*, 119; Horwitz, *Midnight Rising*, 80–81.
10. Anderson, *A Voice from Harper's Ferry*, 34, 38, 52; Jean Libby, ed., *John Brown Mysteries* (Missoula: Pictorial Histories, 1999), 36; Hannah Geffert (with Jean Libby), "Regional Black Involvement in John Brown's Raid on Harpers Ferry," in *Prophets of Protest: Reconsidering the History of American Abolitionism*, ed. Timothy Patrick McCarthy and John Stauffer (New York: New Press, 2006), 165–82; Dangerfield quoted

in Richard J. Hinton, *John Brown and His Men* (New York: Funk & Wagnalls, 1894), 300; Anderson, *A Voice from Harper's Ferry*, 37; Phillips, "John Brown's Pikes."

11. Horwitz, *Midnight Rising*; Reynolds, *John Brown, Abolitionist;* Oates, *To Purge This Land with Blood*; Phillips, "John Brown's Pikes."
12. Horwitz, *Midnight Rising,* 179, 163; "Mason Report," 39, 16; Geffert with Libby, "Regional Black Involvement in John Brown's Raid on Harpers Ferry"; Phillips, "John Brown's Pikes." In the 1990s, the gun reappeared in someone's attic beside two 1858-model Harpers Ferry rifles. By tracing the story of these weapons, historians Hannah Geffert and Jean Libby have uncovered a web of black involvement in the raid.
13. For more on the visceral nature of antebellum material cultures, see Michael E. Woods, "Tracing the 'Sacred Relicts': The Strange Career of Preston Brooks's Cane," *Civil War History* 63, no. 2 (June 2017): 111–30.
14. Anonymous to Clerk of Court, Charlestown, October 23, 1859, quoted in William Glover Stanard, ed., "The John Brown Letters: Found in the Virginia State Library in 1901," *Virginia Magazine of History and Biography* 10, no. 1 (July 1902): 30; Thomas Jefferson to John Holmes, April 22, 1820, in Merrill D. Peterson, ed., *The Portable Jefferson* (New York: Penguin, 1975), 568.
15. "An Onlooker" to Henry Wise, undated letter, in Stanard, ed., "The John Brown Letters: Found in the Virginia State Library in 1901," 28; Edward Young, *The Poems of Edward Young*, vol. 1 (Chiswick: C. Whittingham, 1822), 73.
16. Historians of the French Revolution and women's gossip have also shown how rumors demonstrate the agency of oppressed people. Important examples include Georges Lefebvre, *The Great Fear of 1789: Rural Panic in Revolutionary France*, trans. Joan White (1932; Princeton, NJ: Princeton University Press, 2016); Robert Darnton, *The Great Cat Massacre: And Other Episodes in French Cultural History* (New York: Basic Books, 1984); James C. Scott, *Domination and the Arts of Resistance: Hidden Transcripts* (New Haven, CT: Yale University Press, 1990); Sherna Berger Gluck and Daphne Patai, eds., *Women's Words: The Feminist Practice of Oral History* (New York: Routledge, 1991); Steven Hahn, "'Extravagant Expectations' of Freedom: Rumour, Political Struggle, and the Christmas Insurrection Scare of 1865 in the American South," *Past and Present* 157 (November 1997): 122–58; Bernard Capp, *When Gossips Meet: Women, Family, and Neighbourhood in Early Modern England* (New York: Oxford University Press, 2003); Rebecca Griffin, "Courtship Contests and the Meaning of Conflict in the Folklore of Slaves," *Journal of Southern History* 71, no. 4 (November 2005): 769–802.
17. Henry Ward Beecher, "The Nation's Duty to Slavery," in Beecher, *Patriotic Addresses* (New York: Fords, Howard, & Hulbert, 1887), 204.
18. Colonel Robert E. Lee's Report, October 19, 1859, quoted in Stanard, ed., "The John Brown Letters: Found in the Virginia State Library in 1901," *Virginia Magazine of History and Biography* 11, no. 1 (July 1902): 22.
19. James William to Henry Peter Brougham, February 1861, quoted in Stauffer and Trodd, *The Tribunal*, 345–46.
20. "WIL" to John Brown, November 29, 1859, quoted in Stanard, ed., "The John Brown Letters: Found in the Virginia State Library in 1901," *Virginia Magazine of History and Biography*. 11, no. 1 (July 1903): 27; Amanda Virginia Edmonds diary, November 11, 1859, Amanda Virginia Edmonds Papers, 1857–1886, VHS.

21. November 17, 1859 entry (first quotation), November 11, 1859 entry (second and third quotations), Amanda Virginia Edmonds Papers, 1857–1886, VHS; Richard K. Call to John S. Littell, February 12, 1861, quoted in Stauffer and Trodd, *The Tribunal*, 343–44; Edmund Ruffin diary, November 2, 1859 (ninth quotation), 6 February 26, 1861 (tenth through twelfth quotations), quoted in William Kauffman Scarborough, ed., *The Diary of Edmund Ruffin*, vol. 1 (Baton Rouge: Louisiana State University Press, 1972), 351, 556–57.
22. Samuel F. B. Morse, *Foreign Conspiracy against the Liberties of the United States* (New York: Leavitt, Lord, 1835), 14, 95, 96. According to Richard Hofstadter, the common enemy in all American conspiracy theories is "a gigantic and yet subtle machinery of influence set in motion to undermine and destroy a way of life." Hofstadter understood that conspiracy theorists do not see shadowy designs occasionally throughout history, but rather "history is a conspiracy." "Northerners and southerners believed that cloaked cabals were menacing their freedom, darkness was overcoming the land, and bloodshed would determine whether good or evil prevailed in the end." Richard Hofstadter, *The Paranoid Style in American Politics and Other Essays* (New York: Vintage, 2008), 29, 31; Daniel Wickberg, "What Is the History of Sensibilities? On Cultural Histories, Old and New," *American Historical Review* 112, no. 3 (June 2007): 678.
23. Reynolds, *John Brown, Abolitionist*, 215, 221, 223; Ralph Waldo Emerson, "Speech at a Meeting to Aid John Brown's Family," November 18, 1859, quoted in Len Gougeon and Joel Myerson, eds., *Emerson's Antislavery Writings* (New Haven, CT: Yale University Press, 1995), 118.
24. Stauffer and Trodd, *Meteor of War*, 122; David Potter, *The Impending Crisis, 1848–1861* (New York: Harper & Row, 1976), 466–67.
25. Harriet Prescott Spofford, "Six by Seven," *The Knickerbocker: Or, New York Monthly Magazine* (January 1860): 17–36 (quotations on pp. 31, 17).
26. Edmund Ruffin diary, December 2, 1859, Scarborough, *Diary of Edmund Ruffin*, vol. 1, 368–71 (quotation).
27. Brown quoted in Horwitz, *Midnight Rising*, 251; Thomas J. Jackson to Mary Anna Jackson, December 2, 1829, in Stauffer and Trodd, *The Tribunal*, 283; John Preston to Margaret Junkin Preston, December 2, 1859, in Stauffer and Trodd, *The Tribunal*, 286.
28. John Brown, December 2, 1859, in Stauffer and Trodd, *Meteor of War*, 159; Hebrews 9:20, *King James Bible*; John Brown interview with Senator James Mason and others, October 18, 1859, in Stauffer and Trodd, *The Tribunal*, 46.
29. Edmund Ruffin diary, January 12, 1860, in Scarborough, *Diary of Edmund Ruffin*, vol. 1, 391; Edmund Ruffin, "Incidents of My Life," vol. 2, quoted in David F. AllmendingerJr., ed., *Incidents of My Life: Edmund Ruffin's Autobiographical Essays* (Charlottesville: University Press of Virginia, 1990), 91 (second quotation), 243 n. 166.
30. William Gwathmey diary, December 2–4, 1859, Gwathmey Family Papers, VHS.
31. Adrienne Cole Phillips, "The Mississippi Press's Response to John Brown's Raid," *Journal of Mississippi History* 48, no. 2 (May 1986): 119–34; Anderson, *A Voice from Harper's Ferry*, 7.
32. December 10, 1859 entry, Robert A. Granniss diary, 1858–1861, VHS.
33. Ibid.
34. Stauffer and Trodd, *Meteor of War*, 132 (quotation), 159, 124.

35. Sarah Frances Williams to her parents, November 7, 11, 1859, in Stauffer and Trodd, *The Tribunal*, 249; Moncure Conway, Sermon, December 4, 1859, in Stauffer and Trodd, *The Tribunal*, 292.
36. Speech of Reuben Davis, December 8, 1859, in Stauffer and Trodd, *The Tribunal*, 295; Theodore Parker to Francis Jackson, November 24, 1859, in Stauffer and Trodd, *The Tribunal*, 135.
37. Ronald G. Walters, *The Antislavery Appeal: American Abolitionism after 1830* (Baltimore: Johns Hopkins University Press, 1976), 26–27; Isaiah 9:5, *King James Bible*.
38. David Walker, *Walker's Appeal, in Four Articles; Together with a Preamble, to the Coloured Citizens of the World, but in Particular, and Very Expressly, to Those of the United States of America*, rev. ed. (Boston: David Walker, 1830), 45, 83; Robert H. Abzug, *Cosmos Crumbling: American Reform and the Religious Imagination* (New York: Oxford University Press, 1994), 147.
39. Benjamin F. Dill to Stephen A. Douglas, November 2, 1859, Stephen A. Douglas Papers, Series 1, Box 24, Regenstein Library, University of Chicago; Stephen Douglas, "Invasion of States" Speech, January 23, 1860, in Stauffer and Trodd, *The Tribunal*, 201; National Democratic Executive Committee, September 1860, in Stauffer and Trodd, *The Tribunal*, 333–34; *Pennsylvania Statesman*, October 20, 1860, in Stauffer and Trodd, *The Tribunal*, 224; "Slaveholders and Non-Slaveholders of the South," *Charleston Mercury*, November 1, 1860. According to sociologist Philip Smith, societies escalate storytelling before going to war. He calls this process "narrative inflation" and argues that apocalyptic narratives are "the most effective at generating and legitimating massive society-wide sacrifice." See Philip Smith, *Why War? The Cultural Logic of Iraq, the Gulf War, and Suez* (Chicago: University of Chicago Press, 2005), 26–27. Because they portend an inevitable clash between good and evil, apocalyptic stories complement paranoid politics and conspiracy theories. As Hofstadter explains, "Like religious millenarians," the conspiracy theorist "expresses the anxiety of those who are living through the last days and he is sometimes disposed to set a date for the apocalypse." Hofstadter, *The Paranoid Style in American Politics*, 30.
40. J. D. Andrus to John Sherman, November 18, 1859, Sherman Papers, Box 9, Library of Congress; Tennessee legislature and *Charleston Mercury* quoted in Elizabeth Varon, *Disunion: The Coming of the American Civil War, 1789–1859* (Chapel Hill: University of North Carolina Press, 2008), 331; *New York Herald*, January 6, 1860, 1–2; "A Slaveholder" to John Sherman, December 10, 1859, John Sherman Papers, Box 9, Library of Congress.
41. Abraham Lincoln, "Address at Cooper Institute," February 27, 1860, Roy Basler, ed., *Collected Works of Abraham Lincoln*, vol. 3 (New Brunswick, NJ: Rutgers University Press, 1953), 536 (first quotation), 538 (second quotation), 540 (third quotation), 541 (fourth through seventh quotations), 542 (eighth quotation).
42. Hinton Rowan Helper, *The Impending Crisis of the South: How to Meet It* (New York: A. B. Burdick, 1860), 181; James M. McPherson, *Battle Cry of Freedom: The Civil War Era* (New York: Oxford University Press, 1988), 199.
43. David M. Potter, *The Impending Crisis, 1848–1861* (New York: Harper and Row, 1976), 387; McPherson, *Battle Cry of Freedom*, 200; Edmund Ruffin diary, December 8–20, 1859, Scarborough, *Diary of Edmund Ruffin*, vol. 1, 376–83; William Gist to William Porcher Miles, December 20, 1859, William Porcher Miles Papers, Southern Historical Collection, University of North Carolina-Chapel Hill (UNC-CH); Alan Nevins,

The Emergence of Lincoln, vol. 2, *Prologue to Civil War, 1859–1861* (New York: Charles Scribner's Sons, 1950), 122; Helper, *Impending Crisis*, 153.

44. Strother quoted in Cecil D. Eby, *"Porte Crayon": The Life of David Hunter Strother* (Chapel Hill: University of North Carolina Press, 1960), 30 (first and second quotations), 32 (third), 36 (fourth), 49 (fifth).
45. David Hunter Strother, "The John Brown Raid, Notes by an eye witness and citizen of the Invaded district," Journal 3, Manuscript Box 1, David Hunter Strother Papers, West Virginia and Regional History Collection, Wise Library, West Virginia University, hereinafter WVU.
46. Ibid.
47. Ibid.; Alexis de Tocqueville, *Democracy in America*, vol. 1, translated by Henry Reeve (New York: George Adlard, 1839), 156.
48. Strother, "The John Brown Raid," Journal 3, Manuscript Box 1, David Hunter Strother Papers, WVU.
49. *Harpers Weekly*, November 19, 1859; Isaiah 2:4, *King James Bible*; Eby, "Porte Crayon," 107.
50. Former slave quoted in Steven Hahn, *A Nation Under Our Feet: Black Political Struggles in the Rural South from Slavery to the Great Migration* (Cambridge, MA: Harvard University Press, 2003), 55; William Lovett to Sallie, November 5, 1859, William Lovett Papers, 1859–1864, Georgia Historical Society; Amanda Virginia Edmonds diary, December 4, 1859, Amanda Virginia Edmonds Papers, 1857–1886, VHS; Susan Bradford Eppes quoted in Stauffer and Trodd, *The Tribunal*, 270, 271.
51. Robert Young Conrad to Catherine Brookes Powell Conrad, November 27, 1859, Holmes Conrad Papers, 1794–959, VHS.
52. Anderson, *A Voice from Harper's Ferry*, 35; Stauffer and Trodd, *The Tribunal*, 119 (Douglass quotations), 281 (Harper quotations), 193 (Hamilton quotations), 160 (Martin quotations), 154 (Garnet quotations).
53. Lydia Maria Child (LMC) to Mrs. S. M. Parsons, December 1859, LMC to Mrs. S. B. Shaw, 1860, in Lydia Maria Child, *Letters of Lydia Maria Child* (Boston: Houghton, Mifflin, 1882), 137, 142; Amanda Virginia Edmonds diary, December 3, 1859, Amanda Virginia Edmonds Papers, 1857–86, VHS.
54. Stauffer and Trodd, *The Tribunal*, 198–99 (Alcott quotations), 89, 251, 302 ("A Woman's View" quotations).
55. Margaretta Mason to Lydia Maria Child, November 11, 1859, Child, *Letters of Lydia Maria Child*, 121.
56. Adam Goodheart, *1861: The Civil War Awakening* (New York: Alfred A. Knopf, 2011), 46–52; Earl J. Hess, *Civil War Infantry Tactics: Training, Combat, and Small-Unit Effectiveness* (Baton Rouge: Louisiana State University Press, 2015), 31; Jon Grinspan, "Young Men for War: The Wide Awakes and Lincoln's 1860 Campaign," *Journal of American History* (September 2009), 357–78.
57. Grinspan, "Young Men for War," 365–66; John W. Lawson James Dewitte Hankins, November 28, 1860, Hankins Family Papers, VHS; Grace Elmore diary, October 18, 1860, Grace Elmore Papers, SHC, UNC-CH.
58. Stephen A. West, "Minute Men, Yeomen, and the Mobilization for Secession in the South Carolina Upcountry," *Journal of Southern History* (February 2005): 75–104; Grace

Elmore diary, October 28, 1860 (first through seventh quotations), October 29, 1860 (eighth quotation), ibid.; John G. Nicolay to Therena Bates, December 19, 1860, John G. Nicolay Papers, Library of Congress.

59. Grace Elmore diary, No date (between November 13 and November 19, 1860), Grace Elmore Papers, SHC, UNC-CH.
60. John Pegram to William Ransom Johnson Pegram, January 25, 1860, Section 1, Pegram-Johnson-McIntosh Family Papers, 1825–941, VHS; William Johnston to Andrew McCollam, May 13, 1860, Andrew McCollam Papers, 1792–935 subseries 1.2, SHC, UNC-CH; Ben Wynne, *Mississippi's Civil War: A Narrative History* (Macon, GA: Mercer University Press, 2006), 19–21.
61. Ellis Turner, "Terrible Swift Sword: The Edged Weapons of John Brown's War on Slavery," *Man at Arms* (December 2012): 35 (B&O quotation); John Hope Franklin, *The Militant South, 1800–1861*(Cambridge, MA: Harvard University Press, 1956), 242; James B. Averett, ed., *The Memoirs of General Turner Ashby and His Compeers* (Baltimore: Selby & Dulany, 1867), 66; Oswald Garrison Villard, *John Brown, 1800–1859: A Biography Fifty Years After* (Boston: Houghton Mifflin, 1910), 527 (Hunter quotation).
62. Kenneth S. Greenberg, ed., *The Confessions of Nat Turner and Related Documents* (Boston: St. Martin's Press, 2005), 106–7 (Floyd quotations), 69–70 (Garrison quotations); Phillips, "John Brown's Pikes."
63. Joseph Anderson to the governors of North Carolina, South Carolina, Georgia, Florida, Alabama, Mississippi, Louisiana, Arkansas, Texas, Tennessee, and Kentucky, December 8, 1859, Tredegar Letterbooks, Library of Virginia; Charles B. Dew, *Ironmaker to the Confederacy: Joseph R. Anderson and the Tredegar Iron Works*, 2nd ed. (Richmond: Library of Virginia, 1999), 64–71 (second quotation, p. 71).
64. As Kariann Yokota writes, "Once they are put into circulation, objects consort with people on both sides of any political divide; their makers cannot control how they will be used or by whom." See Kariann Yokota, *Unbecoming British: How Revolutionary America Became a Postcolonial Nation* (New York: Oxford University Press, 2014), 29; Henry Clay Pate, *John Brown, as Viewed by H. Clay Pate* (New York: Henry Clay Pate, 1859), 38; Simon Harrison, "War Mementos and the Souls of Missing Soldiers: Returning Effects of the Battlefield Dead," *Journal of the Royal Anthropological Institute* (December 2008): 775; Phillips, "John Brown's Pikes."
65. Pate, *John Brown,* 38; *New York Herald,* December 9, 1859, 2; Phillips, "John Brown's Pikes."
66. *New York Herald,* December 9, 1859, 2; Phillips, "John Brown's Pikes."
67. *New York Herald,* December 9, 1859, 2; Phillips, "John Brown's Pikes."

CHAPTER 4

1. Bowie Knife and Sheath, Object number 1983.31, Virginia Historical Society; undated entry, Journal 3, 1857–1859, David Hunter Strother Papers, West Virginia and Regional History Collection, Wise Library, West Virginia University; Jason Phillips, "John Brown's Pikes: Assembling the Future in Antebellum America," *War Matters: Material Culture in the Civil War Era*, ed. Joan Cashin (Chapel Hill: University of North Carolina Press, forthcoming).

2. Undated entry, Journal 3, 1857–1859, Strother Papers; Phillips, "John Brown's Pikes."
3. Robert W. Baylor to Governor Henry Wise, October 18, 1859, in Robert M. De Witt, *The Life, Trial and Execution of John Brown* (New York: Robert M. De Witt, 1859), 43, 38; Ellis Turner, "Terrible Swift Sword: The Edged Weapons of John Brown's War on Slavery," *Man at Arms* (December 2012): 34; Phillips, "John Brown's Pikes." There is conflicting evidence about whether Stuart or Lieutenant Israel Green found the spears and distributed them. John C. Unseld testified that Lieutenant Green found and distributed the weapons, but Robert E. Lee reported that he ordered Green to escort the prisoners to Charlestown and sent Stuart to Brown's headquarters. In his postwar recollection of the raid, Green did not mention finding the spears. See "Mason Report," *U.S. Senate Select Committee Reports*, 1859–1860, II (Washington: no publisher, 1860), 42, 11, 12, and Israel Green, "The Capture of John Brown," *North American Review* (December 1885): 564–65.
4. Harriett Newby to Dangerfield Newby, April 11, 1859 (first quotation), August 16, 1859 (second and third quotations), H. W. Flournoy, ed., *Calendar of Virginia State Papers and Other Manuscripts from January 1, 1836, to April 15, 1869*, vol. 11 (Richmond: James E. Goode, 1893), 310–11; Tony Horwitz, *Midnight Rising: John Brown and the Raid that Sparked the Civil War* (New York: Henry Holt, 2011), 242, 282; James Monroe, *Thursday Lectures, Addresses and Essays* (Oberlin, OH: Edward J. Goodrich, 1897), 170; Diana Ramey Berry, *The Price for Their Pound of Flesh: The Value of the Enslaved, from Womb to Grave, in the Building of a Nation* (Boston: Beacon Press, 2017); Phillips, "John Brown's Pikes."
5. Edmund Ruffin diary, December 8, 1859, December 7, 1859, William Kauffman Scarborough, ed., *The Diary of Edmund Ruffin*, vol. 1 (Baton Rouge: Louisiana State University Press, 1972), 377, 375–76; De Witt, *The Life, Trial, and Execution of John Brown*, 38; Stan Cohen, *John Brown: "Thundering Voice of Jehovah"* (Missoula, MT: Pictorial Histories, 1999), 151; Terry Alford, *Fortune's Fool: The Life of John Wilkes Booth* (New York: Oxford University Press, 2015), 81; Booth quoted in John Rhodehamel and Louise Taper, eds., *"Right or Wrong, God Judge Me": The Writings of John Wilkes Booth* (Urbana: University of Illinois Press, 1997), 60. Edged weapons were at the heart of slave revolts. Toussaint L'Ouverture fashioned iron spears for his 1791 overthrow of French slavers in Santo Domingo. In 1800, Gabriel Prosser's plot for a revolt in Virginia planned to arm slaves with swords made by Gabriel and his brother Solomon, both trained blacksmiths. In 1822, Denmark Vesey planned to raid the Charleston, South Carolina, arsenal to gather and circulate hundreds of pikes and bayonets. In 1831, Nat Turner's insurrection murdered Virginians with knives and sharp farm implements. When authorities captured Turner, he was carrying a sword. Ellis Turner, "Terrible Swift Sword: The Edged Weapons of John Brown's War on Slavery," *Man at Arms* (December 2012), 25; Ruffin diary, December 1, 1859, Scarborough, *Diary of Edmund Ruffin*, 368; Phillips, "John Brown's Pikes."
6. Ruffin quoted in Avery Craven, *Edmund Ruffin, Southerner: A Study in Secession* (Baton Rouge: Louisiana State University Press, 1932), 178, 69. Ruffin diary, December 10, 1859, July 17, 1860 (last quotation), in Scarborough, *Diary of Edmund Ruffin*, 378, 443; Sven Beckert and Seth Rockman, eds., *Slavery's Capitalism: A New History of American Economic Development* (Philadelphia: University of Pennsylvania Press, 2016); Phillips, "John Brown's Pikes."

7. Roberta Barker, "Tragical-Comical-Historical Hotspur," *Shakespeare Quarterly*, 54, no. 3 (Autumn 2003): 299; William Shakespeare, *Henry IV, Part 1*, David Scott Kastan, ed., (London: Arden Shakespeare, 2002), 287; Phillips, "John Brown's Pikes."
8. Albert Rust to Edmund Ruffin, June 21, 1860, Edmund Ruffin Papers, Virginia Historical Society; Ruffin to John Letcher, Ruffin Papers, Virginia Historical Society (VHS); Phillips, "John Brown's Pikes."
9. Jamison quoted in Stephen A. Channing, *Crisis of Fear: Secession in South Carolina* (New York: W. W. Norton, 1974), 82, 83; Jamison quoted in William W. Freehling, *The Road to Disunion*, vol. 2, *Secessionists Triumphant, 1854–1861* (New York: Oxford University Press, 2007), 421; Phillips, "John Brown's Pikes"; Danton quoted in William Jennings Bryan, ed., *The World's Famous Orations*, vol. 2, *Continental Europe, 380–1906* (New York: Funk and Wagnalls, 1906), 130–31.
10. Littleton Dennis Quinton Washington to Edmund Ruffin, January 24, 1860, Edmund Ruffin Papers, 1818–1865, VHS; Laurence Keitt to Susan Sparks Keitt, February 19, 1861, in Elmer Don Herd Jr., "Laurence Keitt's Letters from the Provisional Congress of the Confederacy, 1861," *South Carolina Historical Magazine* 61, no. 1 (January 1960): 22.
11. Ruffin diary, April 7, 1860, in Scarborough, *Diary of Edmund Ruffin*, 413; David F. Allmendinger Jr., *Ruffin: Family and Reform in the Old South* (New York: Oxford University Press, 1990), 111–14; Fred Hobson, "'Anticipations of the Future'; Or the Wish-Fulfillment of Edmund Ruffin," *Southern Literary Journal* 10, no. 1 (Fall 1977): 84–91; Ian Binnington, *Nationalism, Symbolism, and the Imagined South in the Civil War* (Charlottesville: University of Virginia Press, 2013).
12. Ruffin, *Anticipations of the Future*, 8 (first quotation), 55 (second quotation), 56 (third quotation).
13. Ibid., 247 (first quotation), 249 (second quotation).
14. Ibid., 254 (first quotation), 258 (second quotation), 264 (third quotation).
15. Ibid., 295.
16. Ruffin diary, February 29, 1860, in Scarborough, *Diary of Edmund Ruffin*, 408; Coleman Hutchison, *Apples and Ashes: Literature, Nationalism, and the Confederate States of America* (Athens: University of Georgia Press, 2012), 62. As Hutchison explains, "The history of southern literary nationalist discourse in the three decades prior to the American Civil War thus provides a history of the future—or, better, a history of possible futures."
17. Ruffin diary, February 26, 1860, in Scarborough, ed., *Diary of Edmund Ruffin*, 407 (italics in original).
18. John B. Jones, *Wild Southern Scenes: A Tale of Disunion! and Border War!* (Philadelphia: T. B. Peterson and Brothers, 1859).
19. Nathaniel Beverley Tucker, *The Partisan Leader; a Tale of the Future* (Washington: Duff Green, 1836). In 1861, Rudd and Carleton, publishers in New York City, reprinted Tucker's novel as *A Key to the Disunion Conspiracy: The Partisan Leader by Beverly Tucker* (New York: Rudd and Carleton, 1861).
20. According to literary scholar John Grammer, this theme supported two messages that Tucker wanted to convey to readers: "He hoped to urge a return to the principles of the past, but he also wished to express a boundless confidence in the future." John M.

Grammer, *Pastoral and Politics in the Old South* (Baton Rouge: Louisiana State University Press, 1996), 85.

21. Ibid., 92–93. William Henry Trescot, *An American View of the Eastern Question* (Charleston: John Russell, 1854), 3. In the end, Tucker fails to imagine how the southern nation might succeed. His history of the future concludes with Douglas Trevor and his bride captured by Martin Van Buren. Capable friends meet in Washington, DC, to liberate the couple but Tucker does not reveal whether they succeed.
22. Tucker, *Partisan Leader*, 33; Jones, *Wild Southern Scenes*; Ruffin diary, February 29, 1860, in Scarborough, *Diary of Edmund Ruffin*, 406.
23. Robert E. Bonner, *Mastering America: Southern Slaveholders and the Crisis of American Nationhood* (Cambridge: Cambridge University Press, 2009), 180–81; Tucker quoted in Eric H. Walther, *The Fire-Eaters* (Baton Rouge: Louisiana State University Press, 1992), 45. Robert Bonner calls these books "future memories of the heroic present." Bonner writes that "Americans' prevailing orientation toward the future made excessive attention to past achievements a source of anxiety no less than pride" during the sectional crisis.
24. Elliott West, *The Contested Plains: Indians, Goldseekers, and the Rush to Colorado* (Lawrence: University Press of Kansas, 1998), xxiii.
25. Tucker, *Partisan Leader*, 5.
26. These gender insights reinforce Hutchison's argument that southern literary nationalists expressed "great anxiety about the full incorporation of women into the body politic." See Hutchison, *Apples and Ashes*, 47.
27. Tucker, *Partisan Leader*, 117 (first and second quotations), 112 (third and fourth quotations); Jones, *Wild Southern Scenes*, 335–36 (fifth through seventh quotations); Eugene D. Genovese, *The Slaveholders' Dilemma: Freedom and Progress in Southern Conservative Thought, 1820–1860* (Columbia: University of South Carolina Press, 1992).
28. W. Fitzhugh Brundage, *The Southern Past: A Clash of Race and Memory* (Cambridge, MA: Harvard University Press, 2005), 5.
29. Ruffin, *Anticipations of the Future*, vi (first quotation), vii (second quotation); Avery Craven, *Edmund Ruffin, Southerner: A Study in Secession* (New York: D. Appleton, 1932; Baton Rouge: Louisiana State University Press, 1991) 34; Mark A. Noll, *The Civil War as a Theological Crisis* (Chapel Hill: University of North Carolina Press, 2006); Tracy Fessenden, *Culture and Redemption: Religion, the Secular, and American Literature* (Princeton, NJ: Princeton University Press, 2006).
30. Walter Brueggemann, *The Prophetic Imagination*, 2nd ed. (Minneapolis: Fortress Press, 2001), x (first and second quotations). Paul Ricoeur *The Rule of Metaphor: Multi-disciplinary Studies of the Creation of Meaning in Language*, trans. Robert Czerny (Toronto: University of Toronto Press, 1977). For liberation theology, see Gustavo Gutierrez, *A Theology of Liberation: History, Politics and Salvation*, trans., John Eagleson and Caridad Inda (London: Orbis, 1973).
31. "Apostles of disunion" comes from Charles B. Dew, *Apostles of Disunion: Southern Secession Commissioners and the Causes of the Civil War* (Charlottesville: University of Virginia Press, 2001); Brueggemann, *The Prophetic Imagination*, 3, 63 (second and third quotations), Scarborough, *The Diary of Edmund Ruffin*, 416. For the political climate of 1860, see William W. Freehling, *The Road to Disunion*, vol. 2, *Secessionists Triumphant, 1854–1861* (New York: Oxford University Press, 2007).

32. Brueggemann, *The Prophetic Imagination*, 3, 63, 74 (quotations).
33. Ruffin, *Anticipations of the Future*, ix. For an interpretation of Ruffin's novel as an act of wish fulfillment, see Fred Hobson. "'Anticipations of the Future'; Or the Wish-Fulfillment of Edmund Ruffin," *Southern Literary Journal* 10, no. 1 (Fall 1977): 84–91.
34. Brueggemann, *The Prophetic Imagination*, 64; Ruffin, *Anticipations of the Future*, 186; Michael Kammen, *Mystic Cords of Memory: The Transformation of Tradition in American Culture* (New York: Knopf, 1991). Jack Temple Kirby noted that "the first Ruffin 'reform' then was the promotion of Virginia's history, wellspring of place pride," when Ruffin became a founding member of the Historical and Philosophical Society of Virginia. In the early 1850s, Ruffin drafted "The Blackwater Guerilla," a forty-three-page Revolutionary War story. This early attempt at historical fiction may have influenced the battle scenes in *Anticipations*. See Edmund Ruffin, *Nature's Management: Writings on Landscape and Reform, 1822–1859*, ed. Jack Temple Kirby (Athens: University of Georgia Press, 2000), xix.
35. Brueggemann, *The Prophetic Imagination*, 64. Note how Brueggemann argues that a hopeful disposition is deeply rooted within the prophet's culture; it is not propaganda or ideology fabricated for current events. Moreover, collective memory supports prophecy by reminding society of its primal sensibilities during a crisis. Here Brueggemann places prophecy within a broader timescape and a deeper sensibility than most historians consider when studying historical memory. Varon, *Disunion*, 33.
36. Edmund Ruffin, "The Blackwater Guerrilla," 4, Ruffin Papers, VHS.
37. Ibid., 8.
38. Ibid., 16–17.
39. Ibid., 43. By the same reasoning, John Brown and other northern invaders could never be honorable partisans like Ruffin's grandfather. Instead of being a knight of honor, Brown was a "robber & murderer, & villain of unmitigated turpitude." See Ruffin diary, November 30, 1859, in Scarborough, *Diary of Edmund Ruffin*, vol. 1, 366–67.
40. Hunter quoted in Robert M. DeWitt, *The Life, Trial, and Execution of Captain John Brown Known as "Old Brown of Ossawatomie," With a Full Account of the Attempted Insurrection at Harpers Ferry* (New York: Robert M. De Witt, 1859), 93; Albert Taylor Bledsoe, "Liberty and Slavery," in E. N. Elliott, ed., *Cotton Is King, and Pro-Slavery Arguments Comprising the Writings of Hammon, Harper, Christy, String-fellow, Hodge, Bledsoe, and Cartwright on this Important Subject* (Augusta, GA: Pritchard, Abbott, and Loomis, 1860), 405; Benjamin Morgan Palmer, "The South: Her Peril and Her Duty," in Jon L. Wakelyn, ed., *Southern Pamphlets on Secession: November 1860–April 1861* (Chapel Hill: University of North Carolina Press, 1996), 77; Hale quoted in Dew, *Apostles of Disunion*, 99; James Henley Thornwell, "Our Danger and Our Duty," in *The Life and Letters of James Henley Thornwell*, ed. Benjamin Morgan Palmer (Richmond: Whittet & Shepperson, 1875), 583. For more on this subject, see Matthew J. Clavin, *Toussaint Louverture and the American Civil War: The Promise and Peril of a Second Haitian Revolution* (Philadelphia: University of Pennsylvania Press, 2010); Alfred N. Hunt, *Haiti's Influence on Antebellum America: Slumbering Volcano in the Caribbean* (Baton Rouge: Louisiana State University Press, 2006).
41. Mary Howard Schoolcraft, *The Black Gauntlet: A Tale of Plantation Life in South Carolina* (Philadelphia: J. P. Lippincott, 1860; reprinted New York: Negro University Press, 1969),

563 (first through fifth quotations), 564, (sixth through tenth), italics in original, 560 (eleventh and twelfth), 569 (thirteenth). Memories of Haiti fueled a general fear of insurrection that shaped secessionists' prophecies. See Carl Paulus, *The Slaveholding Crisis: Fear of Insurrection and the Coming of the Civil War* (Baton Rouge: Louisiana State University Press, 2017).

42. Marx quoted in Reinhart Koselleck, *Futures Past: On the Semantics of Historical Time* (New York: Columbia University Press, 2004), 52; Stephens quoted in Wakelyn, *Southern Pamphlets on Secession*, 403 (second quotation), 410 (third through fifth quotations); George Bagby, "The Manifest Destiny of the World—Its Republic and Its Empire," *Southern Literary Messenger* (September 1859): 207–9; Henry Timrod, "Ethnogenesis," in *The Collected Poems of Henry Timrod*, ed. Edd Winfield Parks and Aileen Wells Parks (Athens: University of Georgia Press, 1965), 95; Hutchison, *Apples and Ashes*, 9; George Mercer diary, March 30, 1861, Mercer Papers, Georgia Historical Society.
43. Timothy Mason Roberts, *Distant Revolutions: 1848 and the Challenge to American Exceptionalism* (Charlottesville: University of Virginia Press, 2009); Andre Fleche, *The Revolution of 1861: The American Civil War in the Age of Nationalist Conflict* (Chapel Hill: University of North Carolina Press, 2012), 4; Don H. Doyle, *The Cause of All Nations: An International History of the American Civil War* (New York: Basic Books, 2015), 7.
44. Abraham J. Heschel, *The Prophets*, Colophon ed., vol. 1 (New York: Harper and Row, 1962), 22; Koselleck, *Futures Past*, 206; William Carey Crane, "The History of Mississippi," *De Bow's Review* 30 (February 1860), 81–90 (quotations on 81–82).
45. Thomas Jefferson, *The Portable Thomas Jefferson*, ed. Merrill D. Peterson (New York: Penguin, 1975), 235.
46. Ruffin, *Anticipations of the Future*, 281; David F. Allmendinger Jr., *Ruffin: Family and Reform in the Old South* (New York: Oxford University Press, 1990), 22; William Grayson, "The Hireling and the Slave," *De Bow's Review* (August 1855): 214–15.
47. Ruffin speech quoted in clipping from Charleston *Courier*, November 7, 1861, Edmund Ruffin Papers, VHS; John Townsend, *The Doom of Slavery in the Union: Its Safety Out of It* (Charleston: Evans and Cogswell, 1860), 4–5, italics in original.
48. Benedict Anderson, *Imagined Communities: Reflections on the Origin and Spread of Nationalism* (London: Verso, 1983); Edward L. Ayers, *What Caused the Civil War? Reflections on the South and Southern History* (New York: W. W. Norton, 2005), 141; Edmund Ruffin, "Fidelity of Slaves to Their Masters," *De Bow's Review* 30 (January 1861): 118–20; Allen, *This Republic in Time*, 6–7.
49. Craven, *Edmund Ruffin*, 191 (first and second quotations), 196 (third quotation); Jack Turner, "Performing Conscience: Thoreau, Political Action, and the Plea for John Brown," *Political Theory* 33, no. 4 (2005): 449; James Darsey, *The Prophetic Tradition and Radical Rhetoric in America* (New York: New York University Press, 1997), xi.
50. Allmendinger, *Ruffin*, 8–13; Jack Temple Kirby, *Poquosin: A Study of Rural Landscape and Society* (Chapel Hill: University of North Carolina Press, 1995), 137; David Allmendinger, ed., *Incidents of My Life: Edmund Ruffin's Autobiographical Essays* (Charlottesville: University Press of Virginia, 1990), 25–26.
51. Craven, *Edmund Ruffin*, 11–13; Allmendinger, *Ruffin*, 16–17.

52. Craven, *Edmund Ruffin*, 26–35; Christine Heyrman, *Southern Cross: The Beginnings of the Bible Belt* (Chapel Hill: University of North Carolina Press, 1998); Charles Irons, *The Origins of Proslavery Christianity: White and Black Evangelicals in Colonial and Antebellum Virginia* (Chapel Hill: University of North Carolina Press, 2008).
53. Quotations in Ruffin, *Anticipations of the Future*, 392–93; Craven, *Edmund Ruffin*, 4; Allmendinger, *Ruffin*, 17.
54. Allmendinger, *Incidents of My Life*, 4–5, 190 (quotation); Thomas Hale, *The Compleat Body of Husbandry: Containing Rules for Performing, in the Most Profitable Manner, the Whole Business of the Farmer and Country Gentleman* (London, 1758–1759); Allmendinger, *Ruffin*, 16–17, 27, 3–7.
55. Craven, *Edmund Ruffin*, 194 (first quotation); Edmund Ruffin, *An Essay on Calcareous Manures*, 5th ed. (Richmond: J. W. Randolph, 1852), 189; Benjamin R. Cohen, *Notes from the Ground: Science, Soil, and Society in the American Countryside* (New Haven, CT: Yale University Press, 2009).
56. Craven, *Edmund Ruffin*, 39.
57. Ruffin quoted in Craven, *Edmund Ruffin*, 178 (first quotation), 194 (second quotation). *Frank Leslie's Weekly* quoted in Craven, *Edmund Ruffin*, 203; Ruffin diary, November 27, 1860, in Scarborough, *The Diary of Edmund Ruffin*, vol. 1, 505.
58. Ruffin diary, November 3, 1860, in Scarborough, *The Diary of Edmund Ruffin*, vol. 1, 482.
59. Edmund Ruffin Jr. to Edmund Ruffin, November 16, 1860 (first through fifth quotations); Edmund Ruffin Jr. to Edmund Ruffin, November 24, 1860 (sixth and seventh quotations), Edmund Ruffin Papers, VHS.
60. Julian Ruffin to Edmund Ruffin November 17, 1860 (first through fourth quotations); Julian Ruffin to Edmund Ruffin December 22, 1860 (fifth through seventh quotations), Edmund Ruffin Papers, VHS.
61. Mildred Ruffin Sayre to Edmund Ruffin, December 4, 1860 (first and second quotations); Mildred Ruffin Sayre to Edmund Ruffin, January 5, 1861 (third quotation), Edmund Ruffin Papers, VHS.
62. Mildred Ruffin Sayre to Edmund Ruffin, January 5, 1861, (first through fourth quotations); Mildred Ruffin Sayre to Edmund Ruffin, January 21, 1861 (fifth through twelfth), Edmund Ruffin Papers, VHS.
63. Ruffin diary, December 14, 1860, in Scarborough, *Diary of Edmund Ruffin*, 509–10 (first and second quotations); Mildred Ruffin Sayre to Edmund Ruffin, February 19, 1861 (third through sixth), Edmund Ruffin Papers, VHS. Focusing on how Ruffin's children opposed his anticipations should not obscure the people at home who fundamentally undermined his prophecy—his slaves. Edmund Jr., Julian, and Mildred forecasted a darker future than their father, but they still favored secession in some form and were proud of him for finally achieving the recognition he sought. Ruffin's slaves projected a very different future for themselves and Ruffin. When the war came, they seized the opportunity and never looked back. Not even Jem Sykes, Ruffin's most trusted bondsman and occasional overseer, would honor the prophet's vision when that time came.
64. Andrew Wallace Johnson to Ruffin, June 25, 1860, Lewis M. Hatch to Ruffin, July 7, 1860, Edmund Ruffin Papers, 1818–65, VHS; John Izard Middleton to Ruffin, July 15, 1860, Edmund Ruffin Papers, 1818–65, VHS. Ruffin requested and received information about

Charleston's defenses after he published *Anticipations of the Future*. He did not request this information for his book's accuracy. Craven, *Edmund Ruffin*, 214–18.

CHAPTER 5

1. John Brown's Pike, original prototype, Object Number 1920.974, Charles F. Gunther Collection, Chicago History Museum; Ted A. Smith, *Weird John Brown: Divine Violence and the Limits of Ethics* (Stanford, CA: Stanford University Press, 2015), 24; Boyd B. Stutler, "Notes on John Brown's Body in New York," Boyd B. Stutler Collection, West Virginia State Archives; John Brown, Pattern Pike, Boston Public Library Rare Books and Manuscripts Department; William E. Cain, ed., *William Lloyd Garrison and the Fight against Slavery: Selections from The Liberator* (Boston: Bedford/St. Martin's, 1995), 158–59; Massachusetts Historical Society, *Proceedings, October 1910–June 1911*, vol. 44 (Boston: Massachusetts Historical Society, 1911), 217–18; James Brewer Stewart, *Wendell Phillips: Liberty's Hero* (Baton Rouge: Louisiana State University Press, 1998), 203; Jason Phillips, "John Brown's Pikes: Assembling the Future in Antebellum America," in *War Matters: Material Culture in the Civil War Era*, ed. Joan Cashin (Chapel Hill: University of North Carolina Press, forthcoming).
2. Wendell Phillips, "Eulogy for John Brown," in *The Tribunal: Responses to John Brown and the Harpers Ferry Raid*, ed. John Stauffer and Zoe Trodd (Cambridge, MA: Harvard University Press, 2012), 175. Phillips's native state, Massachusetts, was hyperconscious of its Revolutionary legacy, and its reformers and citizens appreciated their roles as historical actors in a developing narrative. See Margot Minardi, *Making Slavery History: Abolitionism and the Politics of Memory in Massachusetts* (New York: Oxford University Press, 2010).
3. Wendell Phillips, *Speeches, Lectures, and Letters* (Boston: Lee and Shepard, 1894), 414; Edmund Ruffin, *Anticipations of the Future: To Serve as Lessons for the Present Time* (Richmond: J. W. Randolph, 1860), 281.
4. Phillips, *Speeches, Lectures, and Letters*, 396, 369, 349, 355; James Francis Darsey, *The Prophetic Tradition and Radical Rhetoric in America* (New York: New York University Press, 1997), 72; Jeremiah 34.17, *King James Bible*; Charles Royster, *The Destructive War: William Tecumseh Sherman, Stonewall Jackson, and the Americans* (New York: Alfred A. Knopf, 1991), 262.
5. *New York Times*, April 21, 1861; McKim and Wigham quoted in Caleb McDaniel, *The Problem of Democracy in the Age of Slavery: Garrisonian Abolitionists and Transatlantic Reform* (Baton Rouge: Louisiana State University Press, 2015), 221–22; George M. Fredrickson, *The Inner Civil War: Northern Intellectuals and the Crisis of the Union* (Urbana: University of Illinois Press, 1993), 65–78.
6. William M. Cash and Lucy Somerville Howorth, eds., *My Dear Nellie: The Civil War Letters of William L. Nugent to Eleanor Smith Nugent* (Jackson: University Press of Mississippi, 1977), 45–46; David Huron, *Sweet Anticipation: Music and the Psychology of Expectation* (Cambridge, MA: MIT Press, 2006), 8. Huron writes, "Imagining an outcome allows us to feel some vicarious pleasure (or displeasure)—as though that outcome has already happened." Likewise, Jacques Attali notes that "music is prophecy," because "it makes audible the new world that will gradually become visible, that will impose itself

and regulate the order of things." Attali, *Noise: The Political Economy of Music*, trans. Brian Massumi (Minneapolis: University of Minnesota Press, 1985), 11.

7. David Carr, *Time, Narrative, and History* (Bloomington: Indiana University Press, 1986), 40–41; Michael J. Hove, Céline Marie, Ian C. Bruce, and Laurel J. Trainor, "Superior Time Perception for Lower Musical Pitch Explains Why Bass-Ranged Instruments Lay Down Musical Rhythms," *Proceedings of the National Academy of Sciences of the United States of America* 111 (July 15, 2014), 10383–88.
8. Sophia Rosenfeld, "On Being Heard: A Case for Paying Attention to the Historical Ear," *American Historical Review* 116, no. 2 (April 2011): 316–34; Andrew McCollam Jr. to his father, October 10, 1860, Andrew McCollam Papers, 1792–935, Southern Historical Collection, University of North Carolina-Chapel Hill (UNC-CH).
9. Mark Smith, *The Smell of Battle, the Taste of Siege: A Sensory History of the Civil War* (New York: Oxford University Press, 2014), 18; Abner Doubleday, *Reminiscences of Forts Sumter and Moultrie in 1860-'61* (New York: Harper and Brothers, 1876), 19; David F. Allmendinger, *Ruffin: Family and Reform in the Old South* (Oxford: Oxford University Press, 1990), 172; Russell diary, April 17, 1861, in William Howard Russell, *My Diary North and South*, vol. 1 (London: Bradbury and Evans, 1863), 143–44; George Templeton Strong diary, April 18, 1862, in Allan Nevins and Milton Halsey Thomas, eds., *The Diary of George Templeton Strong*, vol. 3 (New York: Macmillan, 1952), 124.
10. Frank Moore, ed., *The Rebellion Record: A Diary of American Events*, vol. 4 (New York: George P. Putnam, 1862), 29; Franny Nudelman, *John Brown's Body: Slavery, Violence, and the Culture of War* (Chapel Hill: University of North Carolina Press, 2004); Frank Moore, ed., *Lyrics of Loyalty* (New York: George P. Putnam, 1864), 190, 24; Theodore Winthrop, "New York Seventh Regiment," *Atlantic Monthly* 7 (June 1861): 745; Chandler Gillam to his wife, June 2, 1861, Chandler B. Gillam Papers, Library of Congress (LOC).
11. James Ryder Randall, "Maryland, My Maryland," in J. D. McClatchy, ed., *Poets of the Civil War* (New York: Library of America, 2005), 181; Veteran quoted in Christian McWhiter, *Battle Hymns: The Power and Popularity of Music in the Civil War* (Chapel Hill: University of North Carolina Press, 2012), 80; Jesse Walton Reid diary, November 28, 1861, in J. W. Reid, *History of the Fourth Regiment of S. C. Volunteers* (Greenville, SC: Shannon, 1892), 60.
12. Charles F. Herberger, ed., *A Yankee at Arms: The Diary of Lieutenant Augustus D. Ayling, 29th Massachusetts Volunteers* (Knoxville: University of Tennessee Press, 1999), 11; "Interesting Bird's Eye View of the Seat of War," Map, 1861, Virginia Historical Society (VHS); Robert G. Evans, ed., *The 16th Mississippi Infantry: Civil War Letters and Reminiscences* (Jackson: University Press of Mississippi, 2002), 4. Mary Chesnut mocked men who stayed home and claimed to be an authority on the war's developments by calling them "seat-of-war men." See Isabella D. Martin and Myrta L. Avary, eds., *A Diary from Dixie* (New York: D. Appleton, 1905), 424.
13. Timothy J. Orr, ed., *Last to Leave the Field: The Life and Letters of First Sergeant Ambrose Henry Hayward, 28th Pennsylvania Infantry* (Knoxville: University of Tennessee Press, 2010), 9 (first through third quotations), 10 (fourth), 11 (fifth), 12 (sixth), 17 (seventh), 16 (eighth), 34 (ninth).
14. Carpenter quoted in Thomas R. Bright, "Yankees in Arms: The Civil War as a Personal Experience," *Civil War History* 19 (1973): 199 (first, second quotations); Jesse Walton

Reid to his wife, June 8. 1861, in Reid, *History of the Fourth Regiment of South Carolina Volunteers* (Greenville, SC: Shannon, 1892), 9; Frederick D. Williams, ed., *The Wild Life of the Army: Civil War Letters of James A. Garfield* (East Lansing: Michigan State University Press, 1964), 6, 9.

15. Hugh Buckner Johnston, "Josiah Solomon Pender," in *Dictionary of North Carolina Biography*, vol. 5, *P–S*, ed. William S. Powell (Chapel Hill: University of North Carolina Press, 1994), 62–63; Robert J. DriverJr. *5th Virginia Cavalry* (Lynchburg, VA: H. E. Howard, 1997), 241–42.

16. Orlando Poe to Andrew Poe, August 16, 1852, Orlando M. Poe Papers, LOC; Gerald F. Linderman, *Embattled Courage: The Experience of Combat in the American Civil War* (New York: Free Press, 1989), 26; and Phillips, *Speeches, Lectures, and Letters*, 305, 318.

17. Frank Moore, ed., *The Rebellion Record: A Diary of American Events, with Documents, Narratives, Illustrative Incidents, Poetry, Etc.*, vol. 1 (New York: G. P. Putnam, 1861), 324. Charles Royster, *The Destructive War: William Tecumseh Sherman, Stonewall Jackson, and the Americans* (New York: Alfred A. Knopf, 1991), 266.

18. August Kautz, August 2, 1861, Memoir of 1861–1862, August V. Kautz Papers, LOC; McClellan quoted in Stephen W. Sears, *George B. McClellan: The Young Napoleon* (New York: Ticknor and Fields, 1988), 96; Poe to his fiancée, May 1, 1861, May 20, 1861, Orlando M. Poe Papers, LOC.

19. Matthew Harper, "Emancipation and African American Millennialism," in *Apocalypse and the Millennium in the American Civil War Era*, ed. Ben Wright and Zachary W. Dresser (Baton Rouge: Louisiana State University Press, 2013), 155; Leon F. Litwack, *Been in the Storm So Long: The Aftermath of Slavery* (New York: Vintage Books, 1980), xiii. As Litwack argues, "The war and freedom injected into their lives the excitement of anticipation, [and] encouraged a new confidence in their own capabilities."

20. James Oakes, *Freedom National: The Destruction of Slavery in the United States, 1861–1865* (New York: W. W. Norton, 2013), 95.

21. Edward L. Pierce, *Enfranchisement and Citizenship: Addresses and Papers* (Boston: Roberts Brothers, 1896), 24–25; Steven Hahn, *A Nation under Our Feet: Black Political Struggles in the Rural South from Slavery to the Great Migration* (Cambridge, MA: Harvard University Press, 2003), 69–71; Chandra Manning, *Troubled Refuge: Struggling for Freedom in the Civil War* (New York: Knopf, 2016).

22. Harry Jarvis interview in John W. Blassingame, ed., *Slave Testimony: Two Centuries of Letters, Speeches, Interviews, and Autobiographies* (Baton Rouge: Louisiana State University Press, 1977), 607–8.

23. Ibid.

24. Crandall Shifflett, ed., *John Washington's Civil War: A Slave Narrative* (Baton Rouge: Louisiana State University Press, 2008), 45, 48, 49.

25. Ibid., 36–37; Henry Clay Bruce, *The New Man: Twenty-nine Years a Slave. Twenty-nine Years a Free Man* (York, PA: P. Anstadt and Sons, 1895), 100.

26. Harper, "Emancipation and African American Millennialism," 154; Pierce, *Enfranchisement and Citizenship*, 48; Kathryn Gin, "'The Heavenization of Earth': African American Visions and Uses of the Afterlife, 1863–1901," *Slavery & Abolition: A Journal of Slave and Post-Slave Studies* 31, no. 2 (June 2010): 207–31. For more on slaves at Fort Monroe, Ira Berlin et al, eds., *Freedom: A Documentary History of Emancipation, 1861–1867*, ser. 1, vol.

1 (New York: Cambridge University Press, 1985), 61, 71; Benjamin Butler, *Butler's Book* (Boston: A. M. Thayer, 1892), 258–65.

27. C. W. D., "Contraband Singing," *Dwight's Journal of Music*, September 7, 1861, Boston, 182; Lockwood quoted in Samuel Charters, *Songs of Sorrow: Lucy McKim Garrison and Slave Songs of the United States* (Jackson: University Press of Mississippi, 2015), 76.
28. Pierce, *Enfranchisement and Citizenship*, 35, 51, 29.
29. J. Miller McKim, *The Freedmen of South Carolina: Address Delivered by J. Miller McKim in Sansom Hall, July 9, 1862* (Philadelphia, 1862), 11–13.
30. Thomas Wentworth Higginson, *Army Life in a Black Regiment* (Boston: Fields, Osgood, 1870), 202, 205, 59, 41.
31. William Francis Allen, Charles Pickard Ware, and Lucy McKim Garrison, *Slave Songs of the United States* (New York: A. Simpson, 1867); McKim, *Freedmen of South Carolina*, 14; *Dwight's Journal of Music* (Boston), September 7, 1861; Frederick Douglass, *Narrative of the Life of Frederick Douglass, an American Slave* (Dublin: Webb and Chapman, 1846), 103.
32. Reid Mitchell, "Soldiering, Manhood, and Coming of Age: A Northern Volunteer," in Catherine Clinton and Nina Silber, eds., *Divided Houses: Gender and the Civil War* (New York: Oxford University Press, 1992), 43–54; Stephen Ash, *The Black Experience in the Civil War South* (Santa Barbara, CA: Praeger, 2010); Stephanie Camp, *Closer to Freedom: Enslaved Women and Everyday Resistance in the Plantation South* (Chapel Hill: University of North Carolina Press, 2004); Earl J. Hess, *The Union Soldier in Battle: Enduring the Ordeal of Combat* (Lawrence: University Press of Kansas, 1997), 2; Pierce, *Enfranchisement and Citizenship*, 46.
33. Eugene D. Genovese, *Roll, Jordan, Roll: The World the Slaves Made* (New York: Vintage, 1976), 97; Yael A. Sternhell, *Routes of War: The World of Movement in the Confederate South* (Cambridge, MA: Harvard University Press, 2012), 93; Edward L. Ayers and Scott Nesbit, "Seeing Emancipation: Scale and Freedom in the American South," *Journal of the Civil War Era* 1 (March 2011): 9.
34. Laura Winthrop Johnson, ed., *The Life and Poems of Theodore Winthrop* (New York: Henry Holt, 1884), 70; Adam Goodheart, *1861: The Civil War Awakening* (New York: Alfred A. Knopf, 2011), 331–32; Randall Fuller, *From Battlefields Rising: How the Civil War Transformed American Literature* (New York: Oxford University Press, 2011), 25–27.
35. Theodore Winthrop, *Cecil Dreeme* (New York: Dodd, Mead, 1861), 13. Townsend quoted in William C. Davis introduction to Spencer C. Tucker, ed., *American Civil War: The Definitive Encyclopedia and Document Collection*, vol. 1, *A–C* (Santa Barbara, CA: ABC Clio, 2013), lv.
36. Theodore Winthrop, "New York Seventh Regiment," *Atlantic Monthly* 7 (June 1861): 745–47.
37. Theodore Winthrop, "Washington as a Camp," *Atlantic Monthly* 8 (July 1861): 106–14; Orlando Poe to his fiancée, May 13, 1861, Orlando M. Poe Papers, LOC.
38. Winthrop, "New York Seventh Regiment," 753; Winthrop, *Cecil Dreeme*, 14, 16; Winthrop, "Washington as a Camp," 118, 110. George William Curtis published Winthrop's private correspondence with him after Winthrop's death as part of a biographical introduction to *Cecil Dreeme*.

39. "Proclamation Calling Militia and Convening Congress, April 15, 1861," in Roy P. Basler, ed., *Collected Works of Abraham Lincoln*, IV (New Brunswick, NJ: Rutgers University Press, 1953), 332, 375, 431–32; Douglas quoted in David Herbert Donald, *Lincoln* (New York: Simon and Schuster, 1995), 296.
40. Basler, *Collected Works of Abraham Lincoln*, 4: 375, 431–32.
41. Winthrop, *Life and Poems*, 289.
42. Ibid., 291; Goodheart, *1861*, 332–33, 336–37.
43. Theodore Winthrop, "Notes of Plan of Attack," Benjamin Butler Papers, LOC.
44. Pierce, *Enfranchisement and Citizenship*, 25; *The War of the Rebellion: A Compilation of the Official Records of the Union and Confederate Armies*, series I, vol. 2 (Washington: Government Printing Office, 1880), 84, 95–96, hereinafter OR.
45. Winthrop, *Life and Poems*, 70.
46. Frank Moore, ed., *Lyrics of Loyalty* (New York: Putnam, 1864), 85; *New York Tribune* quoted in Winthrop, *Life and Poems*, 292.
47. D. H. Hill to Benjamin Butler, July 5, 1861, Benjamin Butler Papers, LOC; Daniel Harvey Hill, *A Consideration of the Sermon on the Mount* (Philadelphia: William S. & Alfred Martien, 1858), 181 (second and third quotations).
48. Robert Bonner, *The Soldier's Pen: Firsthand Impressions of the Civil War* (New York: Hill and Wang, 2006), 46–47.
49. Frank Moore, ed., *The Rebellion Record: A Diary of American Events*, vol. 2 (New York: G. P. Putnam, 1864), 179; Joseph Jacobs and John D. Batten, eds., *English Fairy Tales* (New York: Dover, 1967), 149–50.
50. Oakes, *Freedom National*, 141.
51. Margaret Williams to James Pegram, September 2, 1863, Pegram Family Papers, 1737–954, VHS; Ednah Cheney, *Louisa May Alcott: Her Life, Letters, and Journals* (Boston, 1890), 127, 132; Sarah Morgan Dawson, *A Confederate Girl's Diary* (Boston, 1913), 138–39, 411; Alcott, *Hospital Sketches: An Army Nurse's True Account of Her Experiences during the Civil War* (Boston: J. Redpath, 1863), 90; Drew Gilpin Faust, *Mothers of Invention: Women of the Slaveholding South in the American Civil War* (Chapel Hill: University of North Carolina Press, 1996), 20–21.
52. Sarah Hopper Emerson, ed., *Life of Abby Hopper Gibbons: Told Chiefly through Her Correspondence*, vol. 1 (New York: Putnam's Sons, 1897), 261; Margaret Hope Bacon, *Abby Hopper Gibbons: Prison Reformer and Social Activist* (New York: State University of New York Press, 2000), 82–83.
53. Emerson, *Life of Abby Hopper Gibbons*, 261, 294, 300, 304.
54. Lizzie Gaillard to Mary Ward, January 16, 1861 (first through sixth quotations), Ward Family Papers, LOC; Lizzie Gaillard to Mary Ward, March 11, 1861 (seventh and eighth), Ward Family Papers, LOC.
55. Caroline Kean Hill Davis diary, VHS, April 27, 1861 (first and second quotations), April 30, 1861 (third).
56. Ibid., May 10, 1861 (first through third quotations), June 14, 1861 (fourth through seventh),
57. Daniel Delaney Addison, ed., *Lucy Larcom: Life, Letters, and Diary* (Boston: Houghton, Mifflin, 1894), 89–90, 101, 108.

58. Carrie Esther Spencer and Kathleen Boone Samuels, eds., *A Civil War Marriage in Virginia: Reminiscences and Letters* (Boyce, VA: Carr, 1956), 78, 81–82 (quotations).
59. Stephen W. Berry II, *All that Makes a Man: Love and Ambition in the Civil War South* (New York: Oxford University Press, 2003), 172; Spencer and Samuels, eds., *A Civil War Marriage*, 83; Reid Mitchell, *The Vacant Chair: The Northern Soldier Leaves Home* (New York: Oxford University Press, 1993), 11; Stephanie McCurry, *Confederate Reckoning: Power and Politics in the Civil War South* (Cambridge, MA: Harvard University Press, 2010), 24–25; Aaron Sheehan-Dean, *Why Confederates Fought: Family and Nation in Civil War Virginia* (Chapel Hill: University of North Carolina Press, 2007), 193.
60. Spencer and Samuels, eds., *A Civil War Marriage*, 86, 81, 82–83; McCurry, *Confederate Reckoning*, 82.
61. Randall Allen and Keith S. Bohannon eds., *Campaigning with "Old Stonewall": Confederate Captain Ujanirtus Allen's Letters to His Wife* (Baton Rouge: Louisiana State University Press, 1998), 7 (first and second quotations), 8 (third through ninth).
62. Ibid.
63. Peter H. Clark, *The Black Brigade of Cincinnati: Being a Report of Its Labors and a Muster-Roll of Its Members; Together with Various Orders, Speeches, etc., Relating to It* (Cincinnati: J. B. Boyd, 1864), 5.
64. Ibid., 6.
65. Ibid., 14.
66. Ibid., 11
67. Quotations in James M. McPherson, *The Negro's Civil War: How American Negroes Felt and Acted during the War for the Union* (New York: Pantheon Books, 1965), 20, 21; Horace Greeley, *The American Conflict,* vol. 2 (Hartford: O.D. Case, 1866), 514–15; David R. Roediger, *The Wages of Whiteness: Race and the Making of the American Working Class* (London: Verso, 2007).
68. Jacob Dodson to Simon Cameron, April 23, 1861, Simon Cameron to Jacob Dodson, April 29, 1861, OR, ser. 3, vol. 1, 107, 133; Andrew Rolle, *John Charles Frémont: Character as Destiny* (Norman: University of Oklahoma Press, 1991), 762.
69. McPherson, *The Negro's Civil War*, 3 (first quotation), 11–14 (second through fifth).
70. Ibid., 31 (first quotation), 32 (second and third), 35 (fourth and fifth), 30 (sixth and seventh).
71. Ibid., 32–33.
72. Ibid., 17–18.
73. Henry W. Halleck to D. C. Buell, February 13, 1862, OR, series 1, vol. 7, 609; T. Harry Williams, *Lincoln and His Generals* (New York: Alfred A. Knopf, 1952), 3–14.
74. Winfield Scott to William Seward, March 3, 1861, Winfield Scott and James Buchanan, *The Private Letters of Lieut.-General Scott, and ex-President Buchanan's Reply* (New York: Hamilton, Johnson and Farrelly, 1862), 24, American Civil War Letters and Diaries.
75. OR, series 1, vol. 51, 369.
76. Ibid., 370; *New Hampshire Patriot and State Gazette*, May 1, 1861; *Macon Daily Telegraph*, May 4, 1861, quoting from the Philadelphia *American and Gazette*.
77. Russell Frank Weigley, *The American Way of War: A History of the United States Military Strategy and Policy* (New York: Macmillan, 1973), 76 (quotation), 93.

78. George McClellan to Winfield Scott, April 27, 1861, OR, series 1, vol. 51, part 1, 338.
79. Williams, *Lincoln and His Generals*, 26–27; George B. McClellan, *The Armies of Europe* (Philadelphia: J. B. Lippincott, 1861), 13; Matthew Moten, *The Delafield Commission and the American Military Profession* (College Station: Texas A&M University Press, 2000), 207.
80. McClellan, *The Armies of Europe*, 6; *The North American Review* 94 (January 1861): 271.
81. Winfield Scott to Abraham Lincoln, May 2, 1861, OR, series 1, vol. 51, part 1, 339.
82. Ibid., 370.
83. Weigley, *American Way of War*, 96–97.
84. *Richmond Examiner* quoted in James McPherson, *Battle Cry of Freedom: The Civil War Era* (New York: Oxford University Press, 1989), 337; Charles Royster, *The Destructive War: William Tecumseh Sherman, Stonewall Jackson, and the Americans* (New York: Knopf, 1991).
85. OR, series 1, vol. 28, part. 3, 868 (first quotation); OR, series 1, vol. 29, part. 2, 819; Emory M. Thomas, *Robert E. Lee: A Biography* (New York: W. W. Norton, 1995), 197; Royster, *The Destructive War*, 40.
86. William C. Davis, *Battle at Bull Run: A History of the First Major Campaign of the Civil War* (Garden City, NY: Doubleday, 1977); Ethan Sepp Rafuse, *A Single Grand Victory: The First Campaign and Battle of Manassas* (Wilmington, DE: SR Books, 2002).
87. Avery Craven, *Edmund Ruffin, Southerner: A Study of Secession* (New York: Appleton, 1932).
88. Edmund Ruffin diary, July 23, 1861, William Kauffman Scarborough, ed., *The Diary of Edmund Ruffin*, vol. 2, *The Years of Hope, April, 1861–June, 1863* (Baton Rouge: Louisiana State University Press, 1976), 80, 82; Craven, *Edmund Ruffin*, 232; Edmund Ruffin, *Anticipations of the Future: To Serve as Lessons for the Present Time* (Richmond: J. W. Randolph, 1860), 302.
89. "Speech Bartow gave to the people of Chatham County, delivered at Masonic hall in Savannah, Monday evening Sept. 17 1860," *Savannah Morning News*, September 27, 1860, clipping in Francis Bartow to James M. Green, December 8, 1860, Bartow's wife to his mother, July 22, 1861, all in Francis Stebbins Bartow Papers, Georgia Historical Society.

CHAPTER 6

1. Henry David Thoreau, "A Plea for Captain John Brown," in *The Tribunal: Reponses to John Brown and the Harpers Ferry Raid*, ed. John Stauffer and Zoe Trodd (Cambridge, MA: Harvard University Press, 2012), 108; Henry David Thoreau to H. G. O. Blake, October 31, 1859, ed. Walter Harding and Carl Bode (New York: New York University Press, 1958), 563; James Redpath to Thoreau, February 6, 1860, in *The Correspondence of Henry David Thoreau*, 574; Jason Phillips, "John Brown's Pikes: Assembling the Future in Antebellum America," in *War Matters: Material Culture in the Civil War Era*, ed. Joan Cashin (Chapel Hill: University of North Carolina Press, forthcoming). According to multiple sources, Brown's family gave Thoreau "a huge knife that had belonged to Brown" in 1859. Brown may have tried to give Thoreau the knife himself during his last visit to Concord in August 1859. He wrote John Kagi that he called on a "friend at Concord" but "he was absent from home." Brown said, "The others here," meaning his family in

New York, will "communicate with him." See John Brown to Kagi, August 17, 1859, in H. W. Flournoy, ed., *Calendar of Virginia State papers and Other Manuscripts from January 1, 1836 to April 15, 1869*, vol. 11 (Richmond: James E. Goode, 1893), 325. Brown had a habit of appearing unannounced. I haven't verified that it was Pate's knife; however, Thoreau did admire Pate's knife when he first met Brown in 1857. See Walter Harding, *The Days of Henry Thoreau* (New York: Knopf, 1970), 423; Larry J. Reynolds, "The Cimeter's 'Sweet' Edge: Thoreau, Contemplation, and Violence," in *More Day to Dawn: Thoreau's Walden for the Twenty-First Century*, ed. Sandra Harbert Petrulionis and Laura Dassow Walls (Amherst: University of Massachusetts Press, 2007), 65; and Janet Kemper Beck, *Creating the John Brown Legend: Emerson, Thoreau, Douglass, Child and Higginson in Defense of the Raid on Harpers Ferry* (Jefferson, NC: McFarland, 2009), 163.

2. Henry Clay Pate, *John Brown, as viewed by H. Clay Pate* (New York: The author, 1859), 38; Stephen B. Oates, *To Purge This Land with Blood: A Biography of John Brown* (Amherst: University of Massachusetts Press, 1984), 168–69.
3. David S. Reynolds, *John Brown, Abolitionist: The Man Who Killed Slavery, Sparked the Civil War, and Seeded Civil Rights* (New York: Vintage Books, 2005), 222; Henry David Thoreau to Parker Pillsbury, April 10, 1861, in *The Correspondence of Henry David Thoreau*, 611; Randall Fuller, *From Battlefields Rising: How the Civil War Transformed American Literature* (New York: Oxford University Press, 2010), 34.
4. Robert J. Driver Jr., *5th Virginia Cavalry* (Lynchburg, VA: H. E. Howard, 1997), 76.
5. Ibid., 76–77.
6. Ibid., 77; OR, series 1, vol. 36, part 1, 818.
7. Douglas Southall Freeman, *Lee's Lieutenants*, vol. 3, *Gettysburg to Appomattox* (New York: Charles Scribner's Sons, 1944), 426; Andrew Reid Venable Letter, 1888, Virginia Historical Society.
8. Ruffin diary, May 16, 1864, in *The Diary of Edmund Ruffin*, vol. 3, *A Dream Shattered, June 1863–June 1865*, ed. William Kauffman Scarborough (Baton Rouge: Louisiana State University Press, 1989), 425.
9. Ibid., 426, 428; David F. Allmendinger, *Ruffin: Family and Reform in the Old South* (New York: Oxford University Press, 1990), 270.
10. Louis Menand, *The Metaphysical Club: A Story of Ideas in American* (New York: Farrar, Straus and Giroux, 2001); Mark A. Noll; *The Civil War as a Theological Crisis* (Chapel Hill: University of North Carolina Press, 2006); Drew Gilpin Faust, *This Republic of Suffering: Death and the American Civil War* (New York: Alfred A. Knopf, 2008).
11. Andrew McCollam Jr. to Andrew McCollam Sr., April 18, 1861, Andrew McCollam Papers, 1792–935, Southern Historical Collection, University of North Carolina-Chapel Hill (UNC-CH) ; diary entry, October 29, 1860, Grace Brown Elmore Papers, 1861–72, SHC UNC-CH .
12. Chandler Gillam to his wife, July 24, 1861, Chandler B. Gillam Papers, Library of Congress (LOC); D. Holmes Conrad to William Welsh, July 25, 1861, Holmes Conrad Papers, Virginia Historical Society (VHS).
13. William Wilkins to his wife, undated letter, William D. Wilkins Papers, LOC.
14. Francis Adams Donaldson to Jacob Donaldson, October 15, 1861, in *Inside the Army of the Potomac: The Civil War Experience of Captain Francis Adams Donaldson*, ed. J. Gregory Acken (Mechanicsburg, PA: Stackpole Books, 1998), 23–24.

15. Cyrus Boyd diary, April 6, 1862, in *The Civil War Diary of C. F. Boyd*, ed. Mildred Throne (Iowa City: State Historical Society of Iowa, 1953), 38; William Wilkins to his wife, May 14, 1862, William D. Wilkins Papers, LOC; Sarah Ann Caperton Preston to Harriet Alexander Caperton, December 10, 1861, Caperton Family Papers, 1729–973, VHS. Polish psychiatrist Eugène Minkowski understood how expectations consumed Civil War Americans because he experienced a similar sensation during World War I. In 1918 he wrote an essay titled "How We Live the Future (and Not What We Know of It)." "During the war," Minkowski recalled, "we were waiting for peace hoping to take up again the life that we had abandoned." Minkowski experienced similar moments of watching in frozen fear while fate loomed on the Western Front. He tried to explain wartime expectation to readers who had no experience with it. Expectation "contains a factor of brutal arrest and renders the individual breathless." The future "swoops down on him in a powerful and hostile mass, attempting to annihilate him." "The image of death, suspended in all its destructive power above us and approaching with giant steps, surges in us." "Powerless, we await the fatal annihilation close at hand, to which we are condemned without mercy." Warfare convinced Minkowski that people lived time primarily by focusing on the future instead of concentrating on the fleeting present or recalling a vanished past. In 1933, he developed this idea in his masterpiece *Lived Time*, by dividing human orientations to the future into two major categories, "activity," or anticipations of moving into the future and controlling it, and "expectations," a dreadful sense that an inevitable future rushes toward us. "In activity, we tend toward the future," he explained. "In expectation, on the contrary, we live time in an inverse sense; we see the future come toward us and wait for that (expected) future to become present." Minkowski quoted in Roxanne Panchasi, *Future Tense: The Culture of Anticipation in France between the Wars* (Ithaca, NY: Cornell University Press, 2009), 2; Eugène Minkowski, *Lived Time: Phenomenological and Psychopathological Studies*, trans. Nancy Metsel (Evanston, IL: Northwestern University Press, 1970), 87–88.
16. John Nicolay to Therena Bates, January 13, 1861, John G. Nicolay Papers, LOC; George Strong diary, April 18, 1861, in *The Diary of George Templeton Strong*, vol. 3, ed. Allan Nevins and Milton Halsey Thomas (New York: Macmillan, 1952), 123.
17. Robert W. Johannsen, *Stephen A. Douglas* (Urbana: University of Illinois Press, 1997). Because citizens proposed solutions to the sectional crisis in these letters, it could be argued that they anticipated future developments and believed they could forge a peaceful path. Nonetheless, I read this correspondence as more expectant than anticipatory because of the desperation that citizens expressed and their plea for help from powerful men.
18. "Alabama" to Stephen A. Douglas, January 3, 1861, Stephen A. Douglas Papers, Series 1, Box 33, Folder 24, Regenstein Library, University of Chicago (hereinafter UC).
19. William S. Cunningham to Stephen A. Douglas, March 17, 1861, Stephen A. Douglas Papers, Series 1, Box 36, Folder 17, UC.
20. Thomas Gibson Sr. to Stephen A. Douglas, January 1861 [no day given], Stephen A. Douglas Papers, Series 1, Box 33, Folder 24, UC.
21. A. G. Dickenoff to Stephen A. Douglas, March 15, 1861, Stephen A. Douglas Papers, Series 1, Box 36, Folder 16, UC.
22. "A Friend" to Stephen A. Douglas, January 1, 1861, Stephen A. Douglas Papers, Series 1, Box 33, Folder 24, UC.

23. J. L. Napier to Stephen A. Douglas, January 3, 1861, Stephen A. Douglas Papers, Series 1, Box 33, Folder 24, UC.
24. William M. Morton to Stephen A. Douglas, March 21, 1861, Stephen A. Douglas Papers, Series 1, Box 36, Folder 22, UC.
25. "Alabama" to Stephen A. Douglas, January 3, 1861, Stephen A. Douglas Papers, Series 1, Box 33, Folder 24, UC.
26. W. G. Fullerton to John Crittenden, December 14, 1860, "A genuine Republican" to Crittenden, December 21, 1860, C. B. Haddock to Crittenden, December 15, 1860, all in John Crittenden Papers, LOC.
27. James Robb to Crittenden, December 3, 1860, Thomas Hicks to Crittenden, December 13, 1860, N. P Tallmadge to Crittenden, December 17, 1860, all in John Crittenden Papers, LOC.
28. James F. Robb to John Crittenden, December 3, 1860, John Crittenden Papers, LOC; Michael E. Woods, *Emotional and Sectional Conflict in the Antebellum United States* (New York: Cambridge University Press, 2014). Minkowski argued that prayers illustrate expectations because they seek intercession in an "unreachable future." People who pray confess they are not the masters of their futures. Because not even God can change the past, "prayer is turned essentially toward the future." Even pleas to pardon past acts seek future redemption. See Minkowski, *Lived Time*, 82, 105.
29. Morse to George L. Douglas, January 12, 1861 (first quotation), Morse to Robert Baird, July 16, 1860 (second), Morse to George L. Douglas, December 29, 1860 (third through fifth); Morse to Hamilton Washington, May 10, 1861 (sixth), all in Samuel F. B. Morse Papers, 1793–919, LOC.
30. Morse to Dear Sir, February 11, 1861, Samuel F. B. Morse Papers, 1793–919, LOC; Jon L. Wakelyn, ed., *Southern Pamphlets on Secession, November 1860–April 1861* (Chapel Hill: University of North Carolina Press, 1996), 160–61.
31. Morse to Hamilton Washington, May 10, 1861, Morse Papers, LOC; "B" [Samuel Morse], *The Present Attempt to Dissolve the American Union, A British Aristocratic Plot* (New York: John F. Trow, 1862), 21; Kenneth Silverman, *Lightning Man: The Accursed Life of Samuel F. B. Morse* (New York: Da Capo, 2003), 393.
32. Journal entry, October 4, 1861, David Hunter Strother, Journal 10, Manuscript Box 2, David Hunter Strother Papers, West Virginia and Regional History Collection (WVRHC), West Virginia University (WVU).
33. David Hunter Strother, "Personal Recollections of the War, by a Virginian, First Paper" *Harper's New Monthly Magazine* 33 (June 1867): 14.
34. Journal entry, July 17, 1861, David Hunter Strother, Journal 9, Manuscript Box 2, Strother Papers, WVRHC, WVU.
35. Journal entry, September 7, 1861, David Hunter Strother, Journal 9, Manuscript Box 2, Strother Papers, WVRHC, WVU; Cecil D. Eby Jr., "*Porte Crayon*": *The Life of David Hunter Strother* (Chapel Hill: University of North Carolina Press, 1960), 113–18; William Wilkins to his wife, January 18, 1862, William D. Wilkins Papers, LOC.
36. Ray Allen Billington, ed., *The Journal of Charlotte Forten: A Young Black Woman's Reactions to the White World of the Civil War Era* (New York: W. W. Norton, 1981), 163.
37. Diary entry, October 28, 1860, Grace Brown Elmore Papers, 1861–72, SHC UNC-CH; Carrie Fries to John F. Shaffner, [no date] June 1861, John F. Shaffner Diary and

Papers, North Carolina Department of Archives and History; Journal entry, May 26, 1861, John Q. Anderson, ed., *Brokenburn: The Journal of Kate Stone, 1861–1868* (Baton Rouge: Louisiana State University Press, 1972), 17.

38. Fanny Broderick to Mary Collins, April 25, 1861, Lizzie Collins to Mary Collins, June 3, 1861, both in Collins Family Letters, 1808–1895, 1837–1879 (bulk dates), Special Collections, University of Kentucky; Daniel Delaney Addison, ed., *Lucy Larcom: Life, Letters, and Diary* (Boston: Houghton, Mifflin, 1894), 295.
39. Diary entry, April 18, 1861, John N. Fain, ed., *Sanctified Trial: The Diary of Eliza Rhea Anderson Fain, a Confederate Woman in East Tennessee* (Knoxville: University of Tennessee Press, 2004), 7; Sally G. McMillen, *Motherhood in the Old South: Pregnancy, Childbirth, and Infant Rearing* (Baton Rouge: Louisiana State University Press, 1990); Joan Cashin, ed., *Our Common Affairs: Texts from Women in the Old South* (Baltimore: Johns Hopkins University Press, 1996).
40. Lucy Blair to Ellen McCollam, August 3, 1861, Andrew McCollam Papers, 1792–935, SHC, UNC-CH; Yael Sternhell, *Routes of War: The World of Movement in the Confederate South* (Cambridge, MA: Harvard University Press, 2012), 146.
41. Fain diary entries, July 23, 1861, April 5, 1865, April 24, 1865 in Fain, ed., *Sanctified Trial,* 22–23 (first and second quotations), 309 (third), 322 (fourth and fifth).
42. Fain diary entries, April 1, 1865, February 17, 1865, March 4, 1865, in Fain, ed., *Sanctified Trial,* 308, 299 (second and third quotations); Helen to Anna Mercur, July 15, 1861, Anna Mercur Papers, 1860–930, SHC, UNC-CH.
43. J. M. Crowell to Harriet Beecher Stowe, July 11, 1863, in *Life and Letters of Harriet Beecher Stowe,* ed. Anne Fields (Boston: Houghton, Mifflin, 1897), 272.
44. Harriet Beecher Stowe, "The Chimney Corner, I," *Atlantic Monthly* (January 1865): 111.
45. Stowe quoted in "Days with Mrs. Stowe," *Atlantic Monthly* (August 1896): 149;Annie Fields, ed., *The Life and Letters of Harriet Beecher Stowe* (New York: Houghton Mifflin, 1897); Patricia R. Hill, "Writing Out the War: Harriet Beecher Stowe's Averted Gaze," in *Divided Houses: Gender and the Civil War,* ed. Catherine Clinton and Nina Silber (New York: Oxford University Press, 1992).
46. Beth Maclay Doriani, *Emily Dickinson, Daughter of Prophecy* (Amherst: University of Massachusetts Press, 1996); Christian McWhirter, *Battle Hymns: The Power and Popularity of Music in the Civil War* (Chapel Hill: University of North Carolina Press, 2012), 42.
47. David Homer Bates, *Lincoln in the Telegraph Office: Recollections of the United States Military Telegraph Corps during the Civil War* (New York: Century, 1907), 12.
48. Ibid., 29.
49. Ibid., 124–31.
50. Ibid., 49–53 (quotation on 50).
51. Oliver Wendell Holmes, *The Writings of Oliver Wendell Holmes,* vol. 8 (Boston: Houghton Mifflin, 1891), 16.
52. James Garfield to Harry, April 13, 1861, in *The Wild Life of the Army: Civil War Letters of James A. Garfield,* ed. Frederick D. Williams (East Lansing: Michigan State University Press, 1964), 5.
53. Christanne Miller, *Emily Dickinson: A Poet's Grammar* (Cambridge, MA: Harvard University Press, 1987), 58.

54. Doris Kearns Goodwin, *Team of Rivals: The Political Genius of Abraham Lincoln* (New York: Simon and Schuster, 2005), 557 (first quotation); Bates, *Lincoln in the Telegraph Office,* 121 (second quotation), 139 (third and fourth quotations).
55. Abraham Lincoln to Albert Hodges, April 4, 1864, in Philip Van Doren Stern, ed., *The Life and Writings of Abraham Lincoln*, ed. Philip Van Doren Stern (New York: Modern Library, 1940), 809 (first through third quotations); Allen Guelzo, "Abraham Lincoln and the Doctrine of Necessity," *Journal of the Abraham Lincoln Association* 18, no. 1 (Winter 1997): 57–81 (quotation on 79); J. G. Randall, *Lincoln the President: Springfield to Gettysburg* (New York: Dodd, Mead, 1945); Carl Sandburg, *Abraham Lincoln: The War Years* (New York: Harcourt, Brace, 1940); Stephen B. Oates, *With Malice toward None* (New York: Harper and Row, 1977).
56. Abraham Lincoln, "Second Inaugural Address," Lincoln to Thurlow Weed, March 15, 1865, both in *Life and Writings of Abraham Lincoln*, 841–42, 843.
57. Emily Dickinson, "Suspense—is Hostiler Than Death," #705, http://www.edickinson.org/editions/1/image_sets/236093, accessed April 3, 2016. For the relationship between poetry, trauma, and time, see Gregory Orr, *Poetry as Survival* (Athens: University of Georgia Press, 2002).
58. Emily Dickinson, "My Triumph lasted till the Drums," #1227, in *The Complete Poems of Emily Dickinson*, ed. Thomas E. Johnson (Boston: Little, Brown, 1960); Walt Whitman, "Beat! Beat! Drums!," "Song of the Banner at Daybreak" (last quotation), *Leaves of Grass* (Philadelphia: David McKay, 1883), 222–23.
59. Whitman, "The Wound-Dresser," *Leaves of Grass*, 241; Dickinson, "I dwell in Possibility," #466 http://www.edickinson.org/editions/1/image_sets/235739, accessed April 3, 2016.
60. Jerry Silverman, *Ballads and Songs of the Civil War* (Pacific, MO: Mel Bay, 1993), 126–27; "Weeping, Sad and Lonely" or "When This Cruel War Is Over," lyrics by Charles Carroll Sawyer, music composed and arranged by Henry Tucker (Brooklyn: Sawyer and Thompson, 1863).
61. Dickinson, "Whole Gulfs—of Red, and Fleets—of Red –" #658, *The Complete Poems of Emily Dickinson*. Other Dickinson poems that compare war to a storm or sunset include #152, #1140, #1471, and #1593.
62. Dickinson, "The Future – Never Spoke," #672, *The Complete Poems of Emily Dickinson*; Jerusha Hull McCormack, "Domesticating Delphi: Emily Dickinson and the Electro-Magnetic Telegraph," *American Quarterly* 55 (December 2003): 569–601.
63. Dickinson, "The Brain – is wider than the Sky," #598, *The Complete Poems of Emily Dickinson*; Edward Hitchcock, *The Religion of Geology and Its Connected Sciences* (Boston: Phillips, Sampson, 1857); Dickinson to Thomas Higginson, 1868, *The Letters of Emily Dickinson, 1845–1886*, ed, Mabel Loomis Todd (Boston: Little, Brown, 1906), 313.
64. McCormack, "Domesticating Delphi," 592; "Battle Hymns," 48.
65. Randall Allen and Keith S. Bohannon, eds., *Campaigning with "Old Stonewall": Confederate Captain Ujanirtus Allen's Letters to His Wife* (Baton Rouge: Louisiana State University Press, 1998), 29.
66. Ibid., 12, 13–14.
67. Ibid., 13, 14, 17–18, 39.
68. Ibid., 18, 19, 32, 33, 39.

69. John Hilton to Mary Hilton, September 16, 1862, John Hilton Papers, 1828–903, Special Collections, Virginia Tech.
70. John Hilton to Mary Hilton, October 2, 1862 (first and second quotations), September 16, 1862 (third), Hilton Papers, Virginia Tech.
71. Jane Hilton to John Hilton, October 8, 1862, Hilton Papers, Virginia Tech.
72. John Hilton to Mary Hilton, December 22, 1862, Hilton Papers, Virginia Tech.
73. Discharge Order, January 18, 1863, obituary, both in Hilton Papers, Virginia Tech.
74. February 4, 1861, Aquila Johnson Peyton diary, 1859–1861, VHS.
75. February 23, 1861 (first quotation), February 9, 1859 (second); February 11, 1859 (third), ibid.
76. January 9, 1861 (quotations), January 19, 1861, ibid.
77. April 30, 1861, ibid.
78. May 1, 1861 (first quotation), May 29, 1861 (second through fourth), May 31, 1861 (fifth through eighth), ibid.
79. April 30, 1861 (first quotation), May 31, 1861, June 8, 1861 (second through fourth), June 9, 1861, July 22, 1861, ibid.
80. June 8, 1861 (first quotation), July 17, 1861 (second through fifth), ibid.
81. July 30, 1861, ibid. It appears that Peyton joined Company D, Mount Pleasant Rifles, of 30th Virginia Infantry on August 14, 1861. See Robert Krick, *30th Virginia Infantry* (Lynchburg, VA: H. E. Howard, 1991), 106. His brother was in Company C, Gordon's Rifles, of the 30th Infantry. Peyton says at the end of the diary that he joined Captain Braxton's company, which became Company I of the 30th, but most of its men were coming from Stafford County, not Spotsylvania.
82. Van Alstyne diary, August 19, 1862, in Lawrence Van Alstyne, *Diary of an Enlisted Man* (New Haven: Tuttle, Morehouse, and Taylor, 1910), 1.
83. Van Alstyne diary, August 19, 1862, September 4, 1862, ibid., 2 (first quotation), 15 (second and third).
84. Van Alstyne diary, August 19, 1862, ibid., v (first quotation), 2 (second through fourth).
85. Helen Cross Knight, *Robert Dawson; or, The Brave Spirit* (London: Religious Tract Society, 1847), 16–17; Van Alstyne diary, August 19, 1862, Van Alstyne, *Diary of an Enlisted Man*, 2.
86. Van Alstyne diary, December 16, 1863, ibid., 244.
87. Van Alstyne diary, January 4, 1864, ibid., 256.
88. Van Alstyne diary, January 11, 1864, ibid., 260–61. For more on men who did not succumb to the spirit of 1861 and rush to enlist, see Kenneth W. Noe, *Reluctant Rebels: The Confederates Who Joined the Army after 1861* (Chapel Hill: University of North Carolina Press, 2010).
89. Doriani, *Emily Dickinson, Daughter of Prophecy*, 85; Jonathan W. White, *Midnight in America: Darkness, Sleep, and Dreams during the Civil War* (Chapel Hill: University of North Carolina Press, 2017).
90. Jones diary, June 28, 1861, John B. Jones, *A Rebel War Clerk's Diary at the Confederate States Capital*, vol. 1 (Philadelphia: J. P. Lippincott, 1866), 56.
91. Jones diary, April 12, April 15, April 22, June 25, 1861, ibid., 18 (first through fifth quotations), 19, 26 (sixth and seventh), 55 (eighth).

92. Jones diary, May 2, 1863, ibid., 305.
93. Van Alstyne diary, December 29, 1863, Van Alstyne, *Diary of an Enlisted Man*, 251–52; Sallie Lovett to William Lovett, May 24, 1862, William Lovett papers, 1859–64, MS 503, Georgia Historical Society.
94. November 30, 1863 (first through third quotations), March 29, 1864 (fourth and fifth), Virginia Hammett diary, VHS.
95. March 29, 1864, February 5, 1865, ibid.
96. March 29, 1864, ibid.
97. March 29, 1864, February 5, 1865, ibid.
98. February 5, 1865, ibid.
99. February 8, 1863 (first through third quotations); February 5, 1865 (fourth through sixth), ibid.
100. Carl Sandburg, *Abraham Lincoln: The Prairie Years*, vol. 1 (New York: Harcourt, Brace, 1926), 65–66; White, *Midnight in America*.
101. Bates, *Lincoln in the Telegraph Office*, 215; David Donald, *Lincoln* (New York: Simon and Schuster, 1996), 572.
102. Royster, *Destructive War*, 244–45; Gideon Welles diary, April 14, 1865, Gideon Welles, *Diary of Gideon Welles, Secretary of the Navy under Lincoln and Johnson*, vol. 2, *April 1, 1864–December 31, 1866* (Boston: Houghton Mifflin, 1911), 282–83.
103. Matthew H. Jamison, *Recollections of Pioneer and Army Life* (Kansas City, MO: Hudson Press, 1911), 43.
104. John Rhodehamel and Louise Taper, eds., *"Right or Wrong, God Judge Me": The Writings of John Wilkes Booth* (Urbana: University of Illinois Press, 1997), 58–59.
105. Ibid., 59, 124, 130.
106. Ibid., 125. Though Booth derided John Brown's cause, he considered him "the grandest character of the century." See Asia Booth Clarke, *The Unlocked Book: A Memoir of John Wilkes Booth by His Sister* (New York: G. P. Putnam's Sons, 1938), 124.
107. Rhodehamel and Taper, *Right or Wrong, God Judge Me*, 154–55; J. W. Watson, *Beautiful Snow, and Other Poems* (Philadelphia: Turner Brothers, 1869), 9.
108. Harold Holzer, *The Civil War in 50 Objects* (New York: Viking, 2013), 119–22; Lindsay J. Twa, "Thoughts of Haiti, Thoughts of Liberia: The Shifting Titles and Interpretations of Edwin White's Thoughts of the Future," *American Art* 31, no. 1 (Spring 2017): 72–97; Ross Barrett, *Rendering Violence: Riots, Strikes, and Upheaval in Nineteenth-Century American Art* (Oakland: University of California Press, 2014), 60.
109. Stephanie Camp, *Closer to Freedom: Enslaved Women and Everyday Resistance in the Plantation South* (Chapel Hill: University of North Carolina Press, 2004), 119.
110. Louisa Alexander to Archer Alexander, November 16, 1863, in John Blassingame, ed., *Slave Testimony: Two Centuries of Letters, Speeches, Interviews, and Autobiographies* (Baton Rouge: Louisiana State University Press, 1977), 119.
111. Stephen V. Ash, *The Black Experience in the Civil War South* (New York: Praeger, 2010), 57–58.
112. Blassingame, *Slave Testimony*, 371–72.
113. Ibid.
114. Ibid.

115. "Slave Songs," David Franklin Thorpe Papers, SHC UNC-CH; James Miller McKim, *The Freedmen of South Carolina: Address Delivered by J. Miller McKim in Sansom Hall, July 9, 1862* (Philadelphia: Willis P. Hazard, 1862), 6, 14.
116. Lawrence W. Levine, *Black Culture and Black Consciousness: Afro-American Folk Thought from Slavery to Freedom* (New York: Oxford University Press, 1977), 137 (first quotation); Peter Randolph, *From Slave Cabin to the Pulpit: The Autobiography of Rev. Peter Randolph* (Boston: James H. Earle, 1893), 59–60 (second and third quotations); Rev. L. S. Burkhead, "History of the Difficulties of the Pastorate of the Front Street Methodist Church, Wilmington, NC, for the Year 1865," *An Annual Publication of Historical Papers Published by the Historical Society of Trinity College, Series VIII* (1908–9): 37–43, (fourth and fifth quotations on 42).
117. Burkhead, "History of the Difficulties of the Pastorate of the Front Street Methodist Church," 44 (first quotation); Psalm 9:3–16, 18, *King James Bible*; Levine, *Black Culture and Black Consciousness*, 136–37 (second through fifth).
118. Ruffin diary, May 18, 1862, William Kauffman Scarborough, ed., *The Diary of Edmund Ruffin*, vol. 2, *The Years of Hope, April 1861–June 1863* (Baton Rouge: Louisiana State University, 1976), 307 (first quotation), 301 (second).
119. Edmund Ruffin Jr. to Edmund Ruffin, May 27, 1862, Edmund Ruffin Papers, VHS; Scarborough, *Diary of Edmund Ruffin*, 2, 409–10, 463, 614. See also, *Official Records*, ser. 1, vol. 11, part 2, 946–50; Allmendinger, *Ruffin*, 160.
120. Scarborough, *Diary of Edmund Ruffin*, 2, 420 (first quotation); Avery Craven, *Edmund Ruffin, Southerner: A Study in Secession* (Baton Rouge: Louisiana State University Press, 1991, originally published in 1932), 240 (second); Edmund Ruffin, undated note about the destruction of Beechwood, Edmund Ruffin Papers; Edmund Ruffin Jr. to Edmund Ruffin, May 27, 1862, Edmund Ruffin Papers, VHS.
121. Joanna Baillie, *A Series of Plays: In which It Is Attempted to Delineate the Stronger Passions of the Mind*, vol. 3 (London: Longman, Hurst, Rees, Orme, and Brown, 1821).
122. Ibid., 141 (first quotation), 137 (second), 138 (third), 159 (fourth).

EPILOGUE

1. No author, *The Logan Emancipation Cabinet of Letters and Relics of John Brown and Abraham Lincoln: Being an Article Prepared Specially for the Chicago Tribune* (Chicago: no publisher listed, 1892). Rust parted with his cherished possessions in exchange for a promise from Logan that he would commission a steel engraving of John Brown, the proceeds of which would go to Rust and Brown's family.
2. Lawrence Weschler, *Mr. Wilson's Cabinet of Wonder: Pronged Ants, Horned Humans, Mice on Toast, and Other Marvels of Jurassic Technology* (New York: Vintage, 1995), 60–61; Teresa Barnett, *Sacred Relics: Pieces of the Past in Nineteenth-Century America* (Chicago: University of Chicago Press, 2013).
3. *The Logan Emancipation Cabinet*; Horatio Rust to Kate Fields, January 2, 1892, in *Kate Field's Washington*, vol. 5 (Washington, February 17, 1892), 98–99; "John Brown's Fort in Chicago, 1893," *Journal of the Society of Architectural Historians*, 18 (December 1959): 159; John J. Flinn, *Standard Guide to Chicago* (Chicago: Standard Guide Company, 1893), 132.

4. *The Logan Emancipation Cabinet*, 24 (first quotation), 4 (second and third).
5. Richard J. Hinton, *John Brown and His Men* (New York: Funk and Wagnalls, 1894), 19, 21; John Stauffer, *The Black Hearts of Men: Radical Abolitionists and the Transformation of Race* (Cambridge, MA: Harvard University Press, 2002), 13.
6. Abraham Lincoln, "Address at Cooper Institute," February 27, 1860, in *The Collected Works of Abraham Lincoln*, vol. 3, ed. Roy Basler (New Brunswick: Rutgers University Press, 1953), 538; Adam Gopnik, *Angels and Ages: A Short Book about Darwin, Lincoln, and Modern Life* (New York: Vintage, 2010).
7. A. E. Michael to Andrew McCollam, October 15, 1865, Andrew McCollam Papers, 1792–935, Southern Historical Collection, University of North Carolina-Chapel Hill (UNC-CH); Reid Mitchell, *The Vacant Chair: The Northern Soldier Leaves Home* (New York: Oxford University Press, 1993).
8. Henry Adams, *The Education of Henry Adams: An Autobiography* (Boston: Houghton Mifflin, 1918), 98–99.
9. Mark J. Stegmaier, ed., *Henry Adams in the Secession Crisis: Dispatches to the Boston Daily Advertiser, December 1860–March 1861* (Baton Rouge: Louisiana State University Press, 2012), 64 (first), 87 (second through fifth).
10. August V. Kautz, Memoir of 1861–1862, August V. Kautz Papers, Library of Congress (LOC).
11. August V. Kautz diary, August 1861, August V. Kautz Papers, LOC.
12. David Hunter Strother, "Personal Recollections of the War," *Harper's New Monthly Magazine* (June 1866), 2 (first and second quotations); Strother, "Personal Recollections of the War," *Harper's New Monthly Magazine* (October 1866): 545 (third and fourth). For more on Americans' faith in the "sharp and short" war, see D. H. Dilbeck, *A More Civil War: How the Union Waged a Just War* (Chapel Hill: University of North Carolina Press, 2016).
13. David Hunter Strother, December 16, 1861, War Journal, David Hunter Strother Papers, West Virginia and Regional History Collection, Wise Library, West Virginia University
14. Henry James, *Hawthorne* (London: Macmillan, 1879), 172 (first quotation), 144 (second through fourth).
15. Randall Fuller, *From Battlefields Rising: How the Civil War Transformed American Literature* (New York: Oxford University Press, 2014), 42; Nathaniel Hawthorne, "Chiefly about War Matters," *Atlantic Monthly* 10 (July 1862): 54, 56.
16. Martin Harry Greenberg and Bill Pronzini, eds., *A Treasury of Civil War Stories* (New York: Bonanza Books, 1985), 190 (first), 191 (second), 188 (third), 189 (fourth and fifth); J. Stanley Mattson, "Mark Twain on War and Peace: The Missouri Rebel and 'The Campaign that Failed,'" *American Quarterly* 20 (1968): 783–94.
17. James Wood Davidson, *The Living Writers of the South* (New York: Carleton, 1869), 30; Louis Menand, *The Metaphysical Club: A Story of Ideas in America* (New York: Farrar, Straus and Giroux, 2002); Mark A. Noll, *The Civil War as a Theological Crisis* (Chapel Hill: University of North Carolina Press, 2006).
18. Stephen Davis, "'A Matter of Sensational Interest': The Century 'Battles and Leaders' Series," *Civil War History* 27 (1981): 338–49; Greenberg and Pronzini, *A Treasury of Civil War Stories*, 203.
19. Despite its problems, historian Harold Holzer praised the "editorial integrity, accuracy, and design" of "Battles and Leaders in the Civil War," calling it "a mother lode resource

for historians." Unfortunately, Holzer is in good company. Harold Holzer, ed., *Hearts Touched by Fire: The Best of Battles and Leaders of the Civil War* (New York: Modern Library, 2011), 26, 28; Yael Sternhell, "The Afterlives of a Confederate Archive: Civil War Documents and the Making of Sectional Reconciliation," *Journal of American History* (March 2016): 1025–50.

20. James G. Randall, "The Blundering Generation," *Mississippi Historical Review* 27 (June 1940): 3–28; Avery O. Craven, *The Repressible Conflict, 1830–61* (Baton Rouge: Louisiana State University Press, 1939), and *The Coming of the Civil War* (New York: Charles Scribner's Sons, 1942); Fred Lewis Pattee, *History of American Literature since 1870* (New York: Century, 1915), viii, 175. Van Wyck Brooks also divided American literature at 1865. See *The Flowering of New England* (New York: E. P. Dutton, 1936) and *New England: Indian Summer* (New York: Dutton, 1940). His literary periodization also used 1915 as a demarcation.
21. For example, in *Give Me Liberty*, Eric Foner writes, "Recruits rushed to enlist, expecting a short, glorious war." Foner does not include what women or African Americans expected from the war. Drew Gilpin Faust employs the short war myth in *This Republic of Suffering* to frame her point that Civil War deaths matured the nation. According to Faust, Confederates and Unionists not only anticipated a short war, but "neither side could have imagined the magnitude and length of the conflict that unfolded." Though its perspective is profoundly white and masculine, even historians like Foner and Faust who have expanded the racial and gender dimensions of Civil War scholarship accept the short war myth as an unquestioned fact. Eric Foner, *Give Me Liberty! An American History*, vol. 1 (New York: Norton, 2009), 483; Drew Gilpin Faust, *This Republic of Suffering: Death and the American Civil War* (New York: Alfred A. Knopf, 2008), 3.
22. Hayden White, *Metahistory: The Historical Imagination in Nineteenth-Century Europe* (Baltimore: Johns Hopkins University Press, 1973), ix; Bruce Catton, *The Civil War* (reprint 1960, New York: Fairfax Press, 1980), 1–2.
23. David E. Shi, *Facing Facts: Realism in American Thought and Culture, 1850–1920* (New York: Oxford University Press, 1996); Menand, *The Metaphysical Club*; Heather Cox Richardson, *West from Appomattox: The Reconstruction of America after the Civil War* (New Haven, CT: Yale University Press, 2007); Stephen Kern, *The Culture of Time and Space, 1880–1918* (Cambridge, MA: Harvard University Press, 2003).
24. Francis Fukuyama, *The End of History and the Last Man* (New York: Avon Books, 1992); Jill Lepore, "No, We Cannot: The New Pessimism Comes of Age," *New Yorker* (June 5 and 12, 2017): 102; Lawrence R. Samuel, *Future: A Recent History* (Austin: University of Texas Press, 2009); Simon Schama, *The American Future: A History* (New York: Harper Collins, 2009).
25. Thomas L. Johnson, *Africa for Christ: Twenty-Eight Years a Slave* (London: Yates Alexander and Shepheard, 1882), 16 (first and second quotations); Thomas L. Johnson, *Born Three Times: The Memoirs of an African-American Missionary Who Finds True Liberation in Europe*, ed. Paul Dennis Sporer (Chester, NY: Bylany Press, 2005), 9 (third and fourth).
26. Johnson, *Born Three Times*, 19 (first), 21 (third and fifth); Johnson, *Africa for Christ*, 22 (second); Daniel 11: 13–15 (fourth) *King James Bible.*
27. Johnson, *Born Three Times*, 23.
28. C. Vann Woodward, ed., *Mary Chesnut's Civil War* (New Haven, CT: Yale University Press, 1981), 114.

29. Chesnut quoted in Elisabeth S. Muhlenfeld, *Mary Boykin Chesnut: A Biography* (Baton Rouge: Louisiana State University Press, 1992), 202; Michael O'Brien, *Conjectures of Order: Intellectual Life and the American South, 1810–1860*, vol. 2 (Chapel Hill: University of North Carolina Press, 2004), 1196.
30. Harold Peter Simonson, *Francis Grierson* (New York: Twayne, 1966).
31. Maeterlinck quoted in Edmund Wilson, *Patriotic Gore: Studies in the Literature of the American Civil War* (New York: Oxford University Press, 1962), 74, 75. Grierson quoted in Simonson, *Francis Grierson*, 77, 32.
32. Francis Grierson, *The Invincible Alliance and Other Essays* (London, 1913), 19, 22, 137.
33. Francis Grierson, *The Valley of Shadows* (Boston: Houghton Mifflin, 1909), 216–17 (first through third quotations), 219 (fourth and fifth), 224 (sixth).
34. Ibid., 3.
35. Ibid., 16 (first quotation), 15 (third), 17 (fourth), 47 (fifth); Isaiah 19.20, *King James Bible*
36. Francis Grierson, *Psycho-Phone Messages Recorded by Francis Grierson* (Los Angeles: Austin, 1921), 15.
37. DeVoto quoted in Simonson, *Francis Grierson*, 109; Wilson, *Patriotic Gore*, 84.
38. David Carr, untitled review essay of Koselleck, *Futures Past, History and Theory* 26 (1987): 198; Craven, *Edmund Ruffin*, 191.
39. Edmund Ruffin diary, June 16, 1865, in *The Diary of Edmund Ruffin*, vol. 3, *A Dream Shattered, June 1863–June 1865*, ed. William Kauffman Scarborough (Baton Rouge: Louisiana State University Press, 1989), 944, 946.
40. Ibid., 949.
41. David F. Allmendinger, *Ruffin: Family and Reform in the Old South* (New York: Oxford University Press, 1990), 152–85.

Index

Note: Page numbers in *italics* indicate photographs and illustrations.

CPSIA information can be obtained
at www.ICGtesting.com
Printed in the USA
BVHW052040131221
623940BV00002B/126

9 780190 868161